This time, I tried doing a "Discussion Room" for the first time in a long while. There's a lot of talk, so grab a snack and do your best to read through!

—Katsura Hoshino

Shiga Prefecture native Katsura Hoshino's hit manga series *D.Gray-man* has been serialized in *Weekly Shonen Jump* since 2004. Katsura's debut manga, "Continue," appeared for the first time in *Weekly Shonen Jump* in 2003.

Katsura adores cats.

D.GRAY-MAN
VOL. 24
SHONEN JUMP ADVANCED
Manga Edition

STORY AND ART BY
KATSURA HOSHINO

English Adaptation/Lance Caselman
Translation/John Werry
Touch-up Art & Lettering/Susan Daigle-Leach
Design/Matt Hinrichs
Editor/Gary Leach

D.GRAY-MAN © 2004 by Katsura Hoshino. All rights reserved.
First published in Japan in 2004 by SHUEISHA Inc., Tokyo. English translation rights arranged by
SHUEISHA Inc.

The stories, characters and incidents mentioned in this publication are entirely fictional.

Printed in the U.S.A.

Published by VIZ Media, LLC
P.O. Box 77010
San Francisco, CA 94107

10 9 8 7 6 5 4 3 2 1
First printing, August 2014

www.viz.com

www.shonenjump.com

PARENTAL ADVISORY
D.GRAY-MAN is rated T+ for Older Teen and
is recommended for ages 16 and up. This
volume contains fantasy violence.
ratings.viz.com

On the side of you

vol.24

STORY & ART BY
Katsura Hoshino

D.Gray-man CHARACTERS

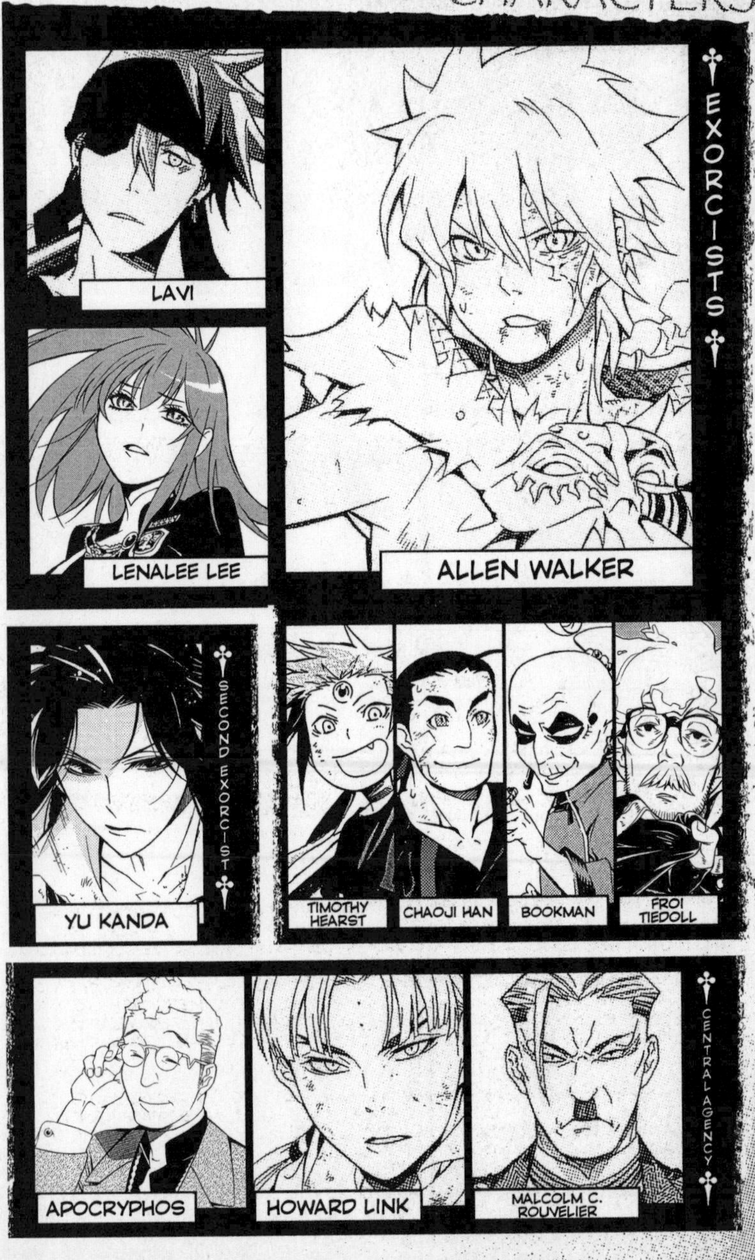
EXORCISTS
ALLEN WALKER
LAVI
LENALEE LEE
FROI TIEDOLL
BOOKMAN
CHAOJI HAN
TIMOTHY HEARST
SECOND EXORCIST
YU KANDA
CENTRAL AGENCY
MALCOLM C. ROUVELIER
HOWARD LINK
APOCRYPHOS

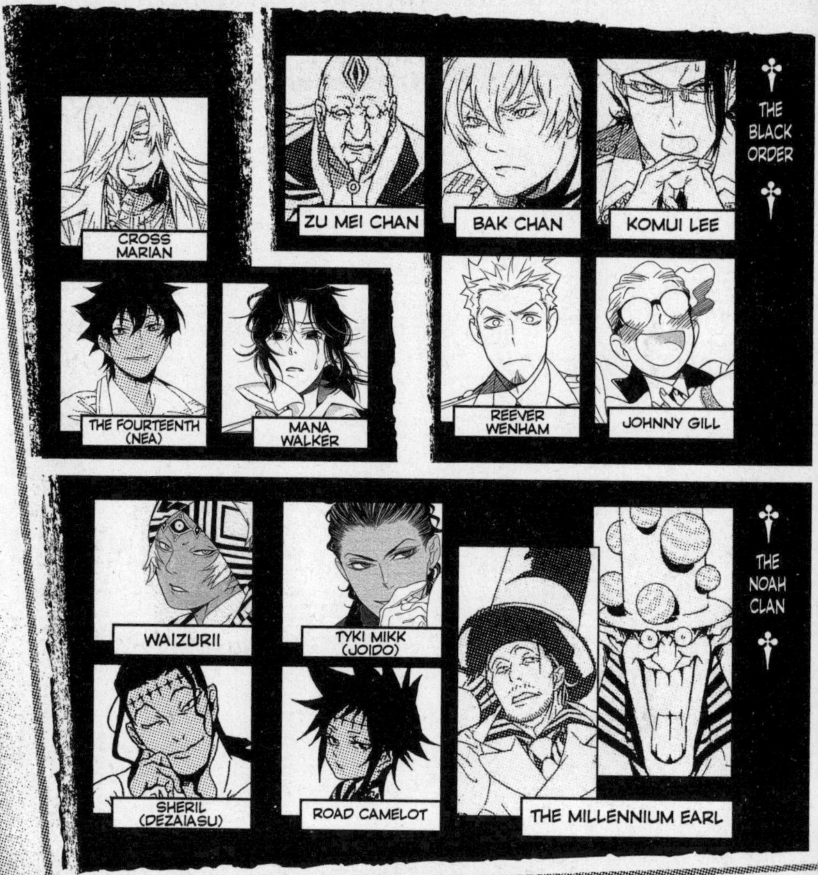
THE BLACK ORDER
KOMUI LEE
BAK CHAN
ZU MEI CHAN
CROSS MARIAN
JOHNNY GILL
REEVER WENHAM
MANA WALKER
THE FOURTEENTH (NEA)
THE NOAH CLAN
THE MILLENNIUM EARL
TYKI MIKK (JOIDO)
WAIZURII
ROAD CAMELOT
SHERIL (DEZAIASU)

STORY

IT ALL BEGAN CENTURIES AGO WITH THE DISCOVERY OF A CUBE CONTAINING AN APOCALYPTIC PROPHECY FROM AN ANCIENT CIVILIZATION AND INSTRUCTIONS IN THE USE OF INNOCENCE, A CRYSTALLINE SUBSTANCE OF WONDROUS SUPERNATURAL POWER. THE CREATORS OF THE CUBE CLAIMED TO HAVE DEFEATED AN EVIL KNOWN AS THE MILLENNIUM EARL BY USING THE INNOCENCE. NEVERTHELESS, THE WORLD WAS DESTROYED BY THE GREAT FLOOD OF THE OLD TESTAMENT. NOW, TO AVERT A SECOND END OF THE WORLD, A GROUP OF EXORCISTS WIELDING WEAPONS MADE OF INNOCENCE MUST BATTLE THE MILLENNIUM EARL AND HIS TERRIBLE MINIONS, THE AKUMA.

WHEN THE MILLENNIUM EARL AND THE NOAH ATTACK THE ORDER, KANDA'S OLD FRIEND ALMA KARMA TRANSFORMS INTO AN AKUMA, CLASHES WITH KANDA AND IS NEARLY KILLED. IN ORDER TO SAVE THEIR LIVES, ALLEN SENDS THEM TO A FARAWAY LAND. LATER, THE INDEPENDENT-TYPE INNOCENCE KNOWN AS APOCRYPHOS TRIES TO FUSE WITH ALLEN AND ALL-OUT BATTLE ENSUES. THE ORDER DECLARES ALLEN TO BE A NOAH, AND HE TAKES HIS LEAVE OF HIS FORMER ALLIES. BUT JOHNNY GILL AND KANDA DECIDE TO FOLLOW HIM, AND THEY SOON DISCOVER THAT ALLEN'S TRANSFORMATION INTO THE FOURTEENTH IS ACCELERATING!

D.GRAY-MAN
Vol. 24

CONTENTS

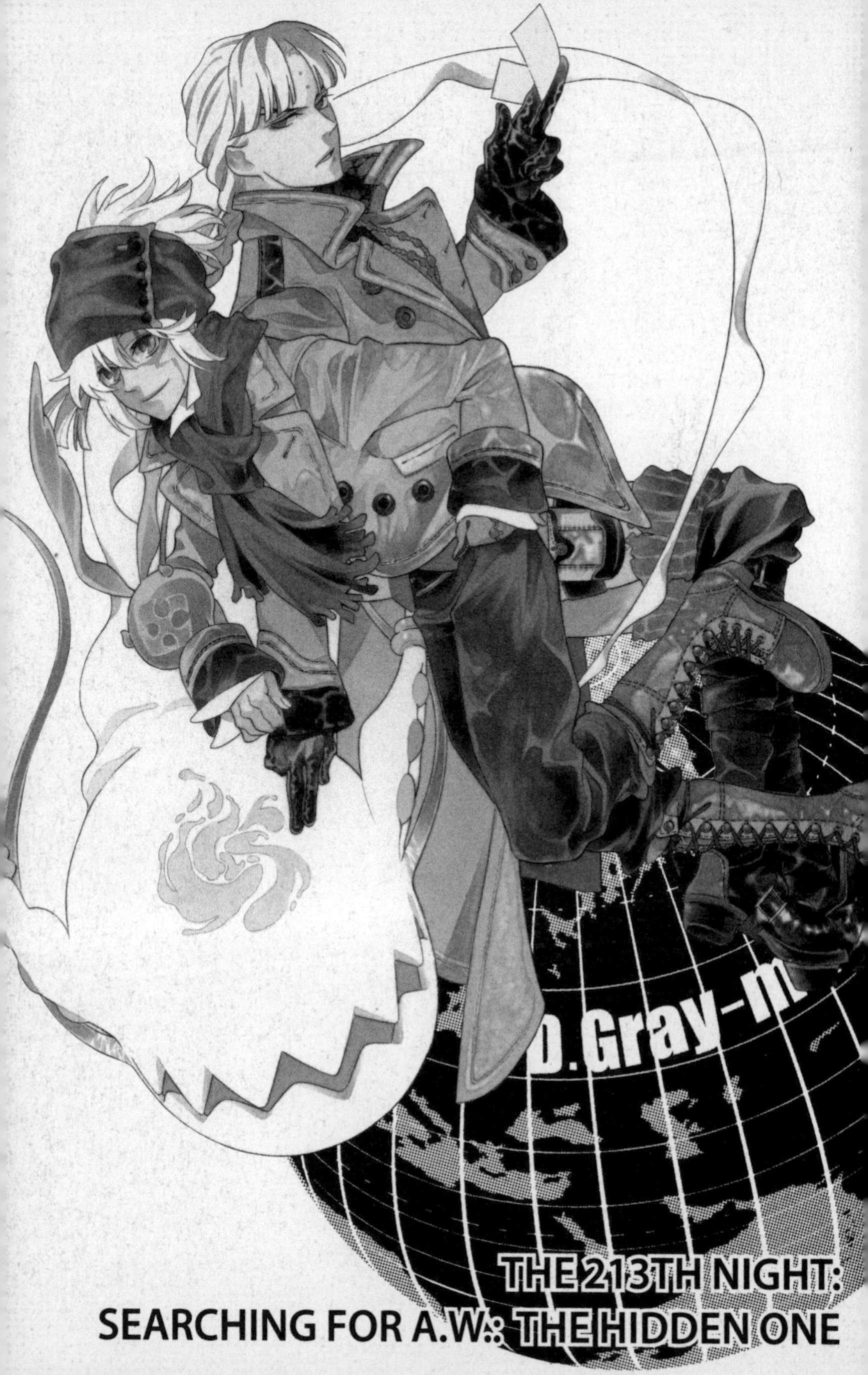
D.Gray-m

THE 213TH NIGHT: SEARCHING FOR A.W.: THE HIDDEN ONE

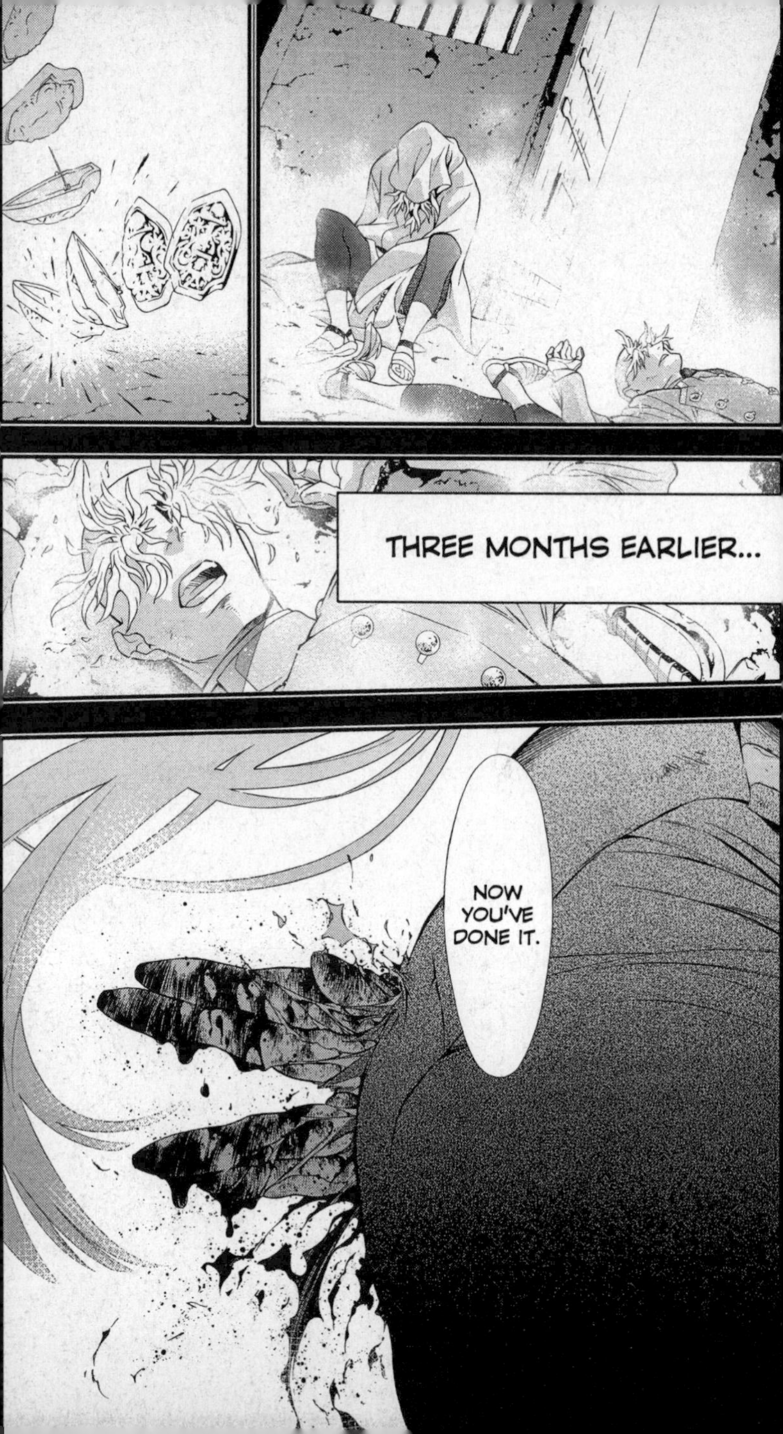
THREE MONTHS EARLIER...
NOW YOU'VE DONE IT.

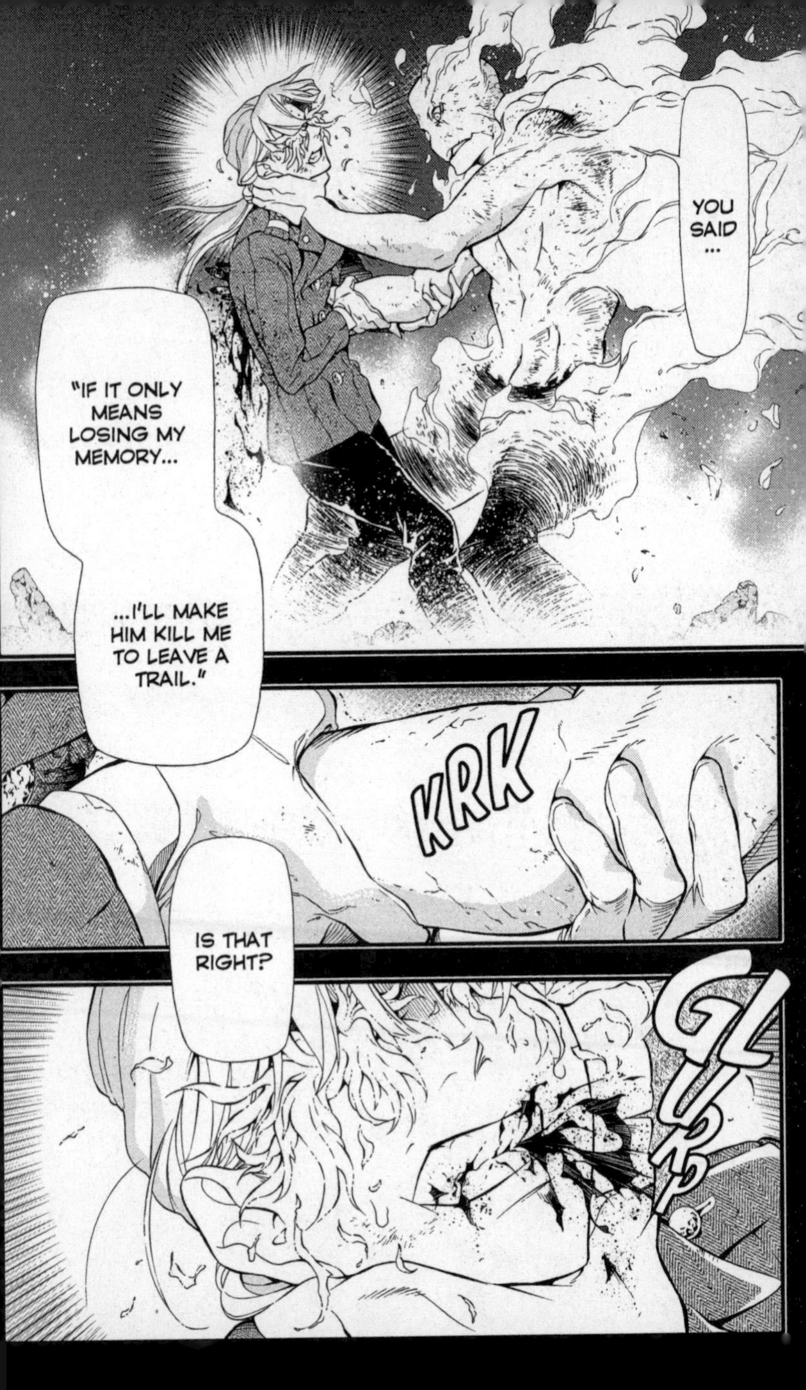
YOU SAID ...
"IF IT ONLY MEANS LOSING MY MEMORY...
...I'LL MAKE HIM KILL ME TO LEAVE A TRAIL."
KRK
IS THAT RIGHT?
GLURP!

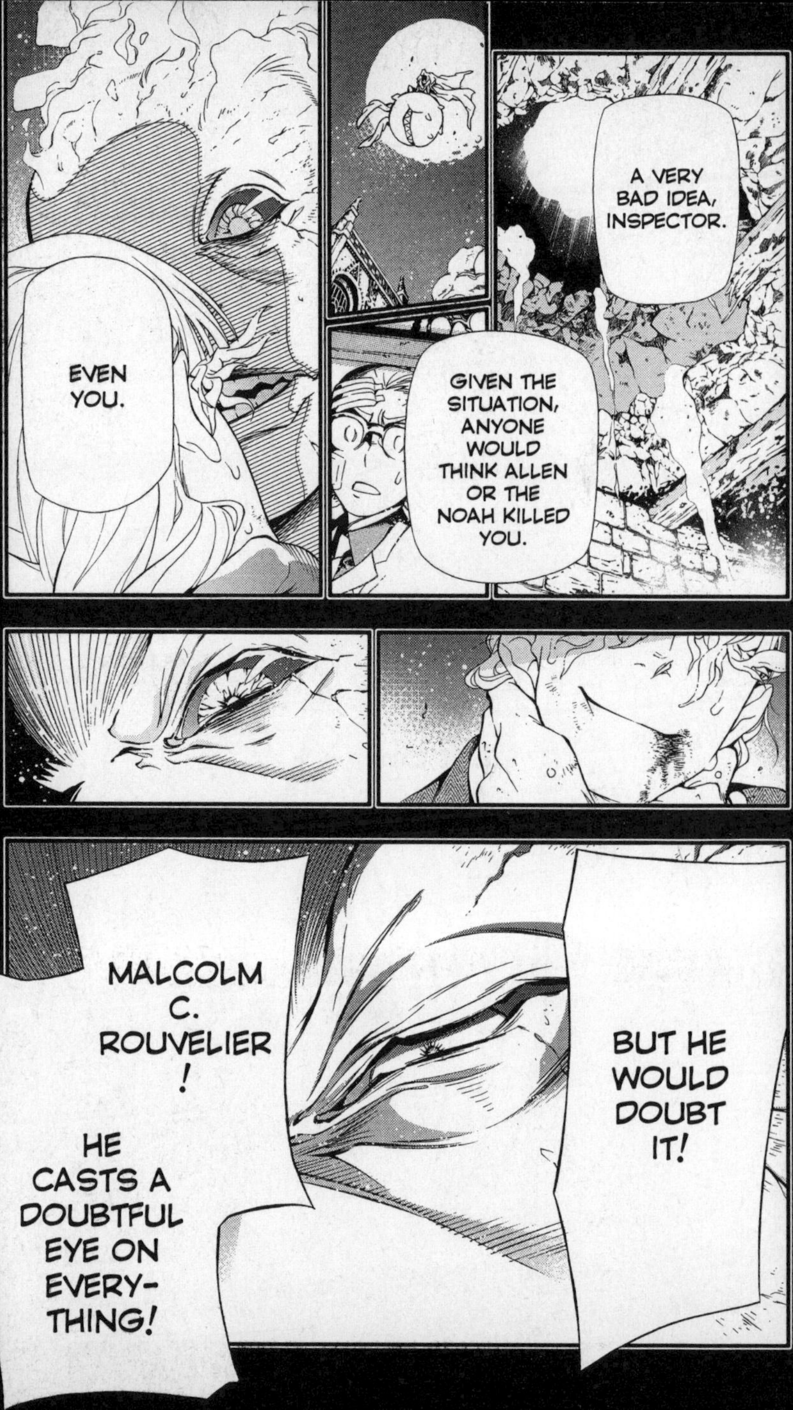
A VERY BAD IDEA, INSPECTOR.
GIVEN THE SITUATION, ANYONE WOULD THINK ALLEN OR THE NOAH KILLED YOU.
EVEN YOU.
BUT HE WOULD DOUBT IT!
MALCOLM C. ROUVELIER!
HE CASTS A DOUBTFUL EYE ON EVERY-THING!

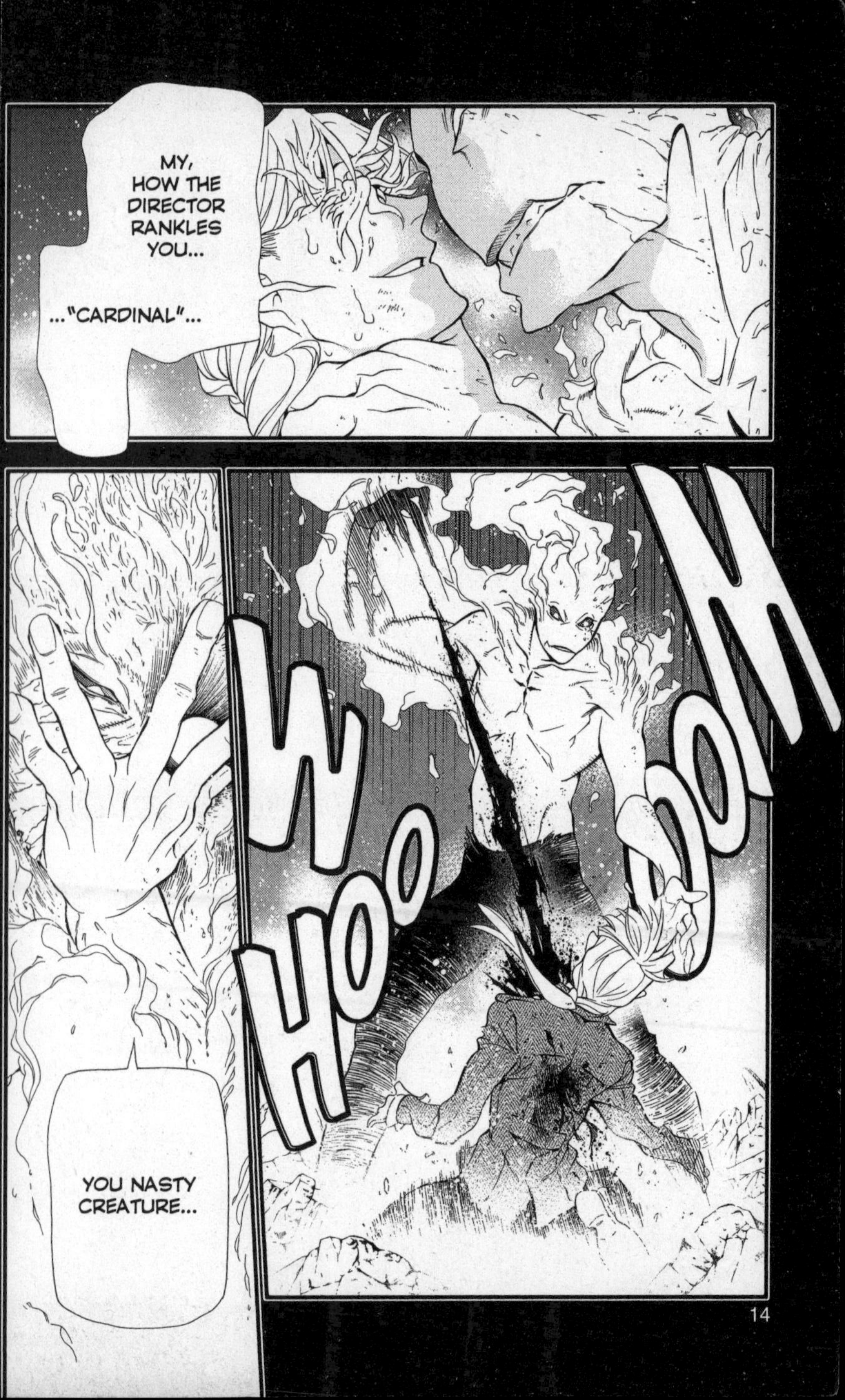
MY, HOW THE DIRECTOR RANKLES YOU...
..."CARDINAL"...
YOU NASTY CREATURE...

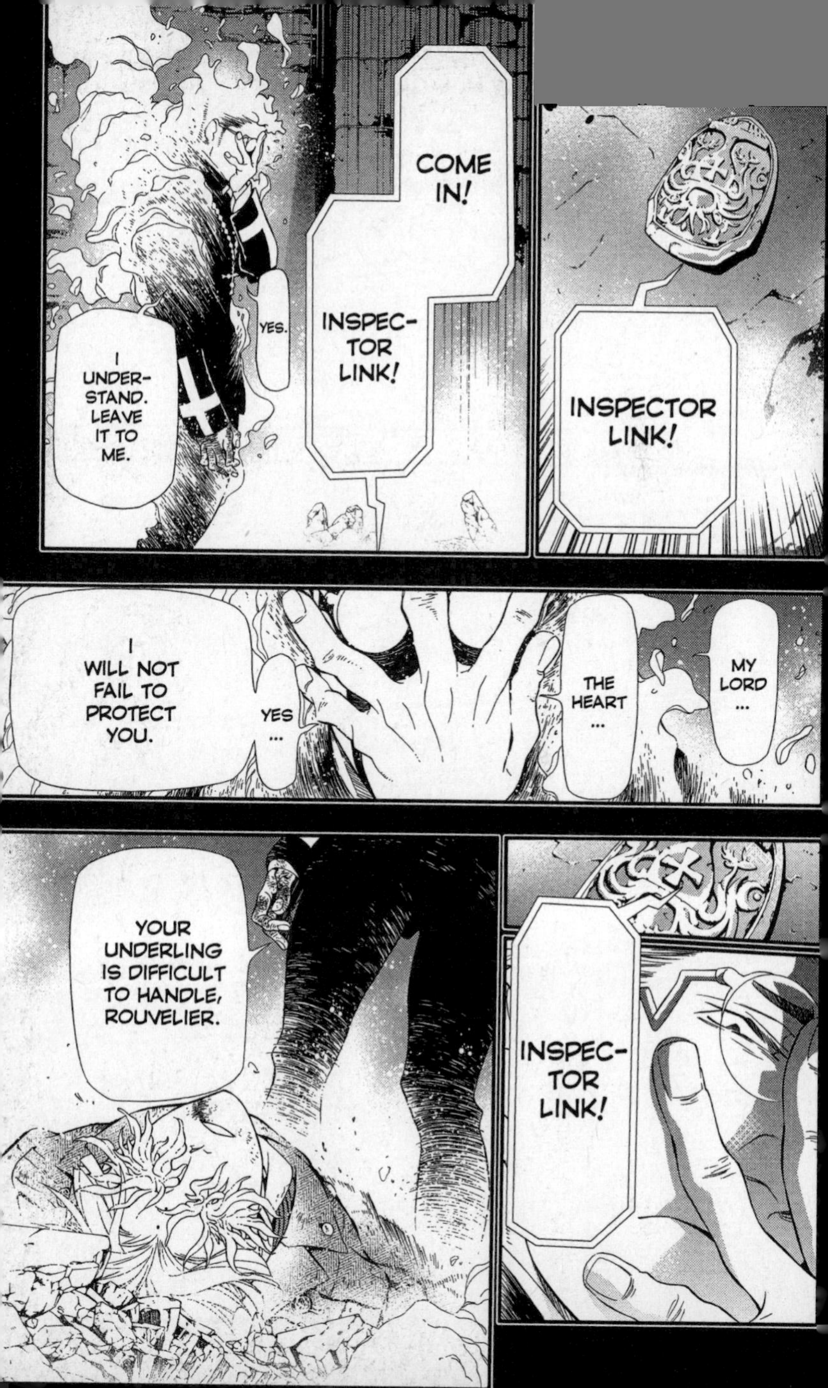
INSPECTOR LINK!
COME IN!
INSPEC-TOR LINK!
YES.
I UNDER-STAND. LEAVE IT TO ME.
MY LORD ...
THE HEART ...
YES ...
I WILL NOT FAIL TO PROTECT YOU.
INSPEC-TOR LINK!
YOUR UNDERLING IS DIFFICULT TO HANDLE, ROUVELIER.

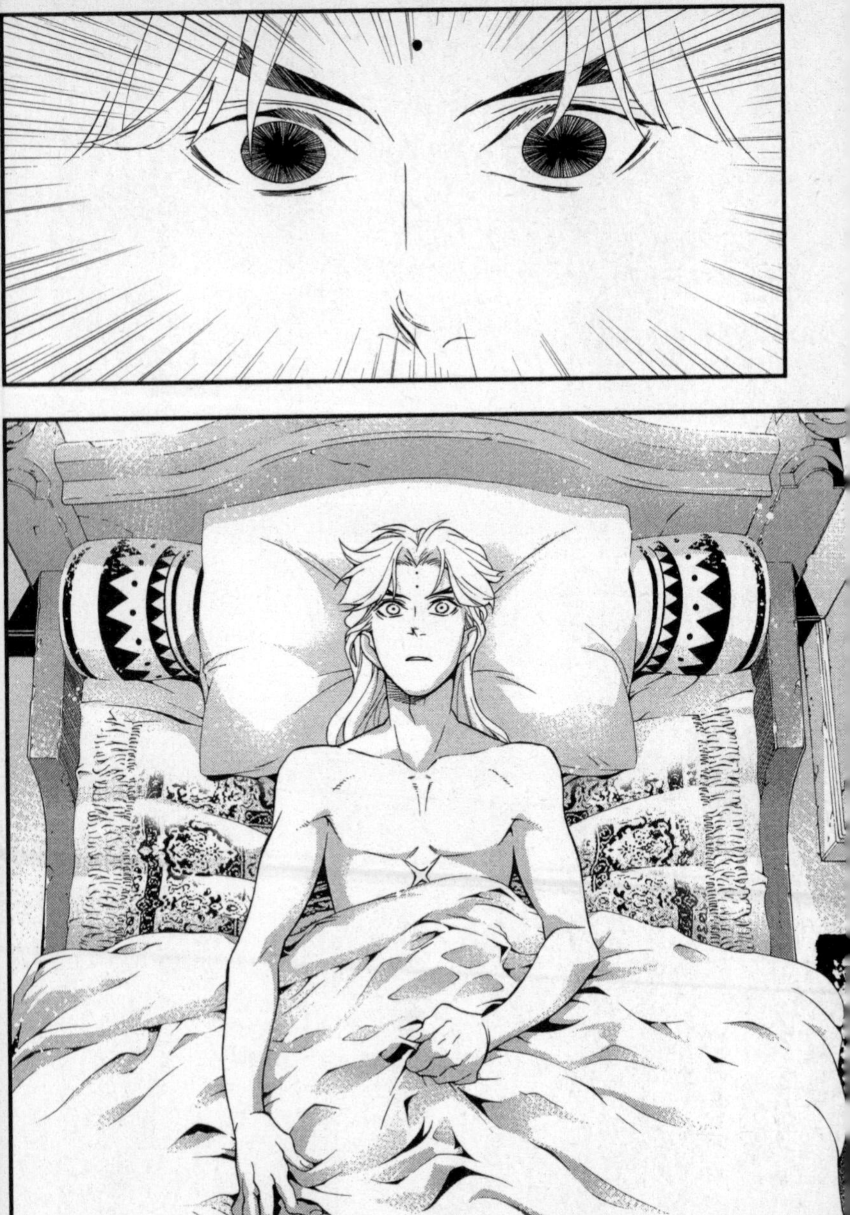

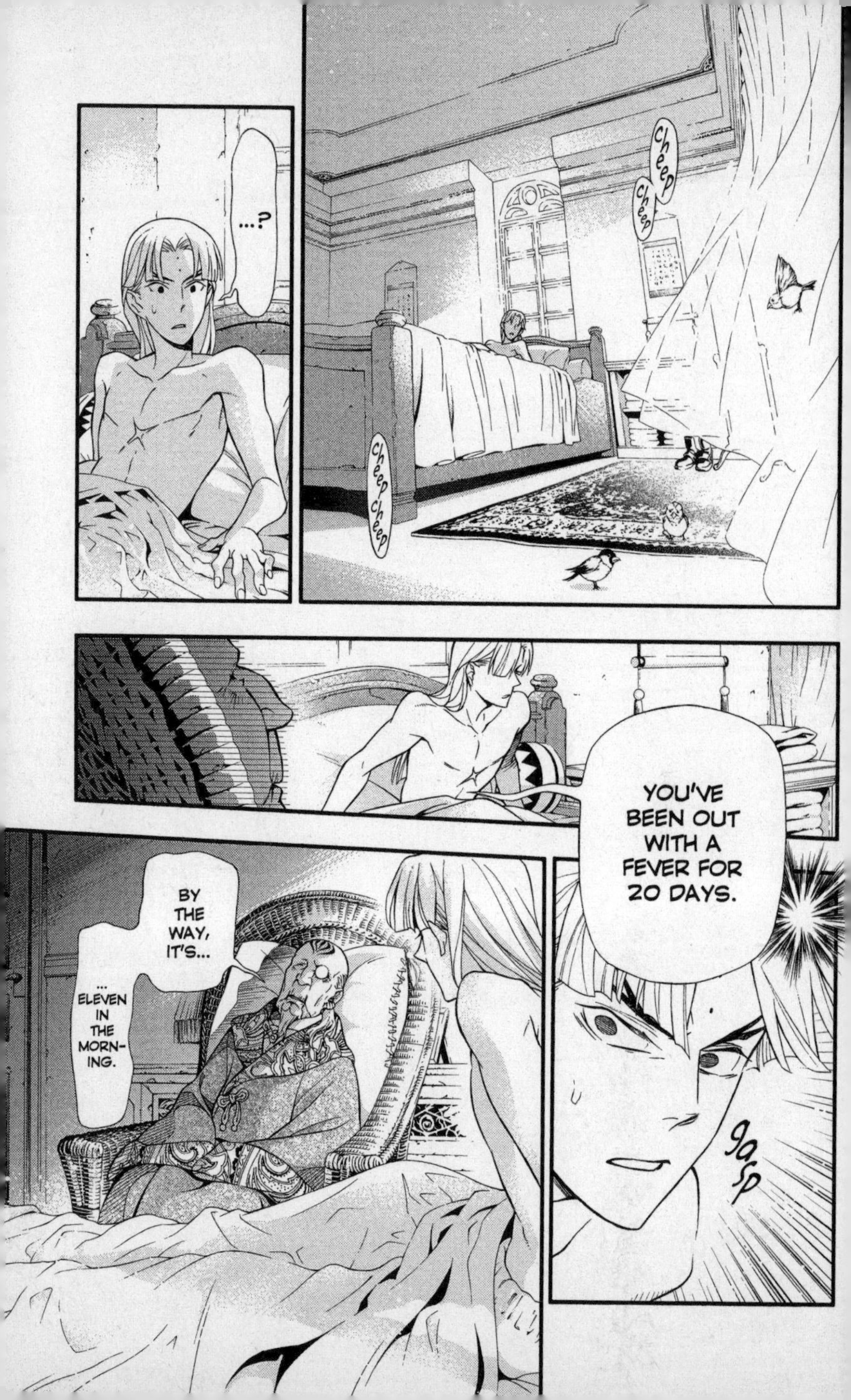
Cheep
Cheep
Cheep cheep
...?
YOU'VE BEEN OUT WITH A FEVER FOR 20 DAYS.
gasp
BY THE WAY, IT'S...
... ELEVEN IN THE MORNING.

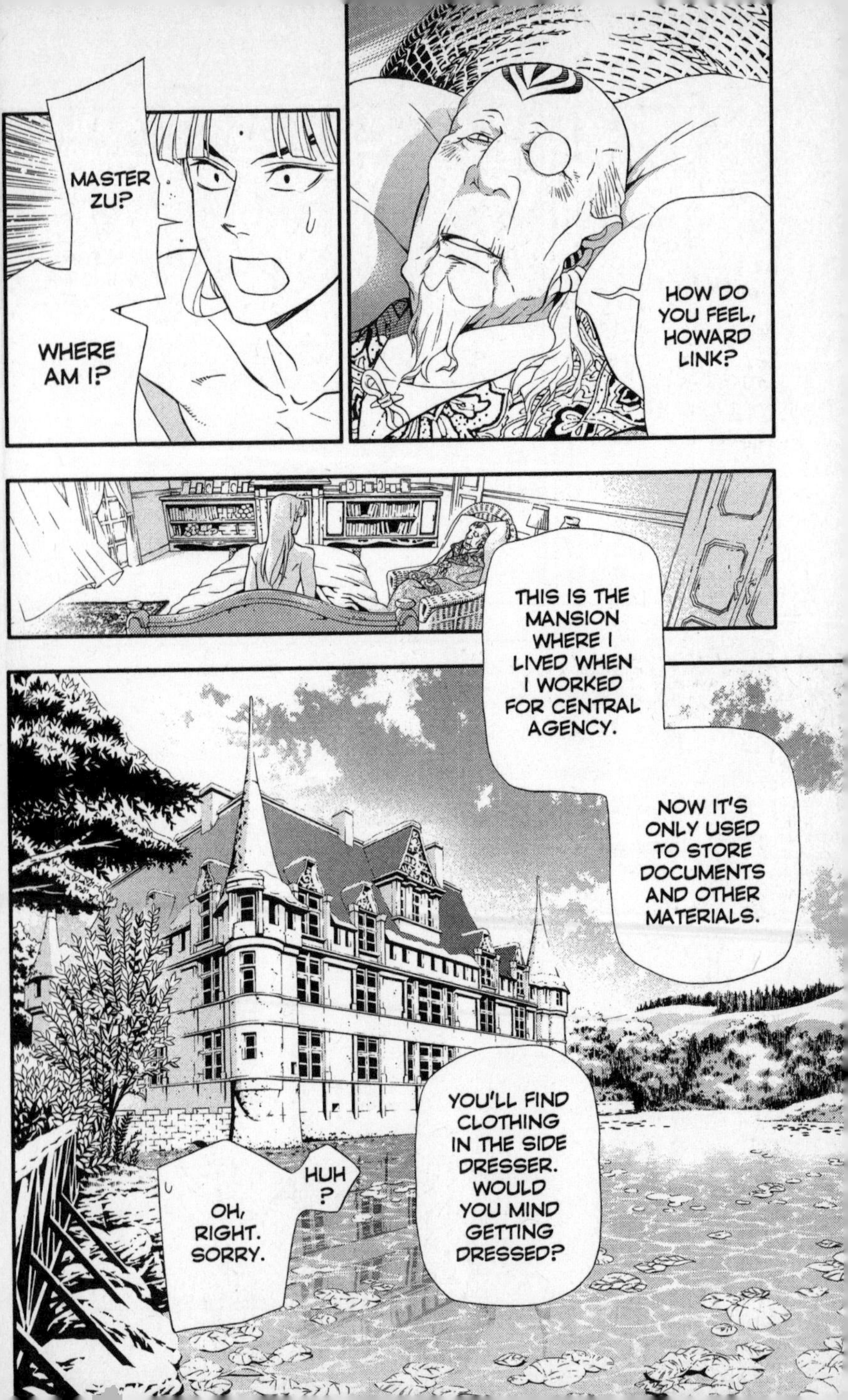
HOW DO YOU FEEL, HOWARD LINK?
MASTER ZU?
WHERE AM I?
THIS IS THE MANSION WHERE I LIVED WHEN I WORKED FOR CENTRAL AGENCY.
NOW IT'S ONLY USED TO STORE DOCUMENTS AND OTHER MATERIALS.
YOU'LL FIND CLOTHING IN THE SIDE DRESSER. WOULD YOU MIND GETTING DRESSED?
HUH?
OH, RIGHT. SORRY.

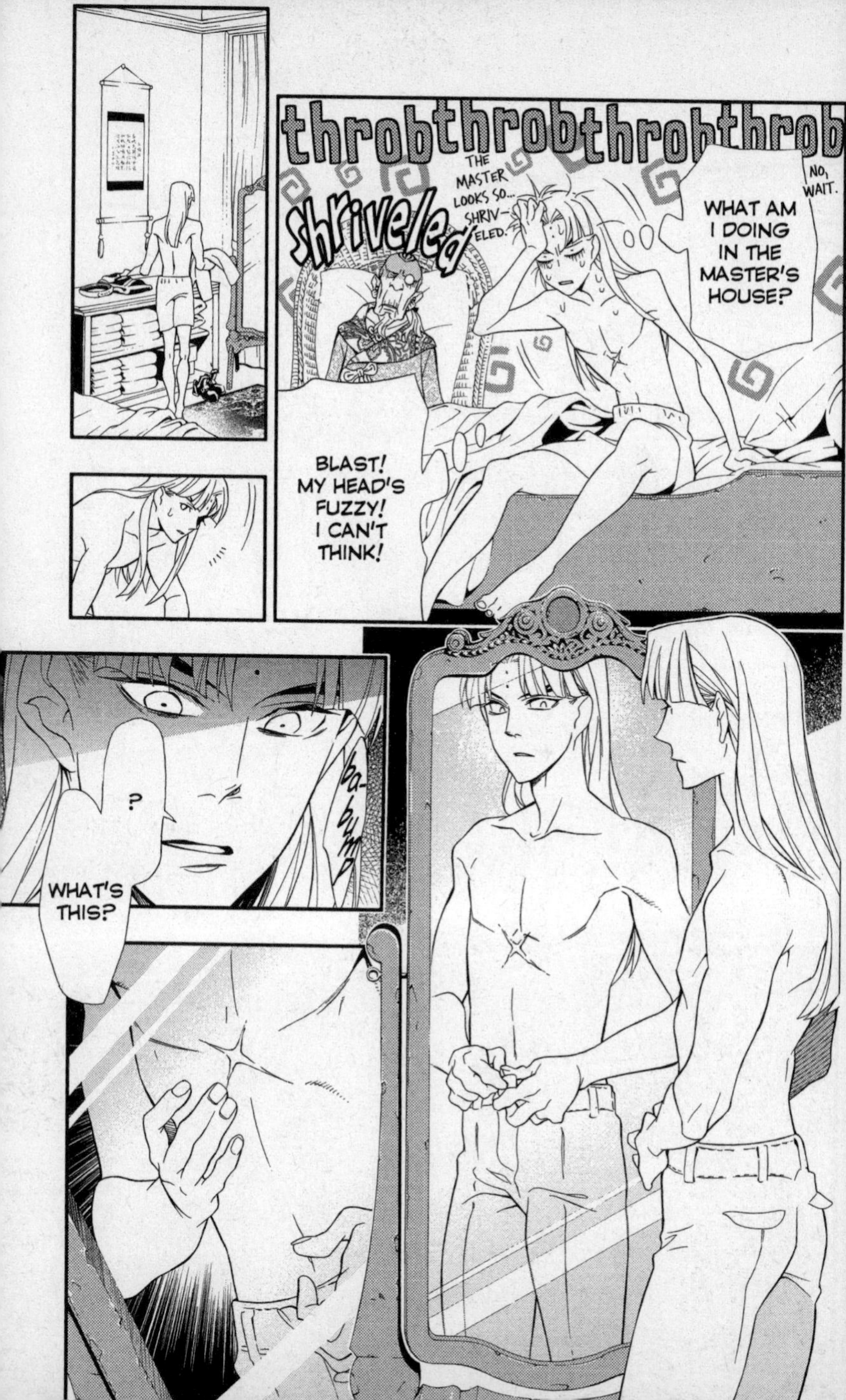
throbthrobthrobthrob
NO, WAIT.
WHAT AM I DOING IN THE MASTER'S HOUSE?
THE MASTER LOOKS SO... SHRIV-ELED.
shriveled
BLAST! MY HEAD'S FUZZY! I CAN'T THINK!
ba-bump
?
WHAT'S THIS?

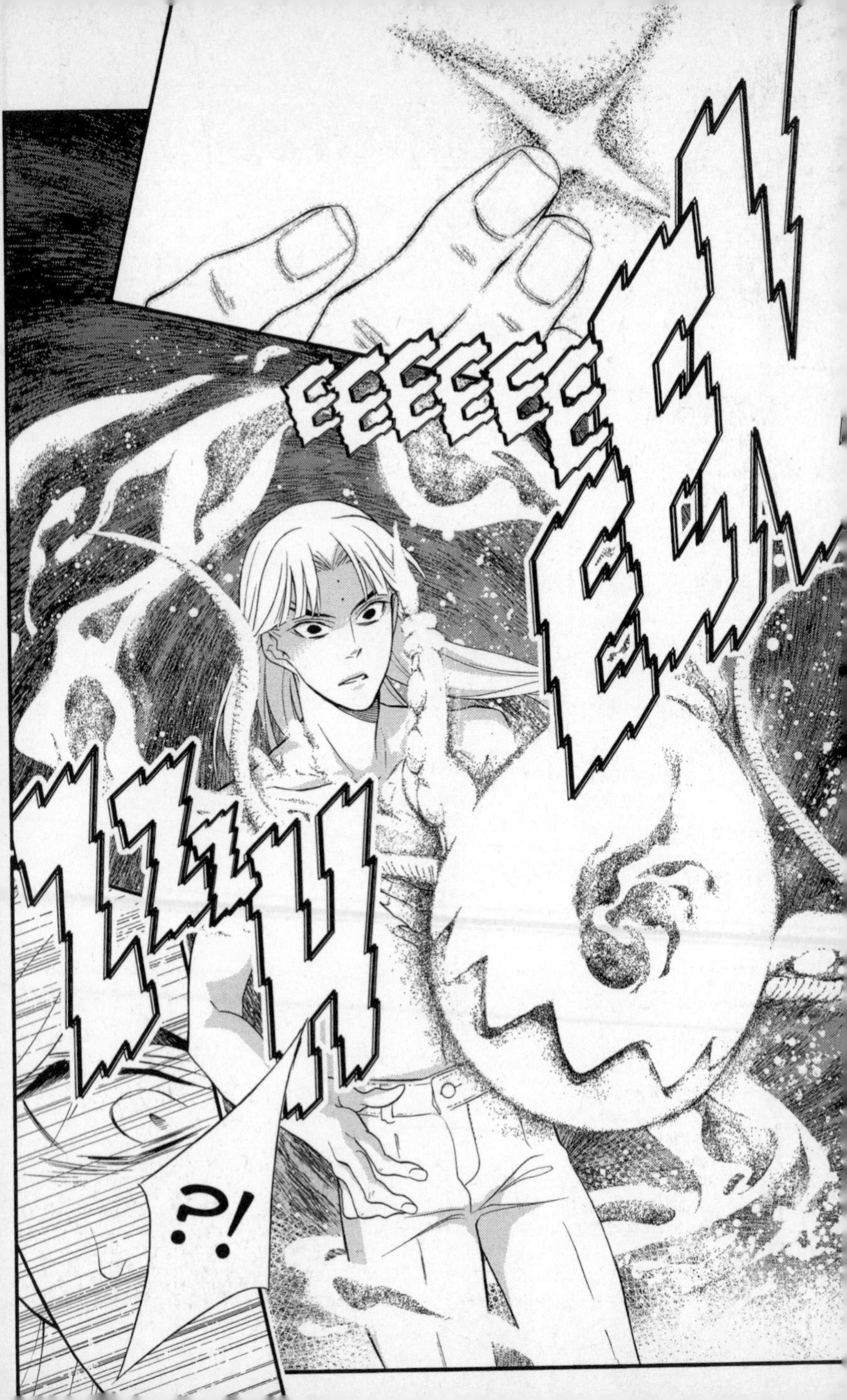
?!

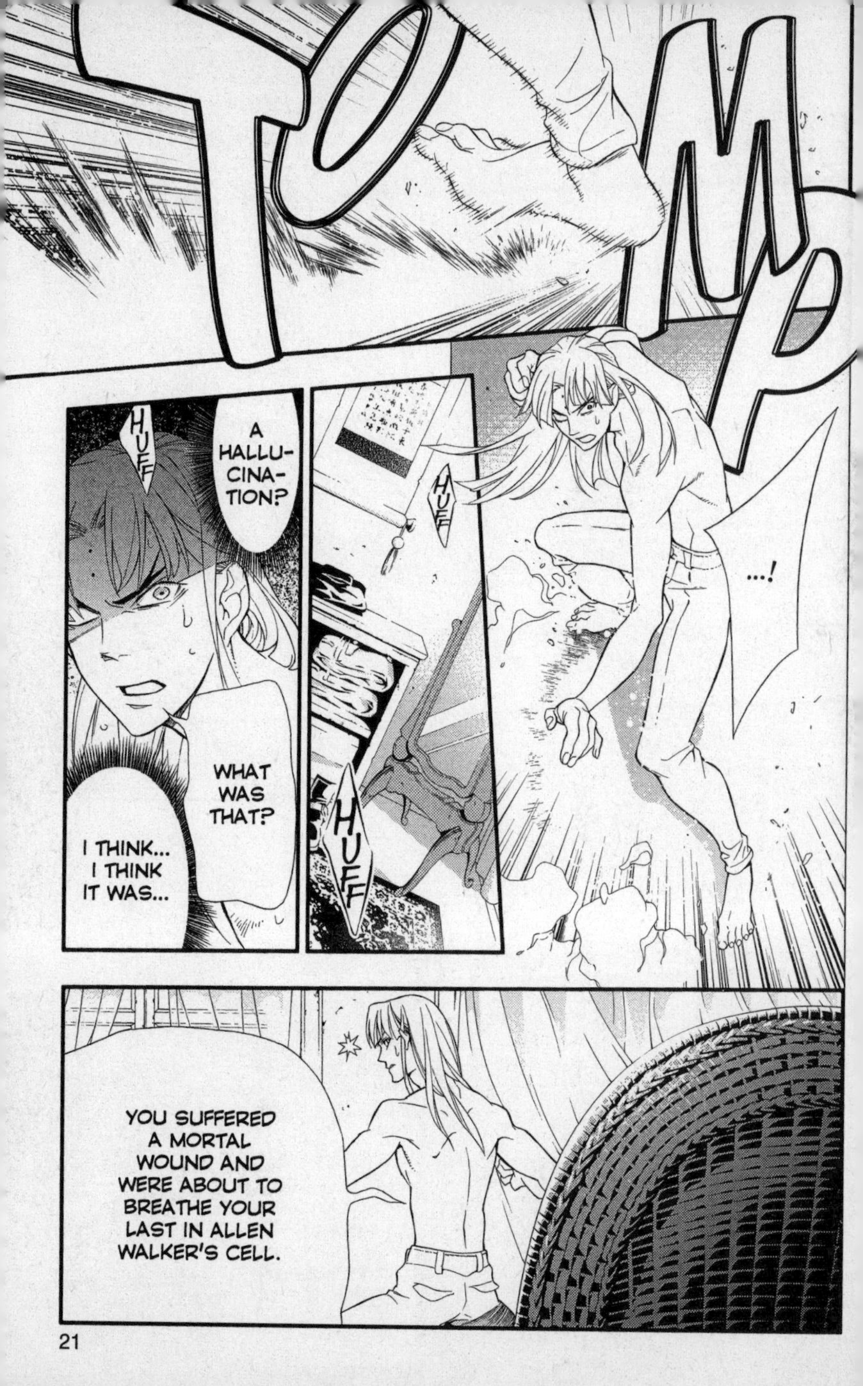
TOMP
...!
HUFF
HUFF
HUFF
A HALLUCINATION?
WHAT WAS THAT?
I THINK... I THINK IT WAS...
YOU SUFFERED A MORTAL WOUND AND WERE ABOUT TO BREATHE YOUR LAST IN ALLEN WALKER'S CELL.

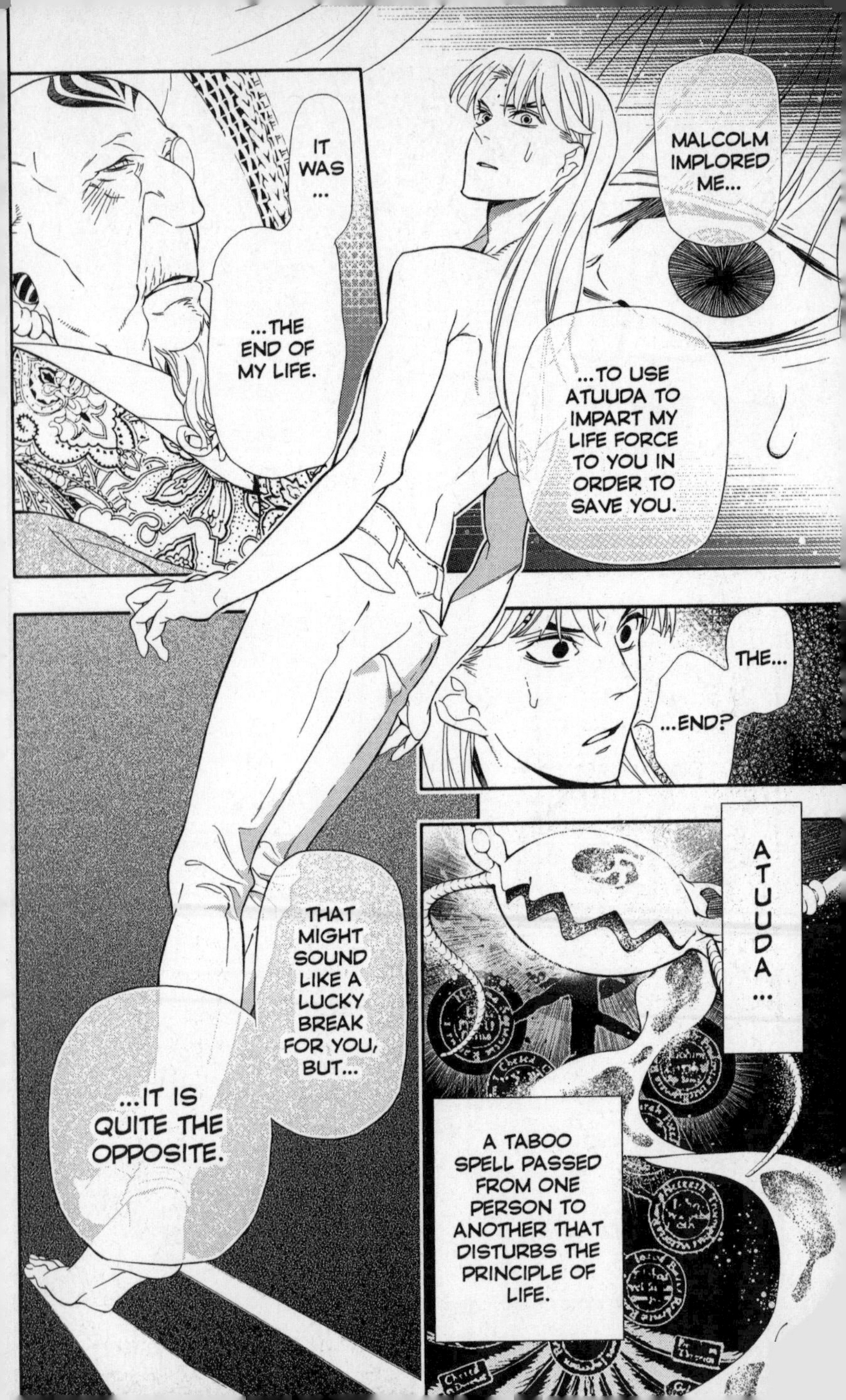
MALCOLM IMPLORED ME...
...TO USE ATUUDA TO IMPART MY LIFE FORCE TO YOU IN ORDER TO SAVE YOU.
IT WAS...
...THE END OF MY LIFE.
THE...
...END?
ATUUDA...
A TABOO SPELL PASSED FROM ONE PERSON TO ANOTHER THAT DISTURBS THE PRINCIPLE OF LIFE.
THAT MIGHT SOUND LIKE A LUCKY BREAK FOR YOU, BUT...
...IT IS QUITE THE OPPOSITE.

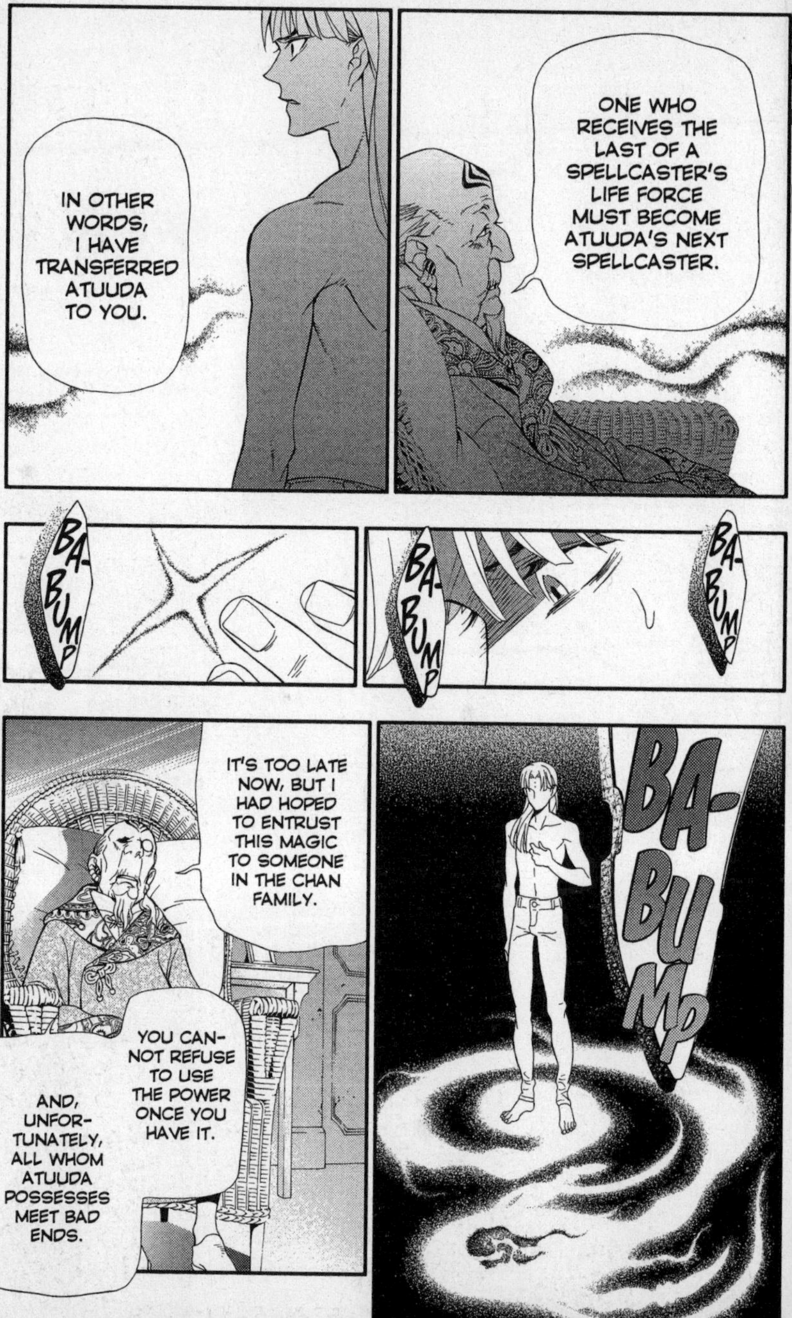
ONE WHO RECEIVES THE LAST OF A SPELLCASTER'S LIFE FORCE MUST BECOME ATUUDA'S NEXT SPELLCASTER.
IN OTHER WORDS, I HAVE TRANSFERRED ATUUDA TO YOU.
BA-BUMP
BA-BUMP
BA-BUMP
BA-BUMP
IT'S TOO LATE NOW, BUT I HAD HOPED TO ENTRUST THIS MAGIC TO SOMEONE IN THE CHAN FAMILY.
YOU CAN-NOT REFUSE TO USE THE POWER ONCE YOU HAVE IT.
AND, UNFOR-TUNATELY, ALL WHOM ATUUDA POSSESSES MEET BAD ENDS.

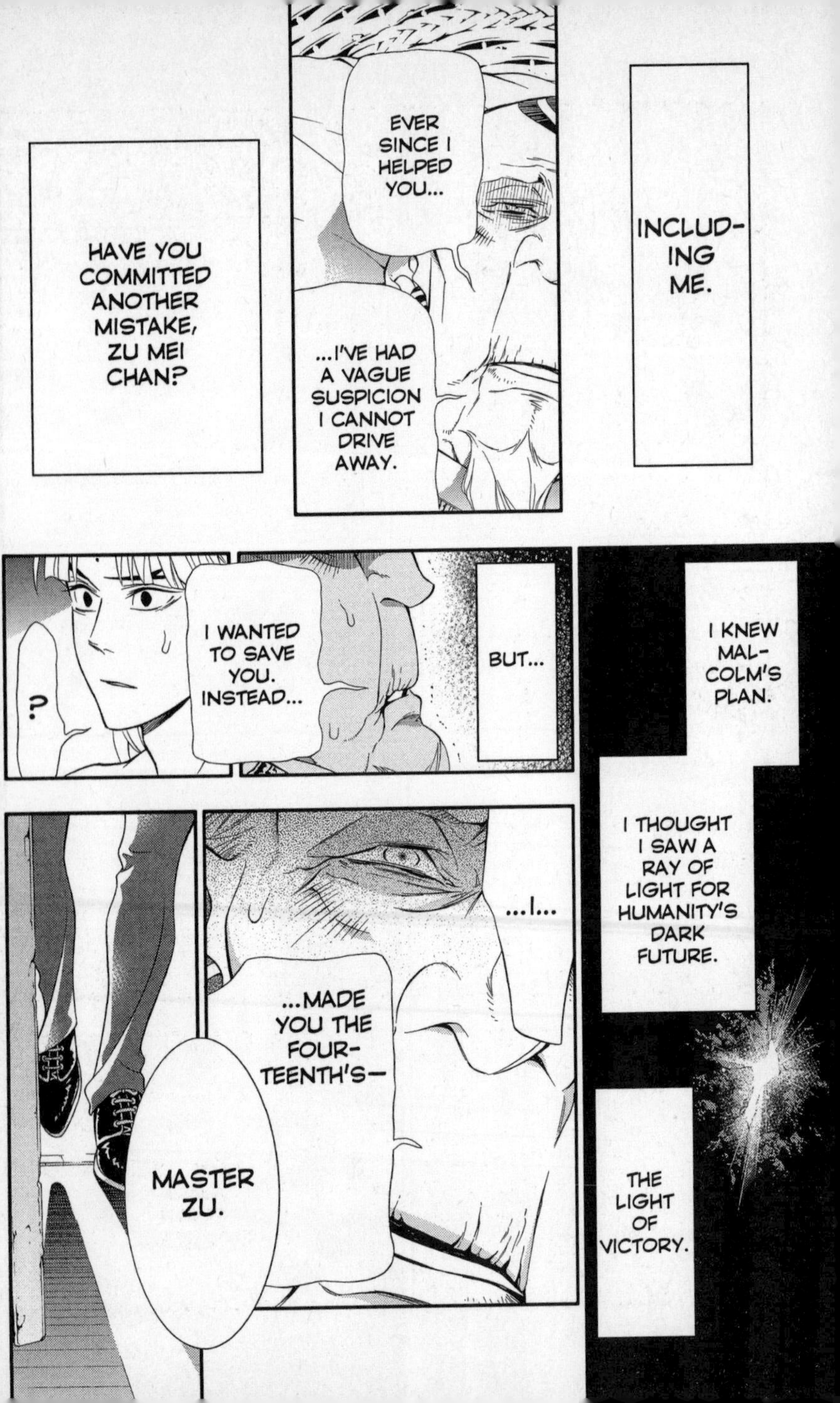
INCLUD-ING ME.
EVER SINCE I HELPED YOU...
...I'VE HAD A VAGUE SUSPICION I CANNOT DRIVE AWAY.
HAVE YOU COMMITTED ANOTHER MISTAKE, ZU MEI CHAN?
I KNEW MAL-COLM'S PLAN.
I THOUGHT I SAW A RAY OF LIGHT FOR HUMANITY'S DARK FUTURE.
THE LIGHT OF VICTORY.
BUT...
I WANTED TO SAVE YOU. INSTEAD...
?
...I...
...MADE YOU THE FOUR-TEENTH'S—
MASTER ZU.

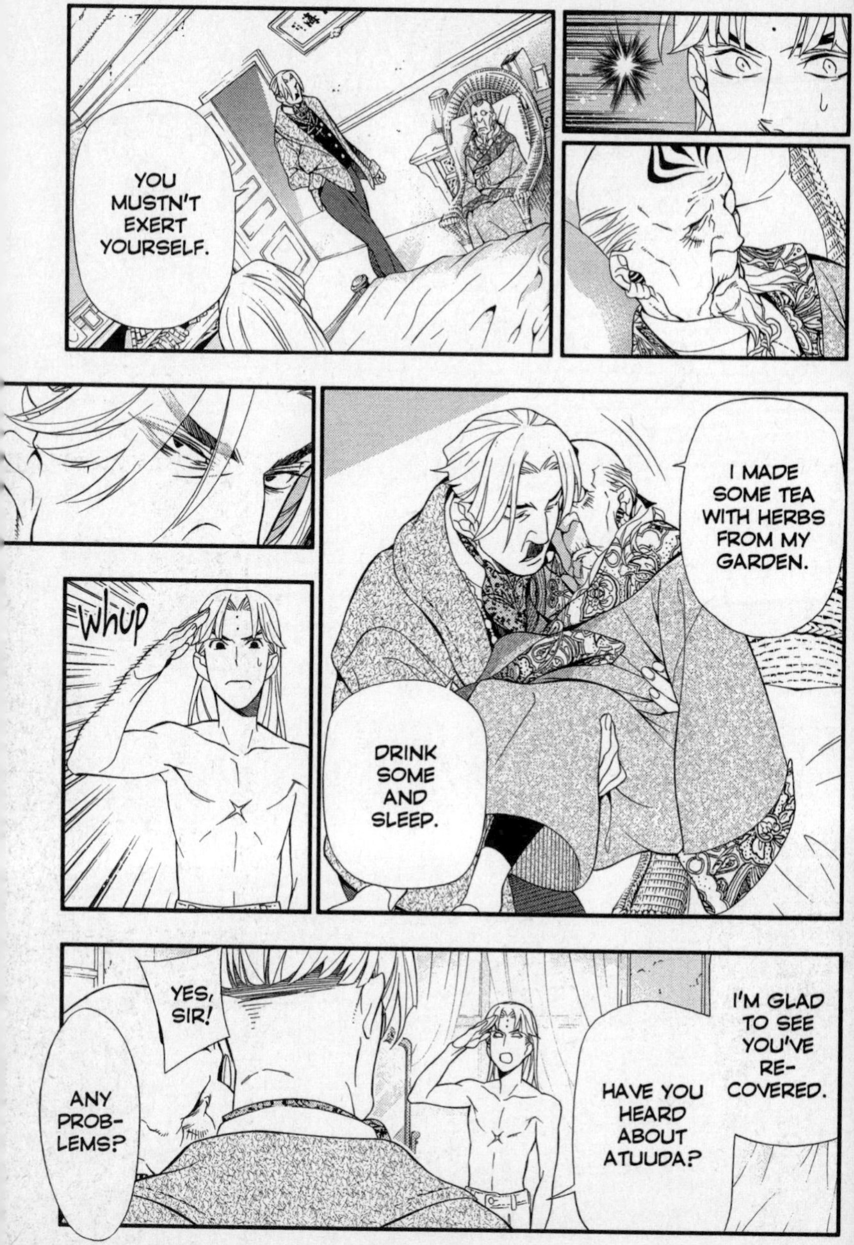
YOU MUSTN'T EXERT YOURSELF.
I MADE SOME TEA WITH HERBS FROM MY GARDEN.
DRINK SOME AND SLEEP.
whup
I'M GLAD TO SEE YOU'VE RE-COVERED.
YES, SIR!
HAVE YOU HEARD ABOUT ATUUDA?
ANY PROB-LEMS?

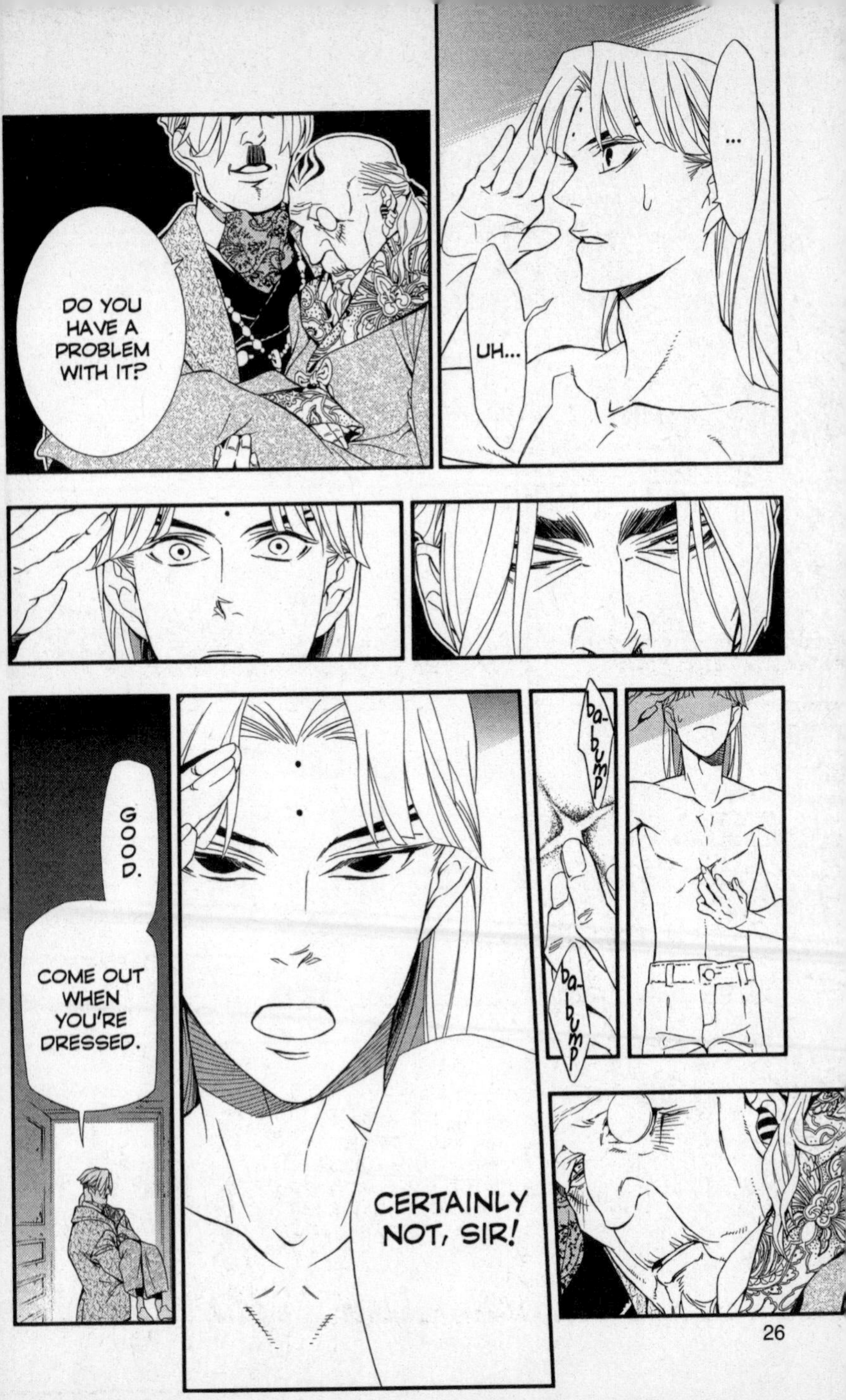
...
UH...
DO YOU HAVE A PROBLEM WITH IT?
ba-bump
ba-bump
CERTAINLY NOT, SIR!
GOOD.
COME OUT WHEN YOU'RE DRESSED.

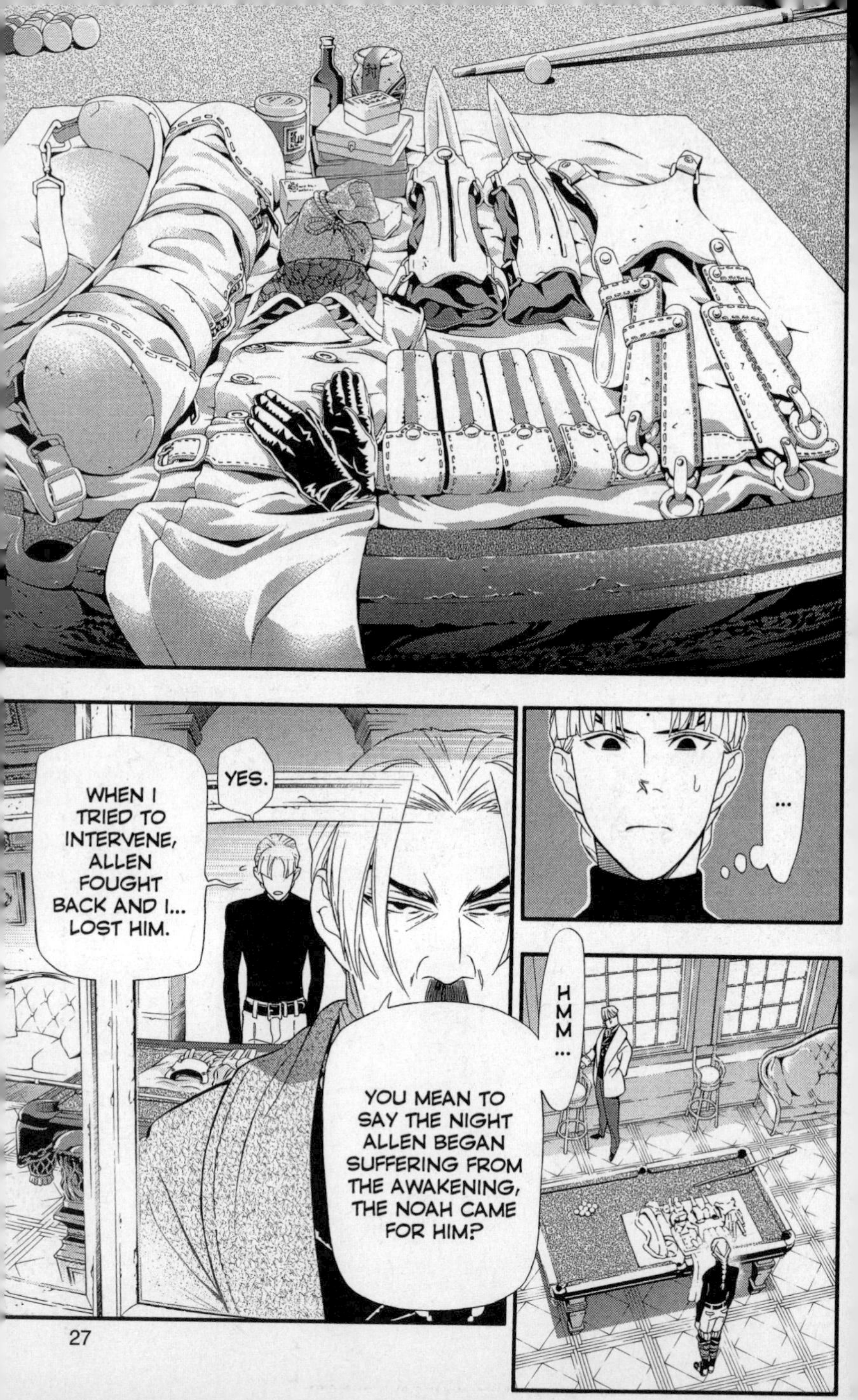
...
HMM...
YOU MEAN TO SAY THE NIGHT ALLEN BEGAN SUFFERING FROM THE AWAKENING, THE NOAH CAME FOR HIM?
YES.
WHEN I TRIED TO INTERVENE, ALLEN FOUGHT BACK AND I... LOST HIM.

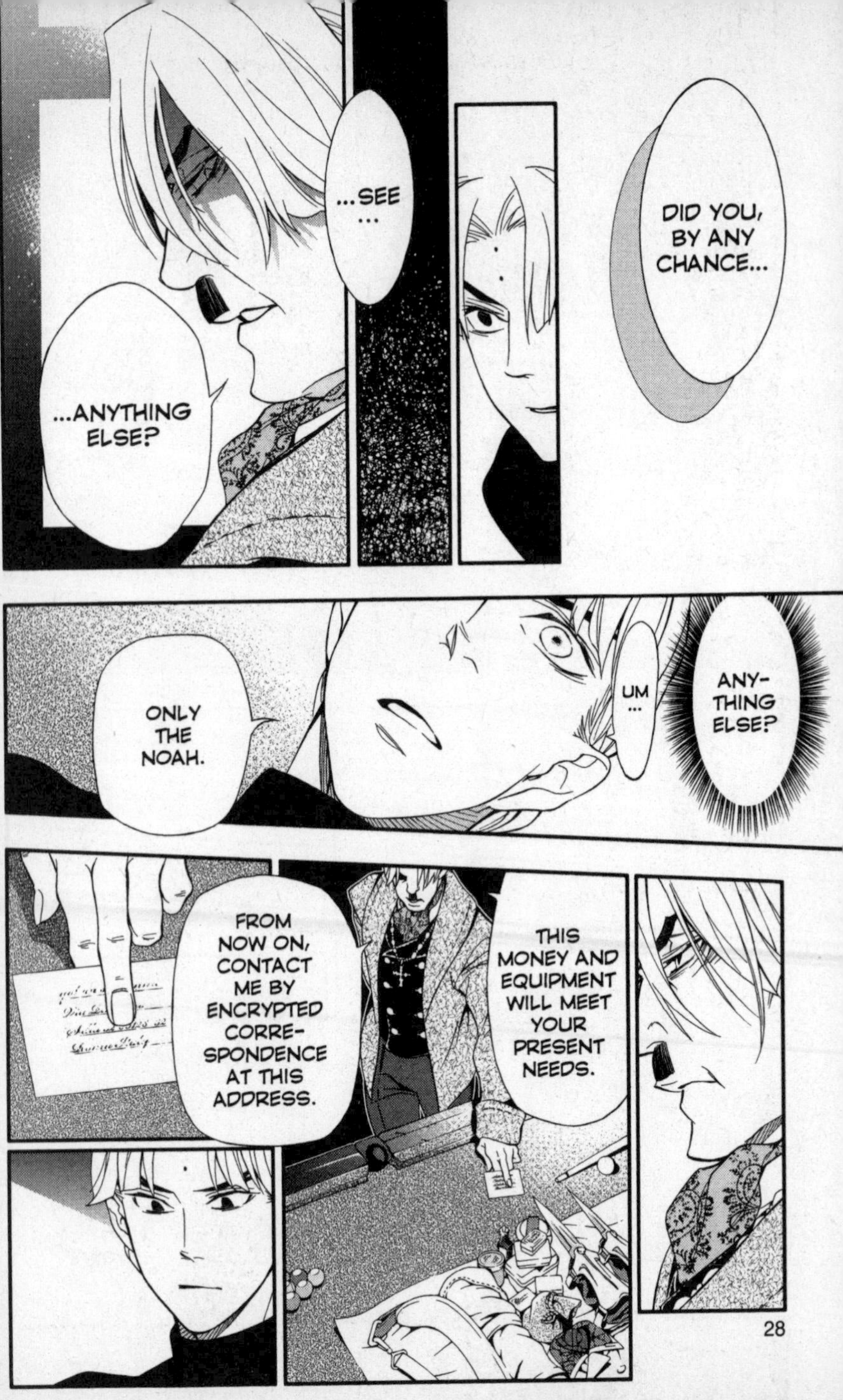
DID YOU, BY ANY CHANCE...
...SEE ...
...ANYTHING ELSE?
ANY-THING ELSE?
UM ...
ONLY THE NOAH.
THIS MONEY AND EQUIPMENT WILL MEET YOUR PRESENT NEEDS.
FROM NOW ON, CONTACT ME BY ENCRYPTED CORRE-SPONDENCE AT THIS ADDRESS.

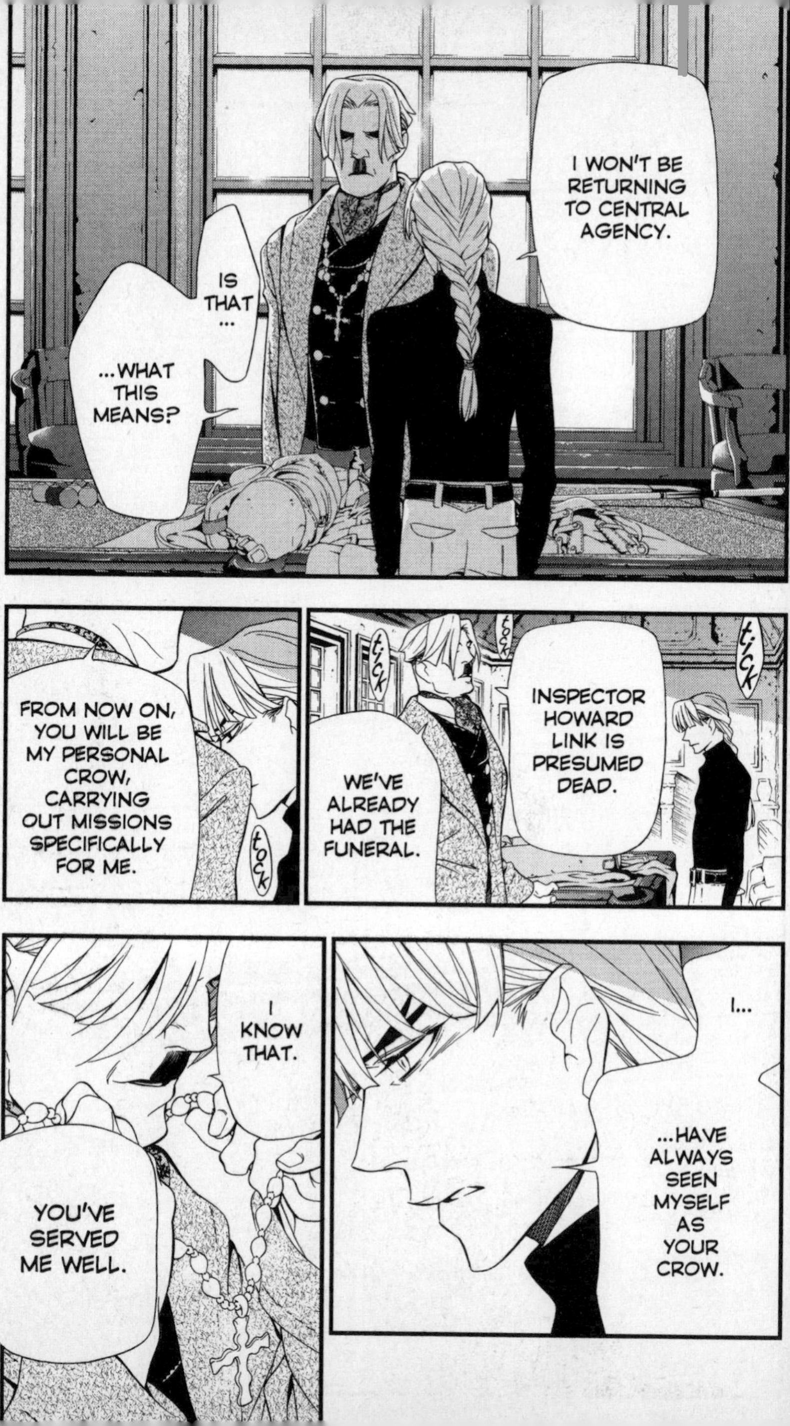
I WON'T BE RETURNING TO CENTRAL AGENCY.
IS THAT ...
...WHAT THIS MEANS?
tick
tock
INSPECTOR HOWARD LINK IS PRESUMED DEAD.
tick
WE'VE ALREADY HAD THE FUNERAL.
FROM NOW ON, YOU WILL BE MY PERSONAL CROW, CARRYING OUT MISSIONS SPECIFICALLY FOR ME.
tock
I...
...HAVE ALWAYS SEEN MYSELF AS YOUR CROW.
I KNOW THAT.
YOU'VE SERVED ME WELL.

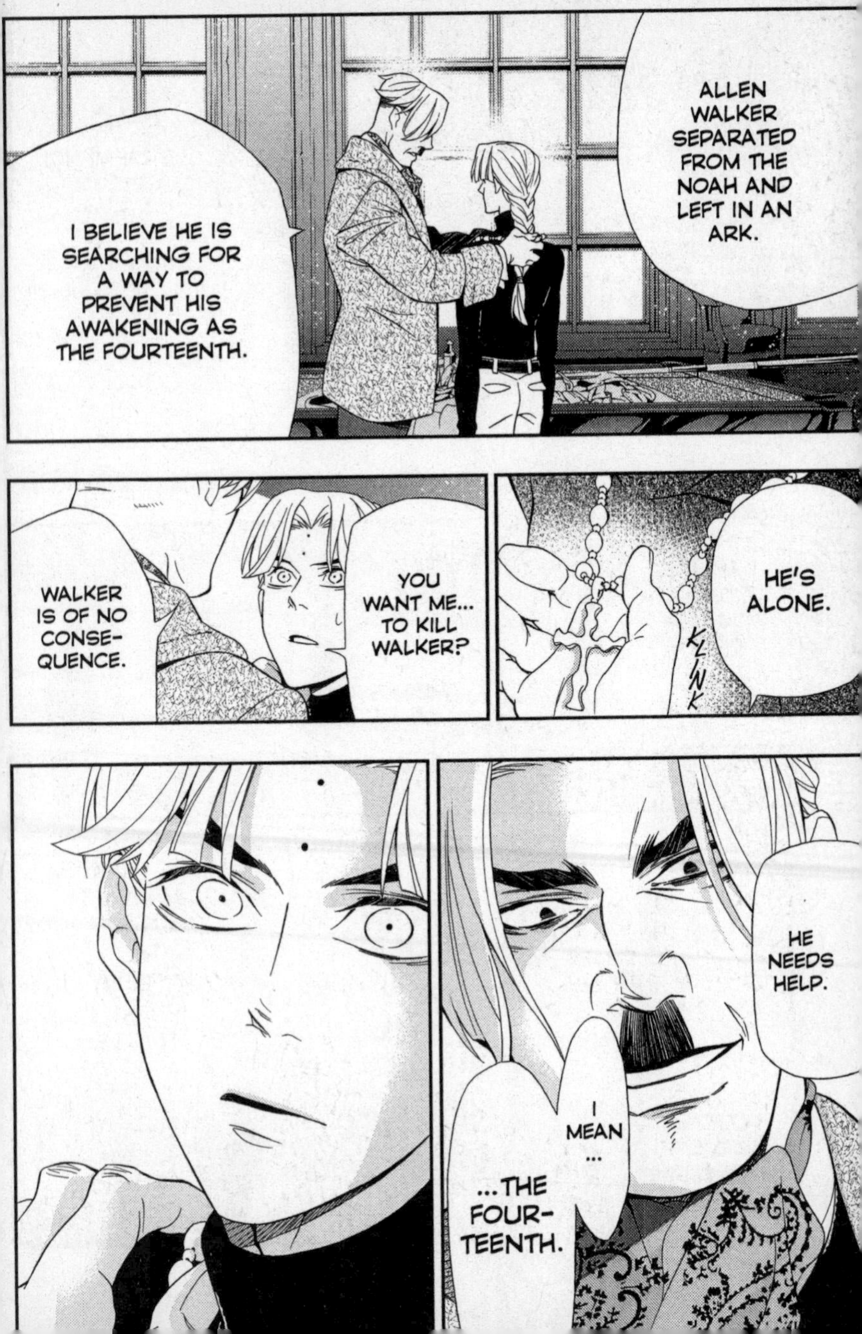
ALLEN WALKER SEPARATED FROM THE NOAH AND LEFT IN AN ARK.
I BELIEVE HE IS SEARCHING FOR A WAY TO PREVENT HIS AWAKENING AS THE FOURTEENTH.
HE'S ALONE.
KLINK
YOU WANT ME... TO KILL WALKER?
WALKER IS OF NO CONSE-QUENCE.
HE NEEDS HELP.
I MEAN...
...THE FOUR-TEENTH.

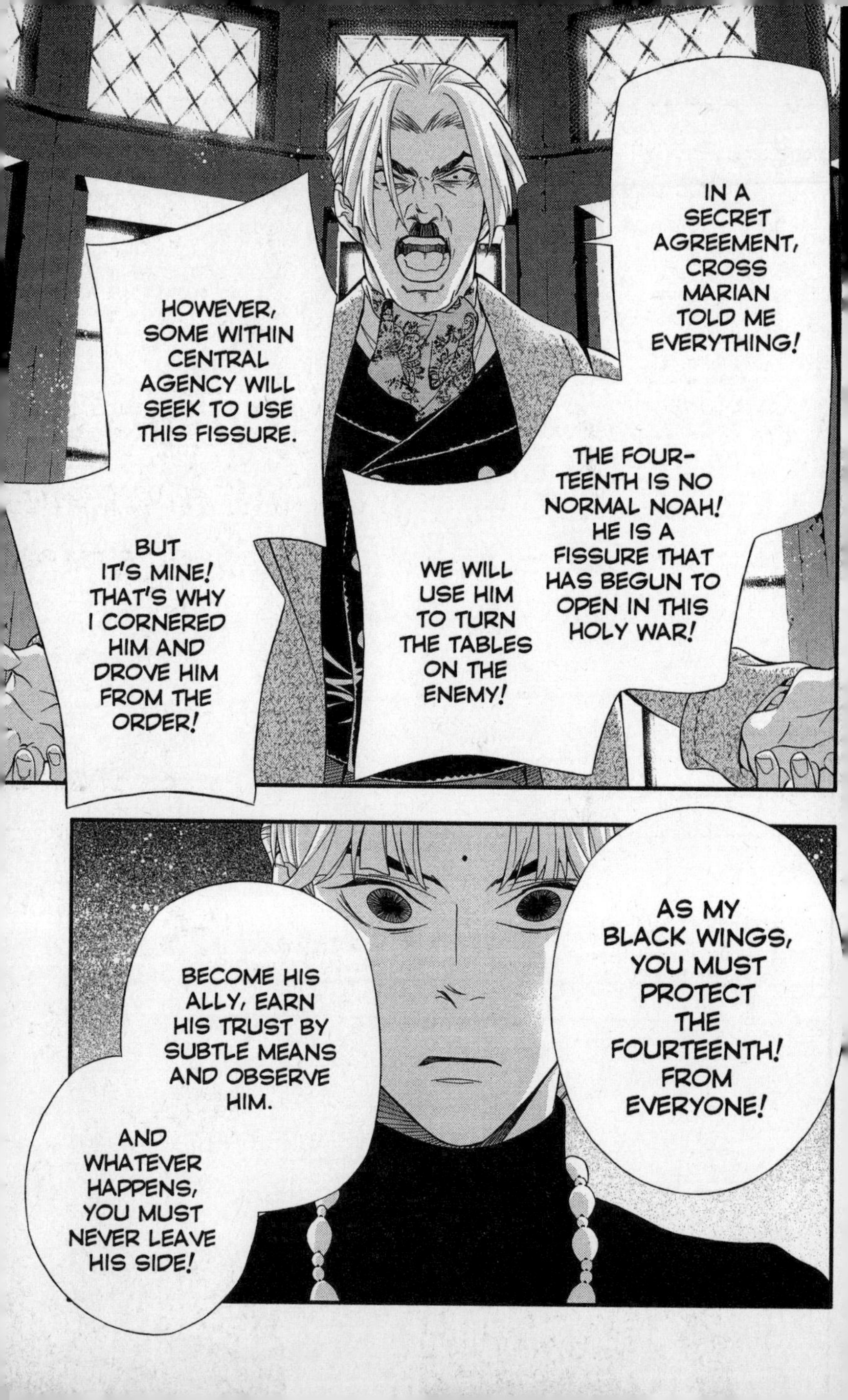
IN A SECRET AGREEMENT, CROSS MARIAN TOLD ME EVERYTHING!
THE FOUR-TEENTH IS NO NORMAL NOAH! HE IS A FISSURE THAT HAS BEGUN TO OPEN IN THIS HOLY WAR!
WE WILL USE HIM TO TURN THE TABLES ON THE ENEMY!
HOWEVER, SOME WITHIN CENTRAL AGENCY WILL SEEK TO USE THIS FISSURE.
BUT IT'S MINE! THAT'S WHY I CORNERED HIM AND DROVE HIM FROM THE ORDER!
AS MY BLACK WINGS, YOU MUST PROTECT THE FOURTEENTH! FROM EVERYONE!
BECOME HIS ALLY, EARN HIS TRUST BY SUBTLE MEANS AND OBSERVE HIM.
AND WHATEVER HAPPENS, YOU MUST NEVER LEAVE HIS SIDE!

WE HUMANS HAVE BEEN MANIPULATED BY THE GREAT HANDS OF OTHERS IN THIS HOLY WAR.

BUT NOW THE FATE OF THE WORLD WILL FINALLY BE IN OUR HANDS!

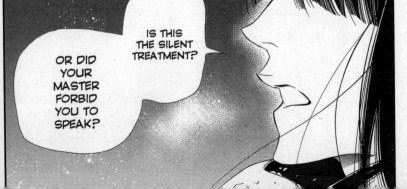

IS THIS THE SILENT TREATMENT?

OR DID YOUR MASTER FORBID YOU TO SPEAK?

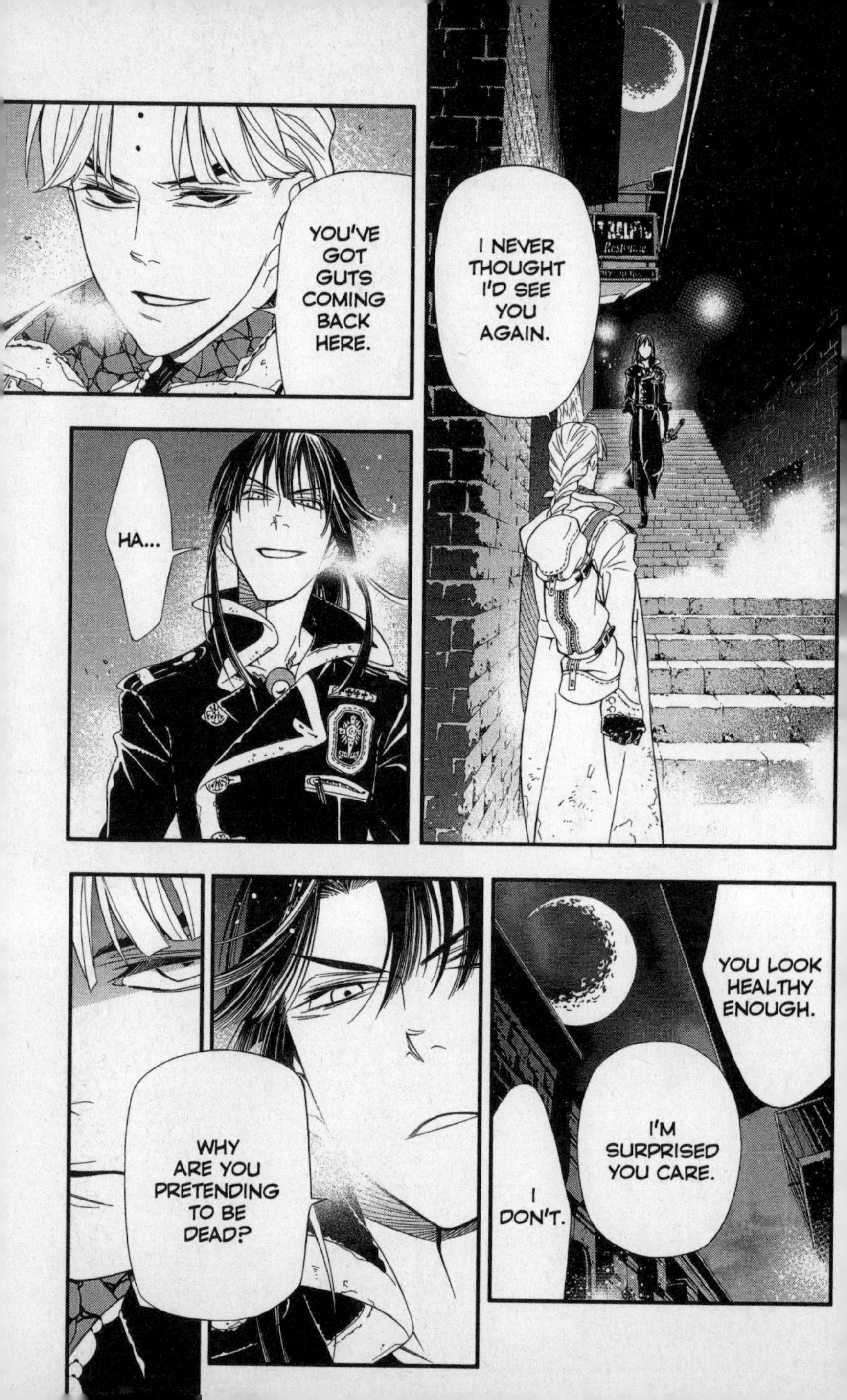
I NEVER THOUGHT I'D SEE YOU AGAIN.
YOU'VE GOT GUTS COMING BACK HERE.
HA...
YOU LOOK HEALTHY ENOUGH.
I'M SURPRISED YOU CARE.
I DON'T.
WHY ARE YOU PRETENDING TO BE DEAD?

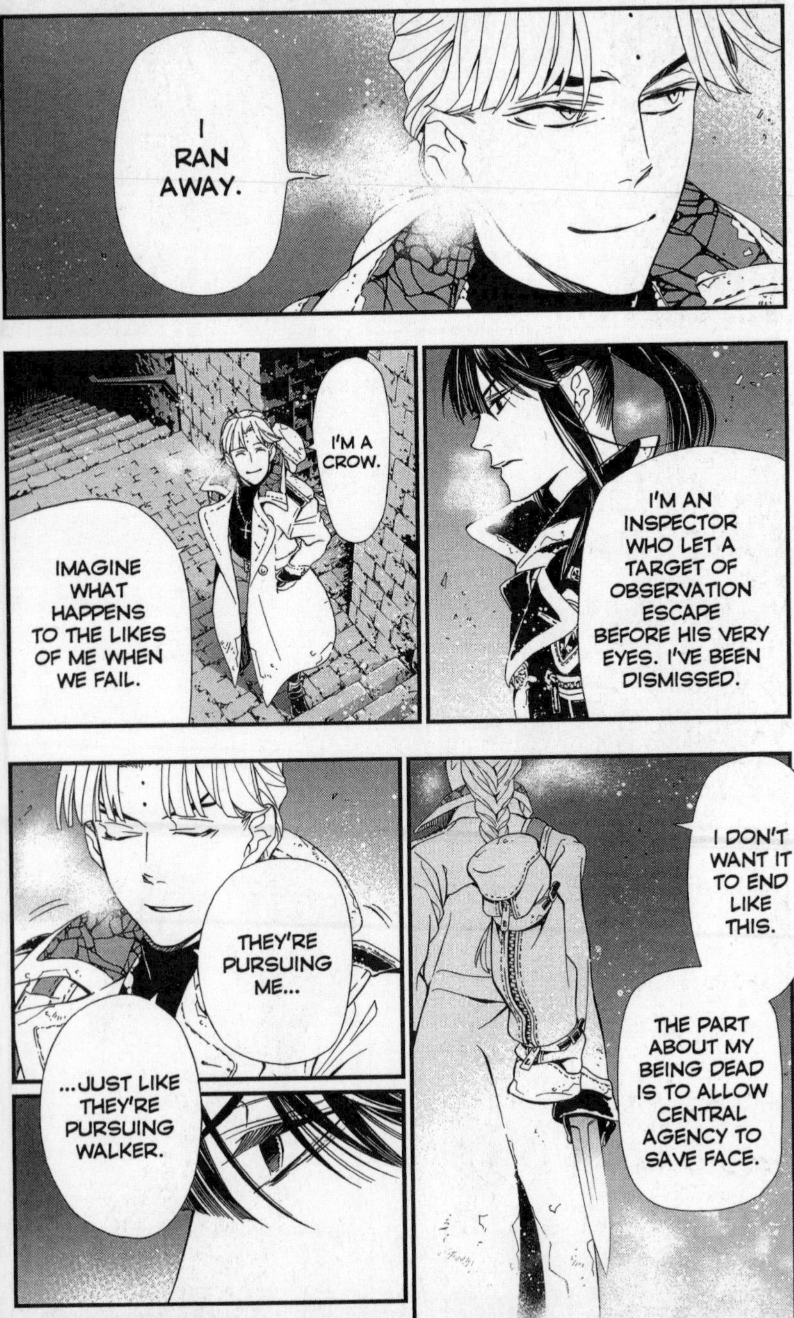
I RAN AWAY.
I'M AN INSPECTOR WHO LET A TARGET OF OBSERVATION ESCAPE BEFORE HIS VERY EYES. I'VE BEEN DISMISSED.
I'M A CROW.
IMAGINE WHAT HAPPENS TO THE LIKES OF ME WHEN WE FAIL.
I DON'T WANT IT TO END LIKE THIS.
THE PART ABOUT MY BEING DEAD IS TO ALLOW CENTRAL AGENCY TO SAVE FACE.
THEY'RE PURSUING ME...
...JUST LIKE THEY'RE PURSUING WALKER.

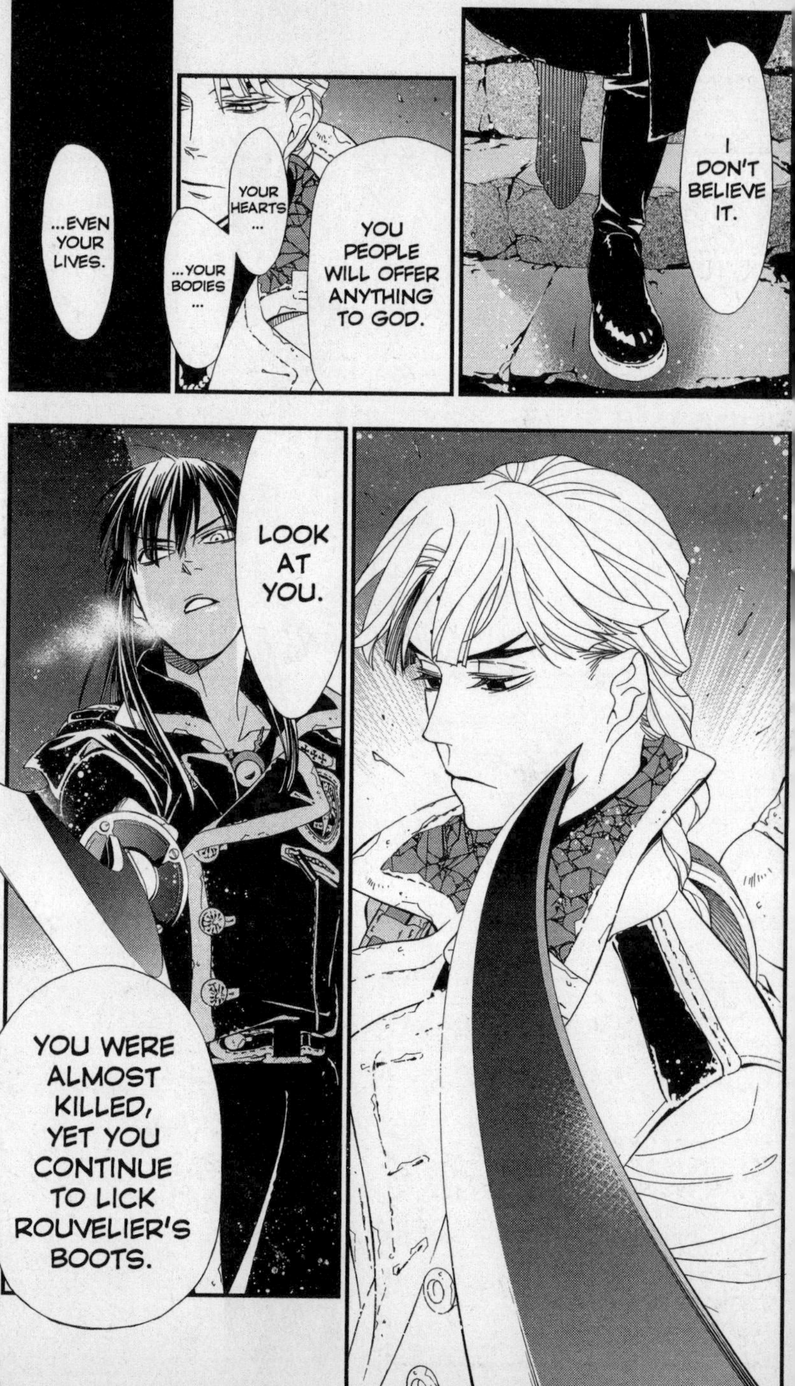
I DON'T BELIEVE IT.
YOU PEOPLE WILL OFFER ANYTHING TO GOD.
YOUR HEARTS...
...YOUR BODIES...
...EVEN YOUR LIVES.
LOOK AT YOU.
YOU WERE ALMOST KILLED, YET YOU CONTINUE TO LICK ROUVELIER'S BOOTS.

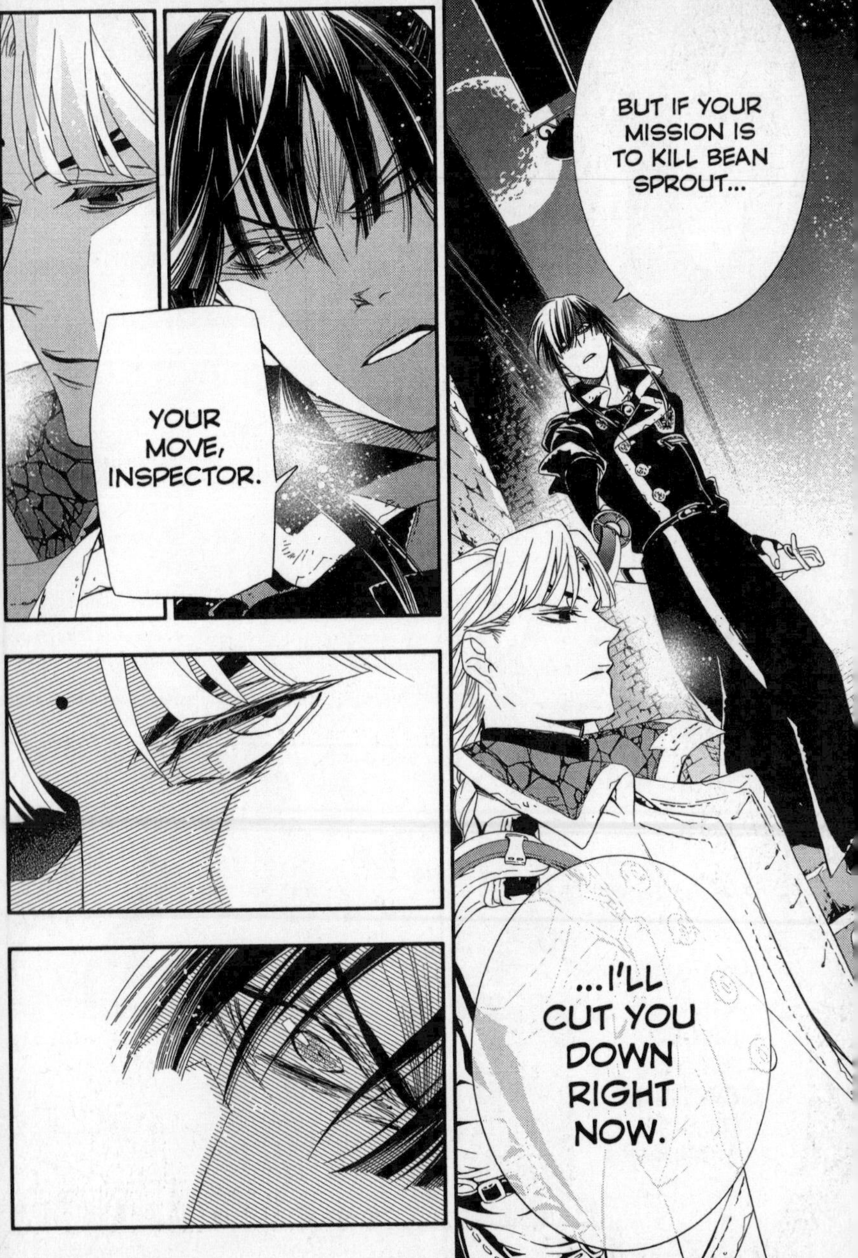
BUT IF YOUR MISSION IS TO KILL BEAN SPROUT...
...I'LL CUT YOU DOWN RIGHT NOW.
YOUR MOVE, INSPECTOR.

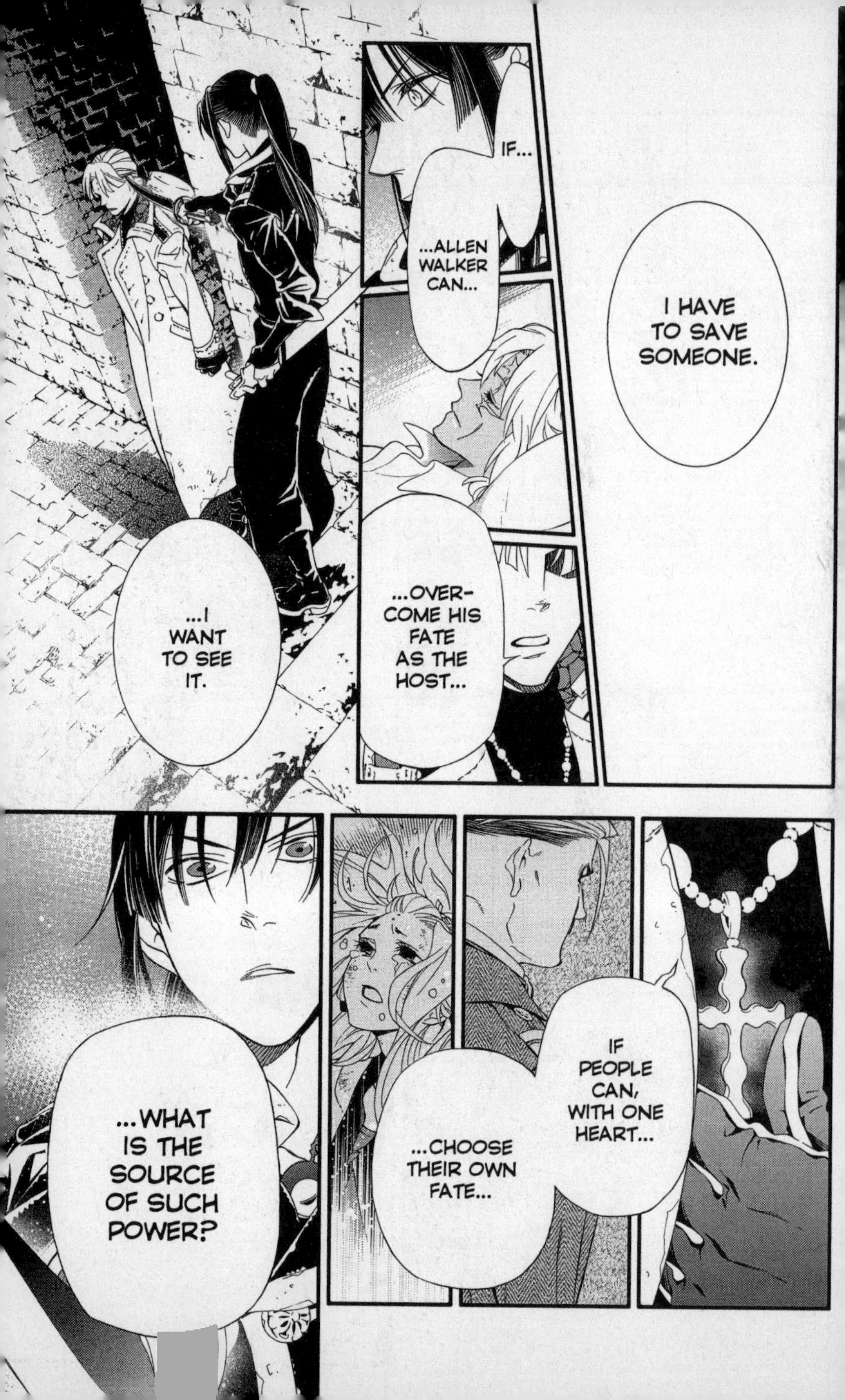
I HAVE TO SAVE SOMEONE.
IF...
...ALLEN WALKER CAN...
...OVER-COME HIS FATE AS THE HOST...
...I WANT TO SEE IT.
IF PEOPLE CAN, WITH ONE HEART...
...CHOOSE THEIR OWN FATE...
...WHAT IS THE SOURCE OF SUCH POWER?

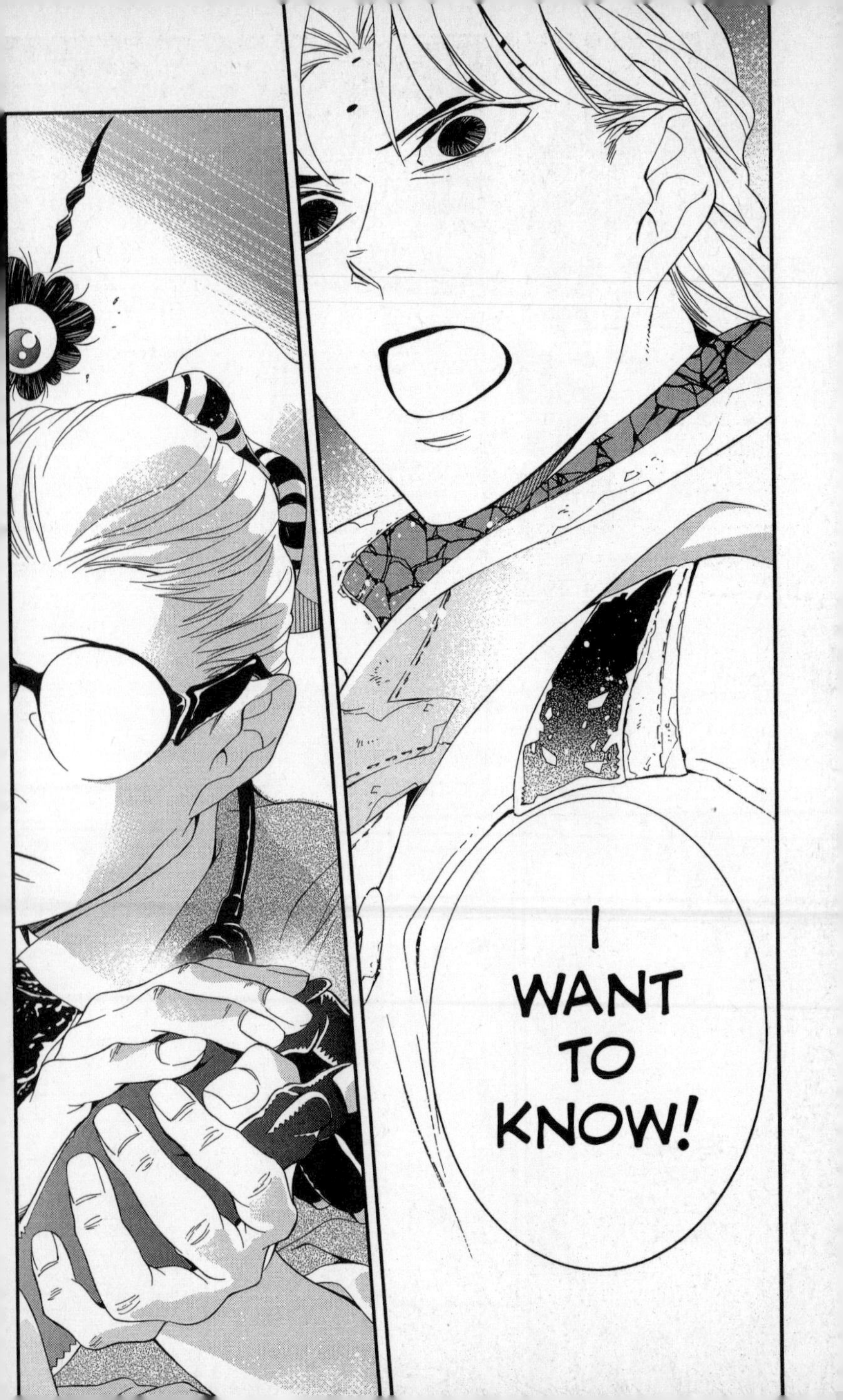
I WANT TO KNOW!

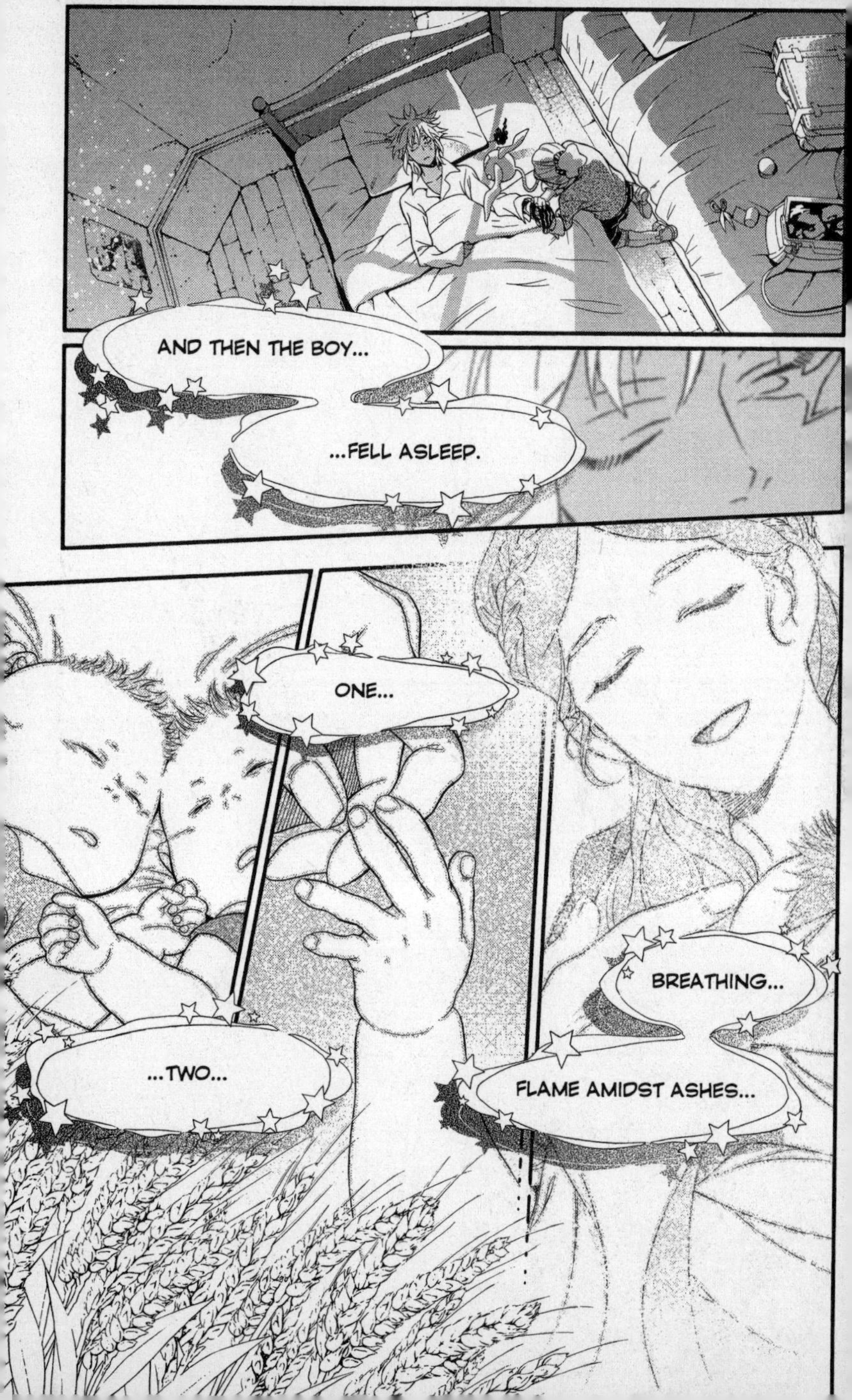
AND THEN THE BOY...
...FELL ASLEEP.
BREATHING...
FLAME AMIDST ASHES...
ONE...
...TWO...

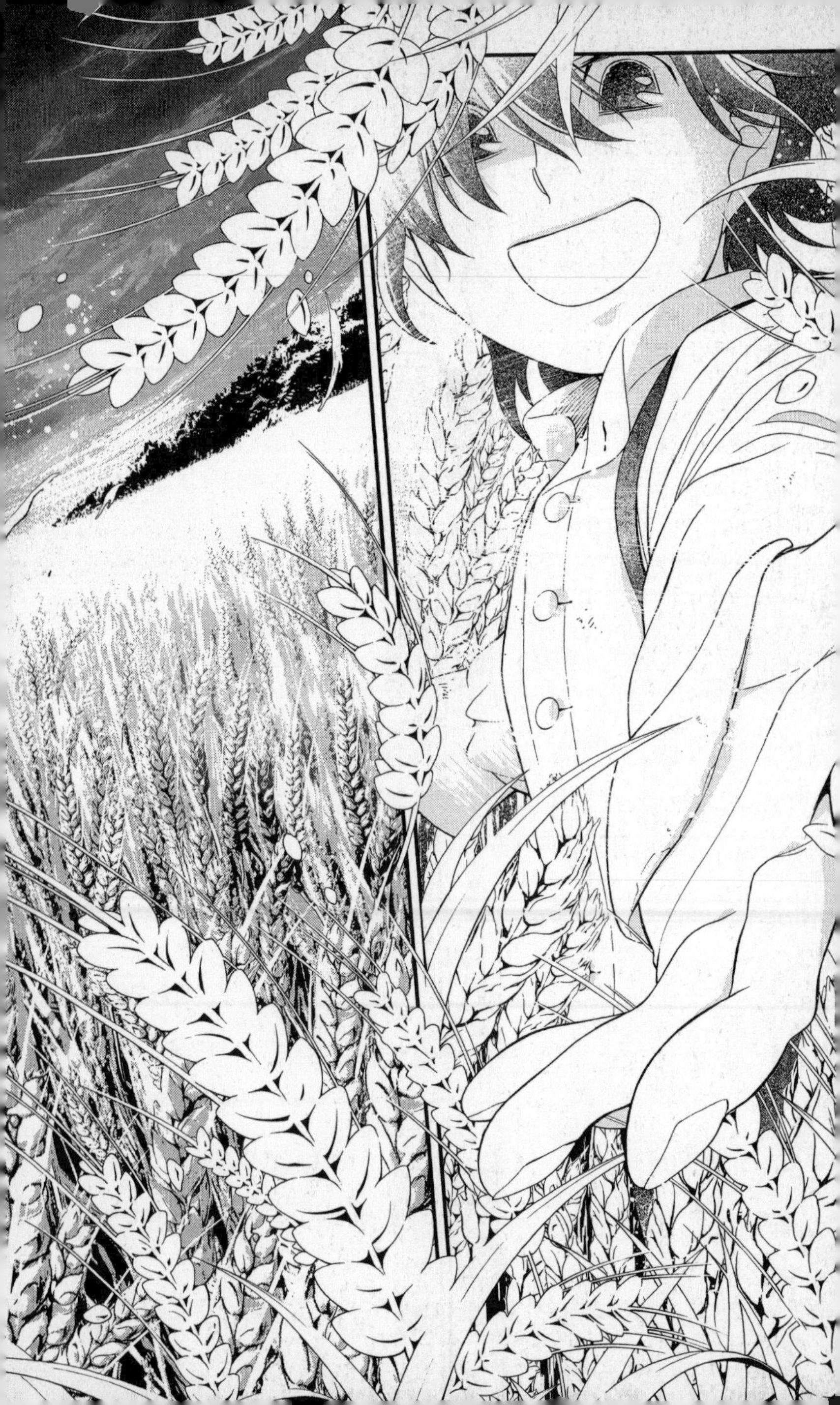

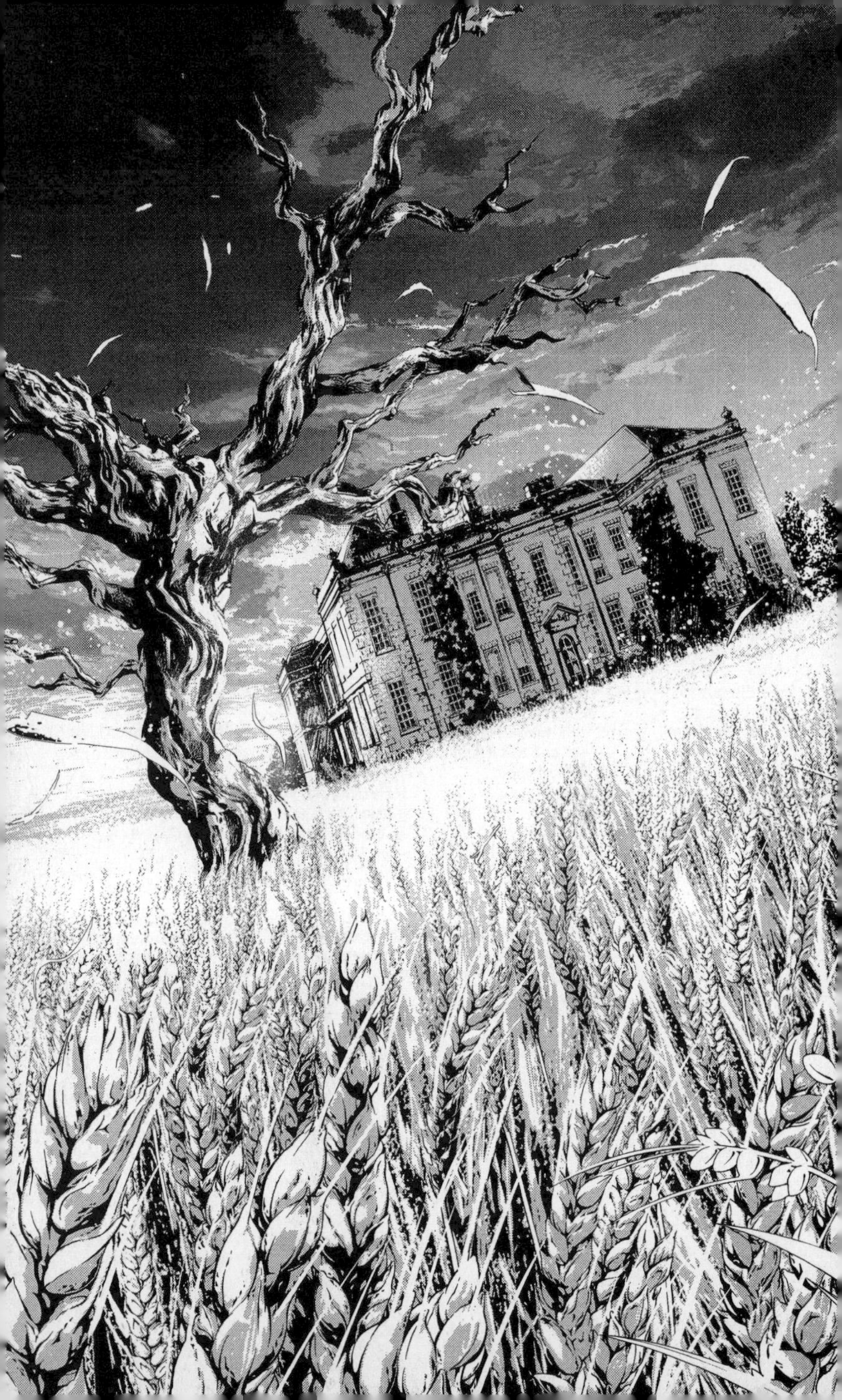

KOMUI'S DISCUSSION ROOM 1

Tim | Link | Tyki | Waizurii | Johnny | Kanda | Allen

Allen
(hereafter "A"):
This segment is affectionately known as "Komui Discussion Room," but Komui never shows up! We received mail asking me to do a discussion again, so for the first time in a while, we're going to chat! We have lots of guests this time!
☆

Kanda
(hereafter "K"):
Hmph! Who sent that mail?

Johnny
(hereafter "J"):
I'm Johnny Gill, once of the Science Department! This is my first time here!

Waizurii
(hereafter "W"):
I'm Waizurii of the Demonic Eyes!
☆

Tyki
(hereafter "Ty"):
I'm Tyki, friend of young boys and the idol of the Noah.
(baffled)
Hey, what's the deal with this script?!

W: You were dragging your feet, so the Millennium Earl wrote it for you.

J: Waaah! N-N-Noah?! (scared)

A: Hey, what are you guys doing there? I wanted Lavi!

W: Chill, Fourteenth! Lavi's busy, so we're taking his place.

A: Don't call me the Fourteenth! (angry)

J: Calm down, Allen! No fighting, or it'll ruin the segment! (frets) Now for the questions, okay? I'll read one...

Q. All the Noah look really fit, but they always seem to be lazing around. Do they go to a gym?

W: A question for the Noah right off the bat! Good thing we're here! ♡

A: (irritated)

J: Allen! Here are some of Chef Jerry's mitarashi dango! ♡ (frets)

A: (takes a bite) Munch munch... I guess I can over- look their impu- dence this time.

K: Food really is your weakness.

A: Sorry. I haven't had a decent meal since I left the Order!

Ty: If you'd asked the Earl,

he would've taken you to a three-star restaurant!

A: Th-Three stars?! Is th-that how you guys always eat?!

J: Allen...

K: Bean Sprout, you're drooling.

W: We're aristocrats; our fine figures are the result of our diet.
♡

Ty: But weren't you homeless, Waizurii?

A: Well, you were too! (glares)

W: Tyki is an aristocrat when he's with the other Noah. When we awaken as Noah, we're reborn on a cellular level, so we defy common sense.

J: You become superhuman?

W: Yes. And we age very slowly. That's why we're beautiful and have such good physiques.

A: Nobody said you were beautiful.

Ty: We're very active, at parties and so forth, which is a real pain. The Earl has been saying it's exhausting to turn

down marriage proposals, so maybe I should accept one! I mean, I want to take it easy! Do you know how long it's been since I saw my miner buddies?!

W: And I hate parties!

J: So it's hard to be a Noah. We have something in common!

A: But you eat at three-star restaurants, right?

K: Oh, get off that!

Ty & W:
The Earl's homemade hamburgers are so much better!

A: Hmph! Jerry's hamburgers beat his! ⊰sob⊱ I wanna see Jerry! (cries)

J: Allen, I'm not Jerry, but I'll make hamburgers for you! (cries)

K: Such a pain...

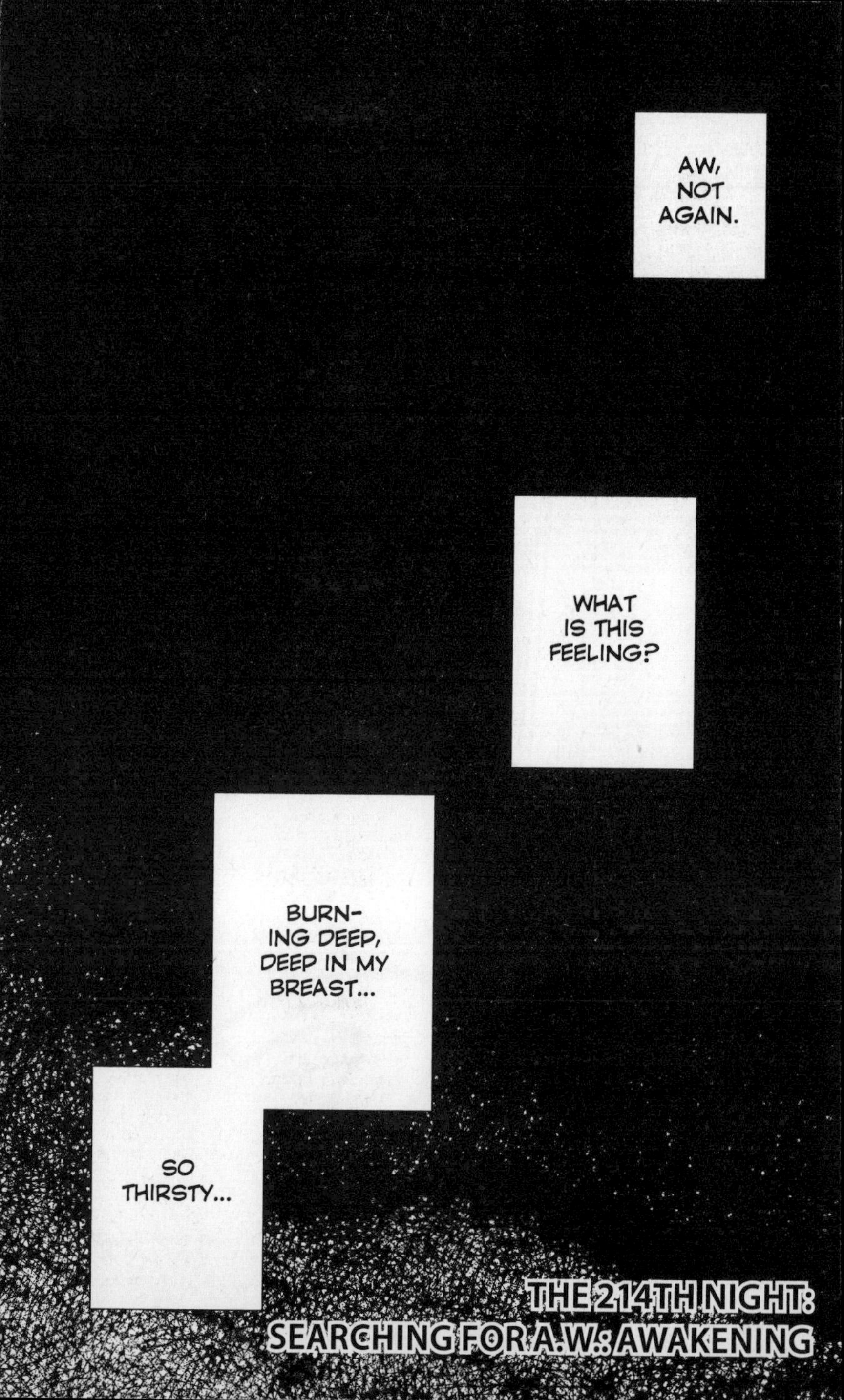
AW, NOT AGAIN.
WHAT IS THIS FEELING?
BURN-ING DEEP, DEEP IN MY BREAST...
SO THIRSTY...
THE 214TH NIGHT: SEARCHING FOR A.W.: AWAKENING

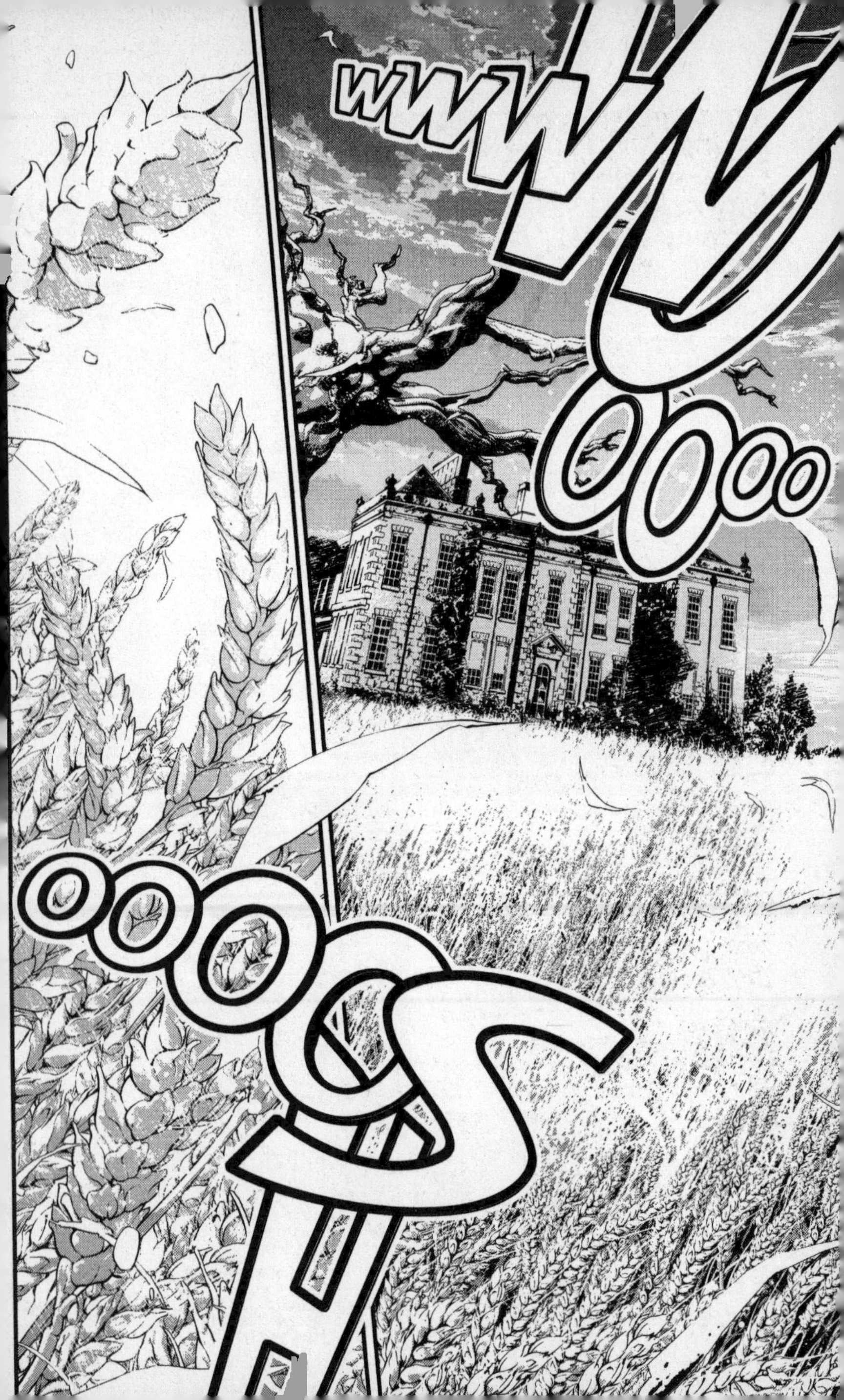
WWWWWOOOO
OOOOSH

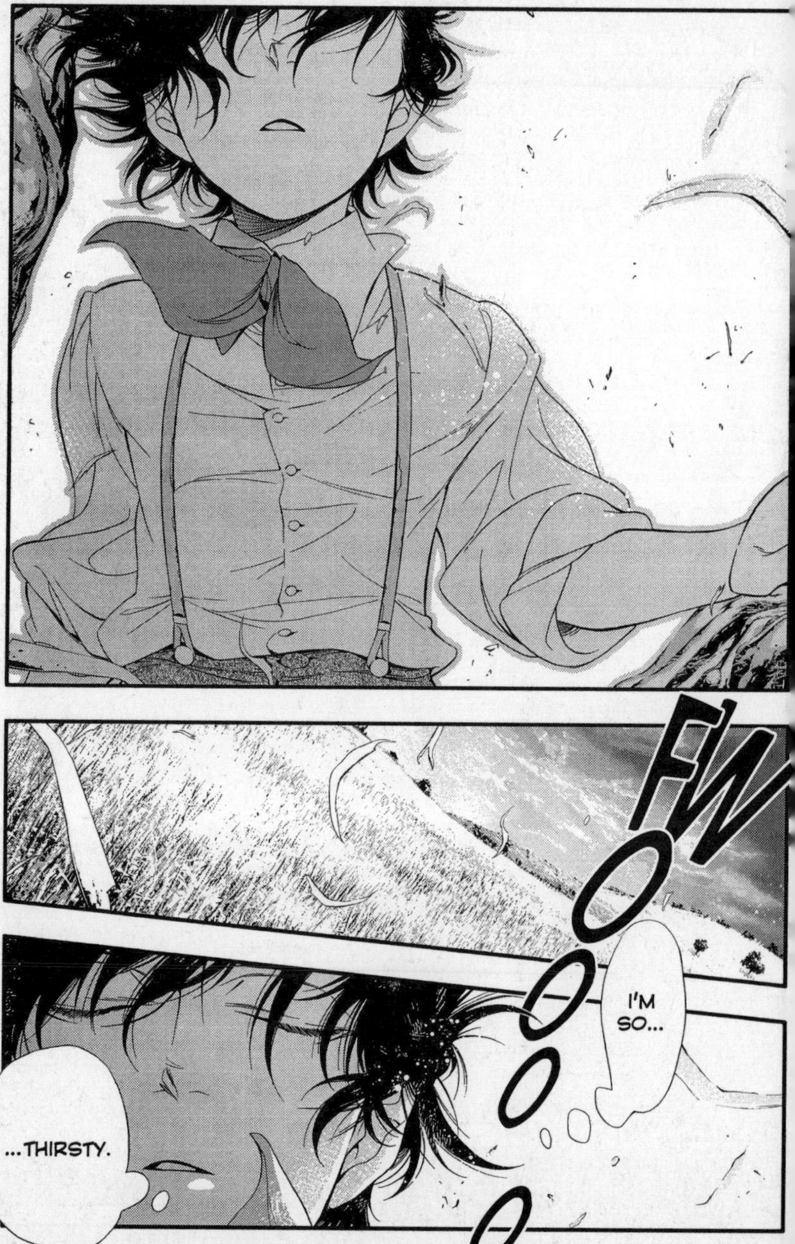
FWOOOOOO
I'M SO...
...THIRSTY.

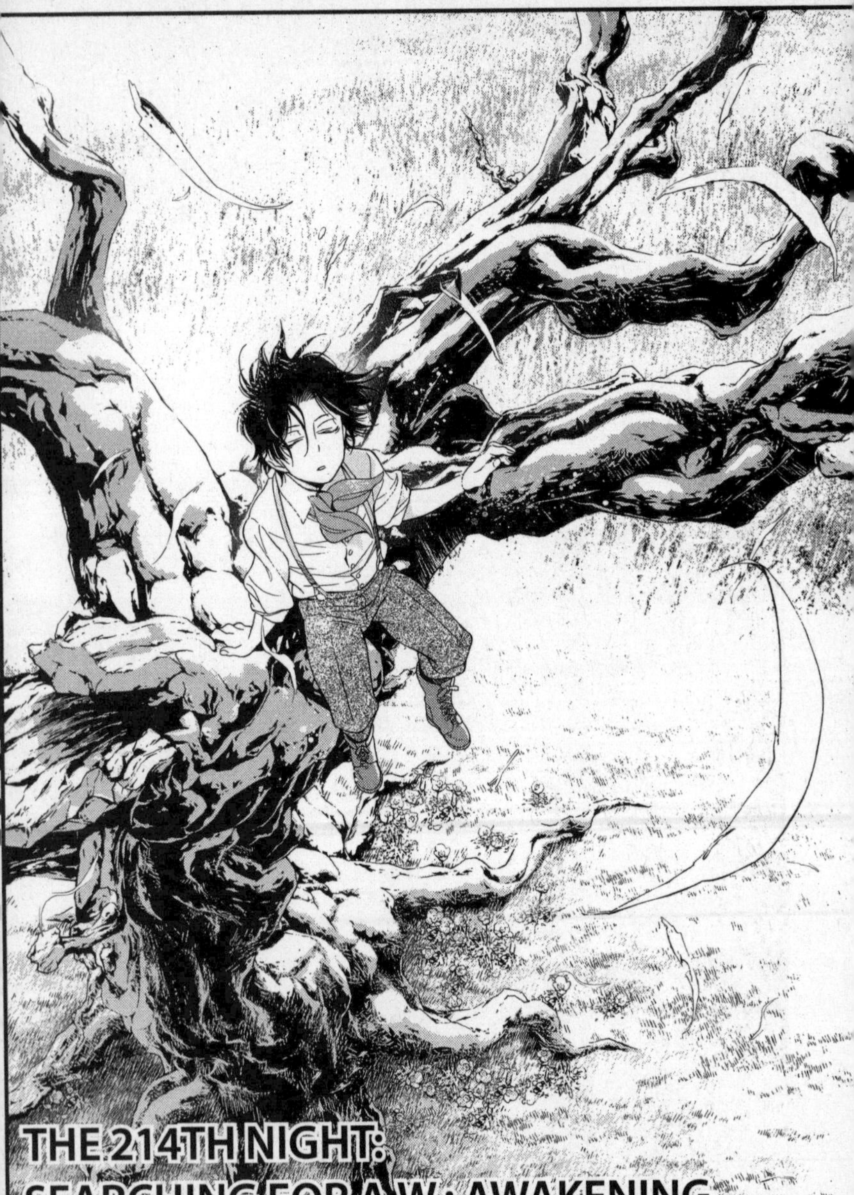
THE 214TH NIGHT:
SEARCHING FOR A.W.: AWAKENING

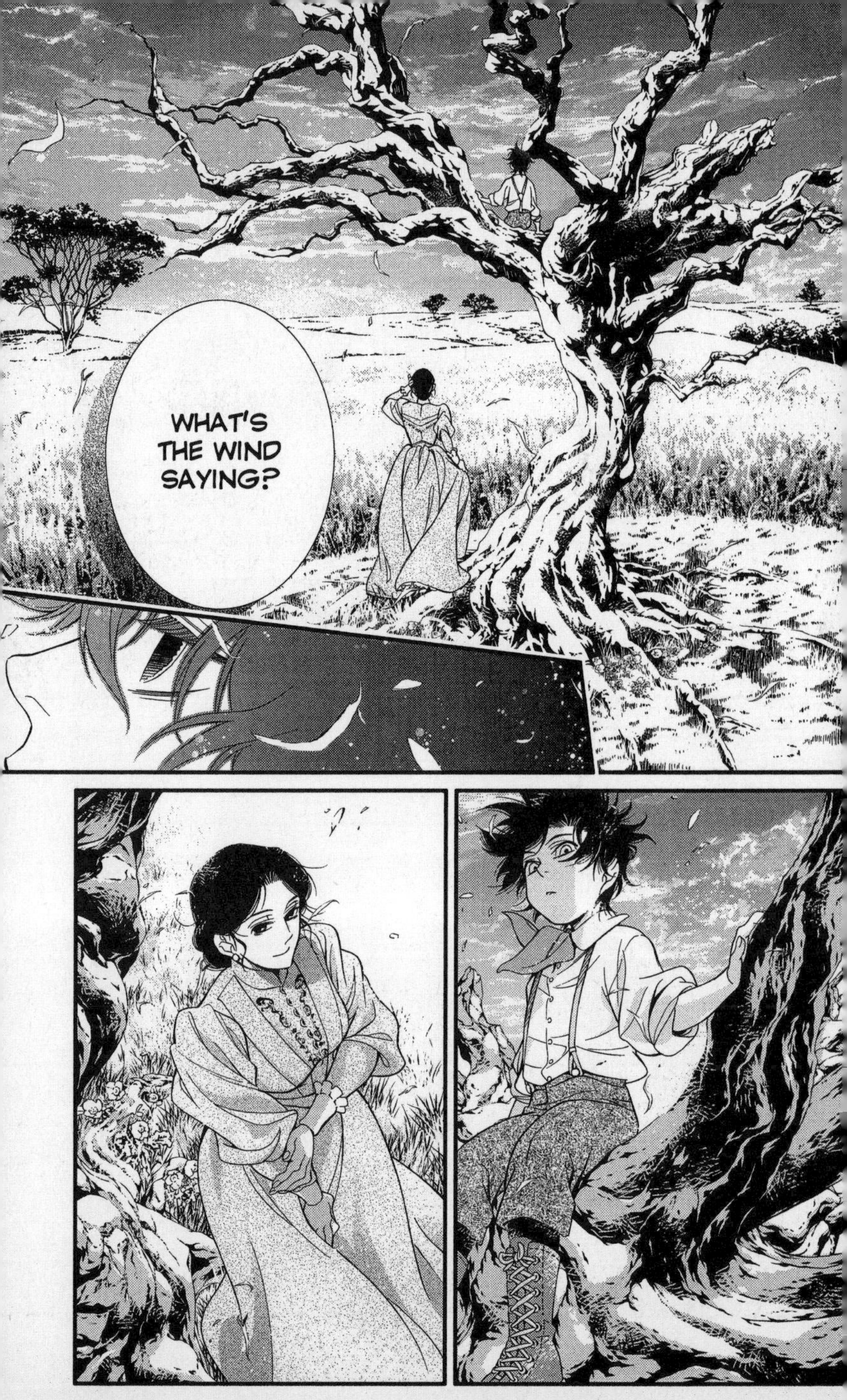
WHAT'S THE WIND SAYING?

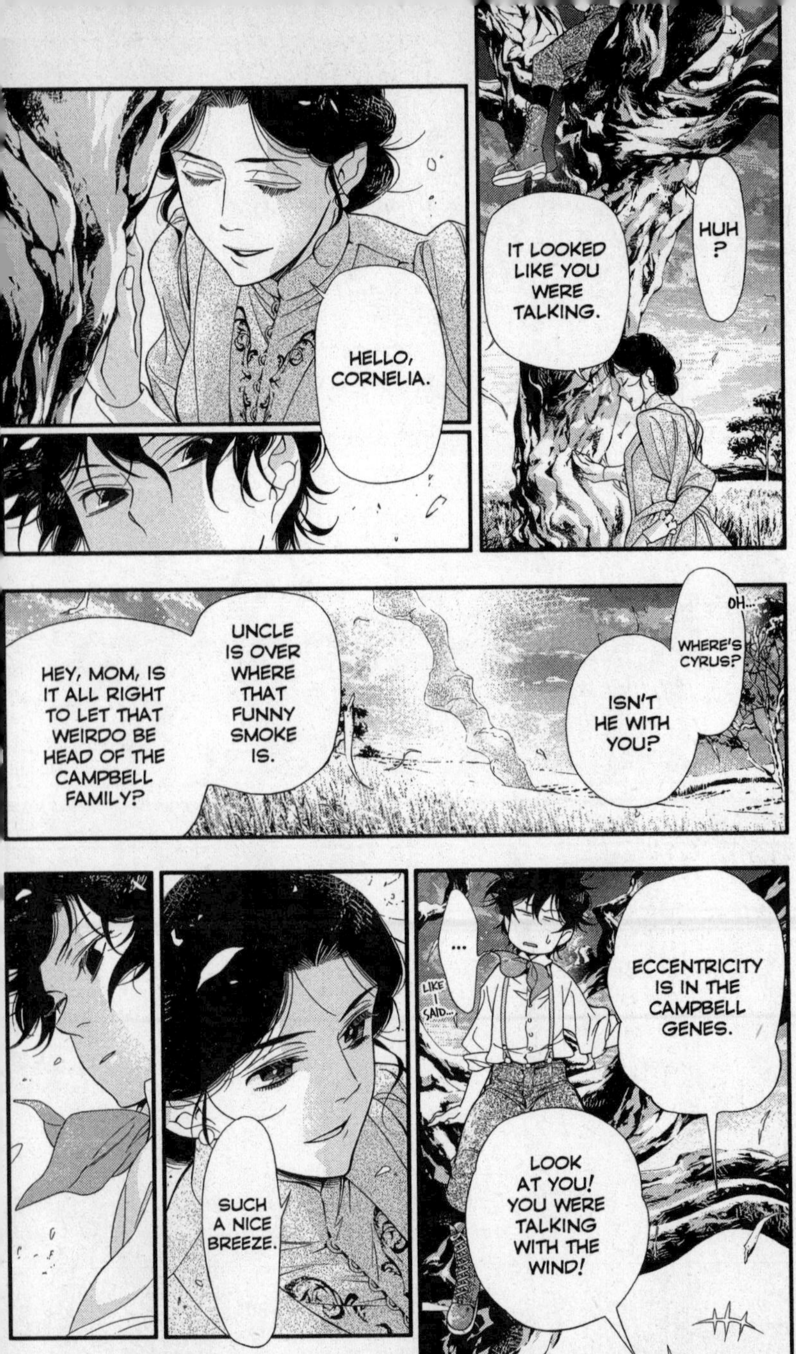
HUH?
IT LOOKED LIKE YOU WERE TALKING.
HELLO, CORNELIA.
OH...
WHERE'S CYRUS?
ISN'T HE WITH YOU?
UNCLE IS OVER WHERE THAT FUNNY SMOKE IS.
HEY, MOM, IS IT ALL RIGHT TO LET THAT WEIRDO BE HEAD OF THE CAMPBELL FAMILY?
ECCENTRICITY IS IN THE CAMPBELL GENES.
...
LIKE I SAID...
LOOK AT YOU! YOU WERE TALKING WITH THE WIND!
SUCH A NICE BREEZE.

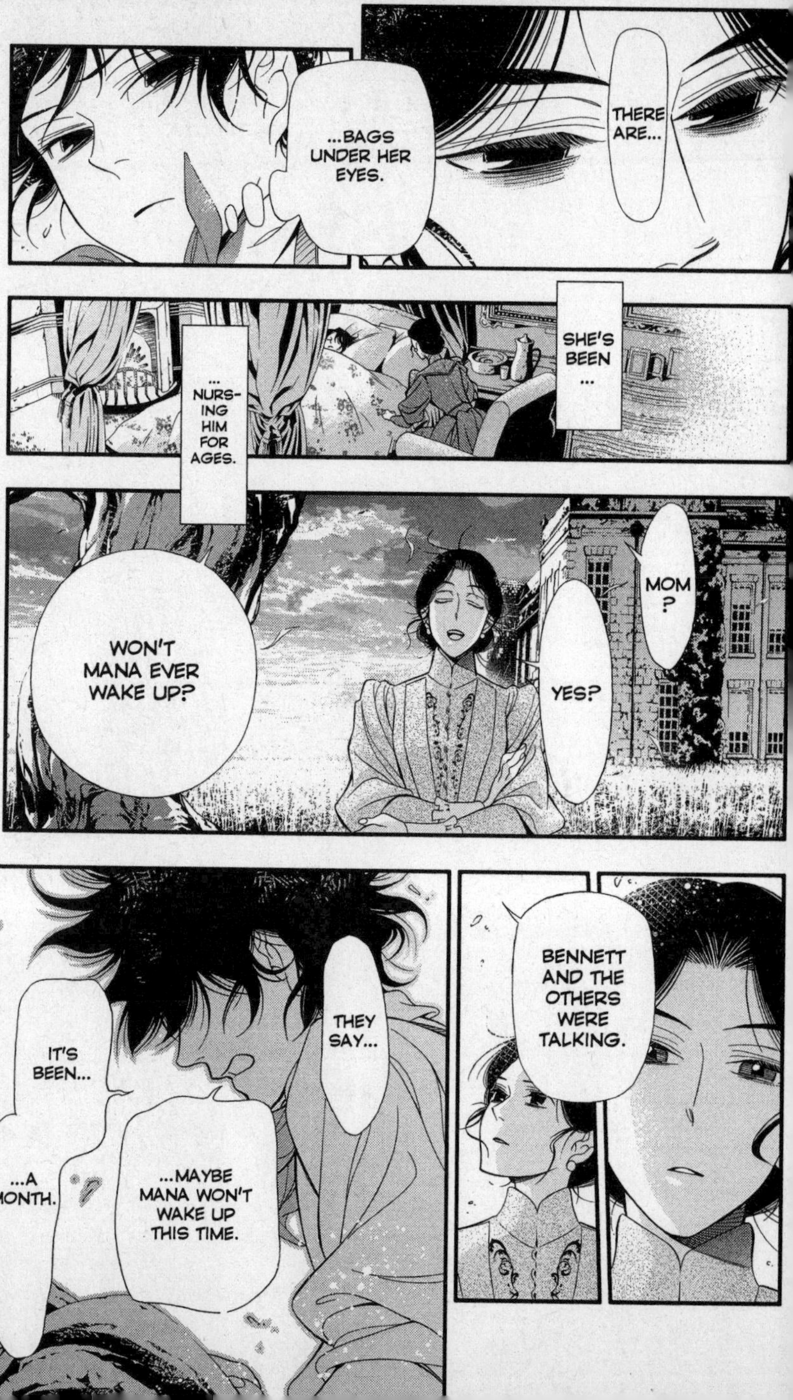
THERE ARE...
...BAGS UNDER HER EYES.
SHE'S BEEN ...
... NURSING HIM FOR AGES.
MOM ?
YES?
WON'T MANA EVER WAKE UP?
BENNETT AND THE OTHERS WERE TALKING.
THEY SAY...
IT'S BEEN...
...A MONTH.
...MAYBE MANA WON'T WAKE UP THIS TIME.

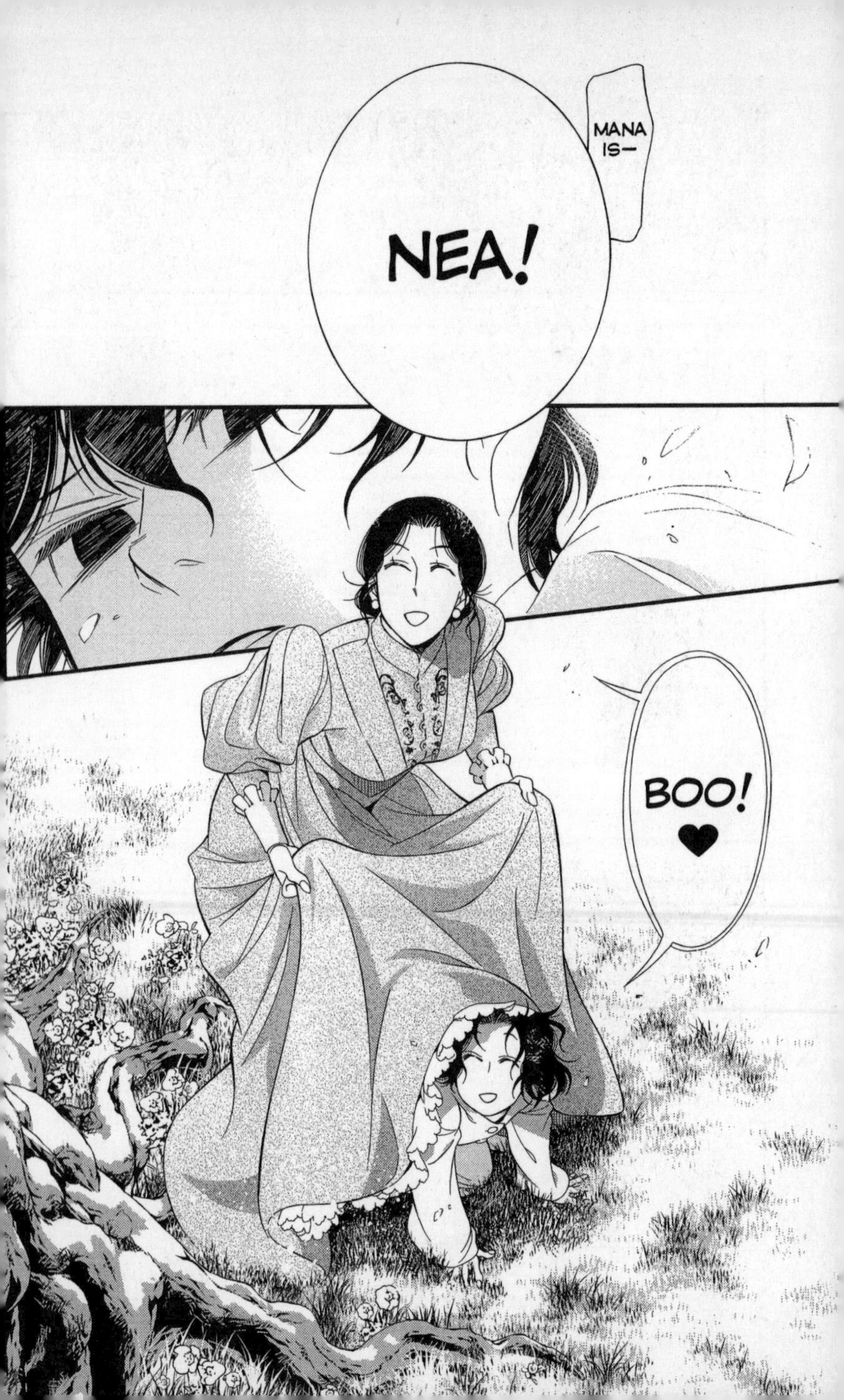
MANA IS—
NEA!
BOO! ♥

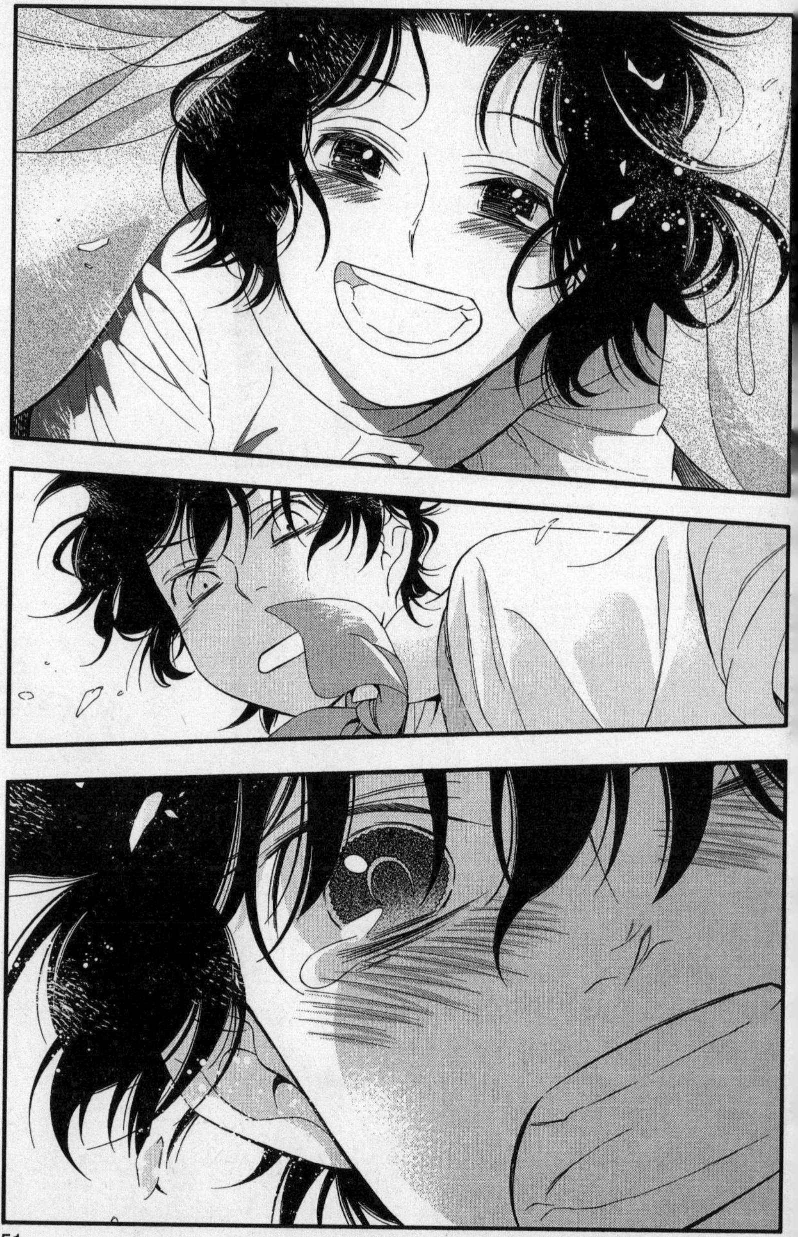

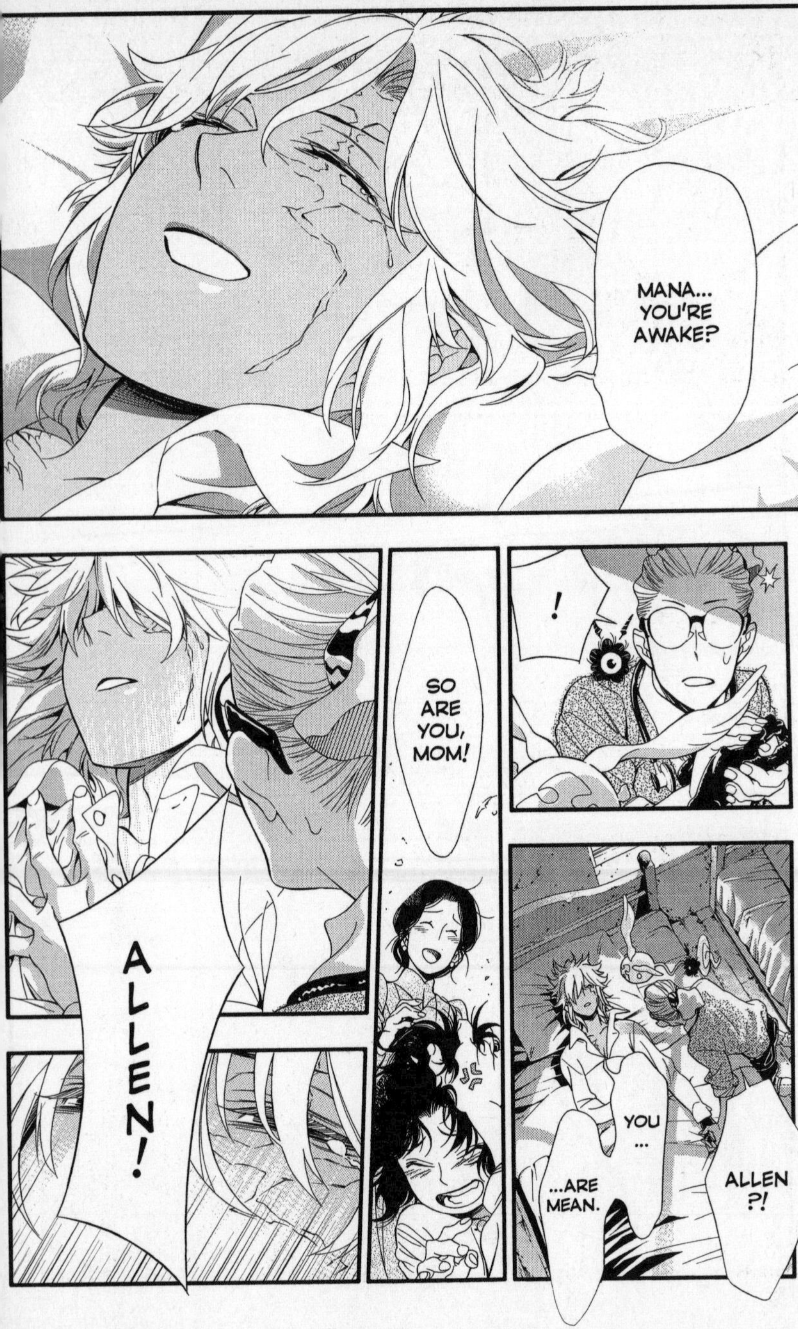
MANA... YOU'RE AWAKE?
!
ALLEN ?!
YOU ...
...ARE MEAN.
SO ARE YOU, MOM!
ALLEN!

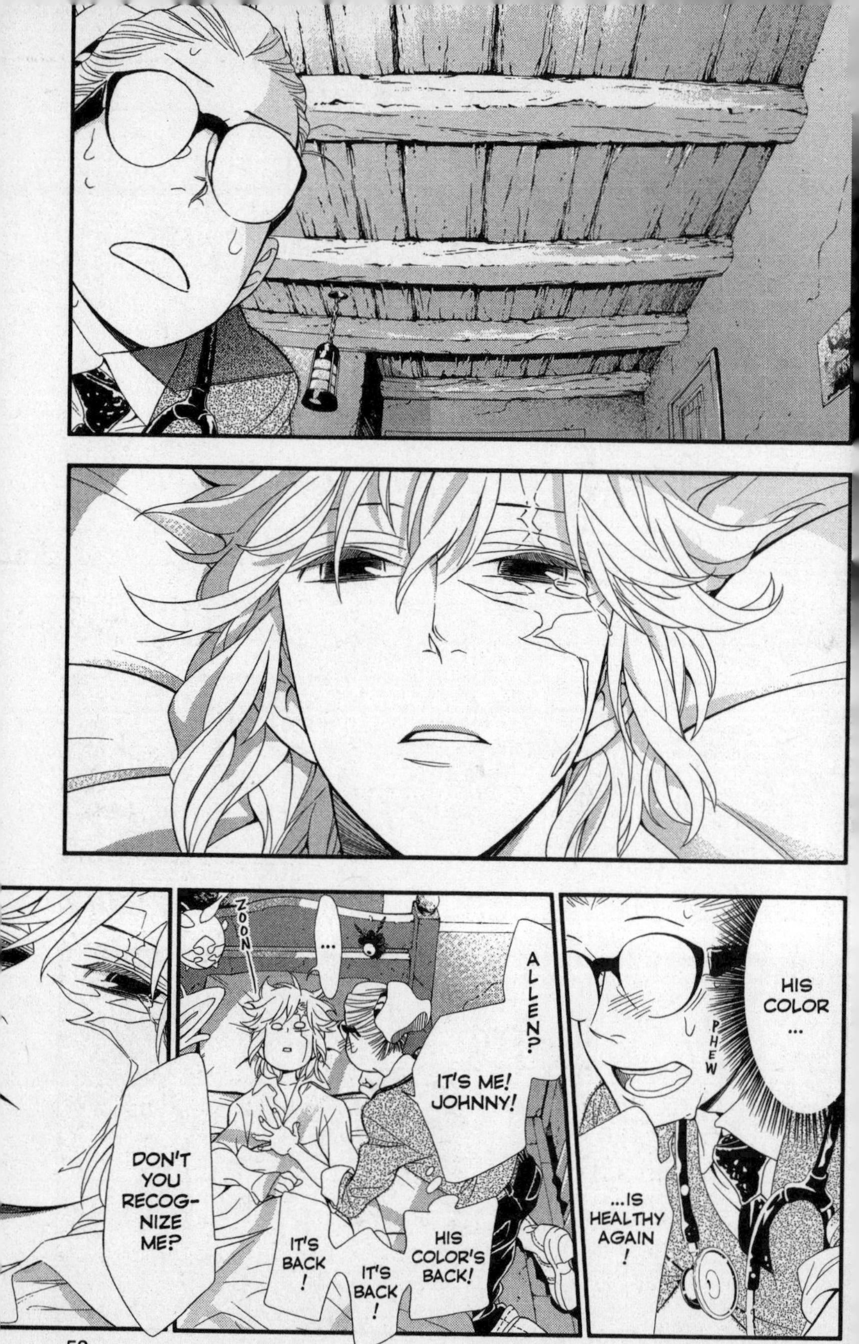
HIS COLOR ...
PHEW
...IS HEALTHY AGAIN!
ALLEN?
IT'S ME! JOHNNY!
...
ZOON
HIS COLOR'S BACK!
IT'S BACK!
IT'S BACK!
DON'T YOU RECOGNIZE ME?

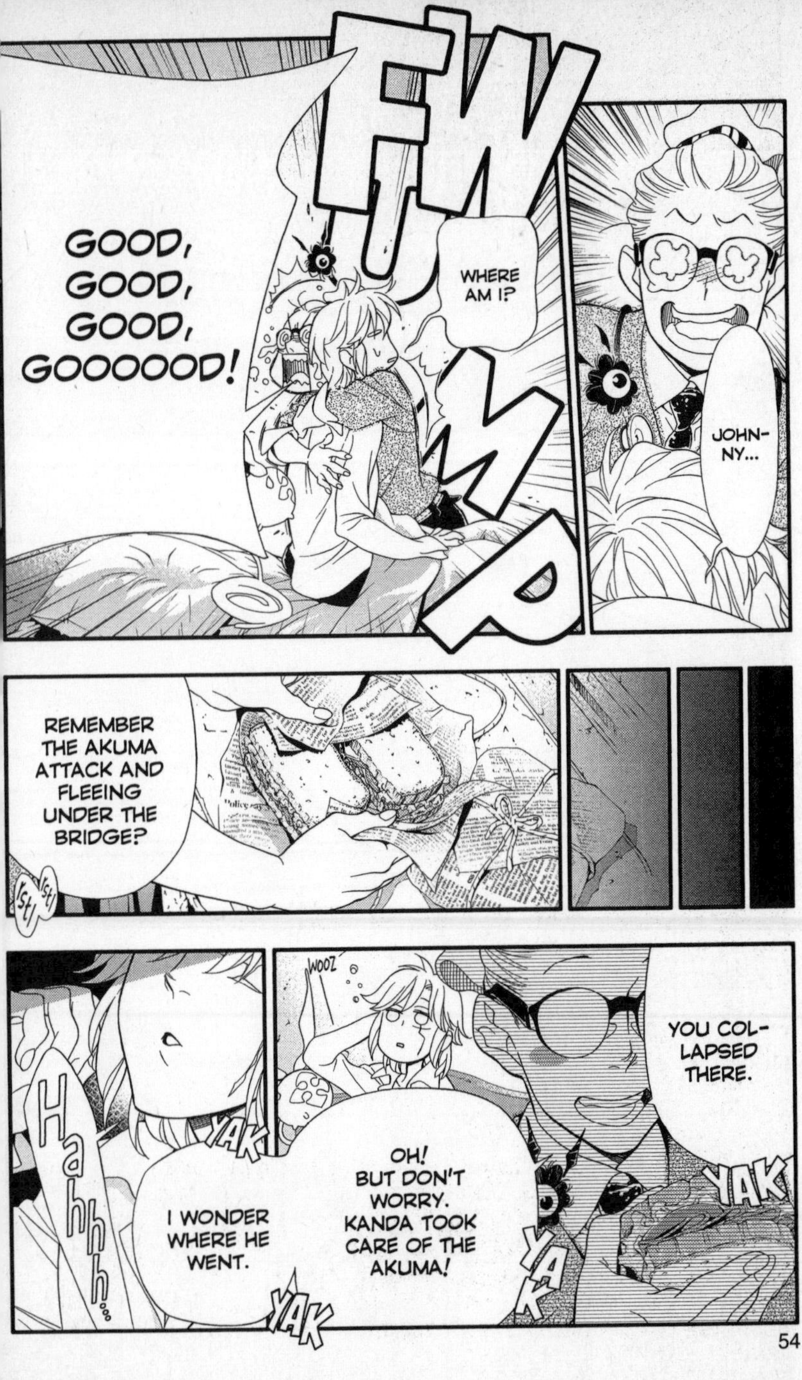
JOHN-
NY...
FWUMP
WHERE AM I?
GOOD, GOOD, GOOD, GOOOOOD!
REMEMBER THE AKUMA ATTACK AND FLEEING UNDER THE BRIDGE?
rst! rst!
WOOZ
YOU COL-
LAPSED THERE.
YAK
YAK
OH! BUT DON'T WORRY. KANDA TOOK CARE OF THE AKUMA!
YAK
YAK
Hahhh...
I WONDER WHERE HE WENT.

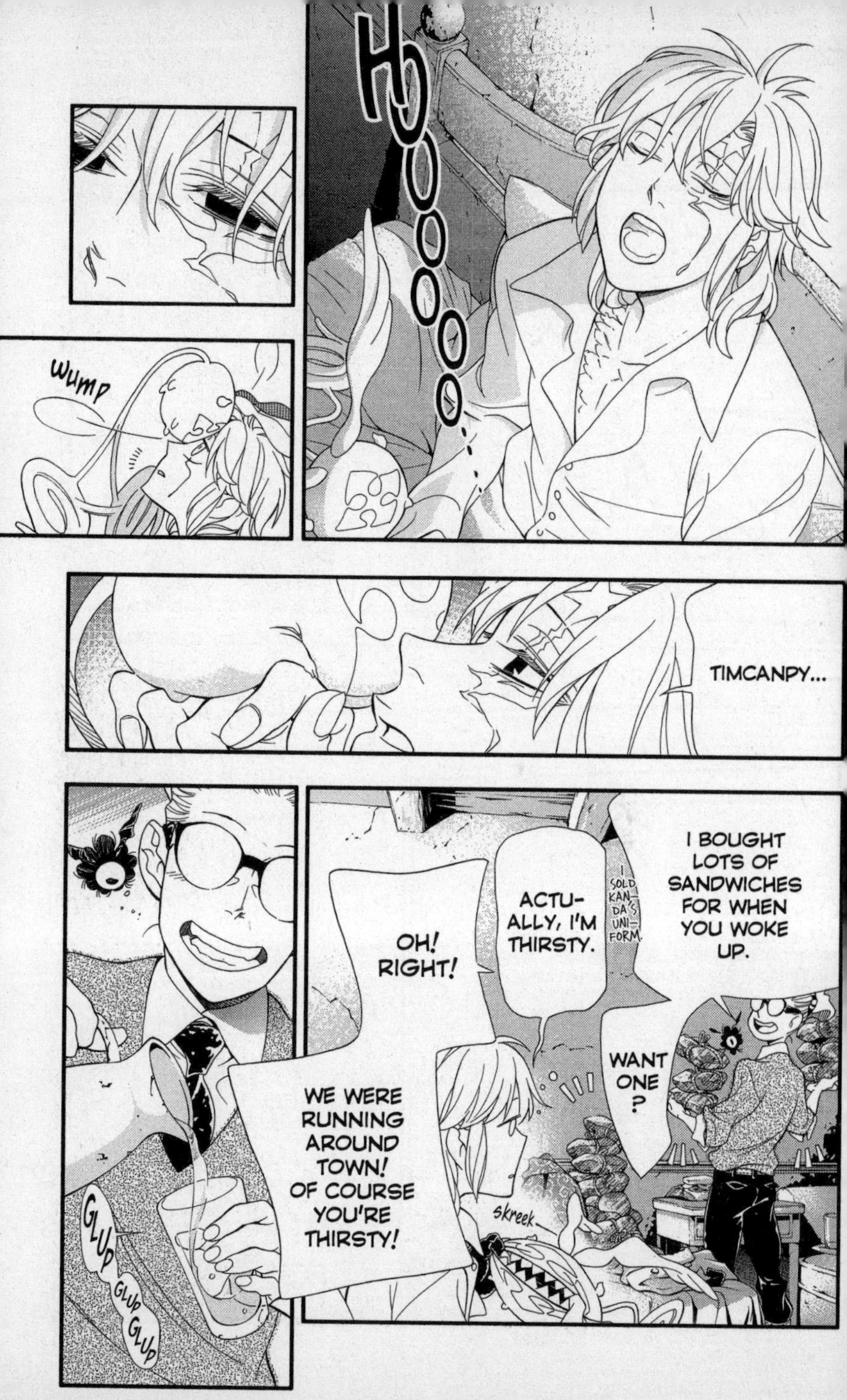
HOOOOOOO...
wump
TIMCANPY...
I BOUGHT LOTS OF SANDWICHES FOR WHEN YOU WOKE UP.
WANT ONE?
I SOLD KANDA'S UNIFORM.
ACTUALLY, I'M THIRSTY.
skreek
OH! RIGHT!
WE WERE RUNNING AROUND TOWN! OF COURSE YOU'RE THIRSTY!
GLUP
GLUP
GLUP

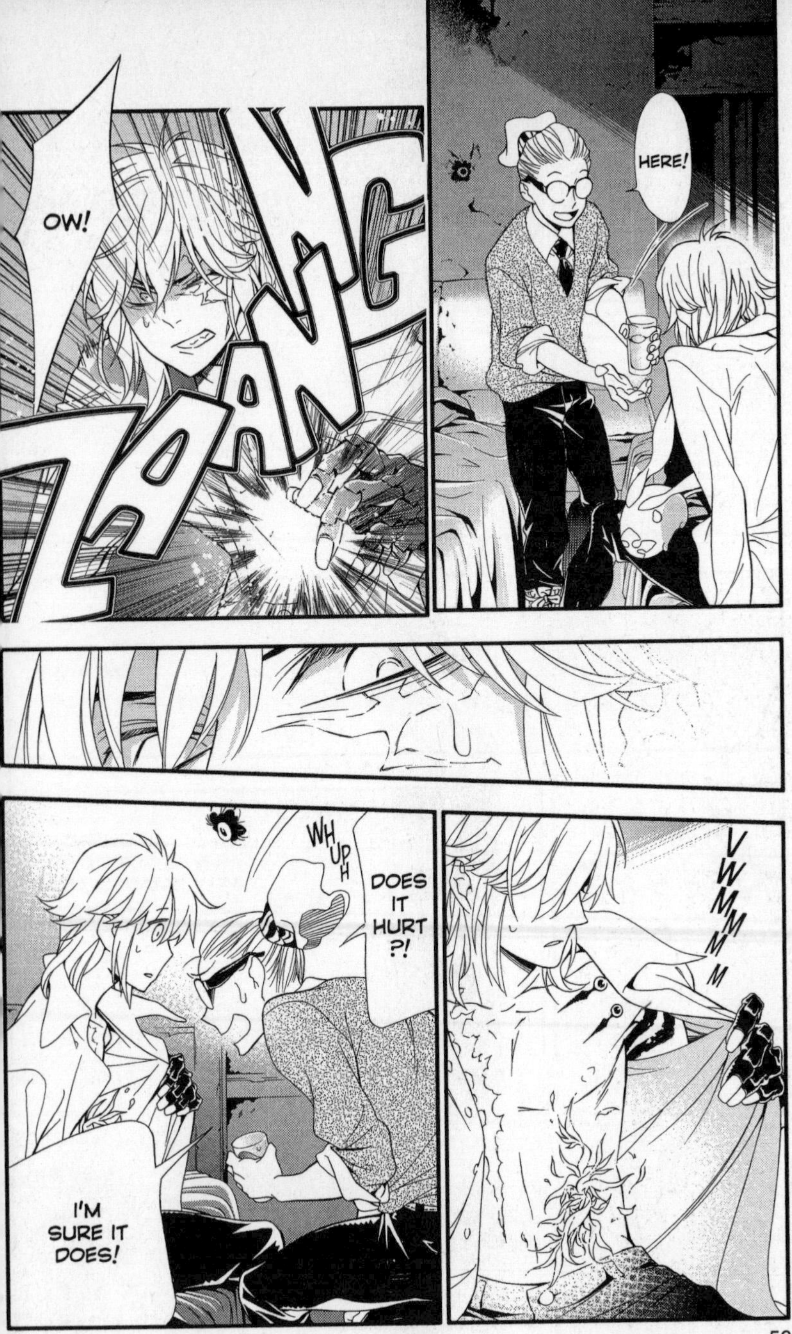

HERE!
OW!
ZAANG
VWMMMM
WHUPH
DOES IT HURT?!
I'M SURE IT DOES!

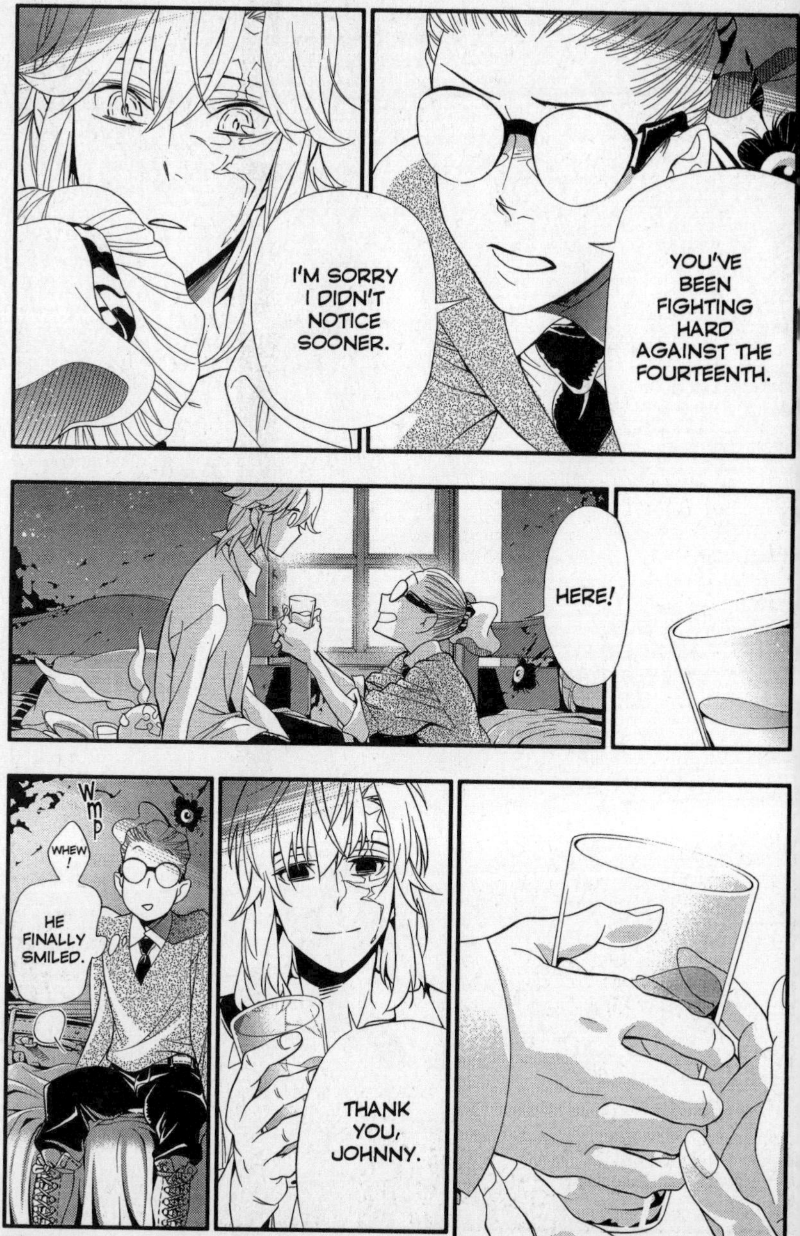
YOU'VE BEEN FIGHTING HARD AGAINST THE FOURTEENTH.
I'M SORRY I DIDN'T NOTICE SOONER.
HERE!
THANK YOU, JOHNNY.
WMP
WHEW!
HE FINALLY SMILED.

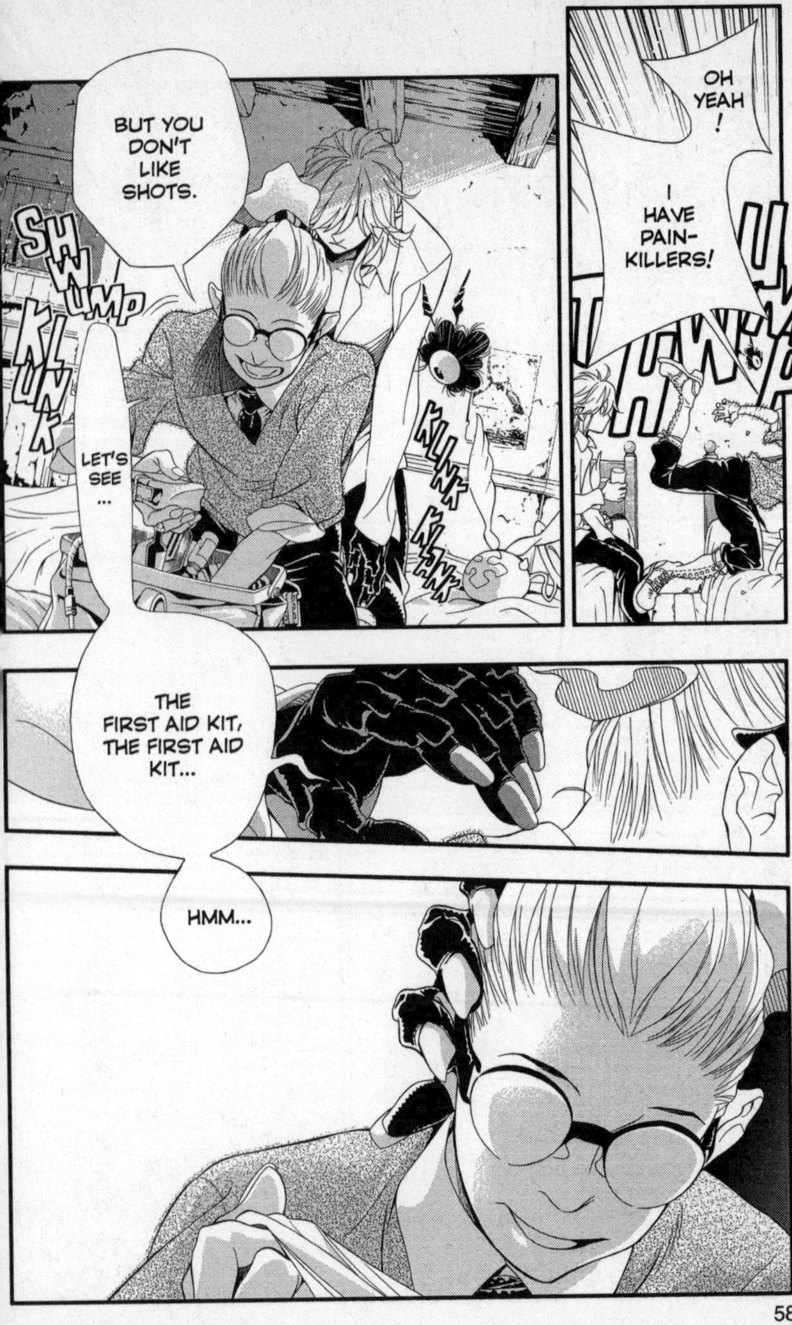
OH YEAH!
I HAVE PAIN-KILLERS!
THWUMP
BUT YOU DON'T LIKE SHOTS.
SHWUMP
KLUNK
KLINK
KLANK
LET'S SEE...
THE FIRST AID KIT, THE FIRST AID KIT...
HMM...

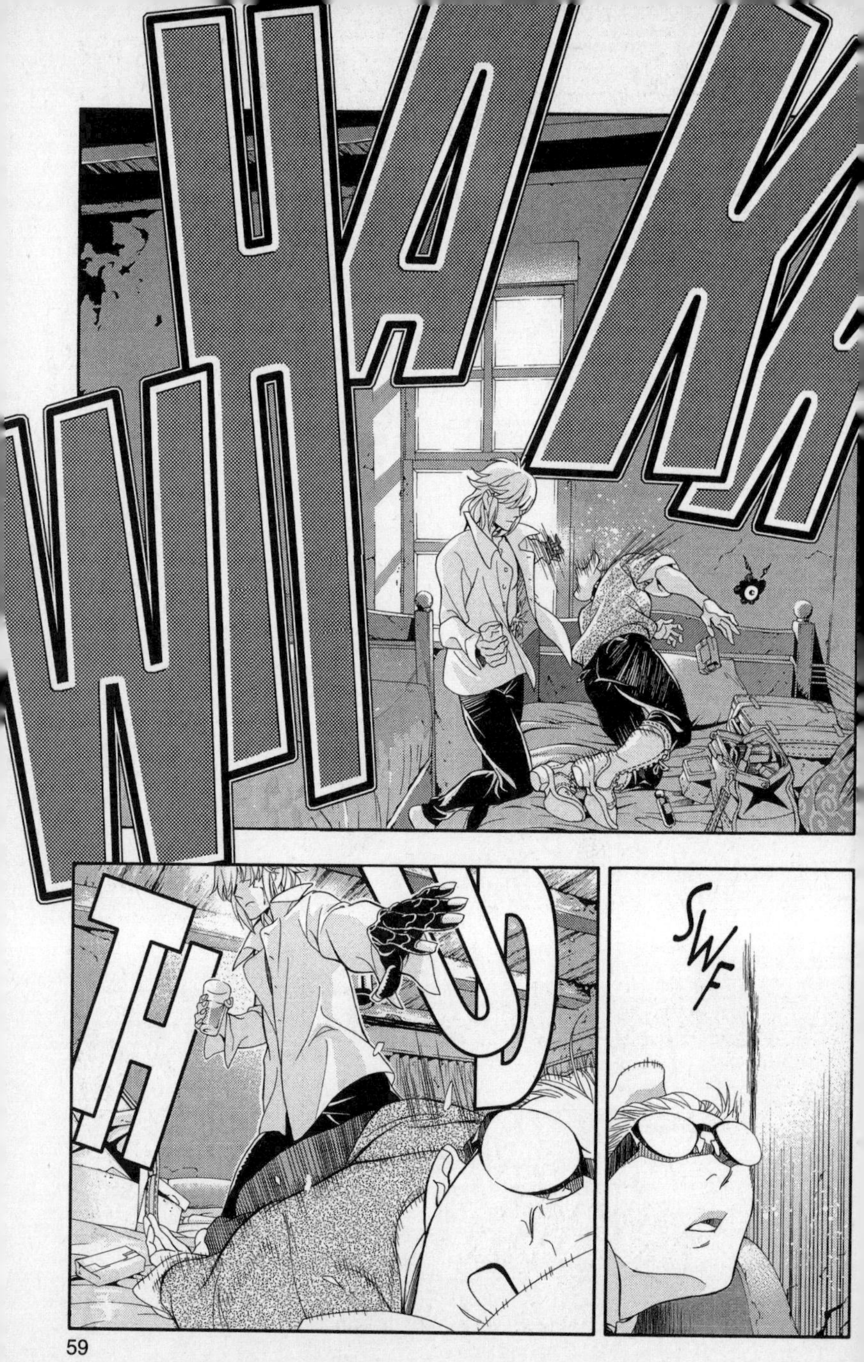
WHAAA
SWF
THUD

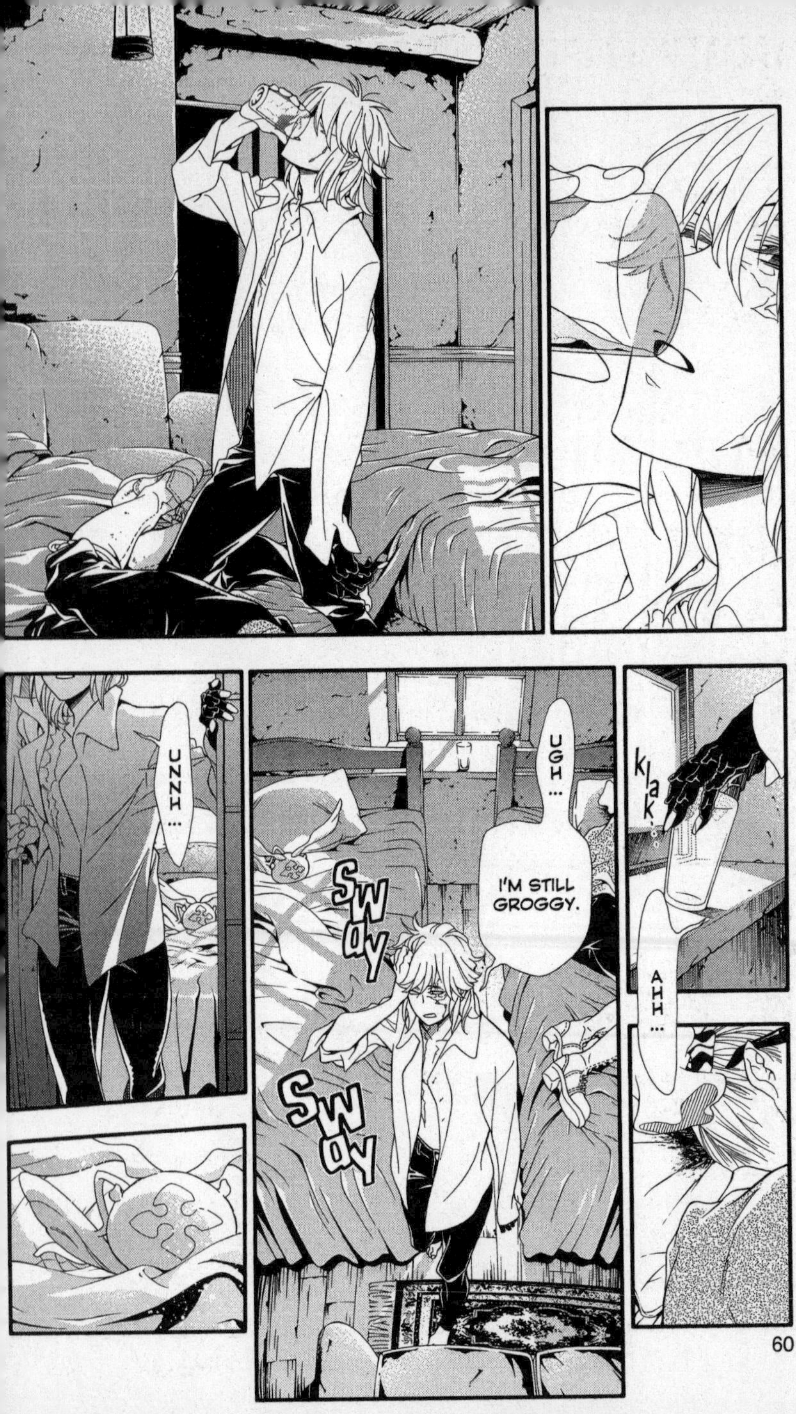
klak
AHH...
UGH...
I'M STILL GROGGY.
SWAY
SWAY
UNNH...

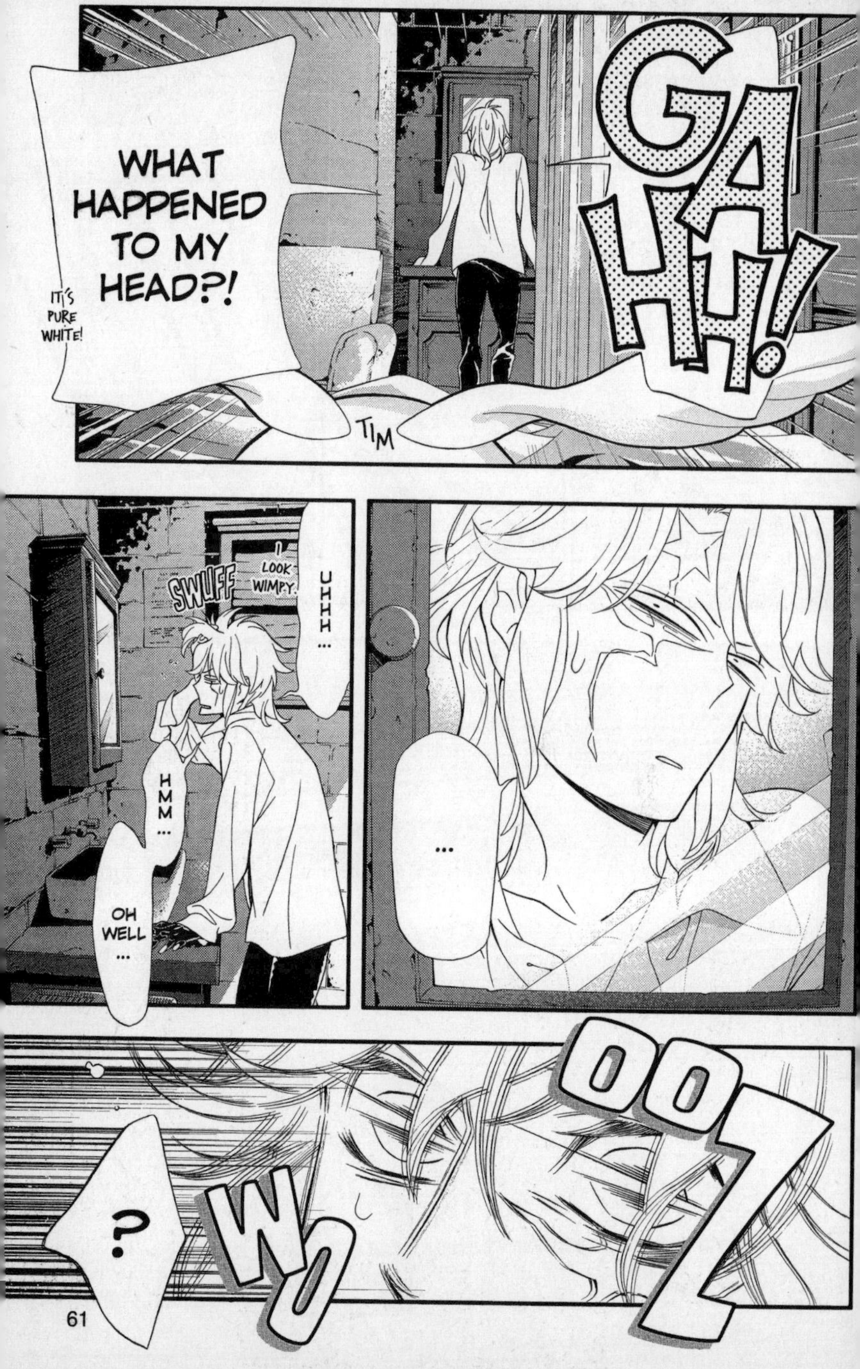
GAHH!!
WHAT HAPPENED TO MY HEAD?!
IT'S PURE WHITE!
TIM
...
UHHH...
SWUFF
I LOOK WIMPY.
HMM...
OH WELL...
WOOOZ
?

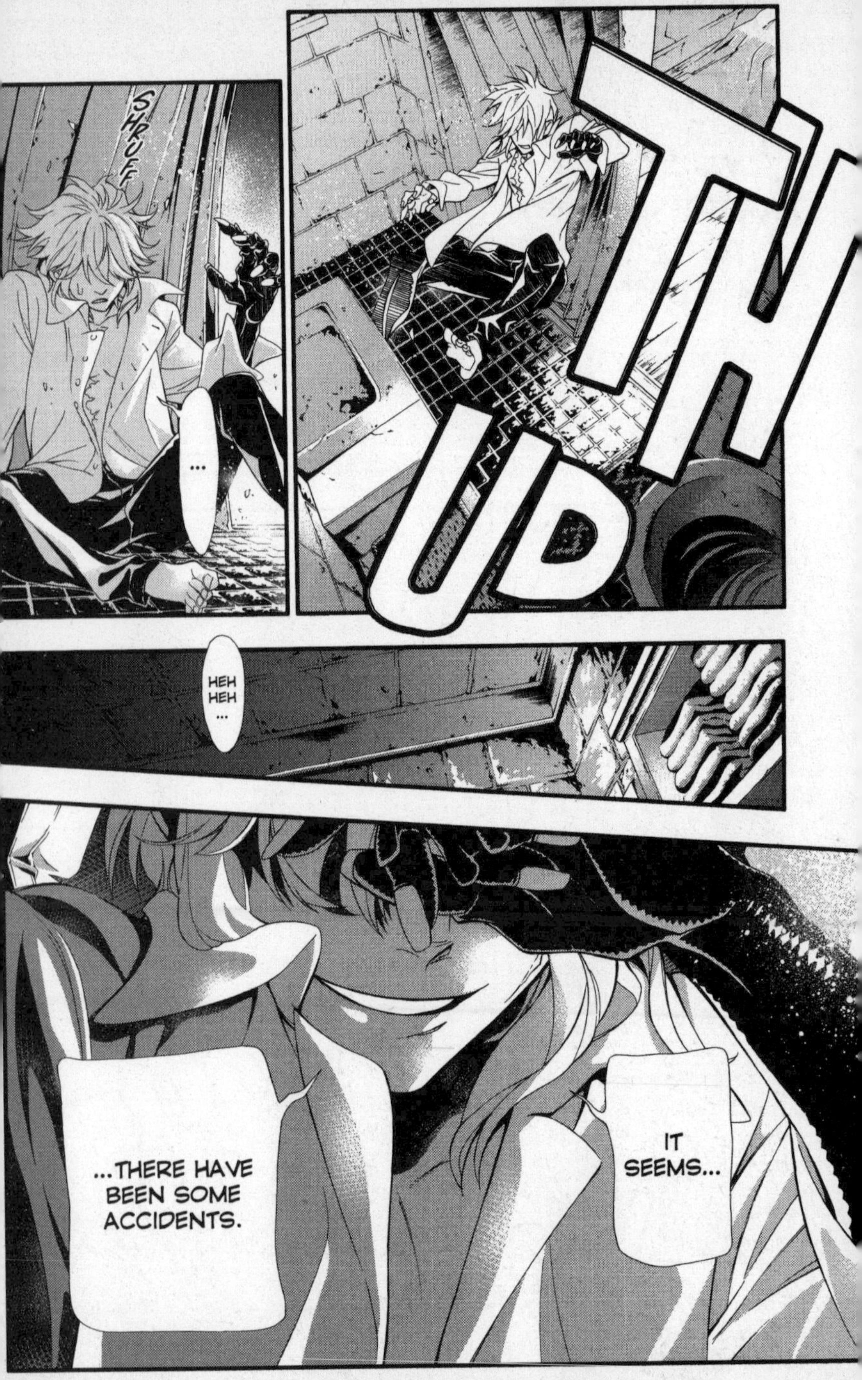
THUD
SHRUFF
...
HEH HEH ...
IT SEEMS...
...THERE HAVE BEEN SOME ACCIDENTS.

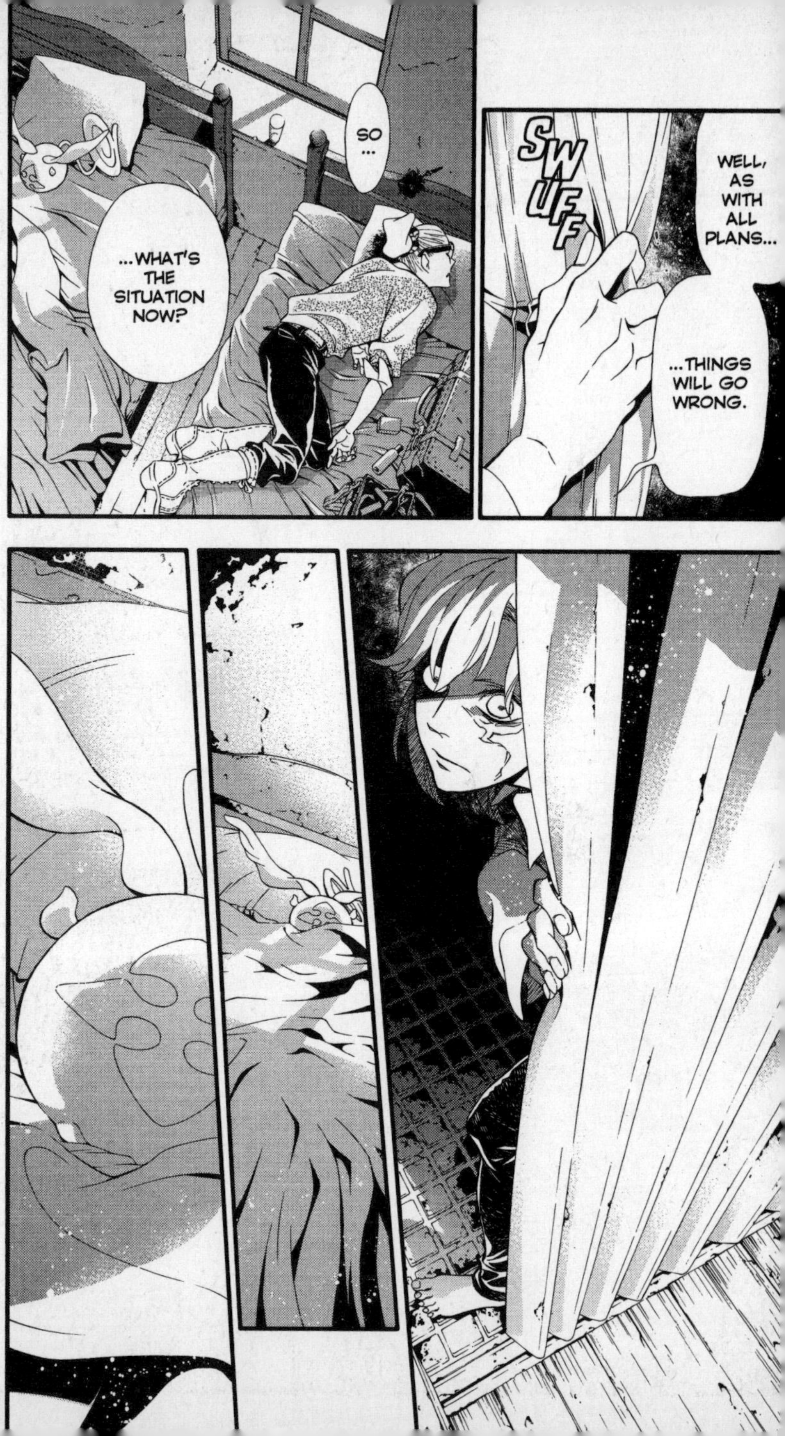
SO ...
...WHAT'S THE SITUATION NOW?
SWUFF
WELL, AS WITH ALL PLANS...
...THINGS WILL GO WRONG.

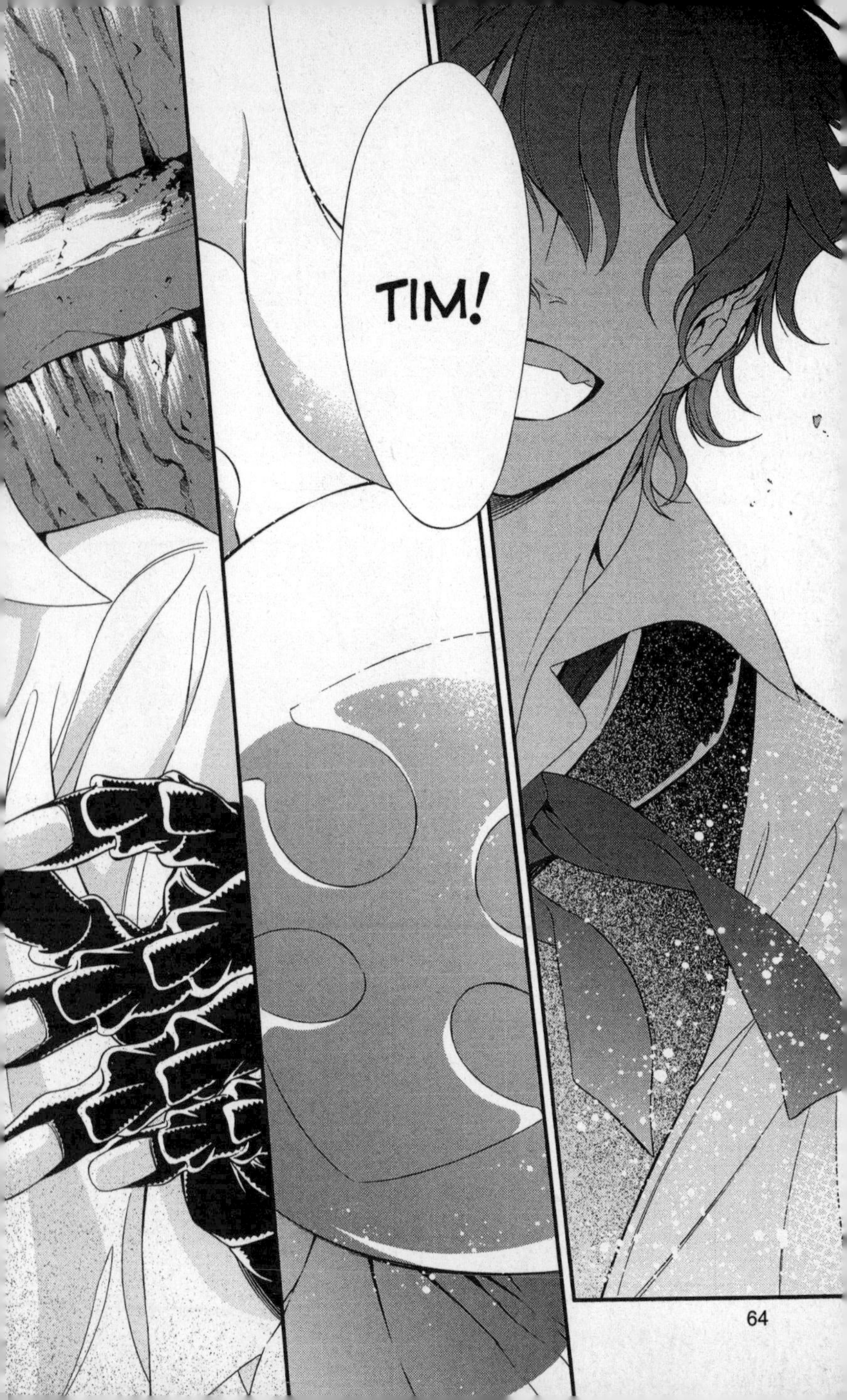
TIM!

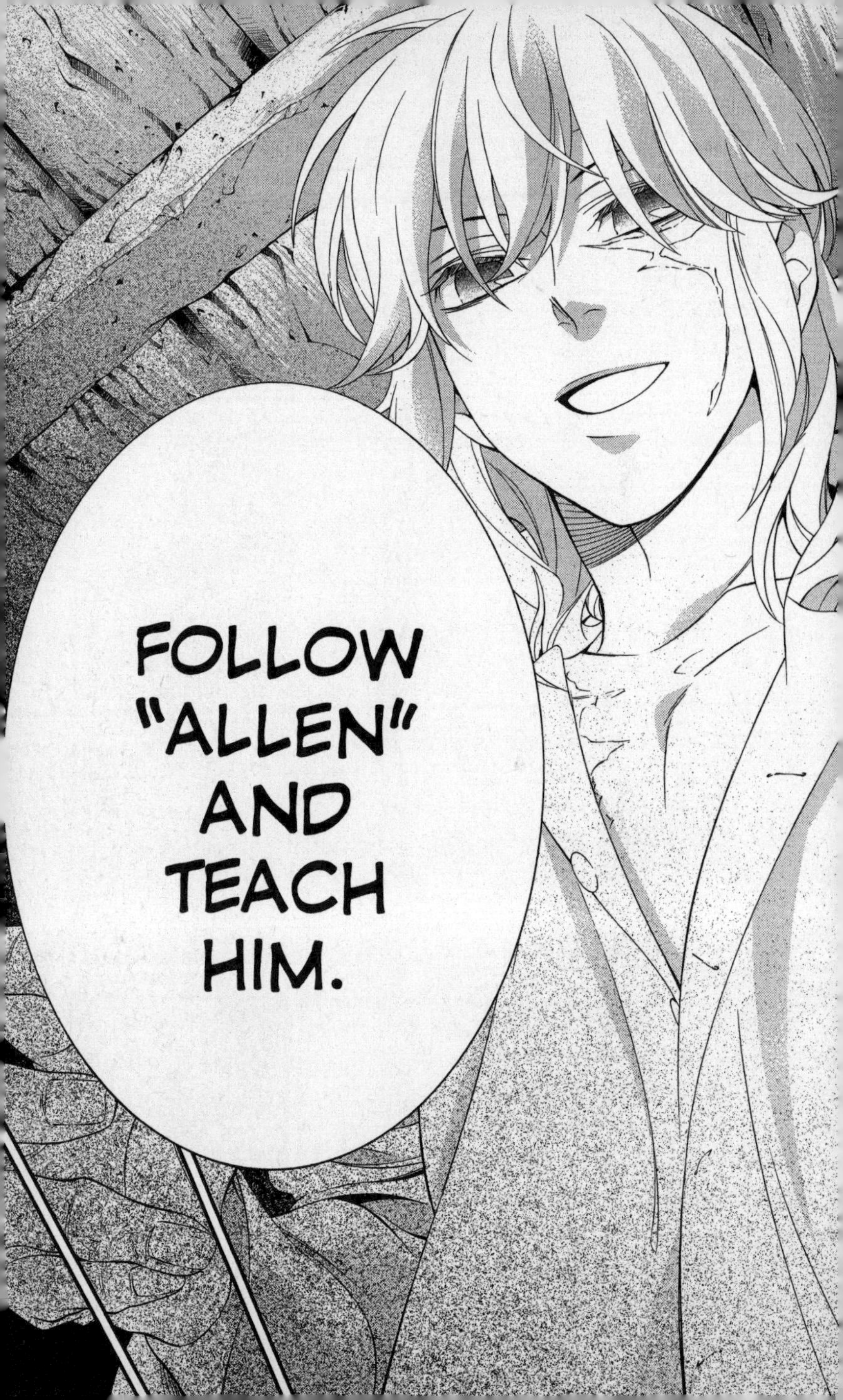
FOLLOW "ALLEN" AND TEACH HIM.

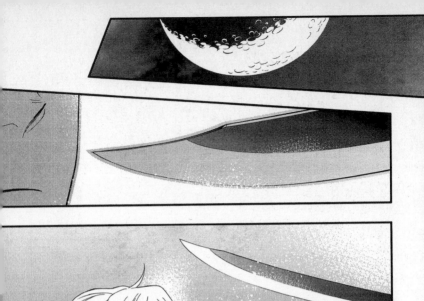

CH

K

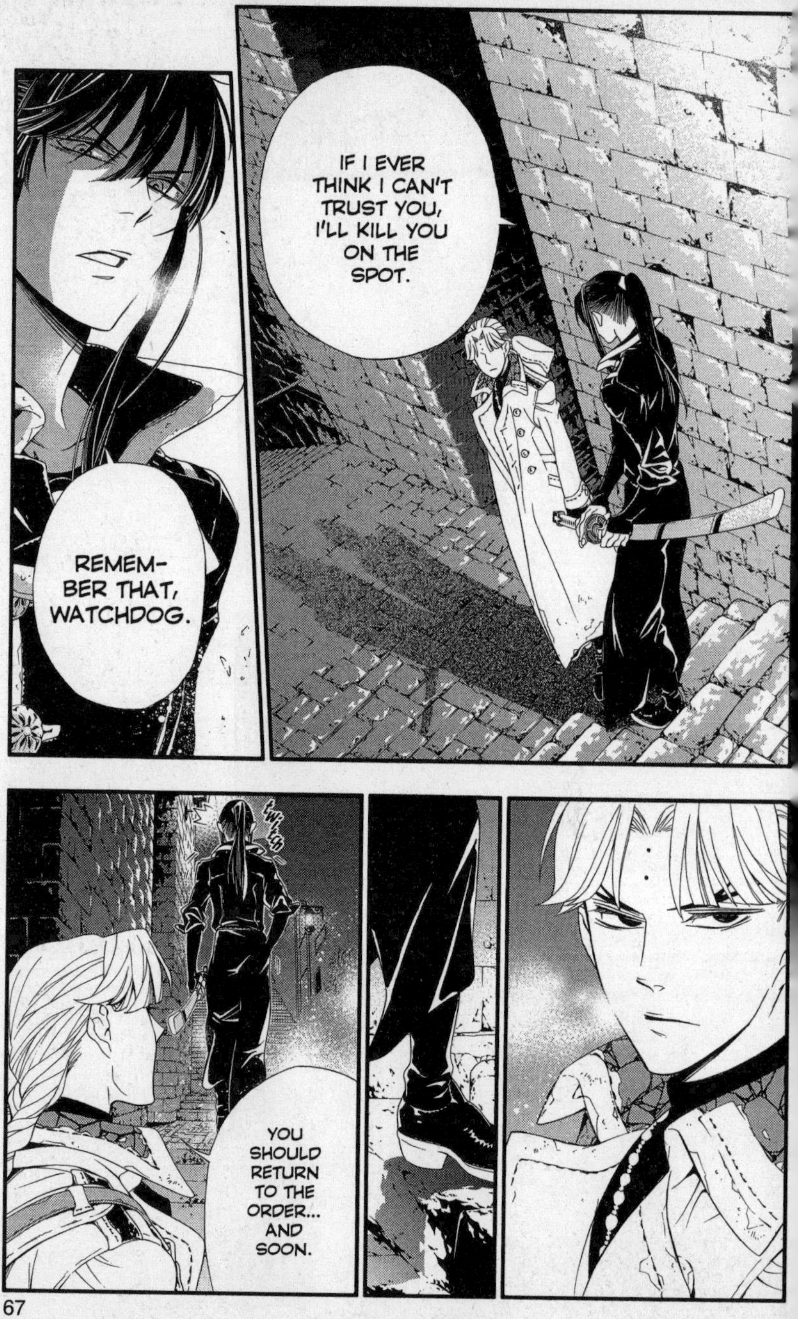
IF I EVER THINK I CAN'T TRUST YOU, I'LL KILL YOU ON THE SPOT.
REMEMBER THAT, WATCHDOG.
YOU SHOULD RETURN TO THE ORDER... AND SOON.

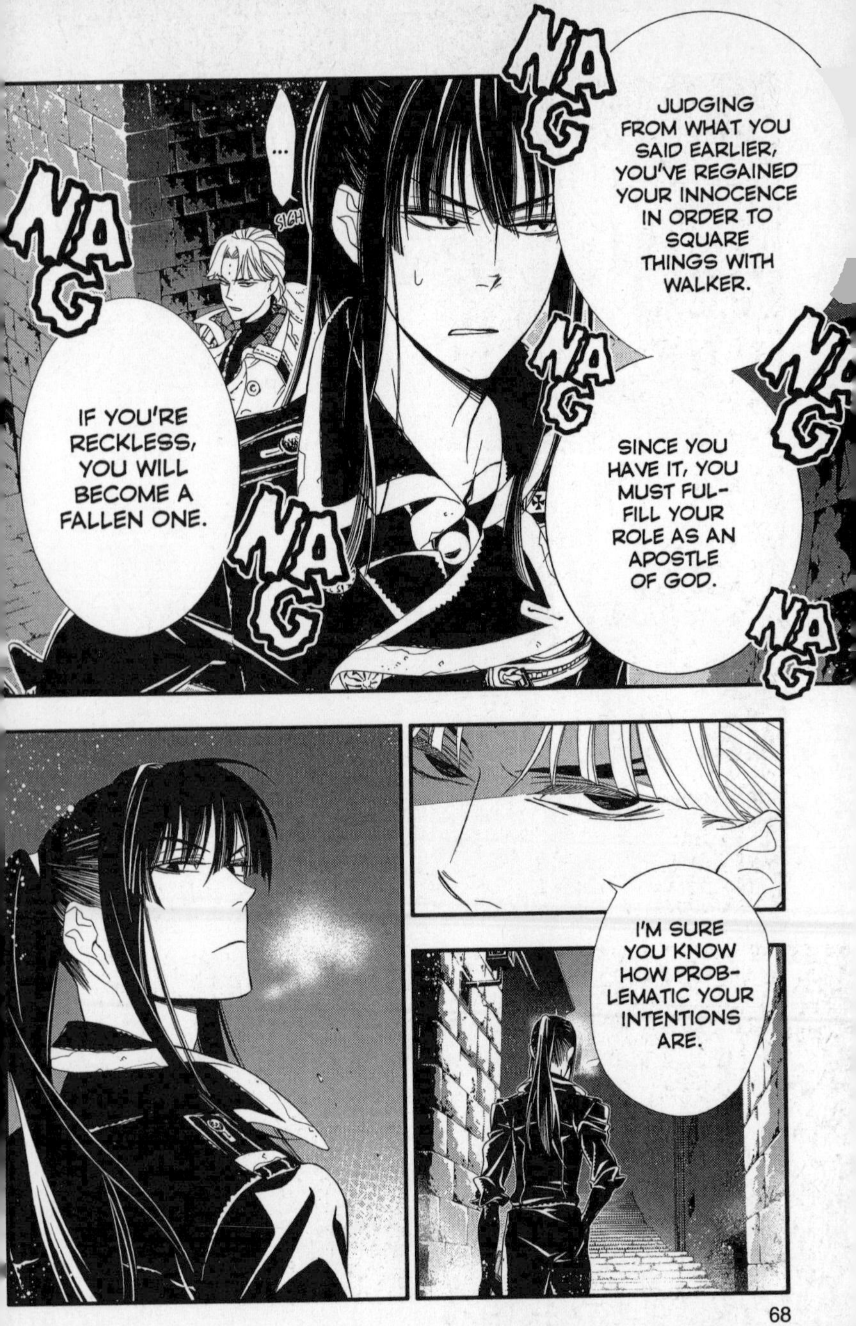
NAG
JUDGING FROM WHAT YOU SAID EARLIER, YOU'VE REGAINED YOUR INNOCENCE IN ORDER TO SQUARE THINGS WITH WALKER.
NAG
NAG
SINCE YOU HAVE IT, YOU MUST FUL-FILL YOUR ROLE AS AN APOSTLE OF GOD.
NAG
NAG
...
SIGH
NAG
IF YOU'RE RECKLESS, YOU WILL BECOME A FALLEN ONE.
I'M SURE YOU KNOW HOW PROB-LEMATIC YOUR INTENTIONS ARE.

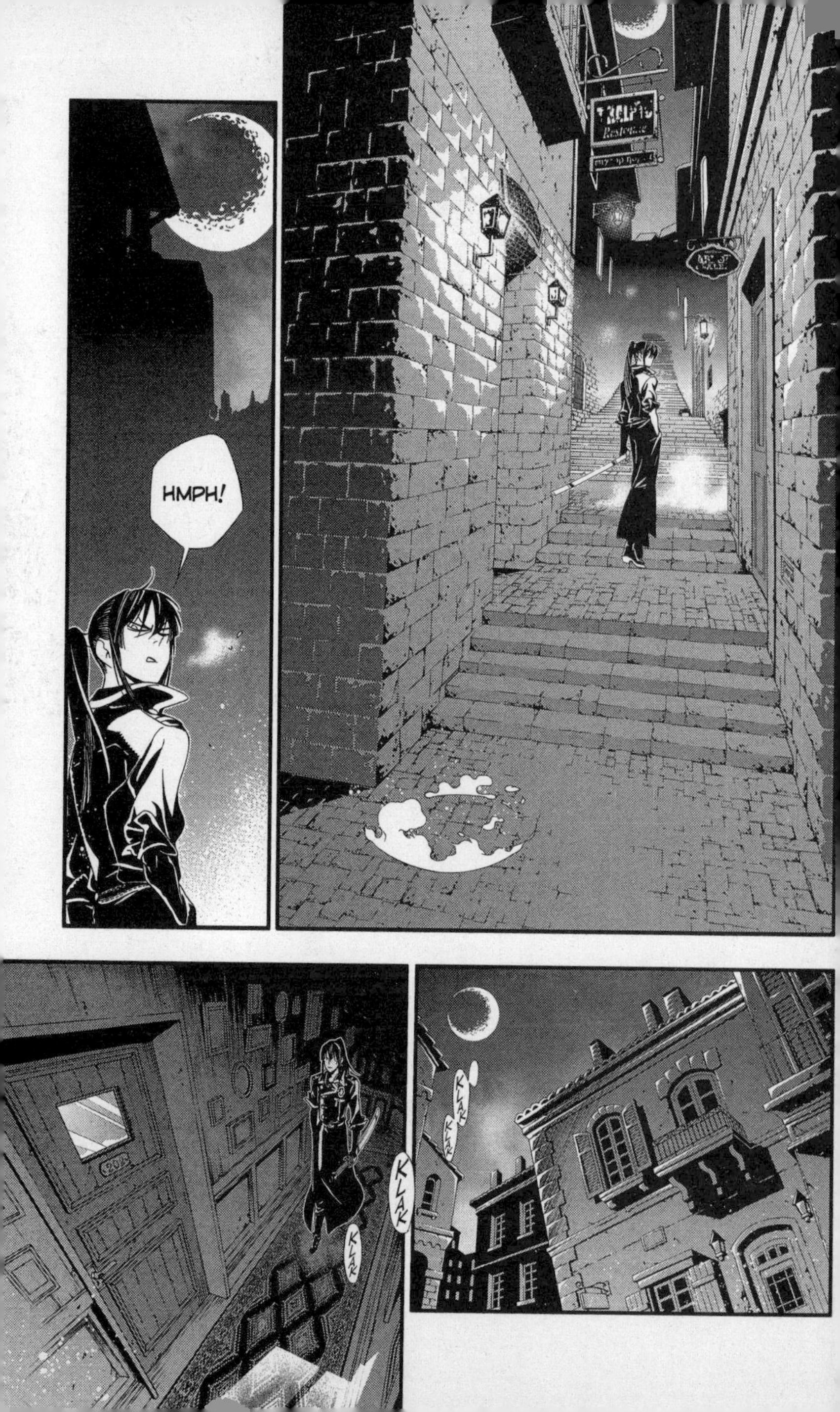
HMPH!
KLAK
KLAK
KLAK
KLAK

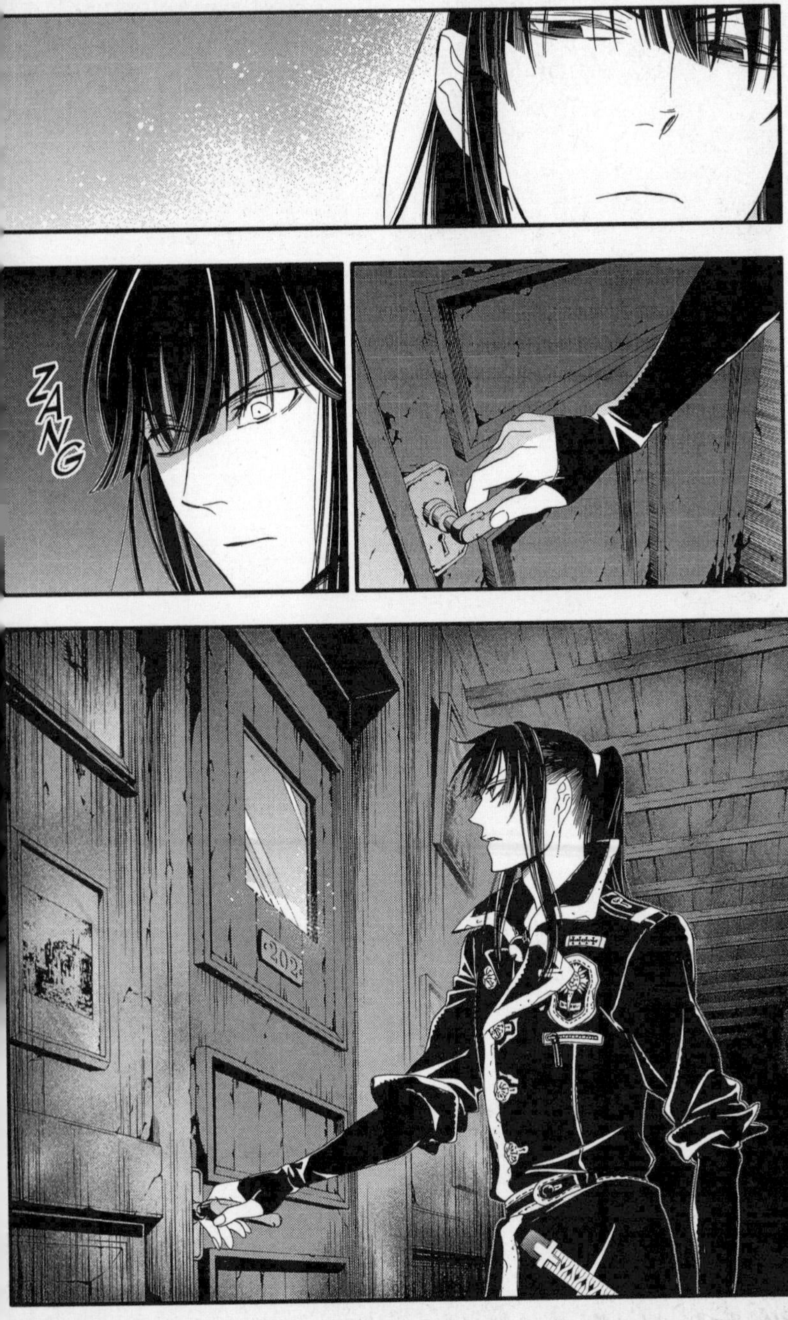
ZANG
202

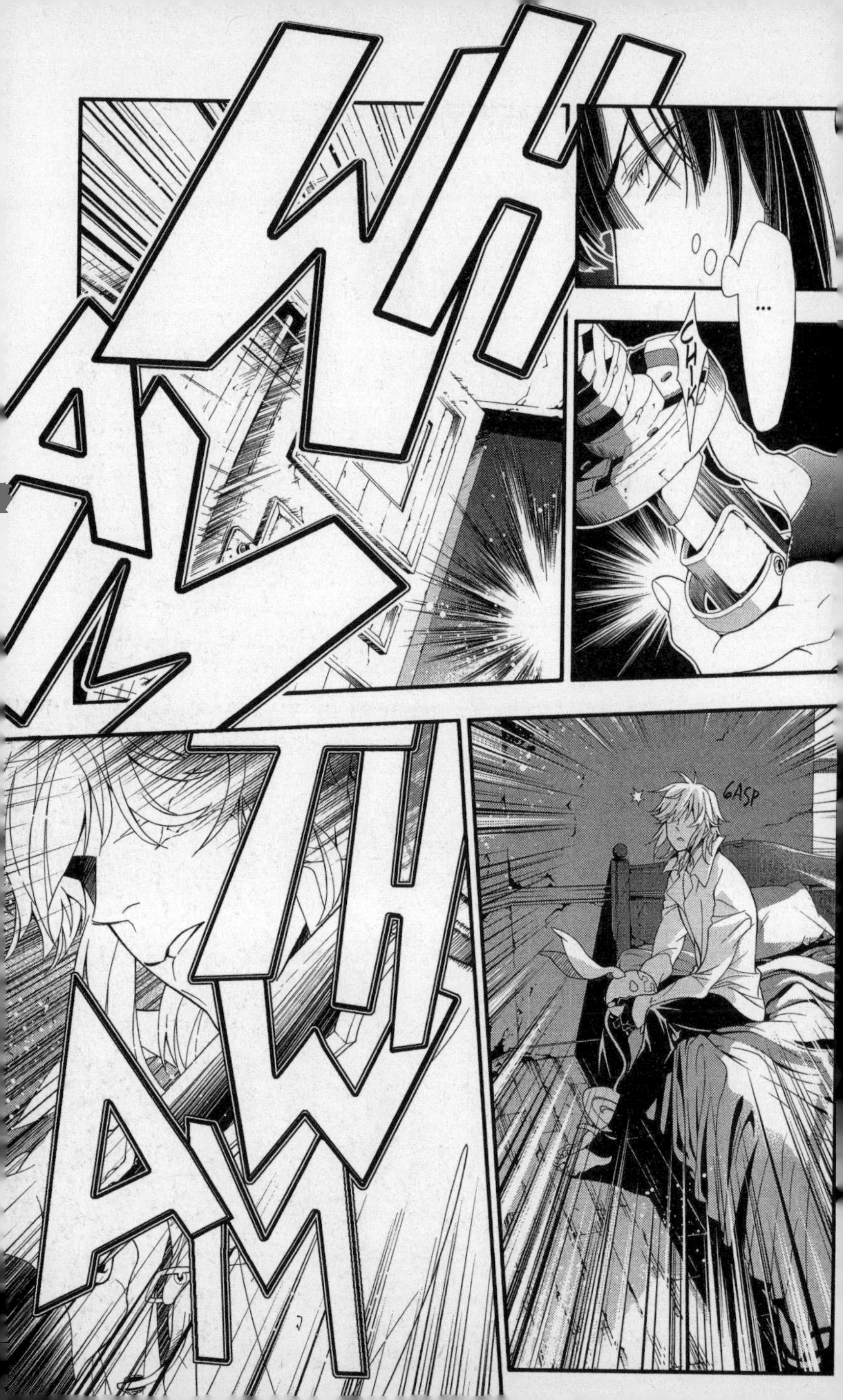
...
CHK
WHAM
GASP
THWAM

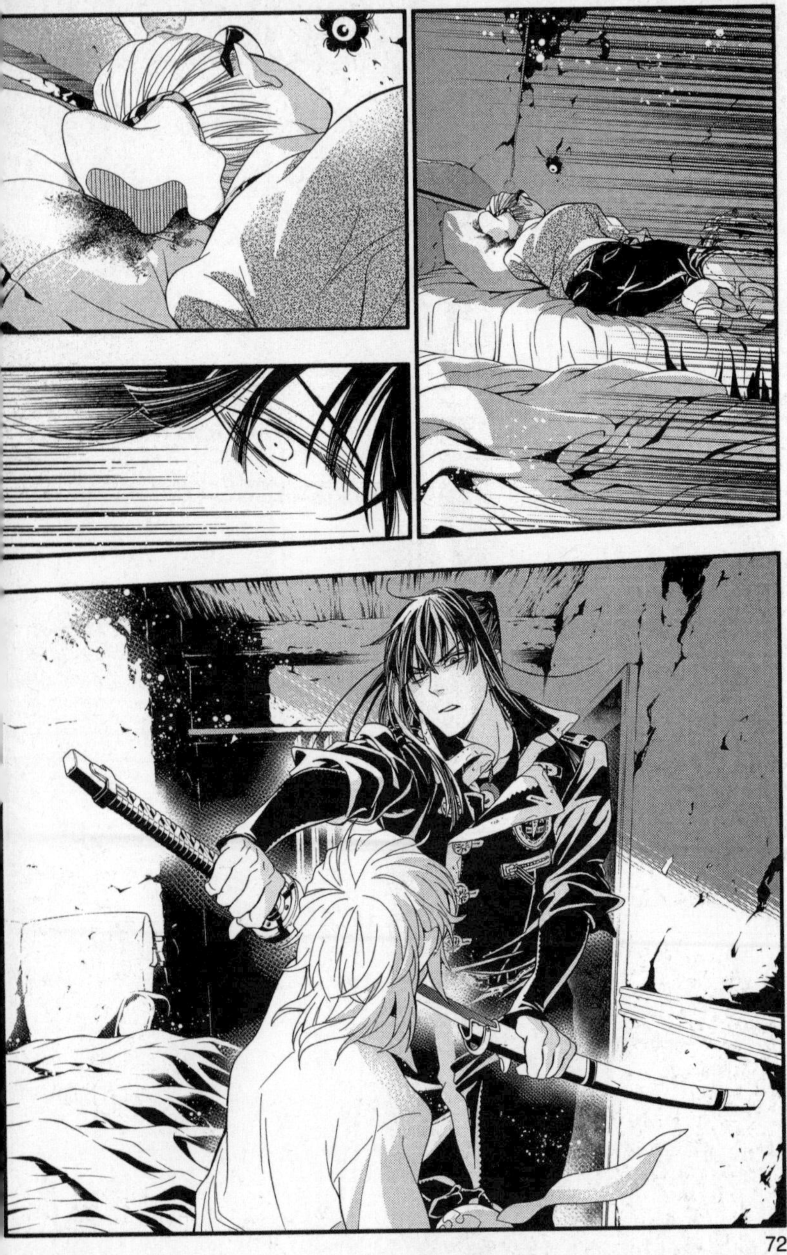

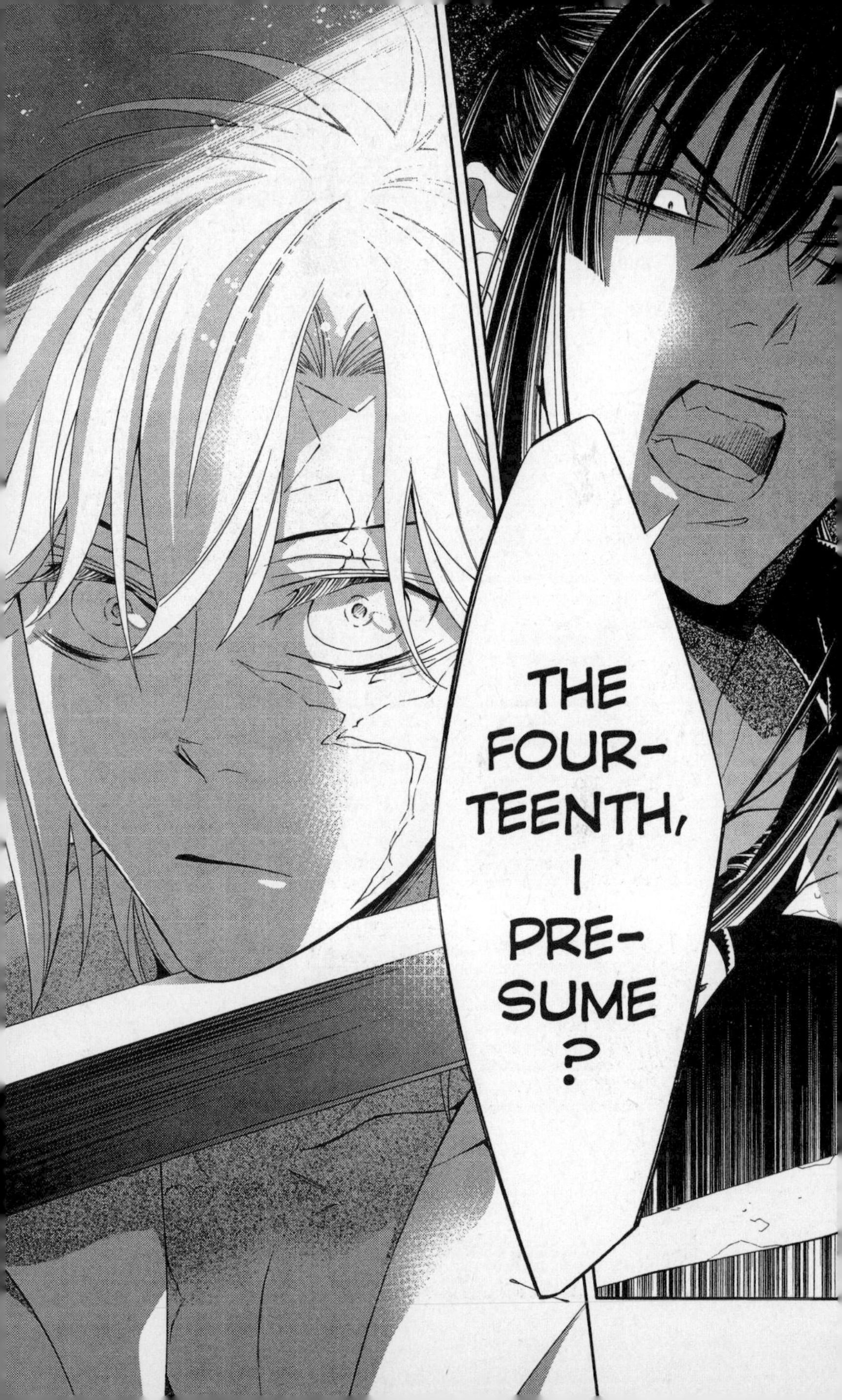
THE FOURTEENTH, I PRESUME?

Tim | Link | Tyki | Waizurii | Johnny | Kanda | Allen

KOMUI'S DISCUSSION ROOM 2

Q. Where did Kanda steal the clothes he wore when he came back to the Order in Volume 22?

K: Hey!

J: They're pretty sure you stole them. (*snicker*)

A: We're talking about Kanda, so it's a given he has no money.

Ty: I've been wondering, boy... are you and Kanda enemies?

W: Kanda didn't steal those clothes, he got them from someone.

K: !

A & J: Huh?

K: You looked into my head! (*draws sword*)

Ty: Sorry. He does that sometimes.

W: It's my Demonic Eye! And I sure wouldn't show restraint against Exorcists!

A & K: Why, you...

J: You "got" them? Surely not from a woman, like General Cross would.

W: It's true. She even fed him. He is a looker after all.

A: Tsk, Kanda! A man should earn his bread!

K: She forced it on me, so I accepted! If I'd hit those small fries and tried to take it, that old woman would've--

J: Old woman?

K: Urgh! Shut up! What's it matter?!

Q. Allen was dressed like a clown similar to Mana. Does he have Mana's clown gear?

Ty: Oh, that getup? When he's bald?

A: It's just a wig! When I left the order, I visited Mother and Mana's belongings were there, so I took them. I was on the run and penniless, but I knew I could manage by street-performing. And with makeup on, my identity was hidden.

I'm not as sloppy as my Master and Kanda.

K: One can survive without money, you know!

A: Sorry, but I can't be friends with a moocher. (*disdainful*)

K: (*This guy annoys me...*)

J: Allen's a good clown! What's your best trick?

W: He's a fair acrobat, but he was once put in a cage with a wild beast, so animal taming is out.

A: Stop using your Eye to answer other people's questions!

Q. Did Allen also earn money by cheating at cards?

J: Is that what you were doing?!

A: Feh! That's no big deal!

K: And you were so self-righteous a minute ago!

W: He's banned from dozens of gambling houses.

Ty: Dangerous business, that!

A: When on the run it's best to have lots of options!

J: But you'll attract the attention of the mafia and other scary types!

A: No one's scarier than my Master.

Ty: What did he do to you?

Link: Twisted as you are, you're still the main character. Consider our readers! They're at an impressionable age!

A: (*Gah!*) Huh? Did someone say something? (*confused*)

J: Nope. Why?

A: I th-thought I heard a voice.

K: ...

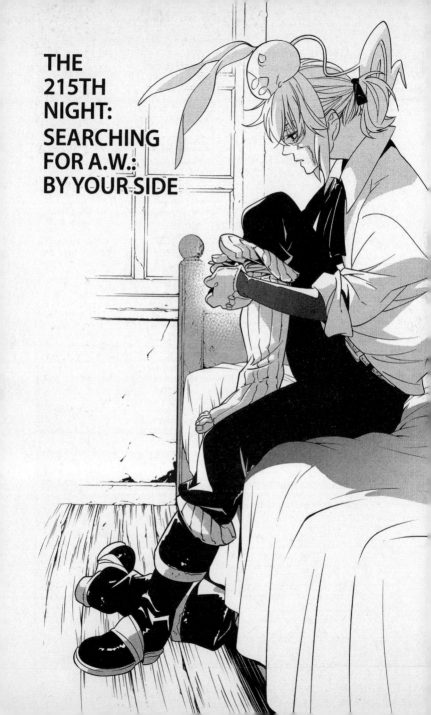

THE 215TH NIGHT: SEARCHING FOR A.W.: BY YOUR SIDE

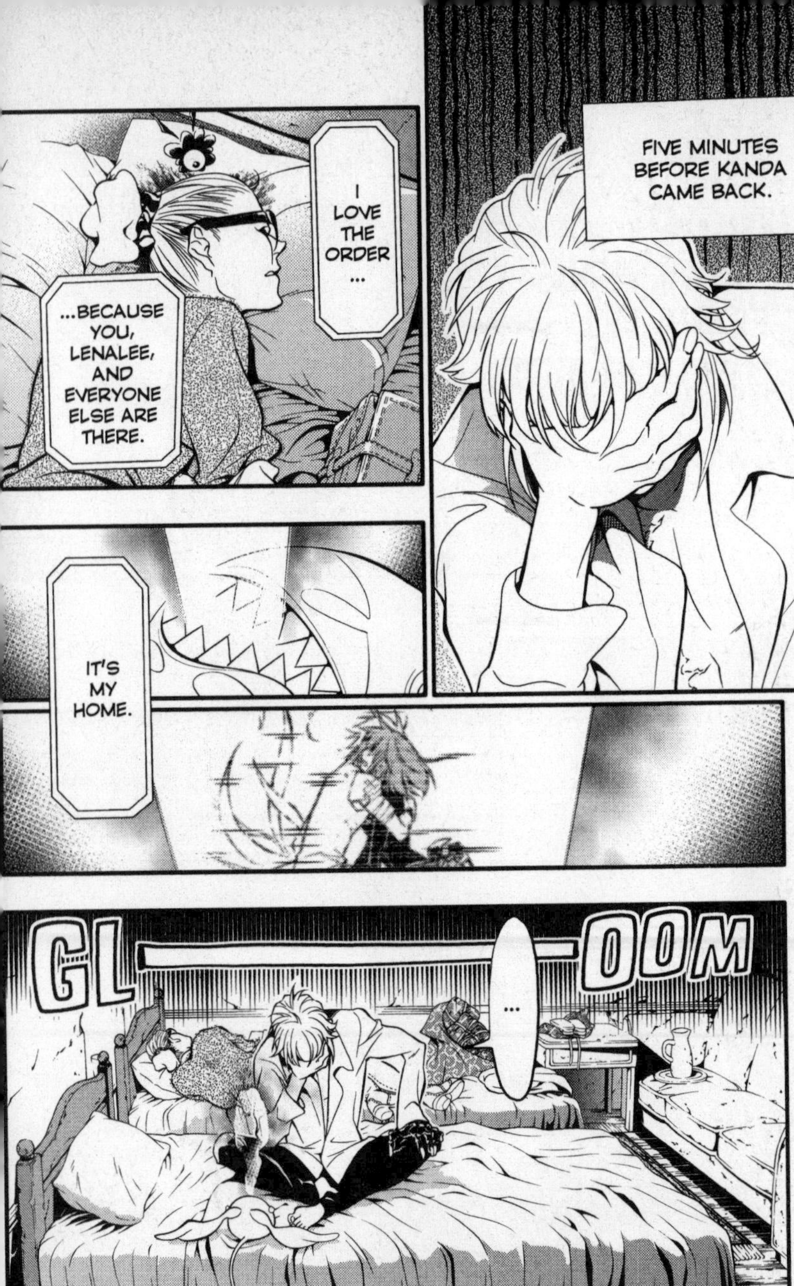
FIVE MINUTES BEFORE KANDA CAME BACK.
I LOVE THE ORDER...
...BECAUSE YOU, LENALEE, AND EVERYONE ELSE ARE THERE.
IT'S MY HOME.
GL—OOM
...

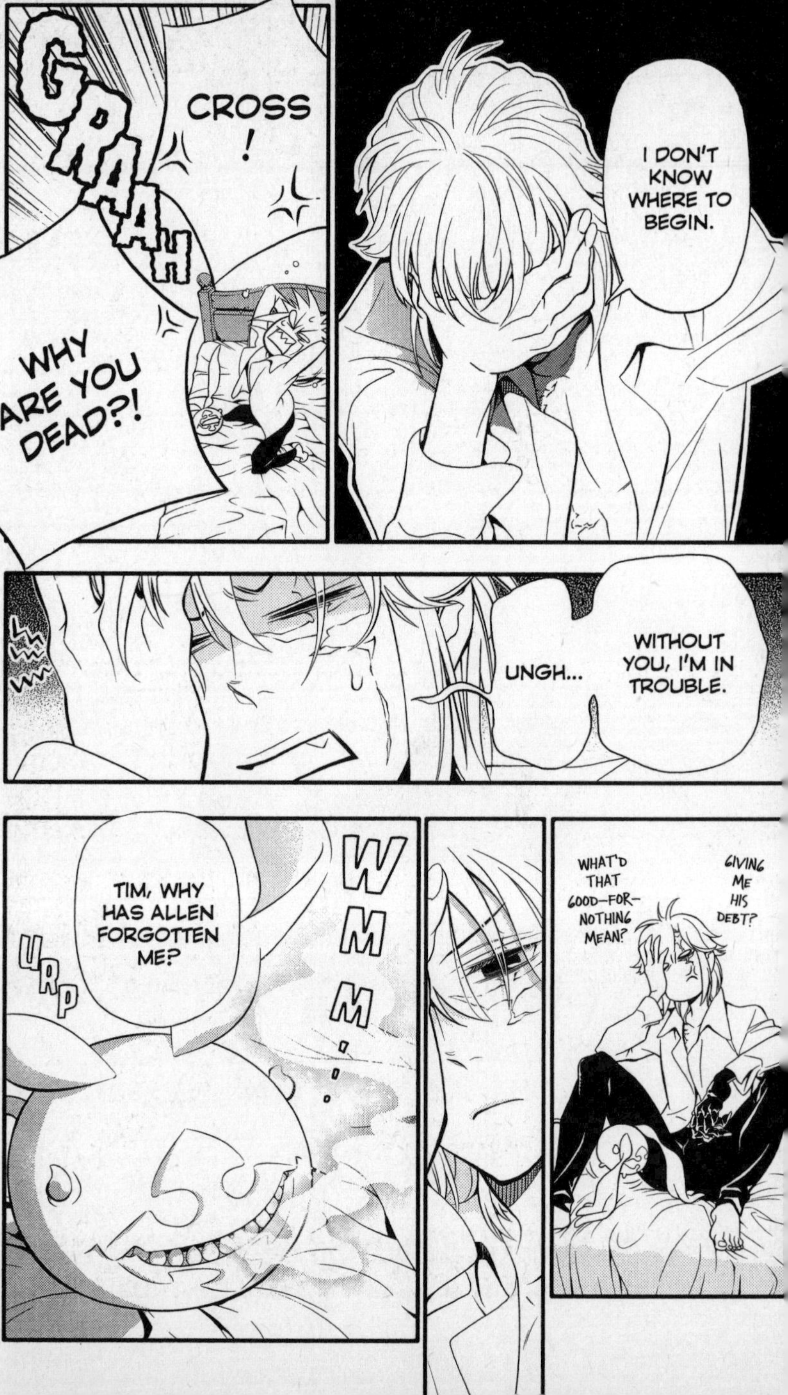

I DON'T KNOW WHERE TO BEGIN.
CROSS!
GRAAH
WHY ARE YOU DEAD?!
WITHOUT YOU, I'M IN TROUBLE.
UNGH...
GIVING ME HIS DEBT?
WHAT'D THAT GOOD-FOR-NOTHING MEAN?
WMM...
TIM, WHY HAS ALLEN FORGOTTEN ME?
URP

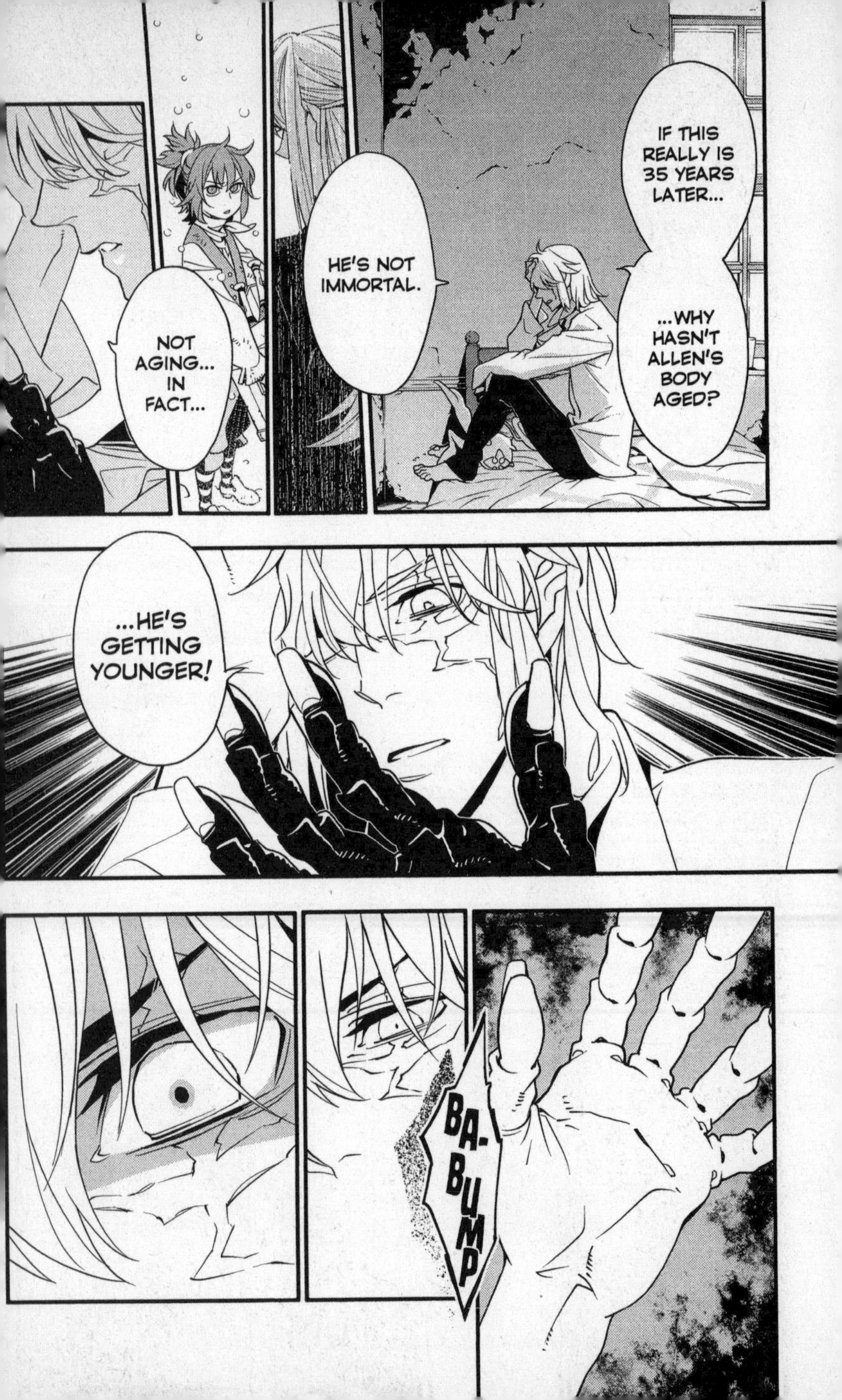
IF THIS REALLY IS 35 YEARS LATER...
...WHY HASN'T ALLEN'S BODY AGED?
HE'S NOT IMMORTAL.
NOT AGING... IN FACT...
...HE'S GETTING YOUNGER!
BA-BUMP

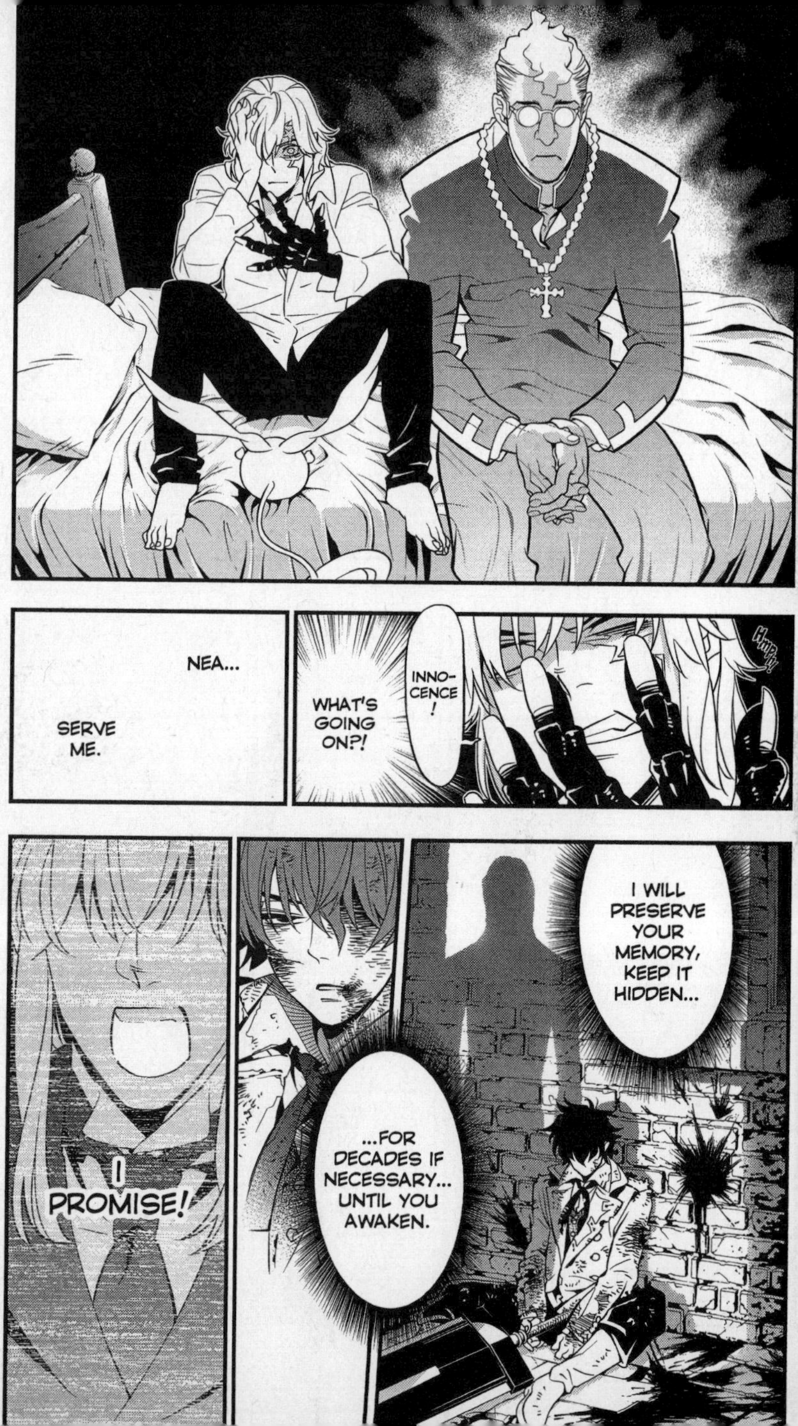
INNO-CENCE!
WHAT'S GOING ON?!
NEA...
SERVE ME.
I WILL PRESERVE YOUR MEMORY, KEEP IT HIDDEN...
...FOR DECADES IF NECESSARY... UNTIL YOU AWAKEN.
I PROMISE!

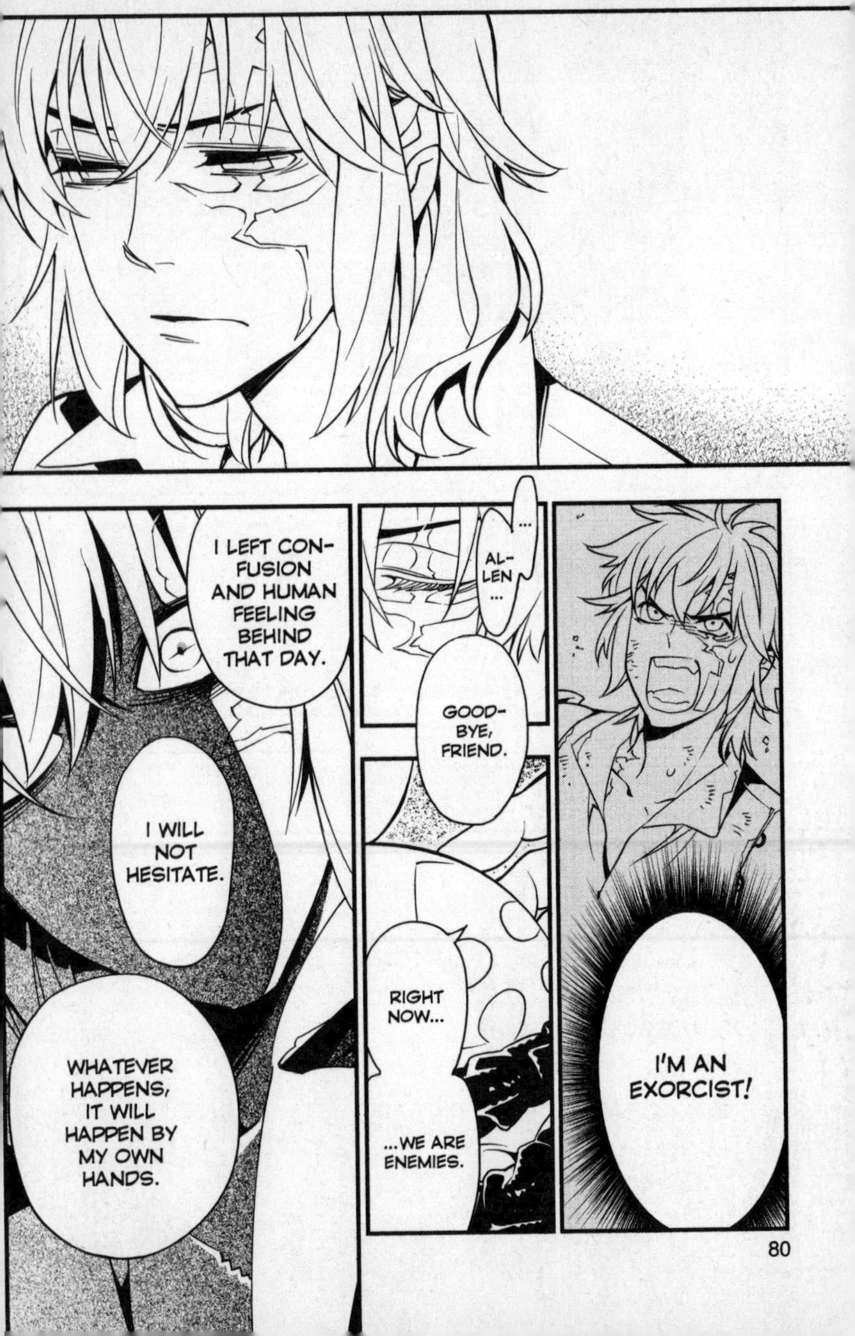
I'M AN EXORCIST!
...
AL-LEN...
GOOD-BYE, FRIEND.
RIGHT NOW...
...WE ARE ENEMIES.
I LEFT CON-FUSION AND HUMAN FEELING BEHIND THAT DAY.
I WILL NOT HESITATE.
WHATEVER HAPPENS, IT WILL HAPPEN BY MY OWN HANDS.

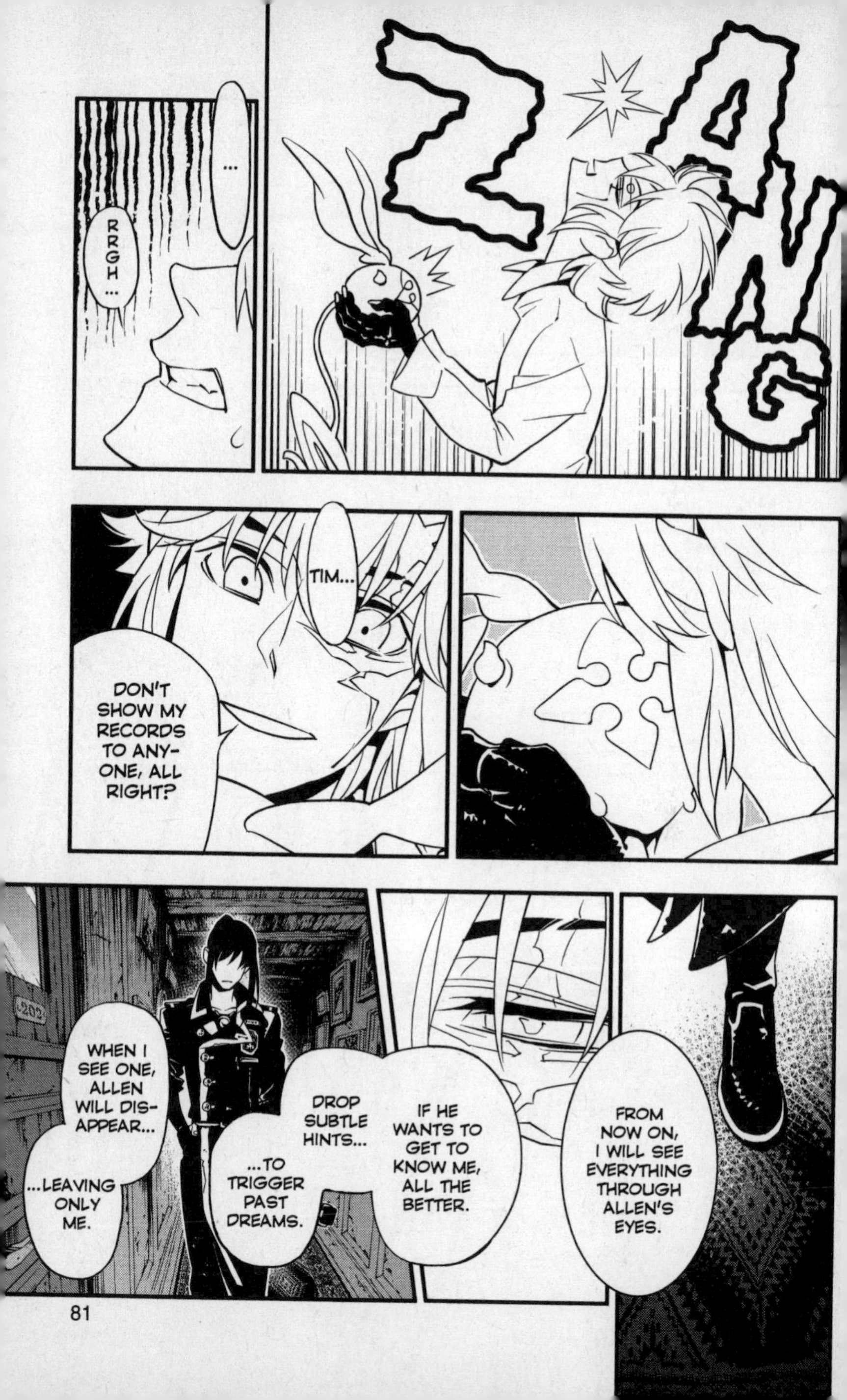
ZANG
...
RRGH...
TIM...
DON'T SHOW MY RECORDS TO ANYONE, ALL RIGHT?
FROM NOW ON, I WILL SEE EVERYTHING THROUGH ALLEN'S EYES.
IF HE WANTS TO GET TO KNOW ME, ALL THE BETTER.
DROP SUBTLE HINTS...
...TO TRIGGER PAST DREAMS.
WHEN I SEE ONE, ALLEN WILL DISAPPEAR...
...LEAVING ONLY ME.

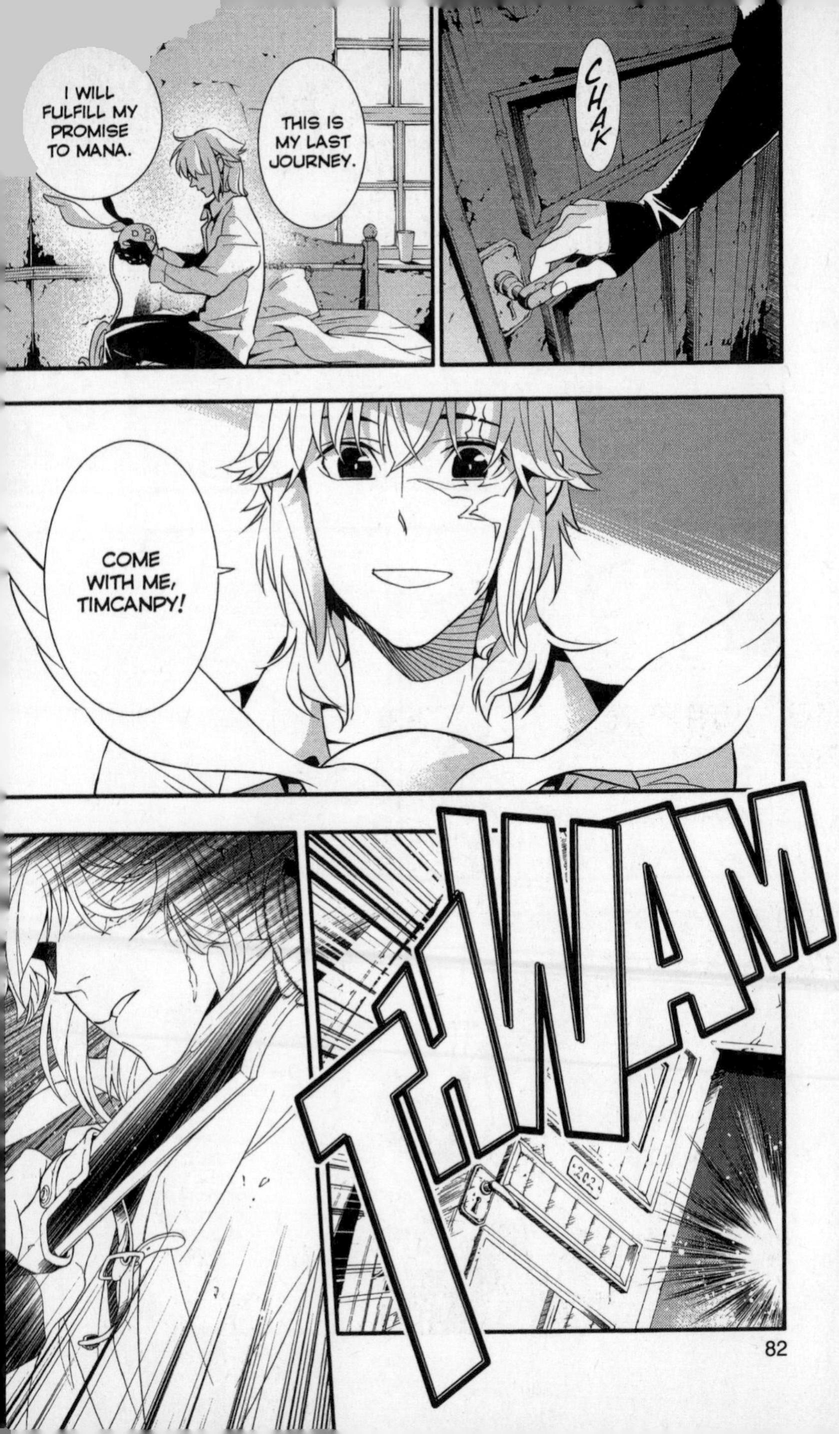
CHAK
THIS IS MY LAST JOURNEY.
I WILL FULFILL MY PROMISE TO MANA.
COME WITH ME, TIMCANPY!
THWAM

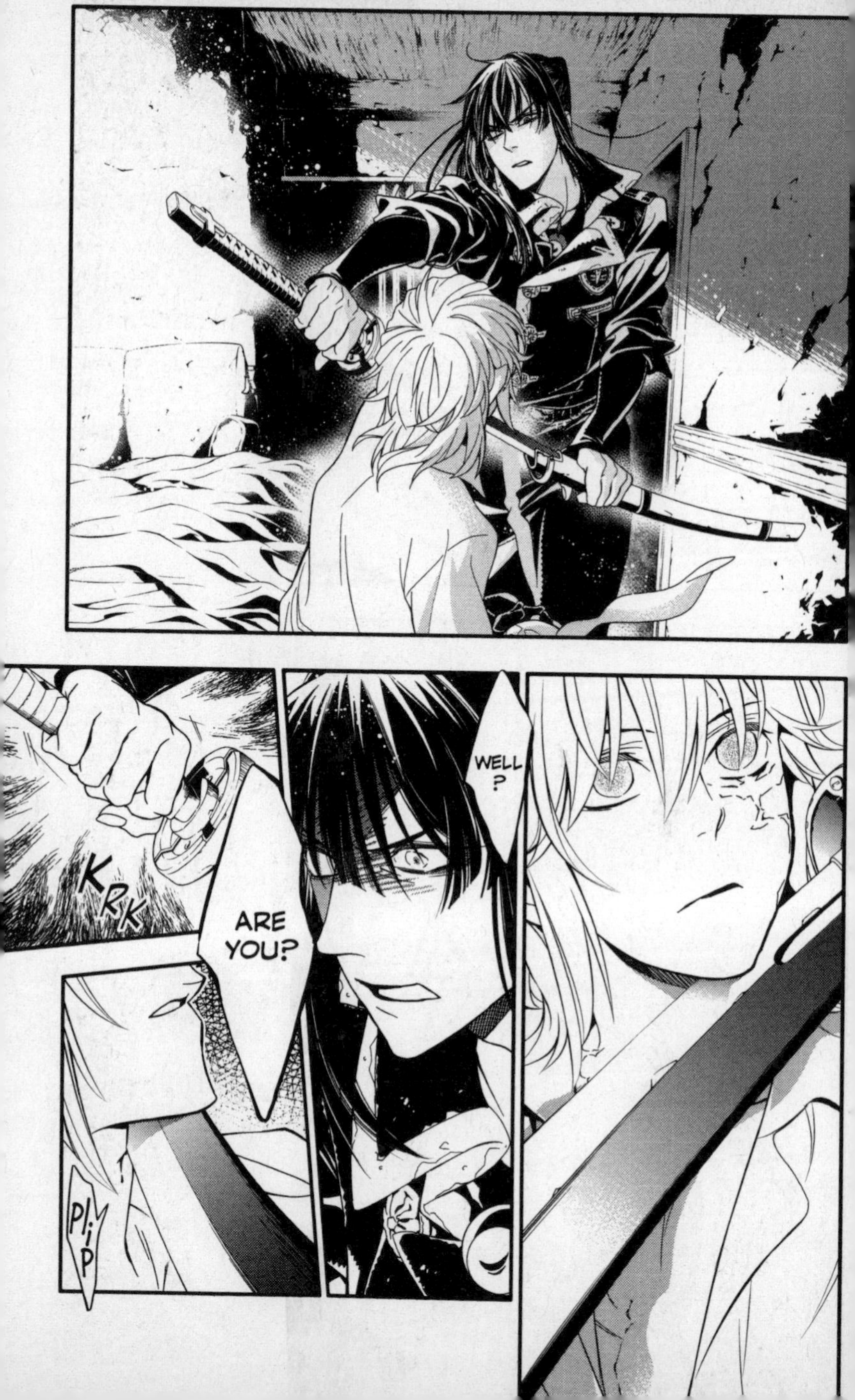
WELL?
ARE YOU?
KRK
PLIP

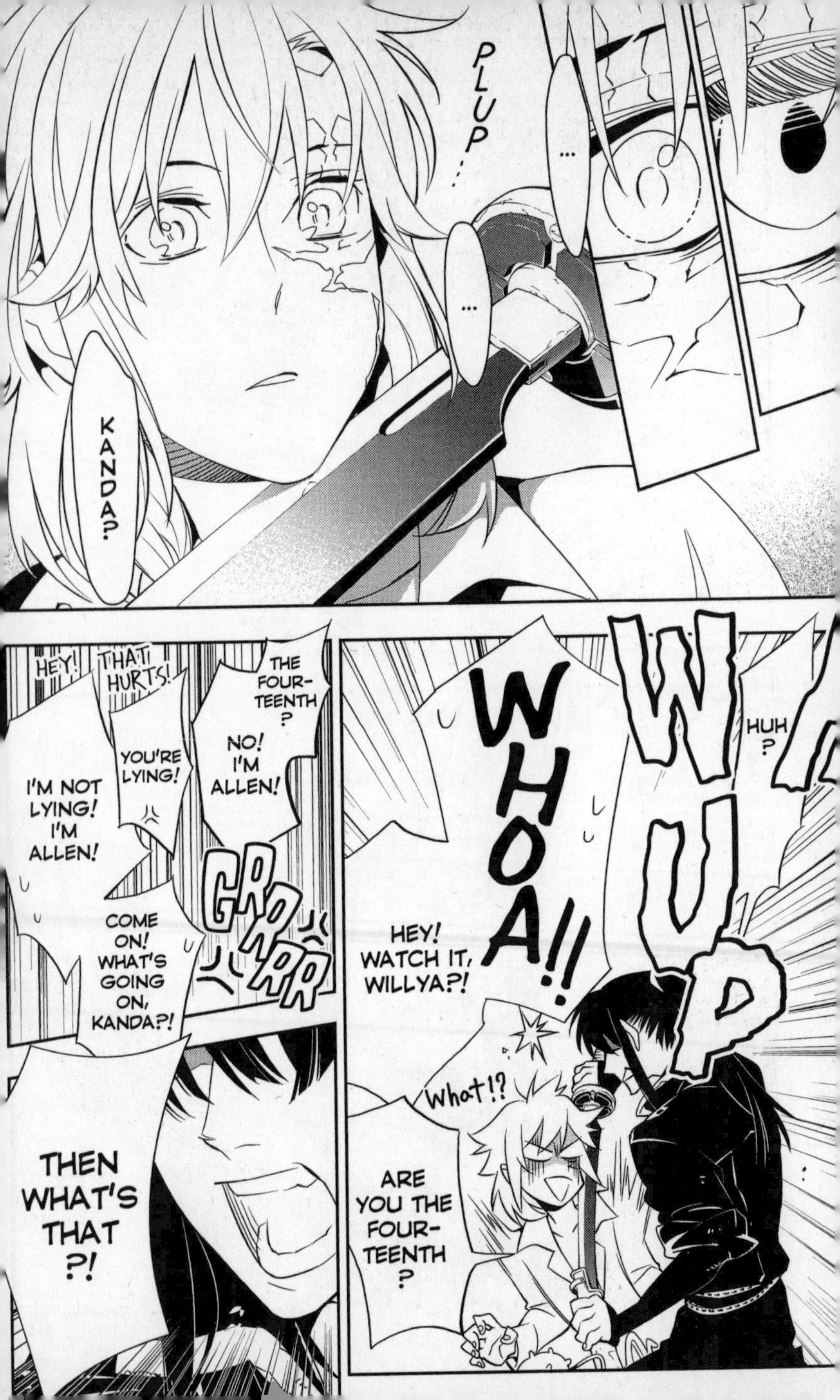
PLUP...
...
...
KANDA?
WHUP
HUH?
WHOA!!
HEY! WATCH IT, WILLYA?!
What!?
ARE YOU THE FOURTEENTH?
THE FOURTEENTH?
NO! I'M ALLEN!
HEY! THAT HURTS!
YOU'RE LYING!
I'M NOT LYING! I'M ALLEN!
GRRRR
COME ON! WHAT'S GOING ON, KANDA?!
THEN WHAT'S THAT?!

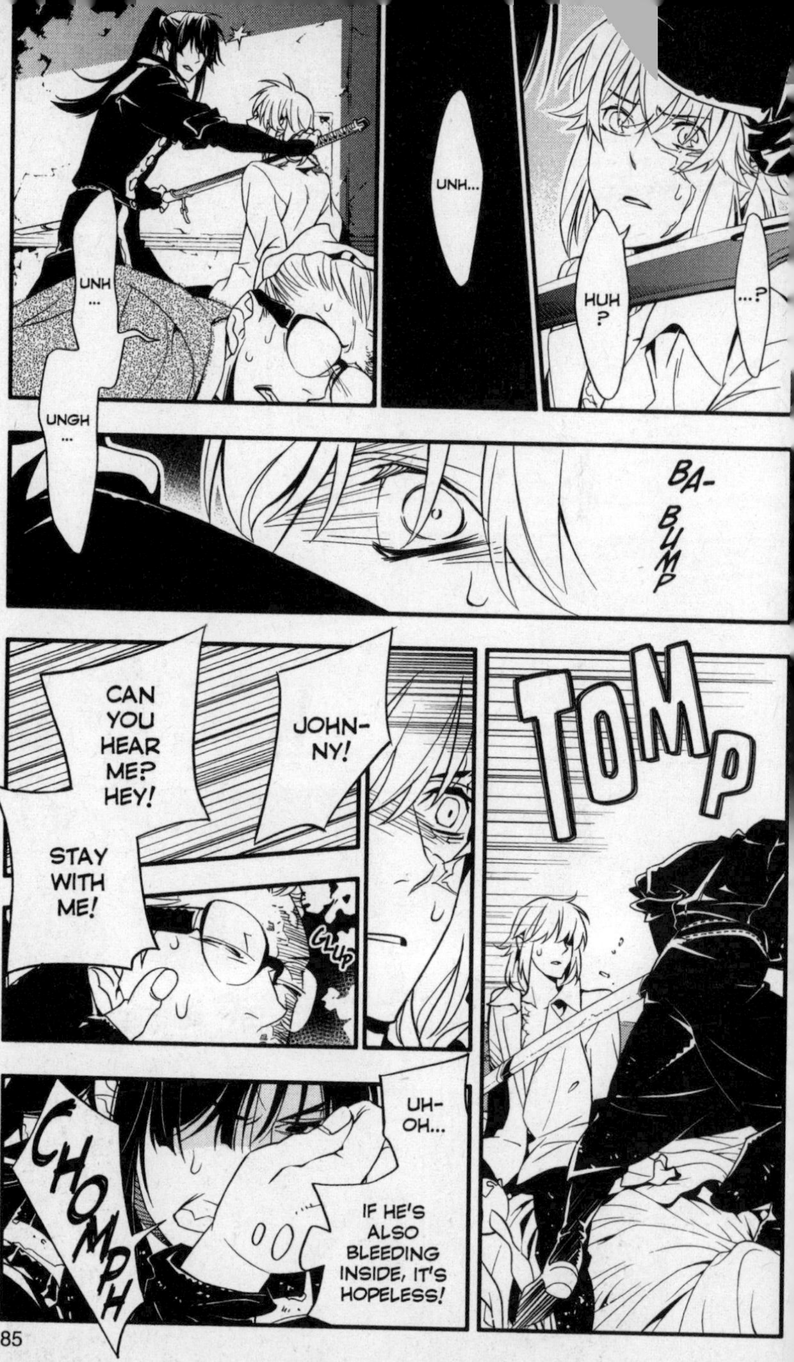
...?
HUH?
UNH...
UNH...
UNGH...
BA-BUMP
TOMP
JOHN-NY!
CAN YOU HEAR ME? HEY!
STAY WITH ME!
GLUP
UH-OH...
IF HE'S ALSO BLEEDING INSIDE, IT'S HOPELESS!
CHOMPH

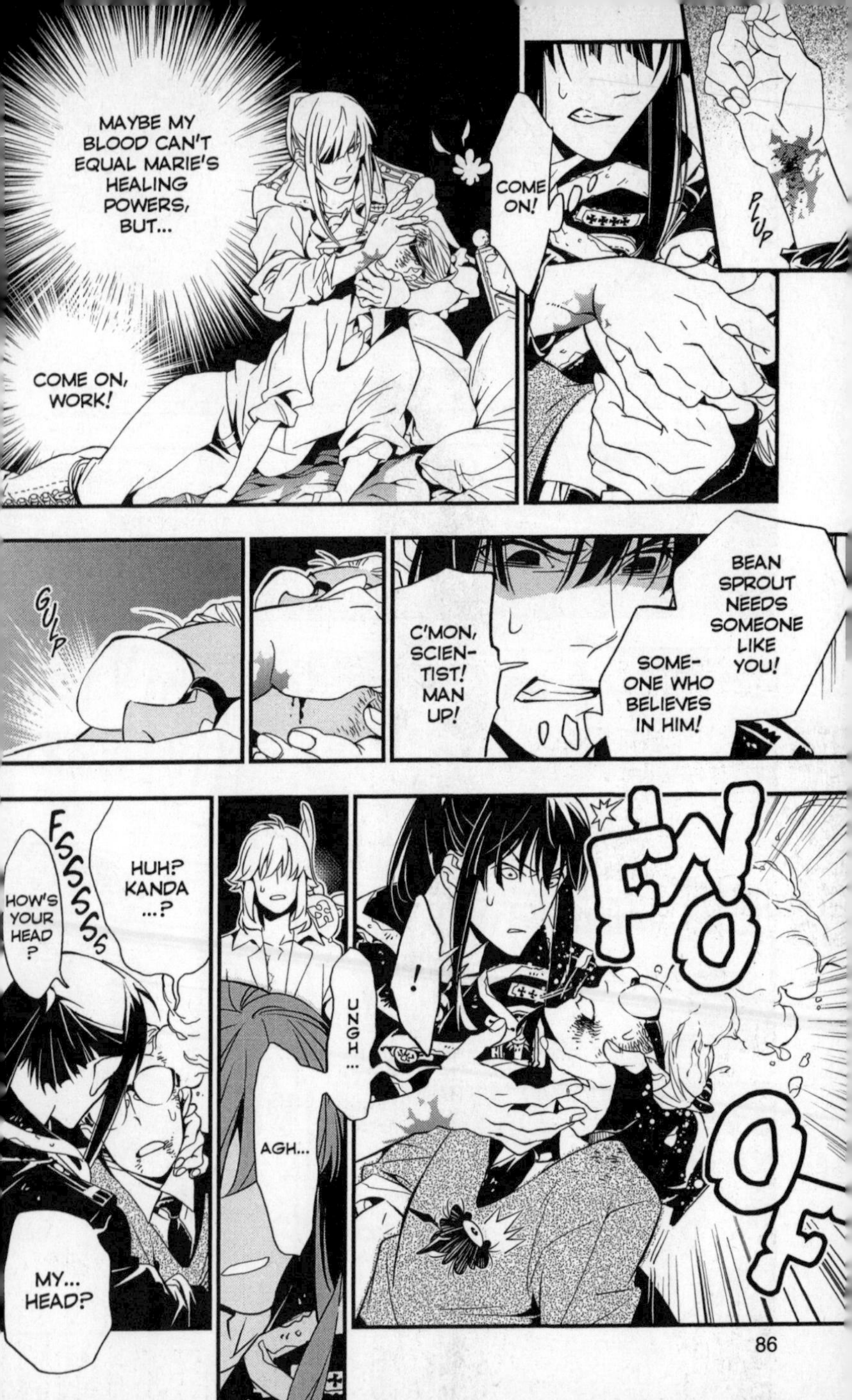
PLUP
COME ON!
MAYBE MY BLOOD CAN'T EQUAL MARIE'S HEALING POWERS, BUT...
COME ON, WORK!
BEAN SPROUT NEEDS SOMEONE LIKE YOU!
SOME-ONE WHO BELIEVES IN HIM!
C'MON, SCIENTIST! MAN UP!
GULP
FWOOF
!
UNGH...
AGH...
HUH? KANDA ...?
FSSSSSS
HOW'S YOUR HEAD?
MY... HEAD?

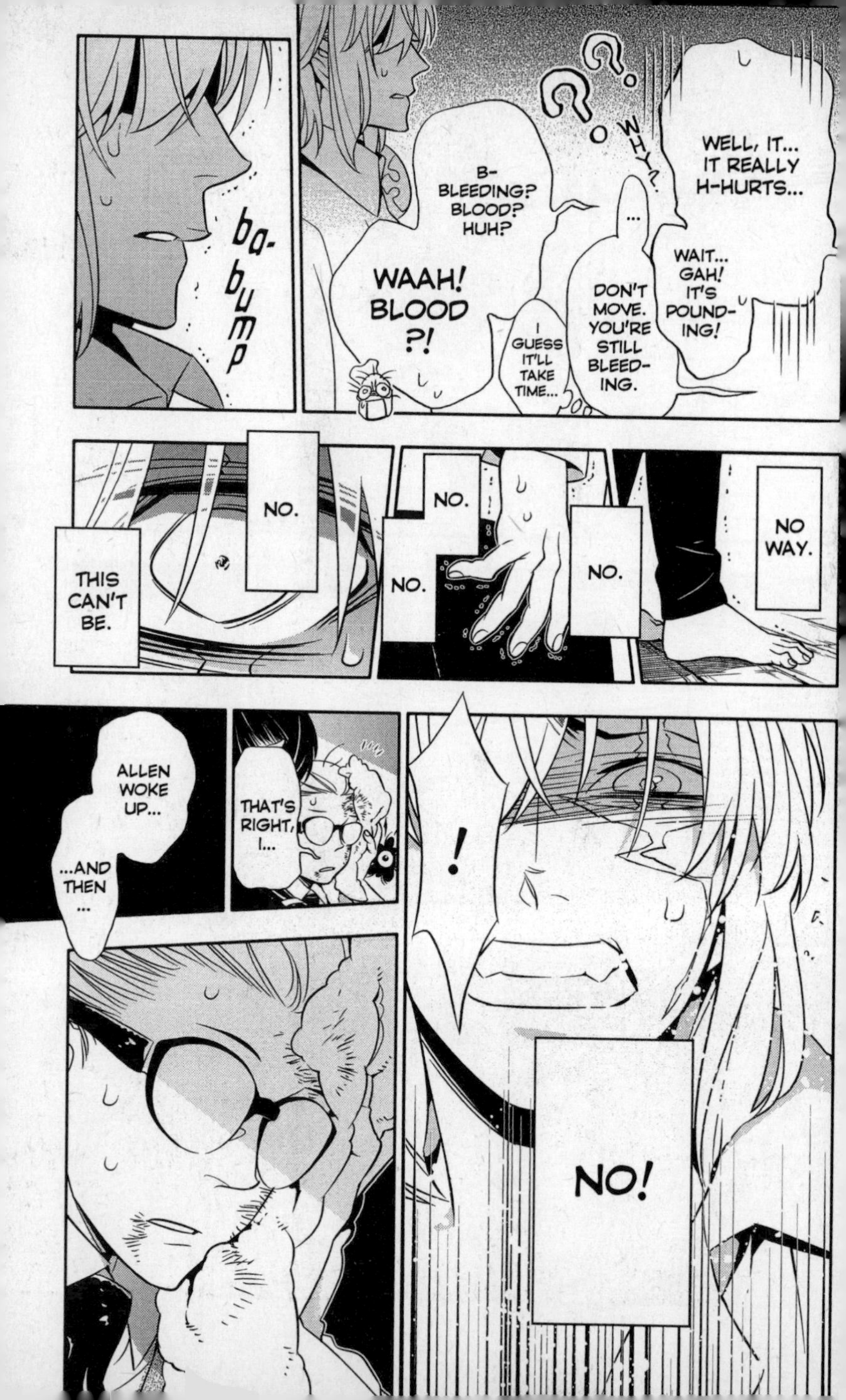
WELL, IT... IT REALLY H-HURTS...
WAIT... GAH! IT'S POUNDING!
WHY?
B-BLEEDING? BLOOD? HUH?
...
DON'T MOVE. YOU'RE STILL BLEEDING.
I GUESS IT'LL TAKE TIME...
WAAH! BLOOD?!
ba-bump
NO WAY.
NO.
NO.
NO.
NO.
THIS CAN'T BE.
!
NO!
THAT'S RIGHT, I...
ALLEN WOKE UP...
...AND THEN ...

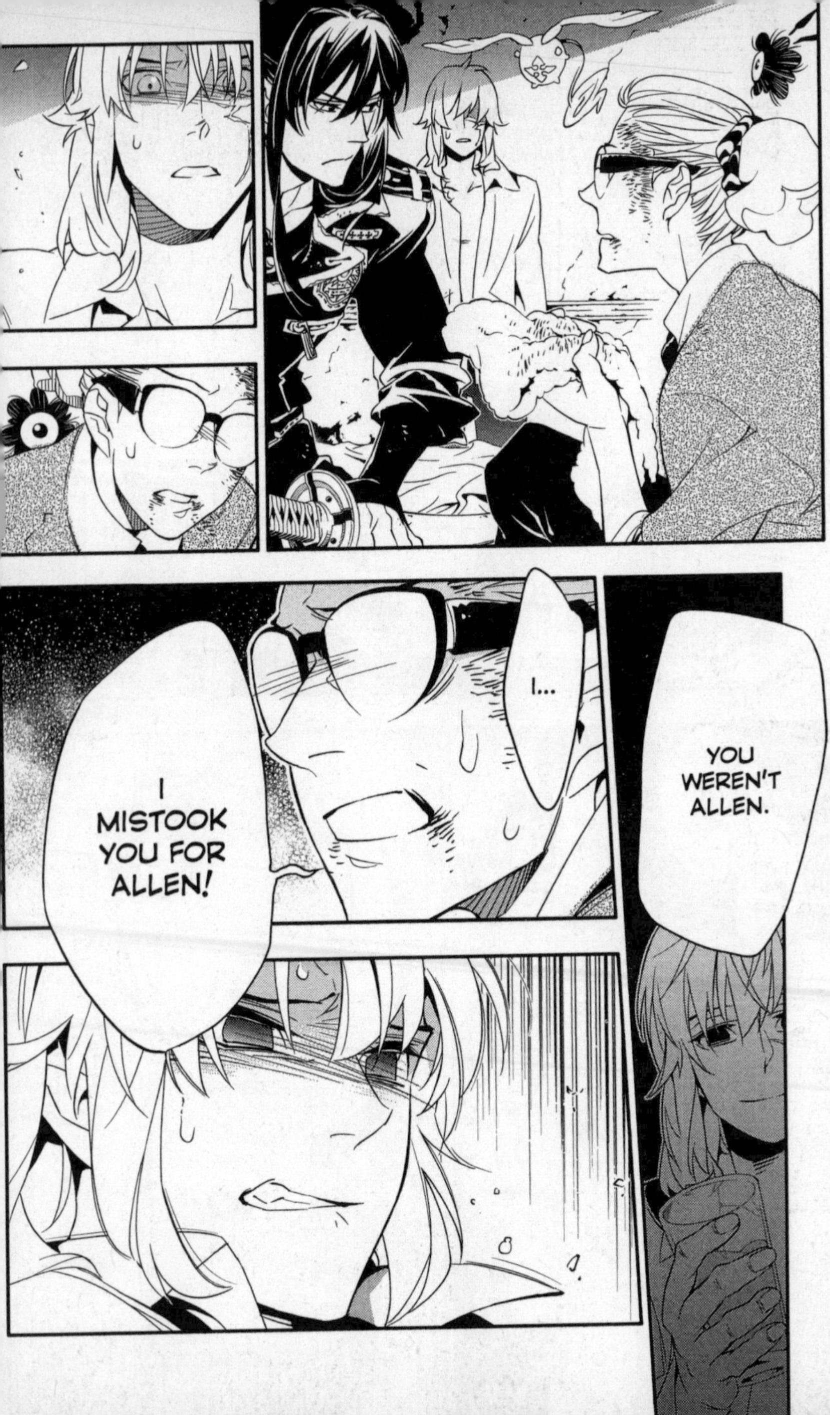
YOU WEREN'T ALLEN.
I...
I MISTOOK YOU FOR ALLEN!

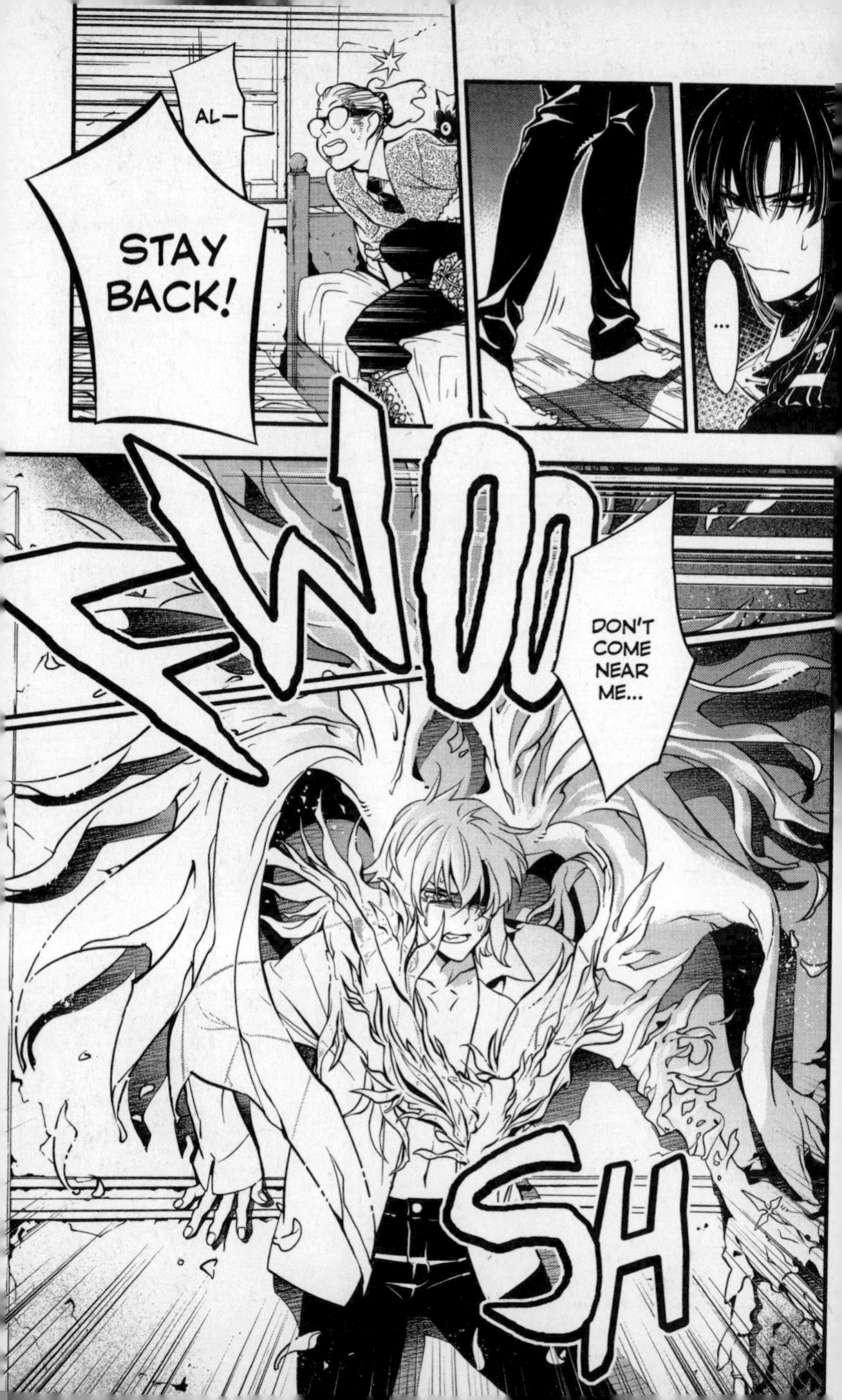
...
AL—
STAY BACK!
WOOSH
DON'T COME NEAR ME...

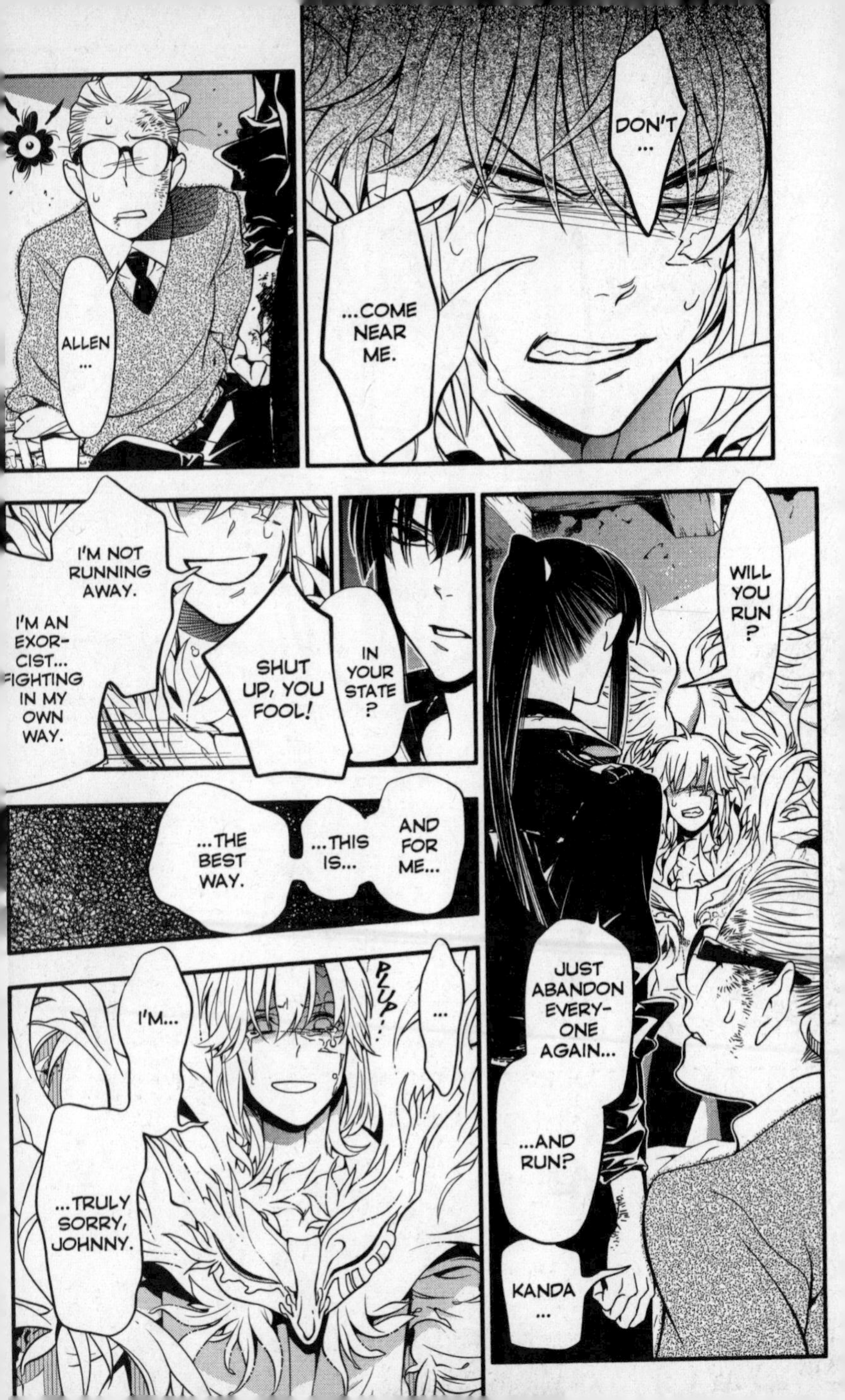
DON'T ...
...COME NEAR ME.
ALLEN ...
WILL YOU RUN ?
JUST ABANDON EVERY-ONE AGAIN...
...AND RUN?
KANDA ...
IN YOUR STATE ?
SHUT UP, YOU FOOL!
I'M NOT RUNNING AWAY.
I'M AN EXOR-CIST... FIGHTING IN MY OWN WAY.
AND FOR ME...
...THIS IS...
...THE BEST WAY.
...
PLUP...
I'M...
...TRULY SORRY, JOHNNY.

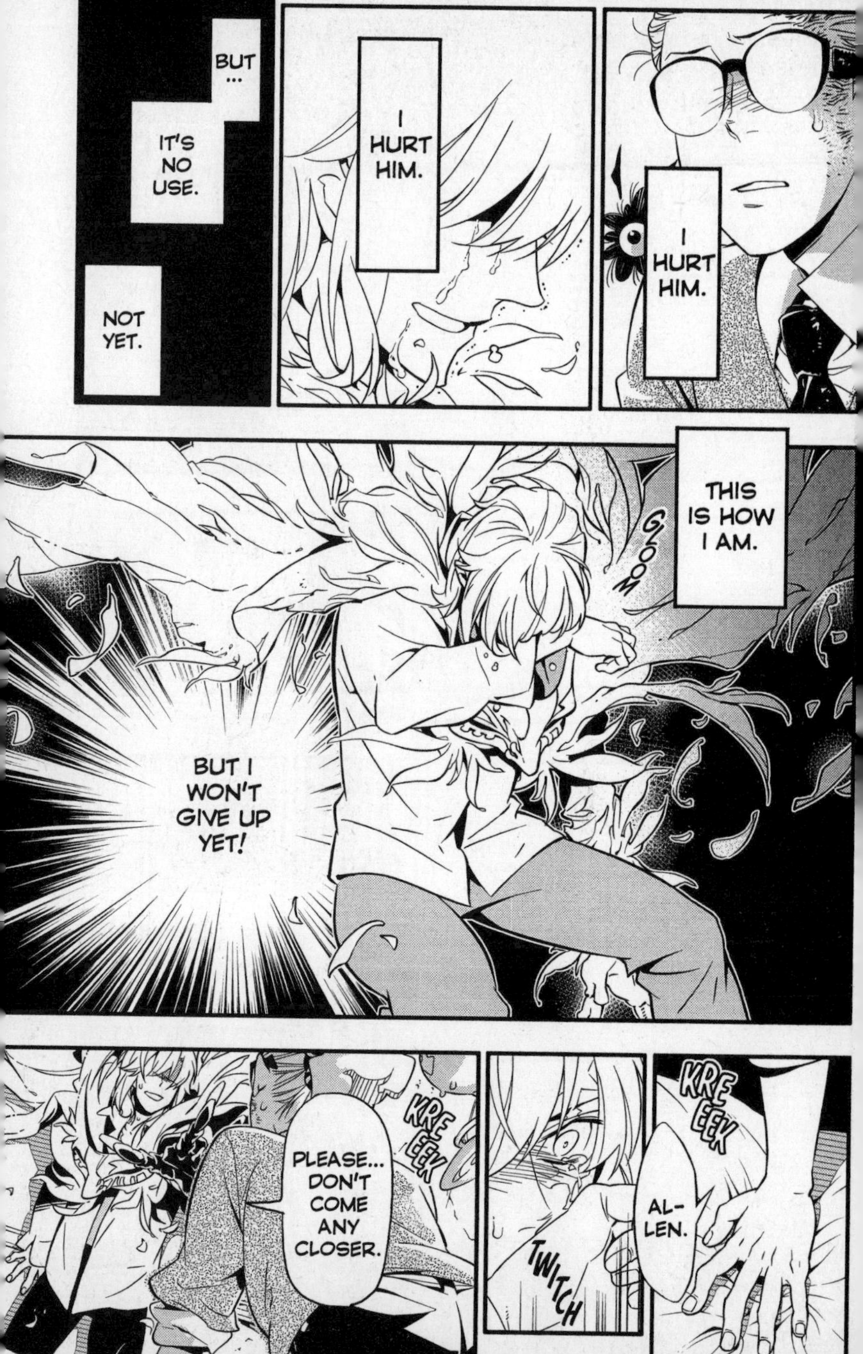
I HURT HIM.
I HURT HIM.
BUT...
IT'S NO USE.
NOT YET.
THIS IS HOW I AM.
GLOOM
BUT I WON'T GIVE UP YET!
KREEEEK
AL-LEN.
TWITCH
KREEEEK
PLEASE... DON'T COME ANY CLOSER.

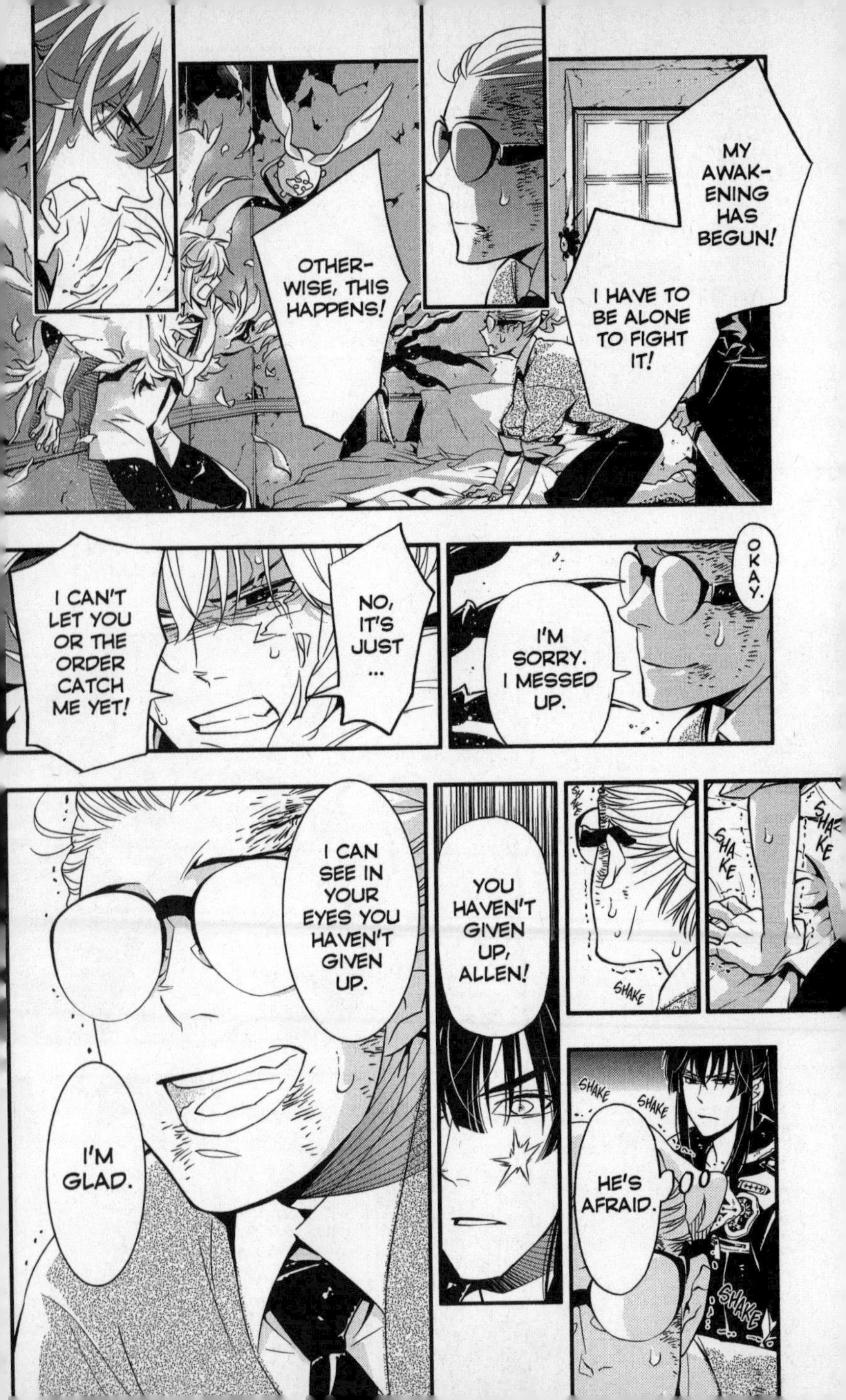
MY AWAKENING HAS BEGUN!
I HAVE TO BE ALONE TO FIGHT IT!
OTHERWISE, THIS HAPPENS!
OKAY.
I'M SORRY. I MESSED UP.
NO, IT'S JUST ...
I CAN'T LET YOU OR THE ORDER CATCH ME YET!
SHAKE SHAKE
SHAKE SHAKE
SHAKE SHAKE
HE'S AFRAID.
SHAKE
YOU HAVEN'T GIVEN UP, ALLEN!
I CAN SEE IN YOUR EYES YOU HAVEN'T GIVEN UP.
I'M GLAD.

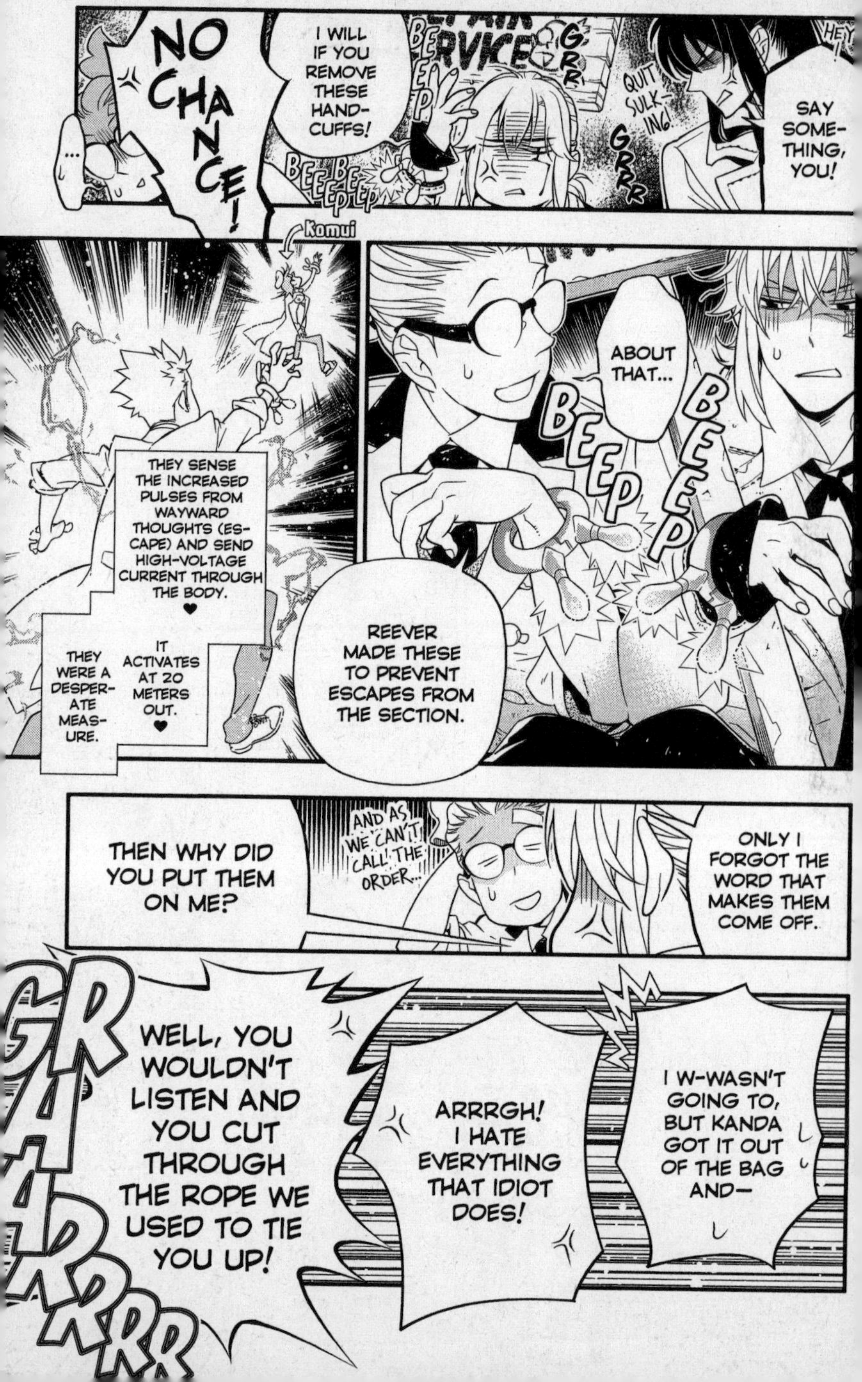

HEY!
SAY SOMETHING, YOU!
QUIT SULKING!
GRRR
GRRR
RVICE
BEEP
I WILL IF YOU REMOVE THESE HANDCUFFS!
BEEEP BEEP
NO CHANCE!
...
ABOUT THAT...
BEEP
BEEP
REEVER MADE THESE TO PREVENT ESCAPES FROM THE SECTION.
Komui
THEY SENSE THE INCREASED PULSES FROM WAYWARD THOUGHTS (ESCAPE) AND SEND HIGH-VOLTAGE CURRENT THROUGH THE BODY. ♥
IT ACTIVATES AT 20 METERS OUT. ♥
THEY WERE A DESPERATE MEASURE.
ONLY I FORGOT THE WORD THAT MAKES THEM COME OFF.
AND AS WE CAN'T CALL THE ORDER...!
THEN WHY DID YOU PUT THEM ON ME?
I W-WASN'T GOING TO, BUT KANDA GOT IT OUT OF THE BAG AND—
ARRRGH! I HATE EVERYTHING THAT IDIOT DOES!
WELL, YOU WOULDN'T LISTEN AND YOU CUT THROUGH THE ROPE WE USED TO TIE YOU UP!
GRAARRRR

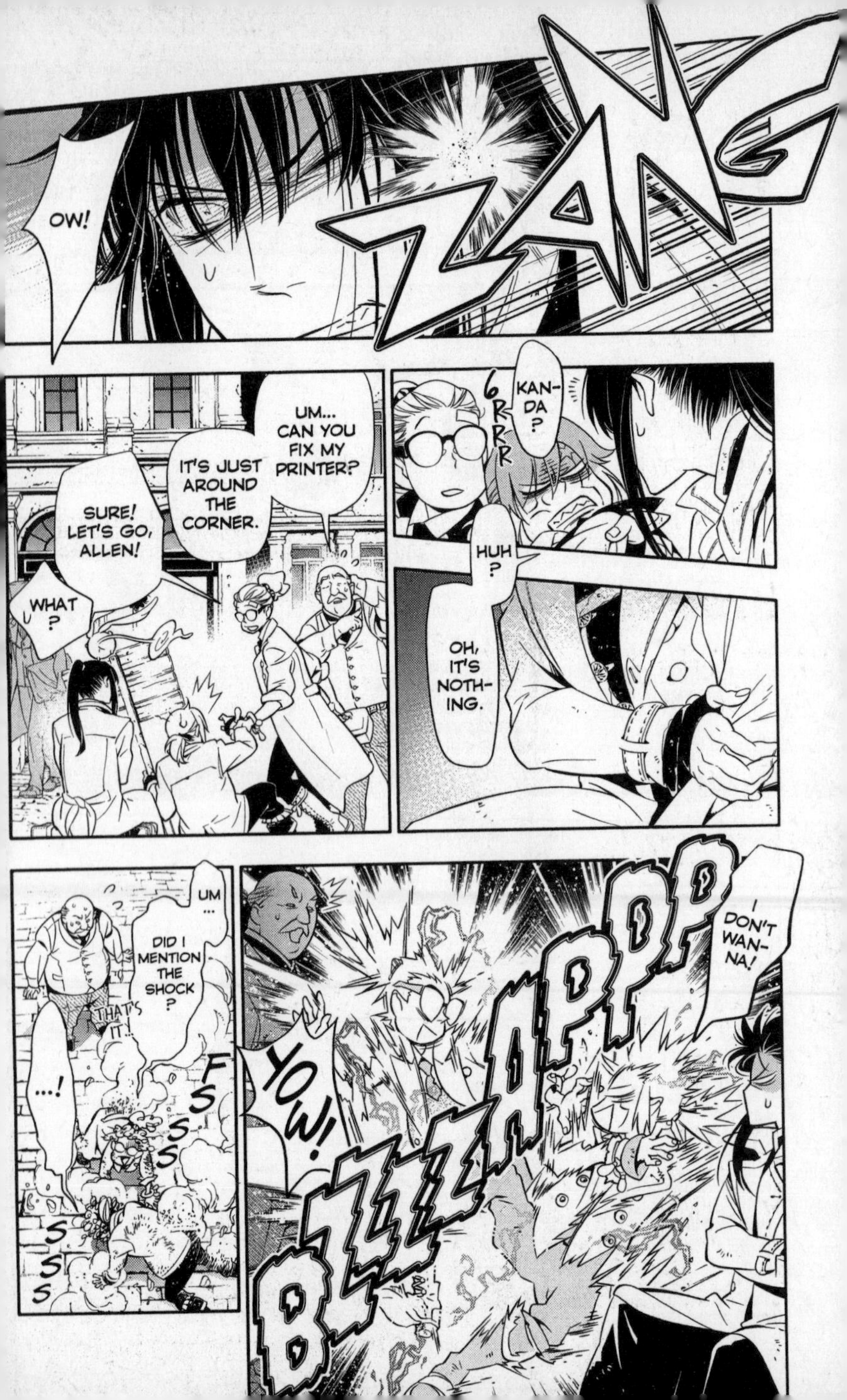
ZANG
OW!
KAN-DA?
GRRR
HUH?
OH, IT'S NOTHING.
UM... CAN YOU FIX MY PRINTER?
IT'S JUST AROUND THE CORNER.
SURE! LET'S GO, ALLEN!
WHAT?
I DON'T WAN-NA!
BZZZAPP
YOW!
UM... DID I MENTION THE SHOCK?
THAT'S IT!
...!
FSSS
SSS

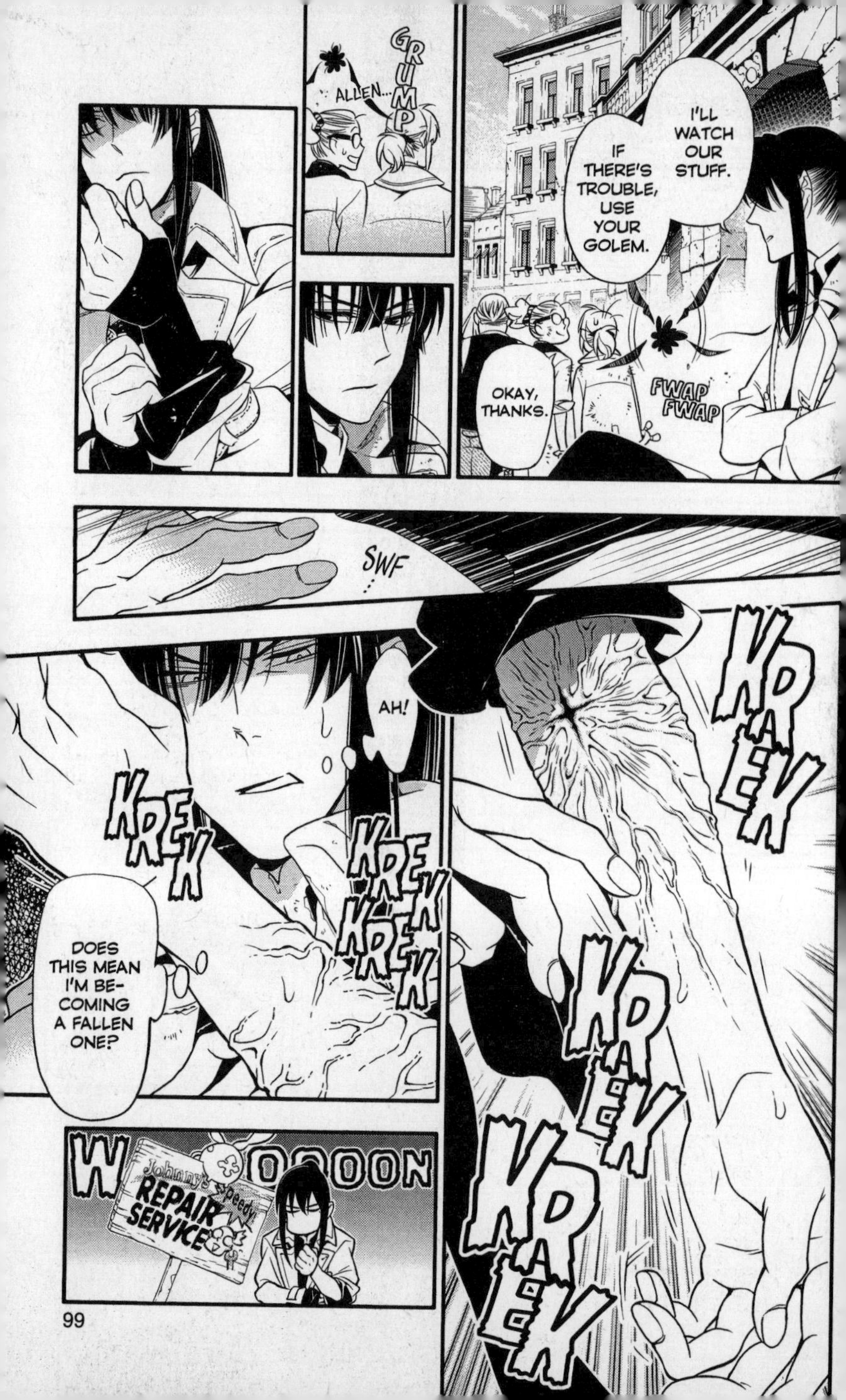
I'LL WATCH OUR STUFF.
IF THERE'S TROUBLE, USE YOUR GOLEM.
FWAP FWAP
OKAY, THANKS.
GRUMP
ALLEN...
SWF
KRAEK
AH!
KREK
KREK KREK KREK KREK
DOES THIS MEAN I'M BE-COMING A FALLEN ONE?
KRAEK
KRAEK
WOOOOON
Johnny's Speedy REPAIR SERVICE

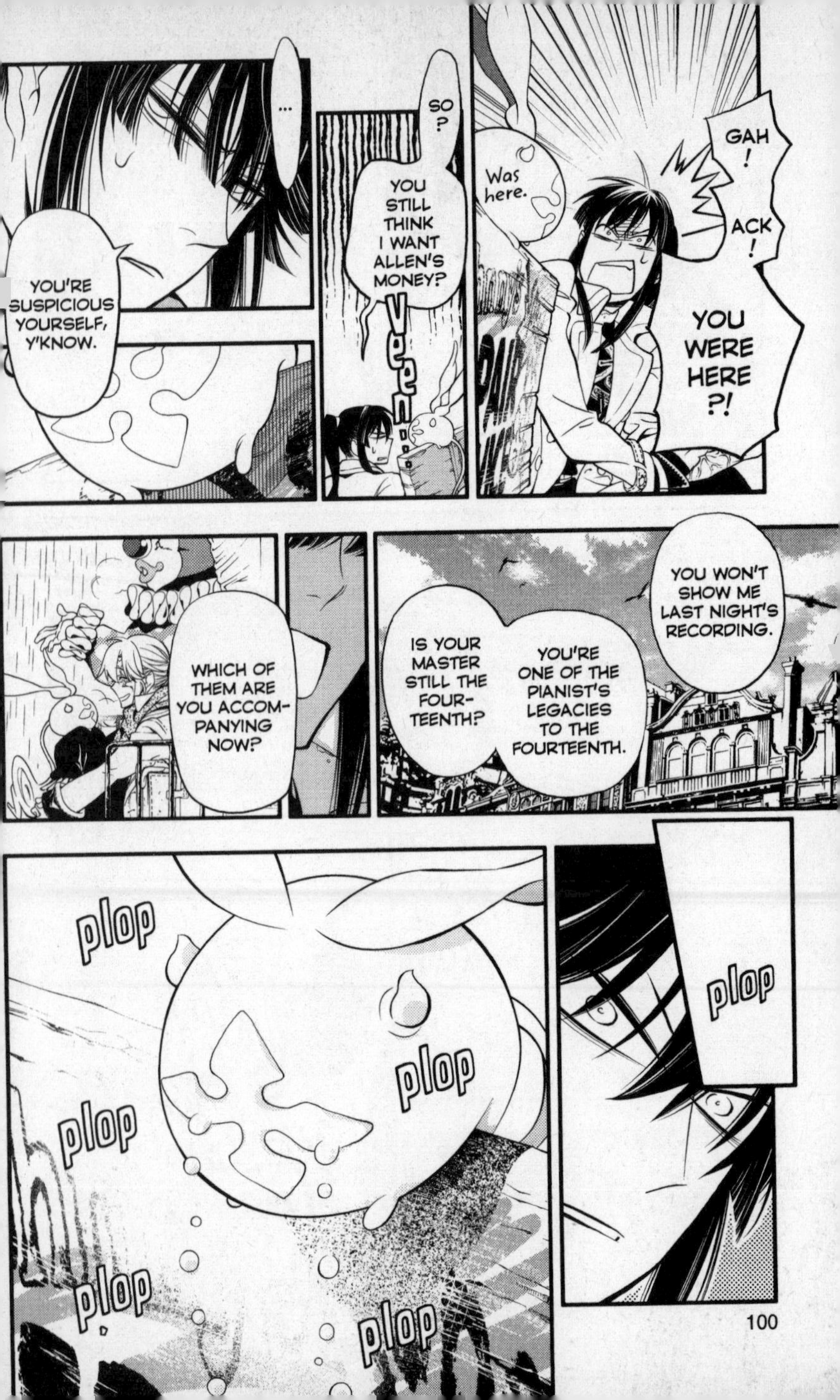
GAH! ACK!
YOU WERE HERE?!
Was here.
SO?
YOU STILL THINK I WANT ALLEN'S MONEY?
...
YOU'RE SUSPICIOUS YOURSELF, Y'KNOW.
YOU WON'T SHOW ME LAST NIGHT'S RECORDING.
YOU'RE ONE OF THE PIANIST'S LEGACIES TO THE FOURTEENTH.
IS YOUR MASTER STILL THE FOURTEENTH?
WHICH OF THEM ARE YOU ACCOMPANYING NOW?
plop
plop
plop
plop
plop
plop

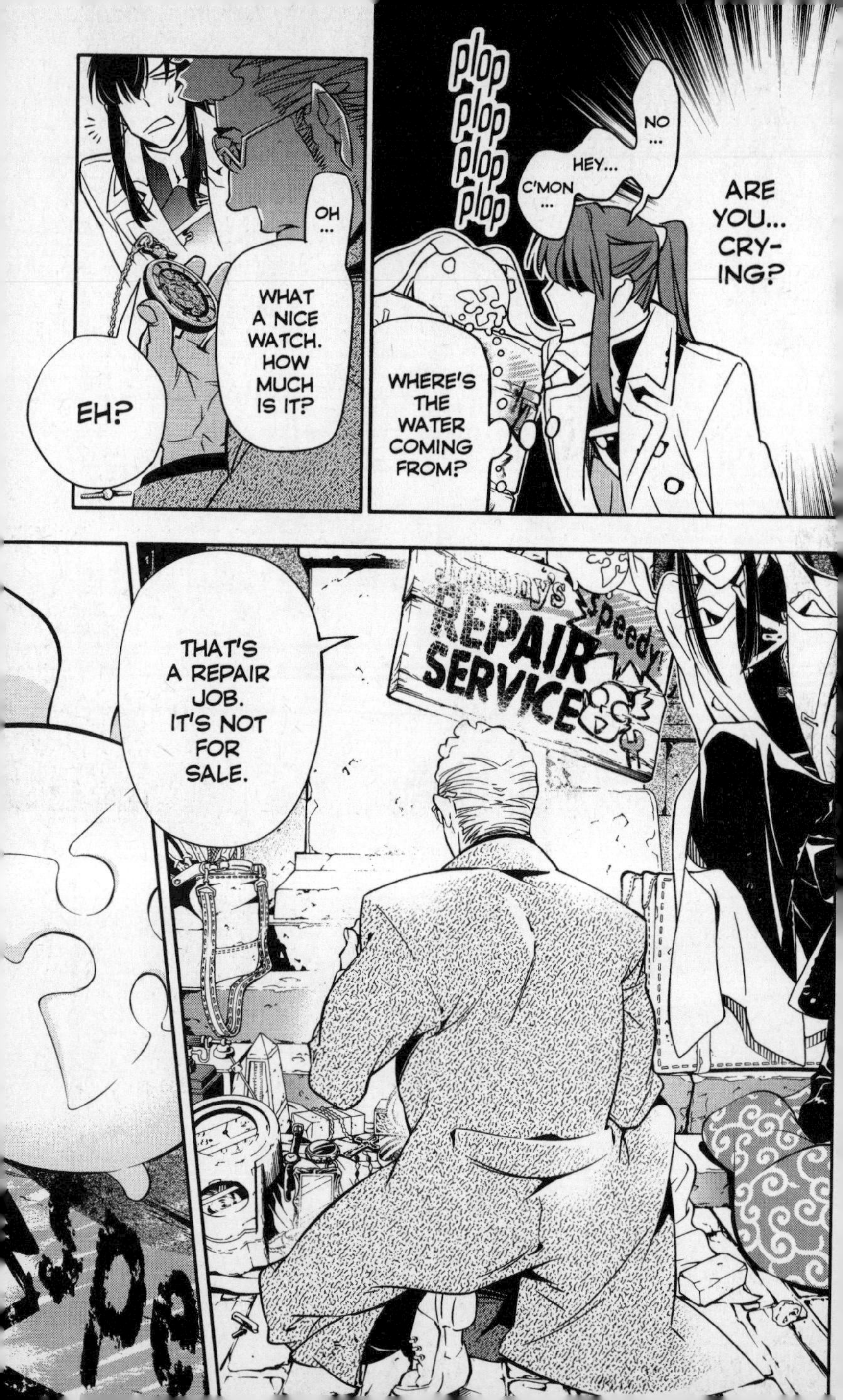
ARE YOU... CRY-ING?
NO ...
HEY... C'MON ...
plop plop plop plop
WHERE'S THE WATER COMING FROM?
OH ...
WHAT A NICE WATCH. HOW MUCH IS IT?
EH?
Johnny's REPAIR SERVICE
Speedy!
THAT'S A REPAIR JOB. IT'S NOT FOR SALE.

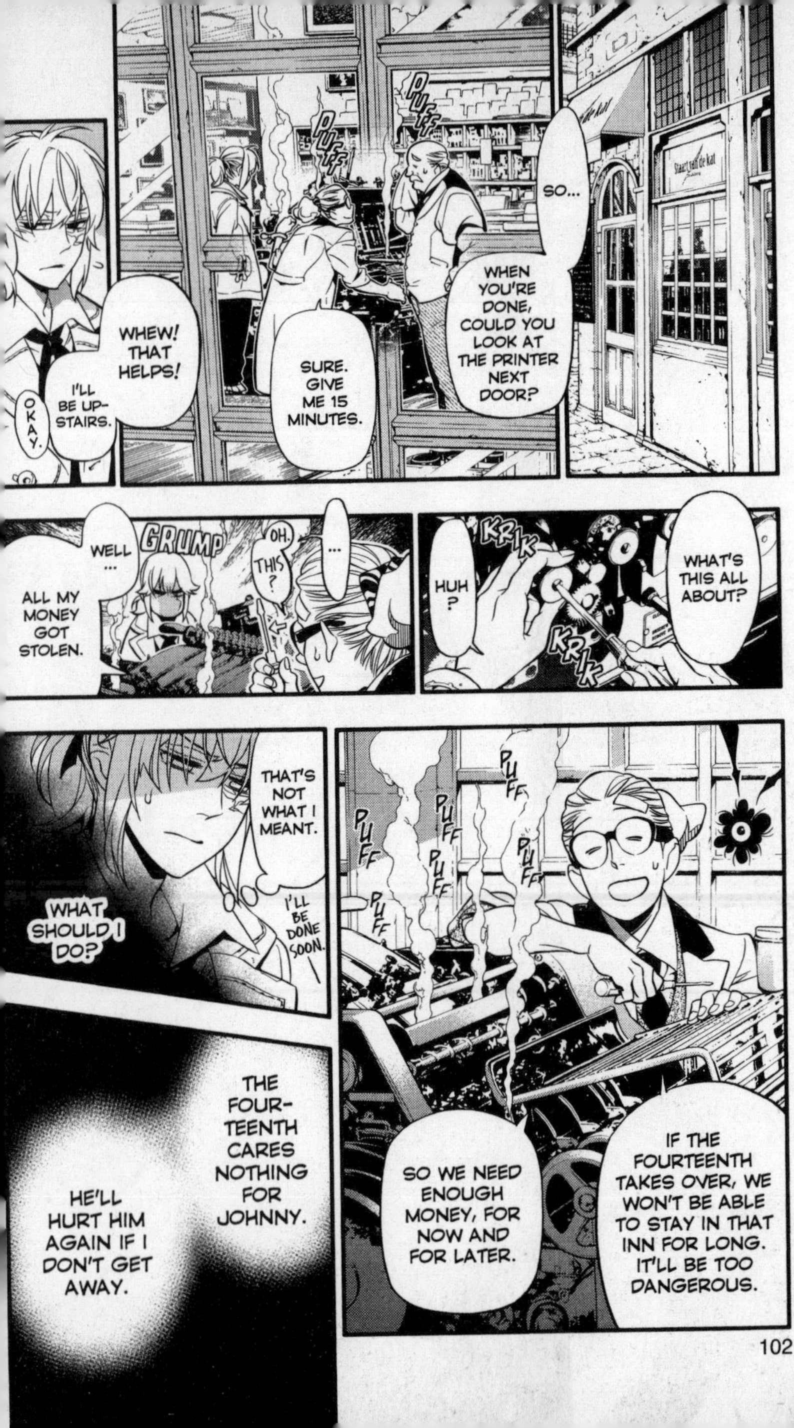
SO...
WHEN YOU'RE DONE, COULD YOU LOOK AT THE PRINTER NEXT DOOR?
PUFF
PUFF
SURE. GIVE ME 15 MINUTES.
WHEW! THAT HELPS!
I'LL BE UP-STAIRS.
OKAY.
WHAT'S THIS ALL ABOUT?
KRIK
HUH?
KRIK
...
OH. THIS?
GRUMP
WELL...
ALL MY MONEY GOT STOLEN.
PUFF
PUFF
PUFF
PUFF
PUFF
PUFF
IF THE FOURTEENTH TAKES OVER, WE WON'T BE ABLE TO STAY IN THAT INN FOR LONG. IT'LL BE TOO DANGEROUS.
SO WE NEED ENOUGH MONEY, FOR NOW AND FOR LATER.
THAT'S NOT WHAT I MEANT.
I'LL BE DONE SOON.
WHAT SHOULD I DO?
THE FOURTEENTH CARES NOTHING FOR JOHNNY.
HE'LL HURT HIM AGAIN IF I DON'T GET AWAY.

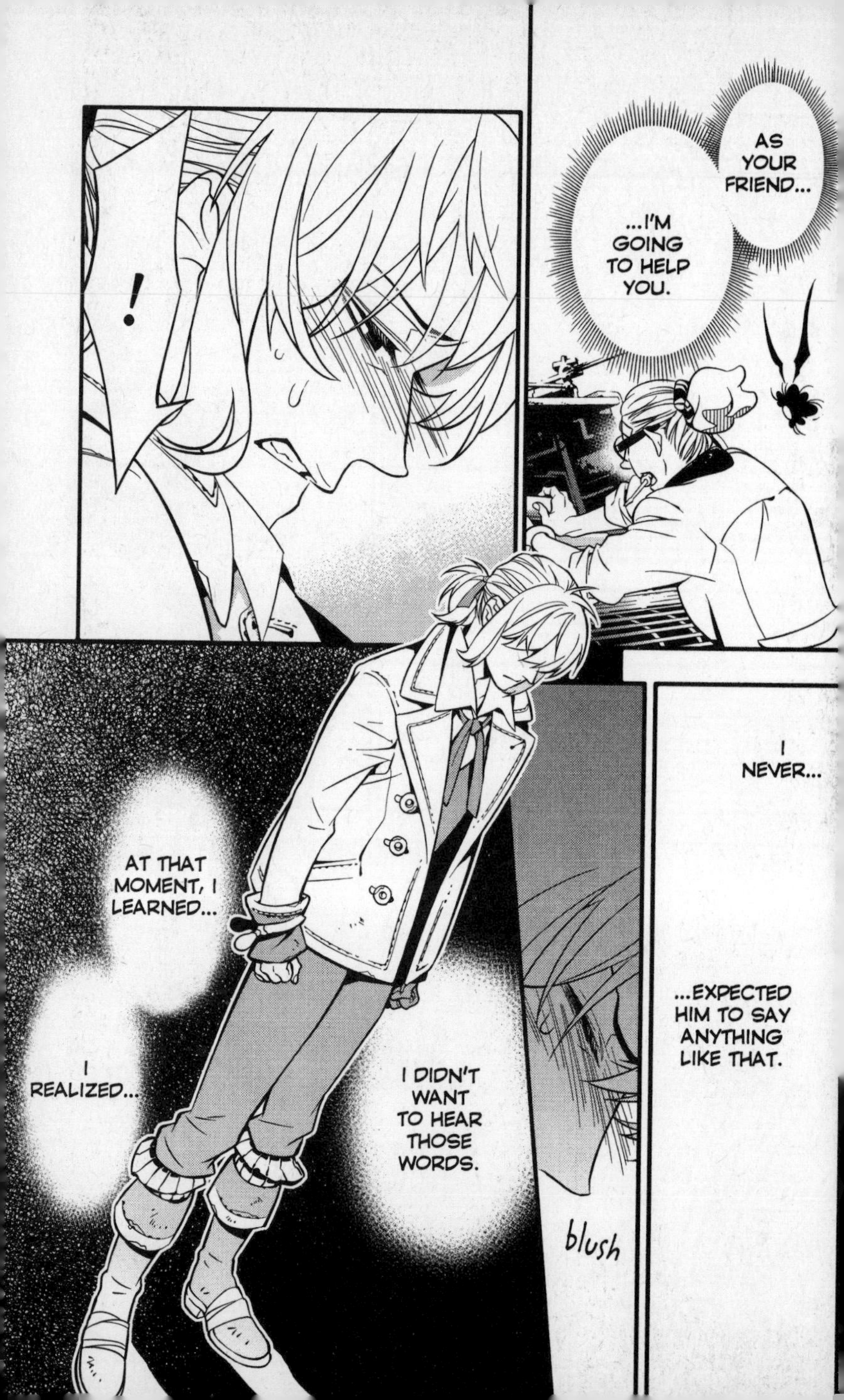
AS YOUR FRIEND...
...I'M GOING TO HELP YOU.
!
I NEVER...
...EXPECTED HIM TO SAY ANYTHING LIKE THAT.
blush
AT THAT MOMENT, I LEARNED...
I REALIZED...
I DIDN'T WANT TO HEAR THOSE WORDS.

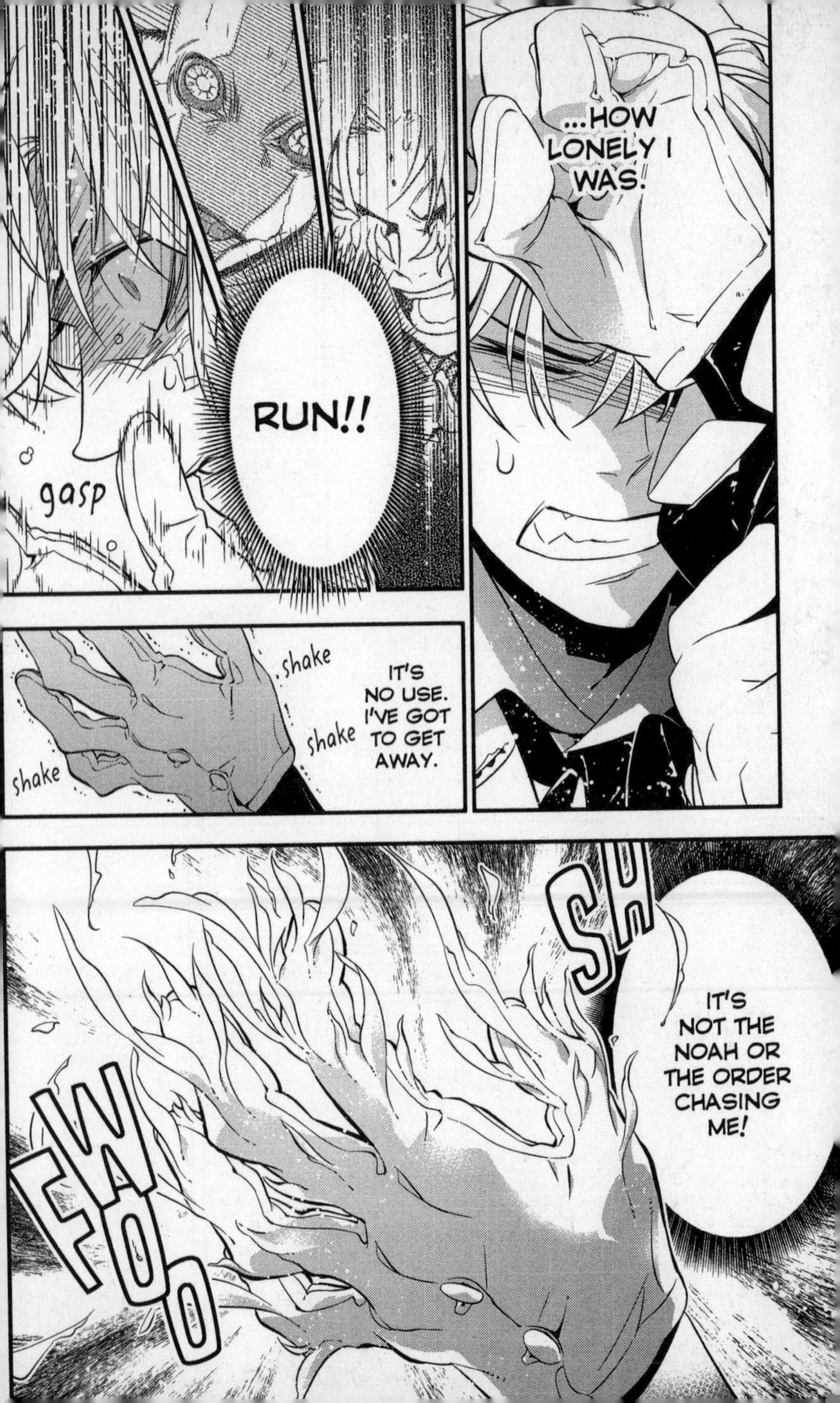
...HOW LONELY I WAS.
RUN!!
gasp
shake
IT'S NO USE. I'VE GOT TO GET AWAY.
shake
shake
SH
IT'S NOT THE NOAH OR THE ORDER CHASING ME!
FWOOO

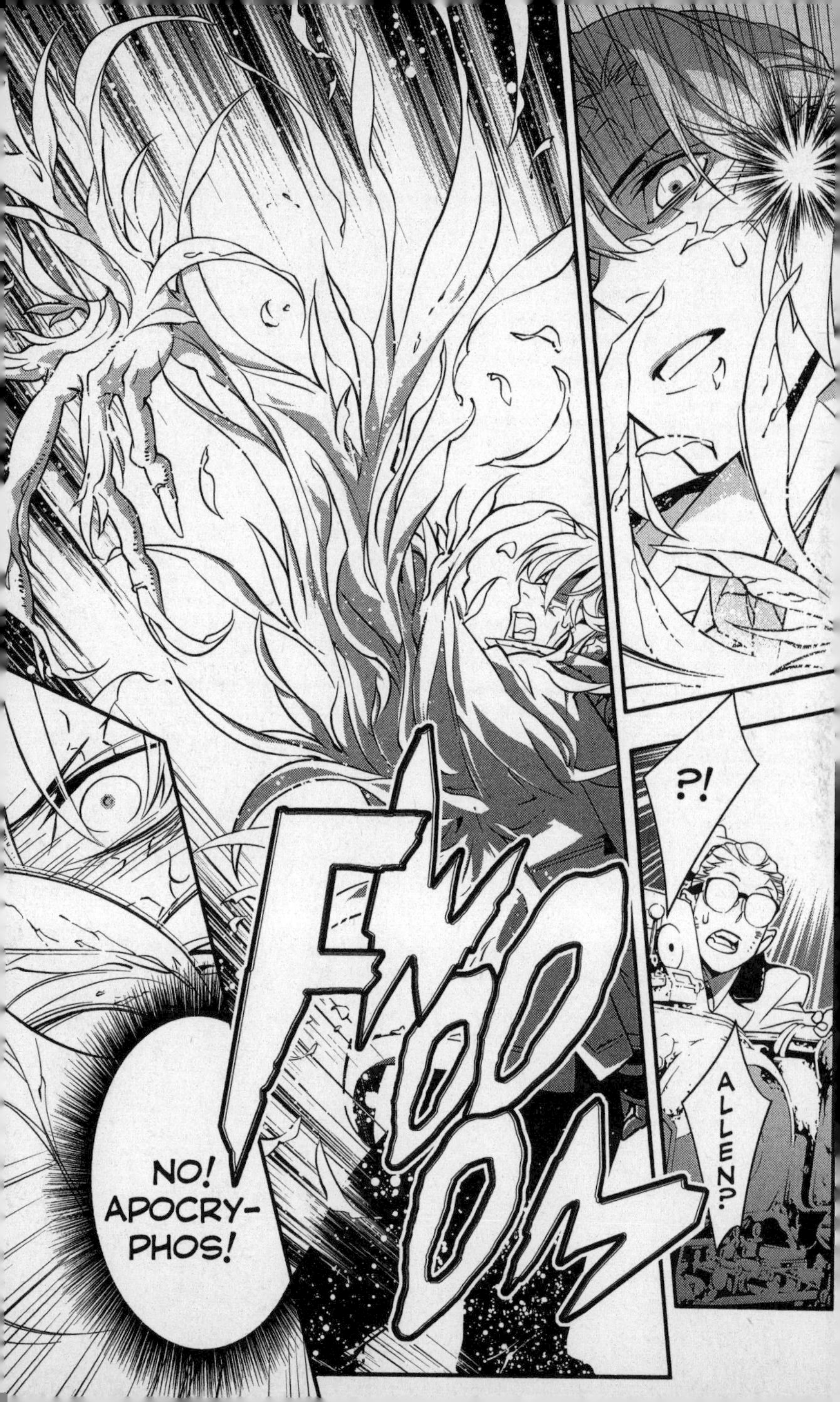
?!
ALLEN?!
FWOOOM
NO! APOCRY-PHOS!

(Tim) (Link) (Tyki) (Waizurii) (Johnny) (Kanda) (Allen)

KOMUI'S DISCUSSION ROOM 3

Q. Does Marie like Miranda?

A: Huh?! Does he?!

K: Does Marie like... (*surprised*) No way! Not her!

A: If you say anything bad about Miranda, I'll beat you silly!

J: But Marie does take care of Miranda a lot, like in a novel, so I'm rooting for him!

K: Marie's nice, he just shouldn't be nice to her!

A: Kanda, you're like a guy whose kid brother stole his sweetheart!

K: Die, Bean Sprout!

Ty: We'll never know unless we ask Marie.

W: I could use my Eye to take a peek if you want.

A, K & J: No peeking!

Q. At the North America Branch, when Allen destroyed the Gate Kanda and Alma Karma escaped through, he chanted "adara." Can he use spells like his master?

J: That surprised me too. Allen, when did you learn how to destroy Gates?

A: Um... (*uncomfortable*) when Kanda stabbed me and the Fourteenth started to awaken. When I want to use the spell, I hear it in my head like the Pianist's songs.

W: That's the Fourteenth's memory. He brought down the old Arks you guys use. They were obsolete. That's why the Earl got rid of them.

J: So that was the Fourteenth's spell? When you chant, your face gets really scary looking.

A: Did I look like the Fourteenth?! (*upset*)

Ty: I wonder more about Cross Marian than you, boy. He seems able to use the same spells as the Earl and the Skulls.

J: And General Cross looks like he's in his late twenties. But given what we know about the Fourteenth, he must at least be in his forties.

W: Hmm... He could be even older, like over 100! Anything to say? You're his protégé, after all.

A: I don't know his real age! He hasn't changed at all since we met! I always knew he was a monster!

Q. How much of his Master's debt has Allen finished paying?

A: ...

J: Allen? (*worried*)

Ty: His eyes are white. That's bad. Waizurii, look into his head.

W: ...

Ty: Did you get a look?

K: How bad is his debt?

W: Look, just let it go. It's better not to know some things. (*looks pale*)

Ty & K: ?! (*worried*)

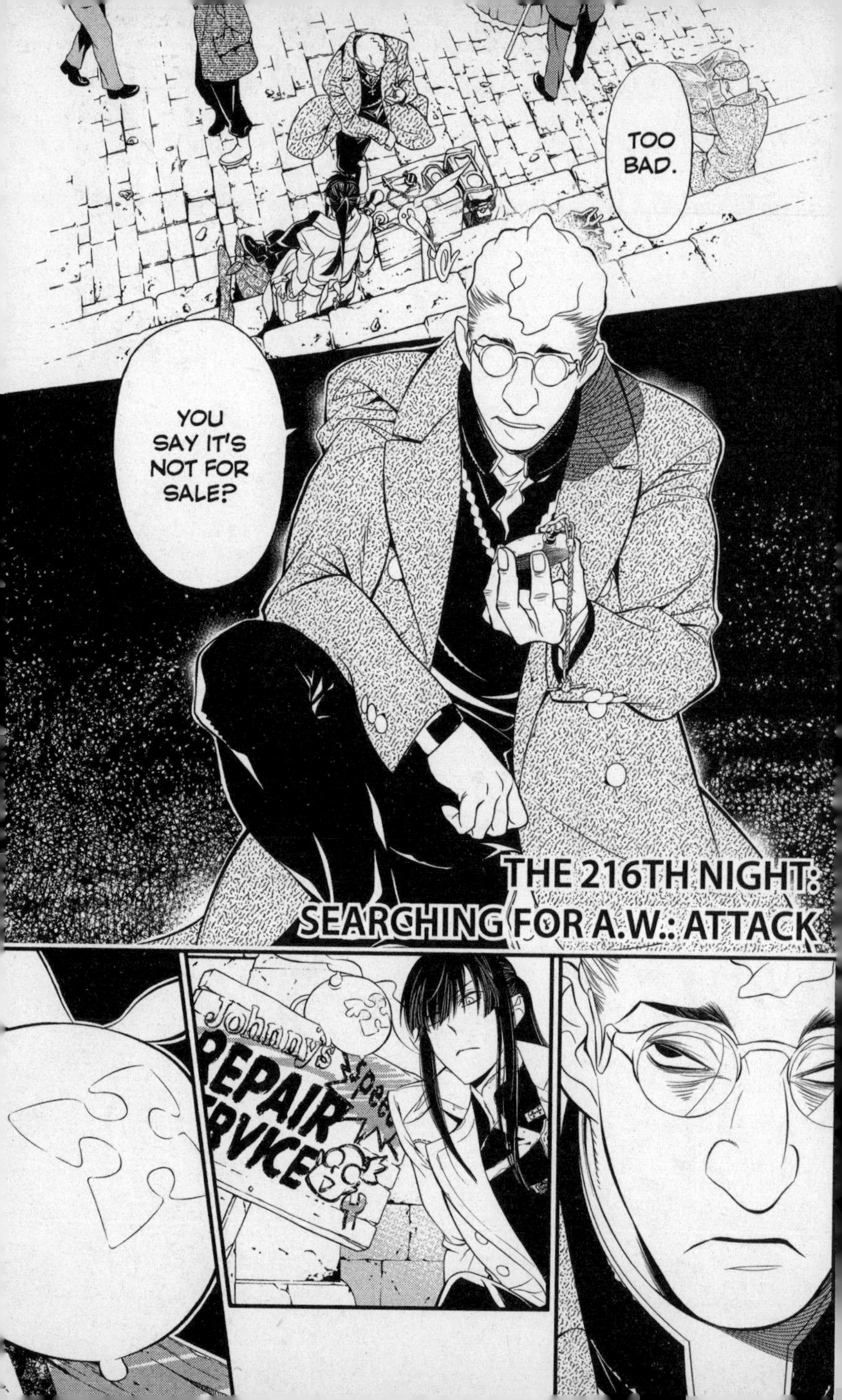
TOO BAD.
YOU SAY IT'S NOT FOR SALE?
THE 216TH NIGHT: SEARCHING FOR A.W.: ATTACK
Johnny's
REPAIR
RVICE

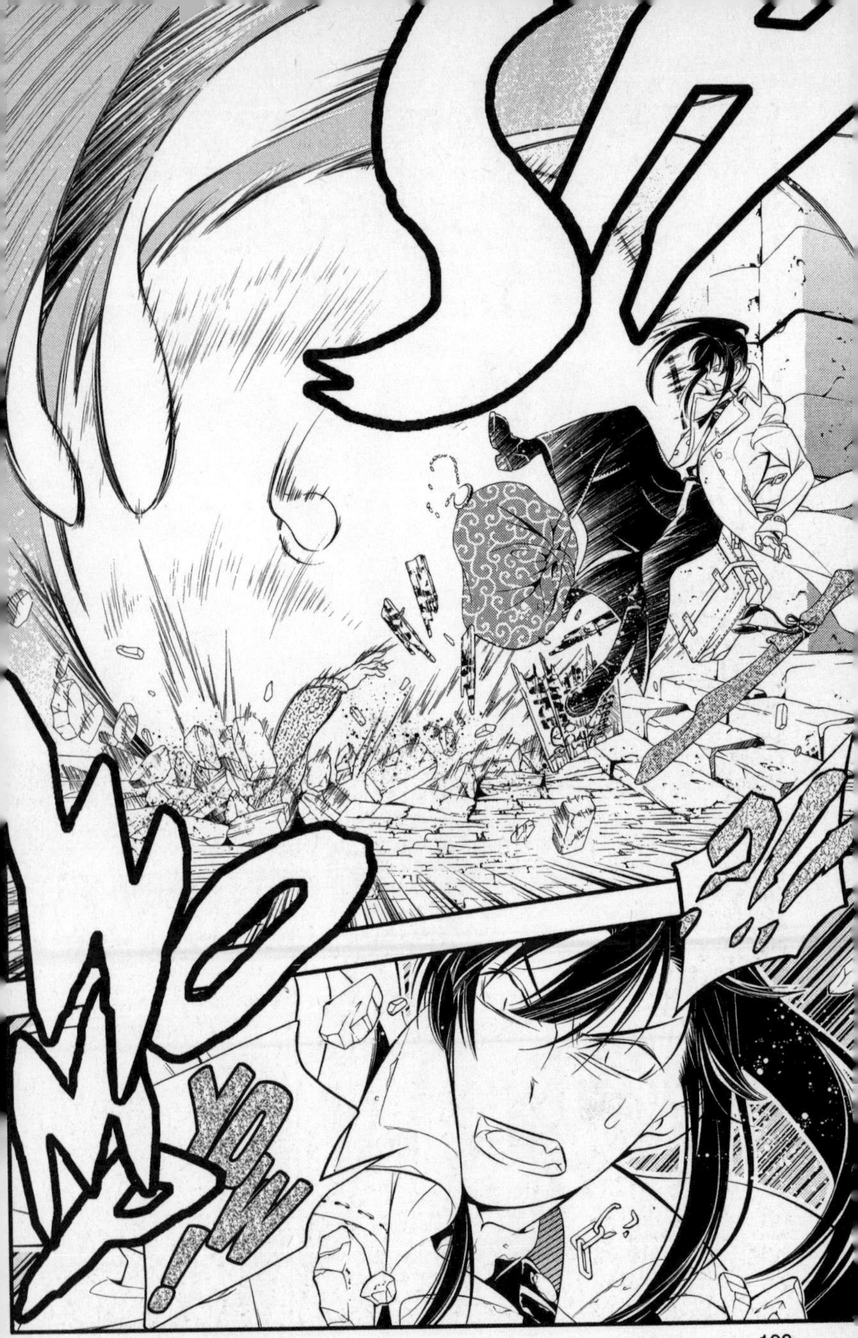
YOW!

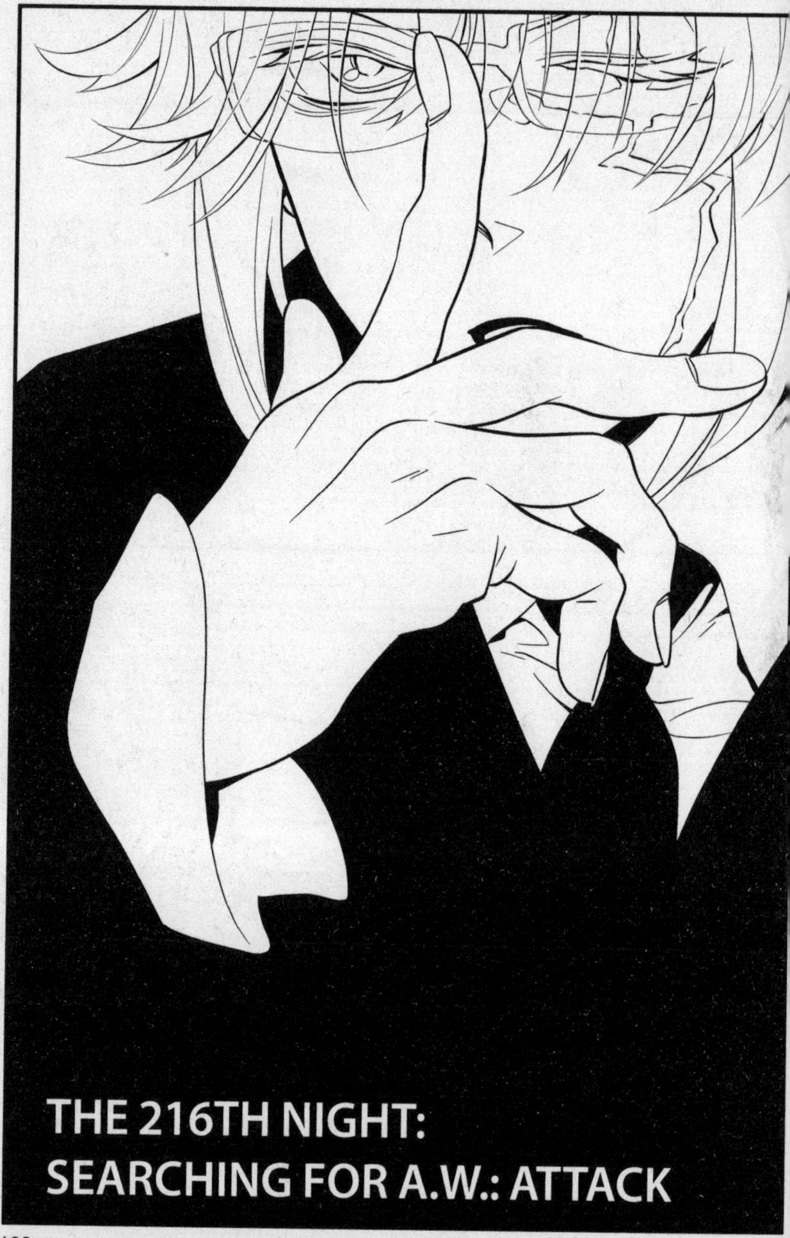
THE 216TH NIGHT:
SEARCHING FOR A.W.: ATTACK

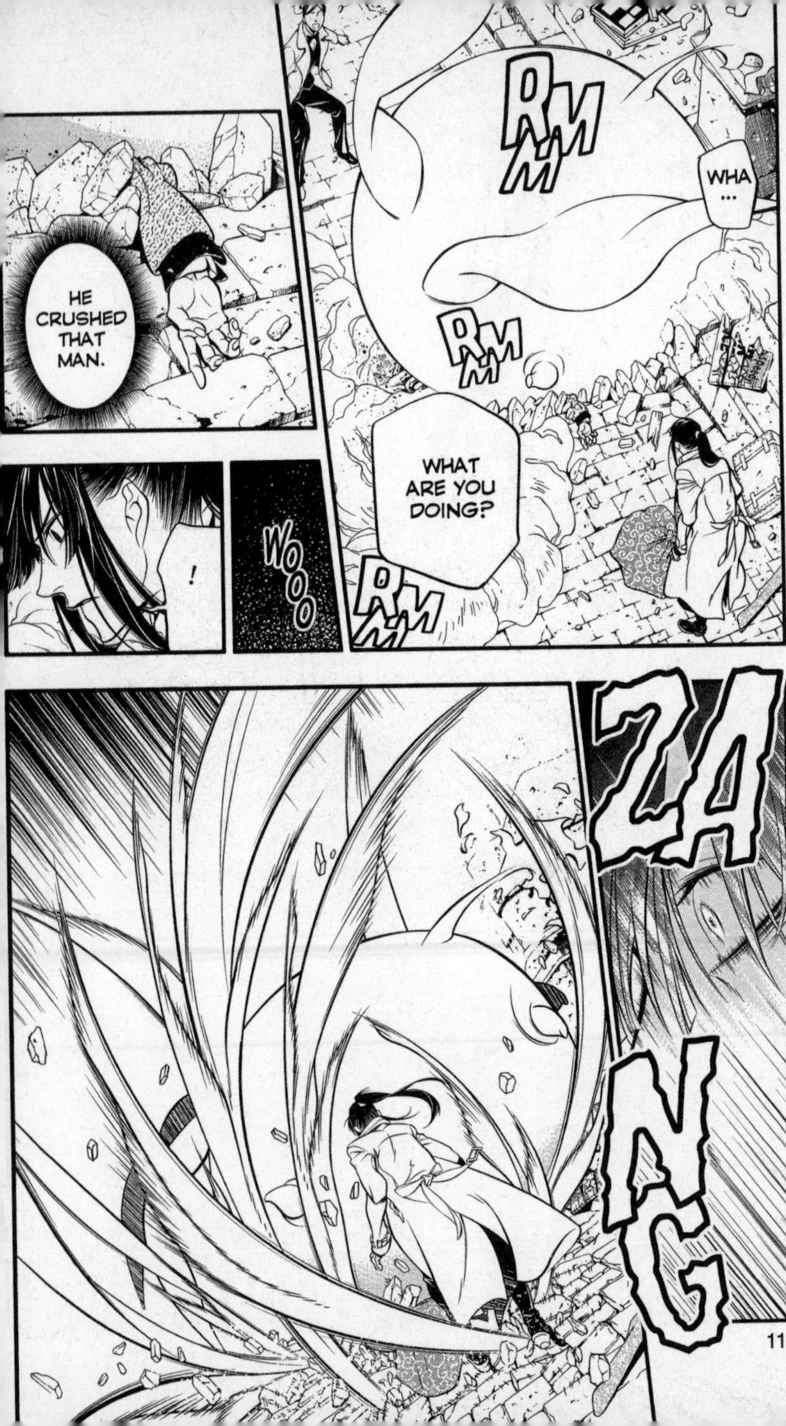
RMMM
WHA ...
RMM
WHAT ARE YOU DOING?
RMM
HE CRUSHED THAT MAN.
WOOO
!
ZANG

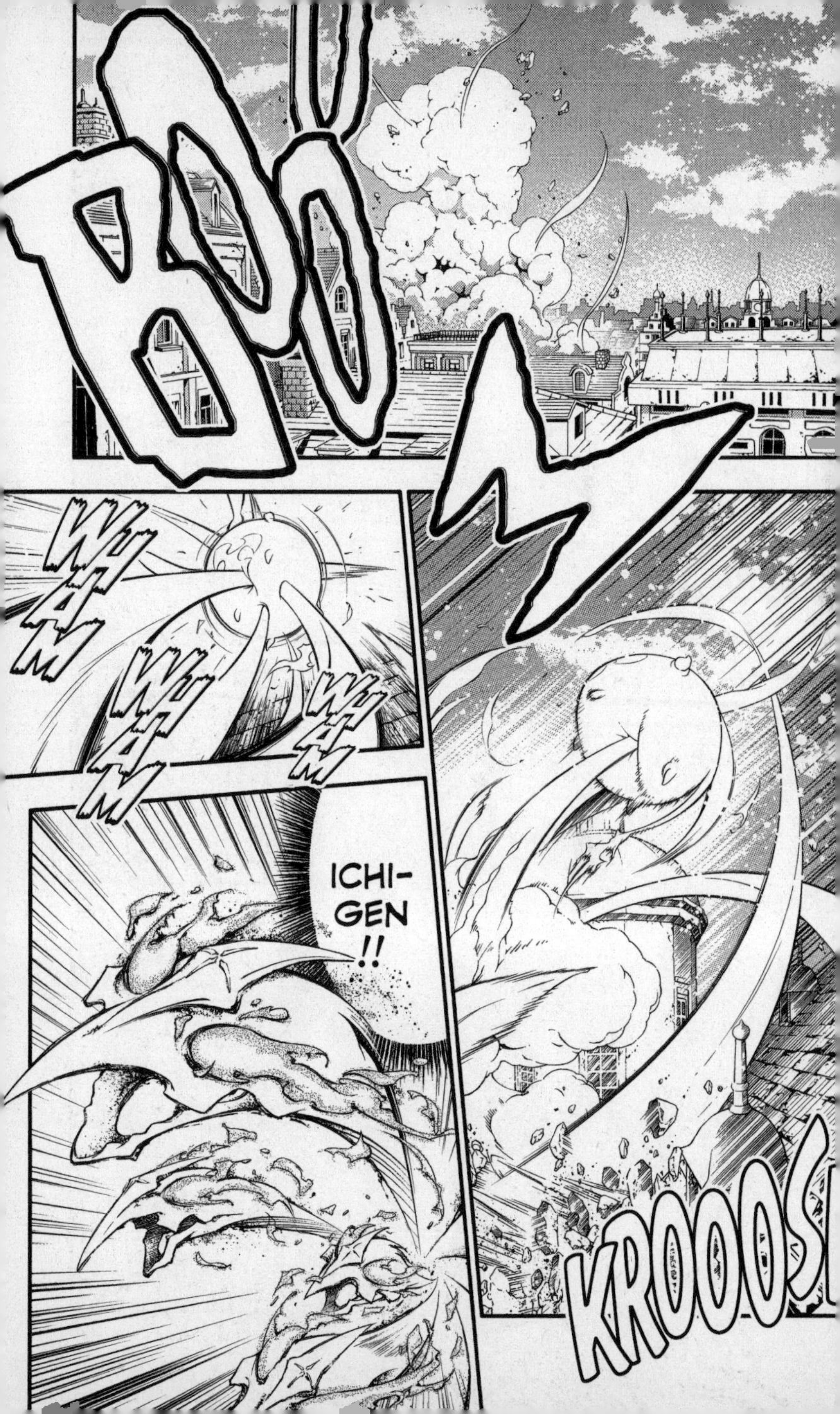
BOOM
KROOOS
WHAM
WHAM
WHAM
ICHI-GEN!!

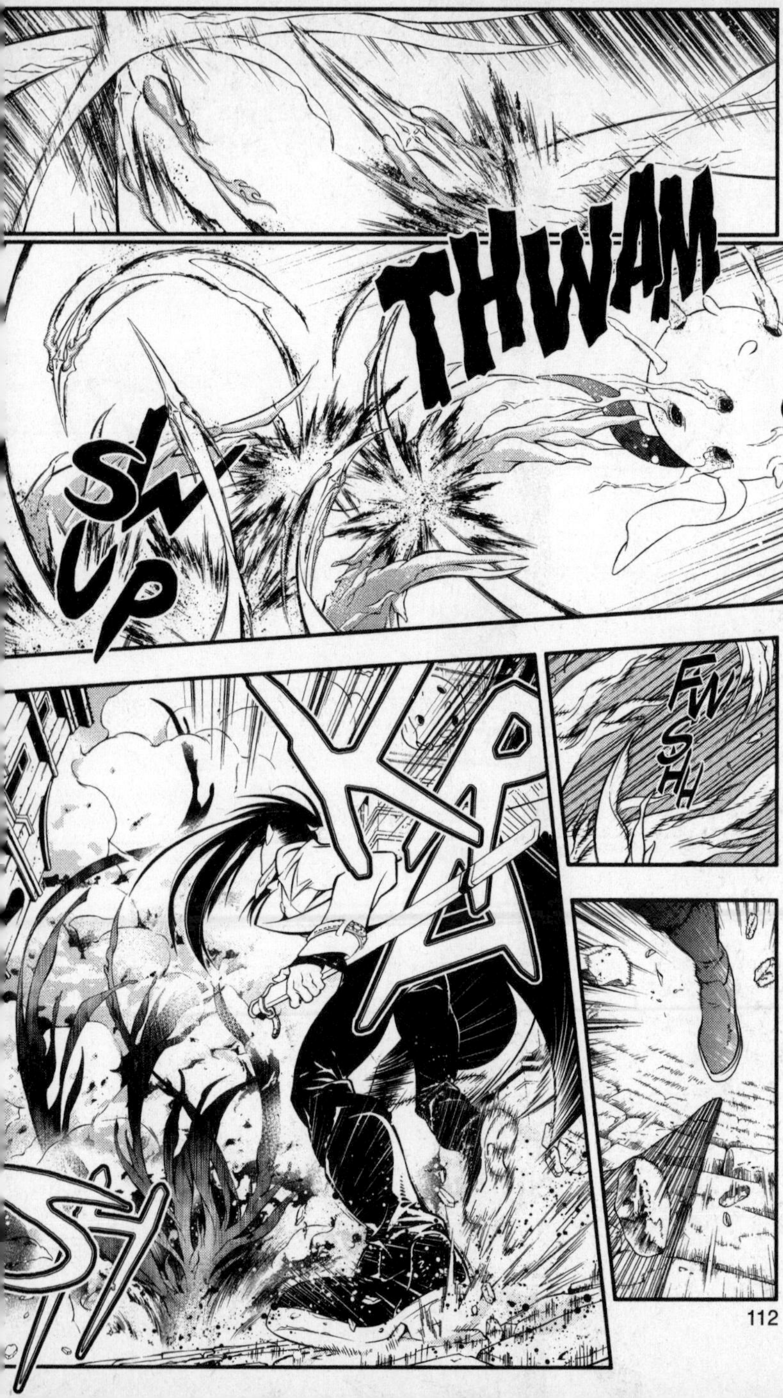
THWAM
SWUP
FWSHH
KA

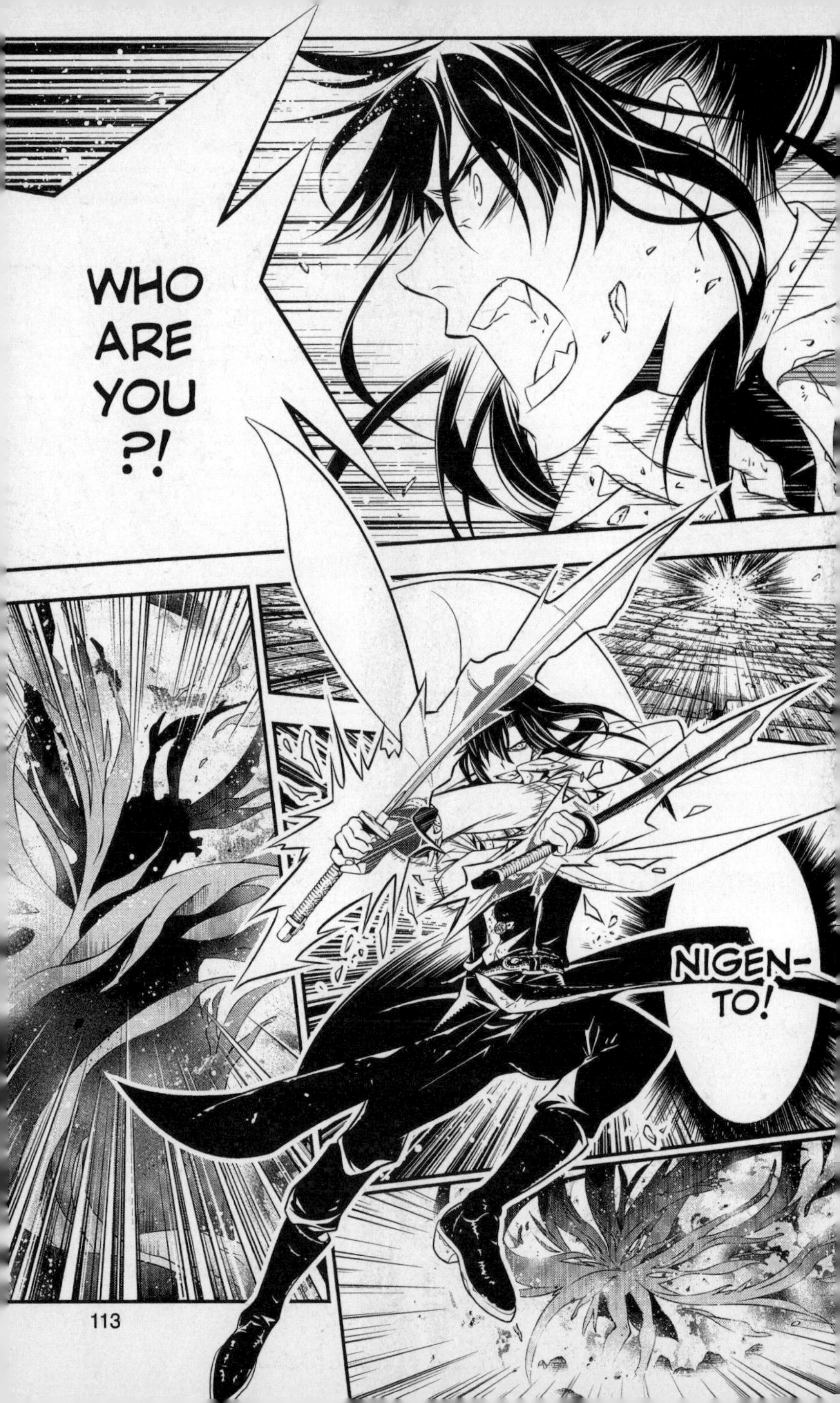
WHO ARE YOU ?!
NIGEN-TO!

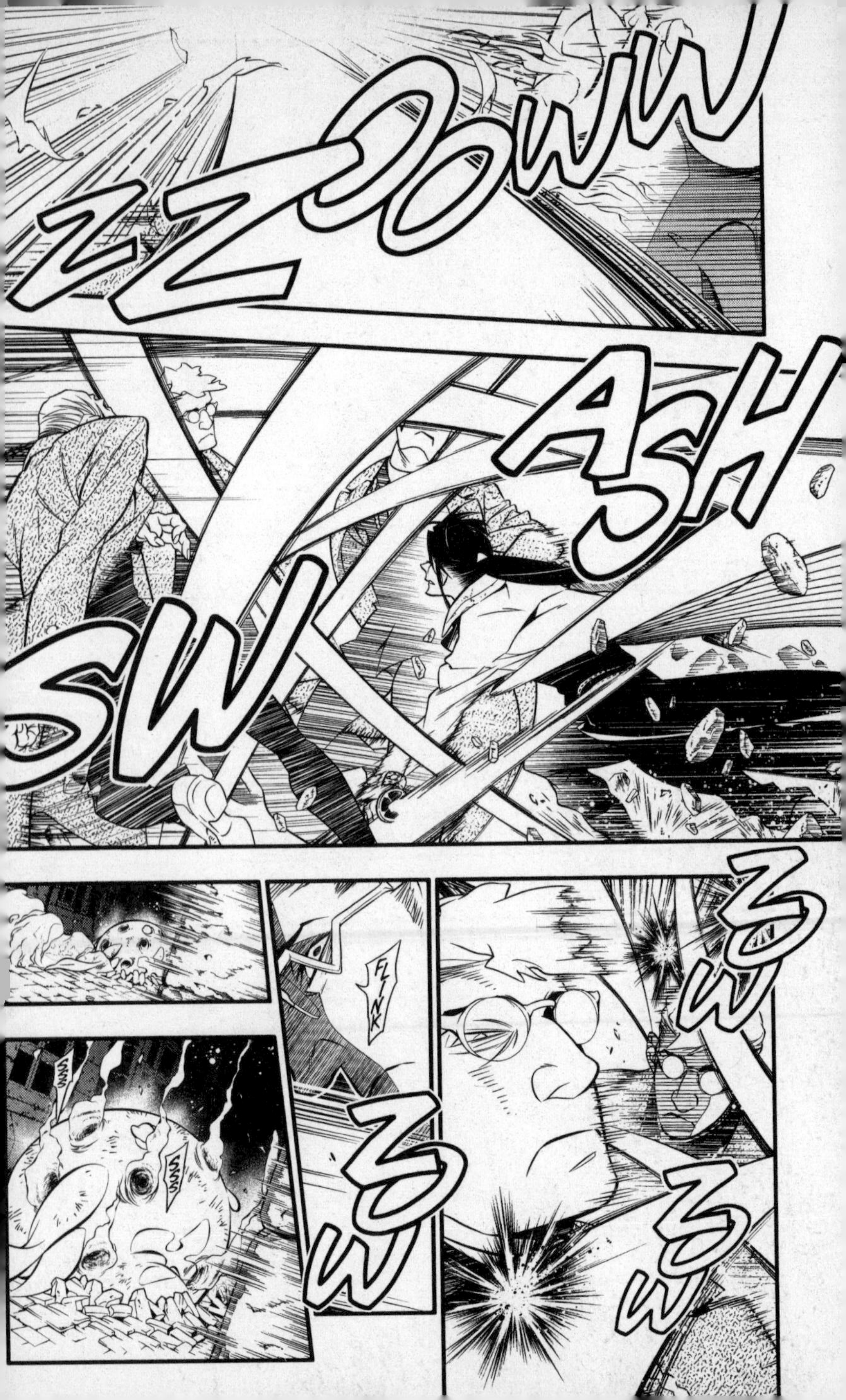
ZZOOWN
SWASH
ZOW
ZOW
FLINK
ZOW

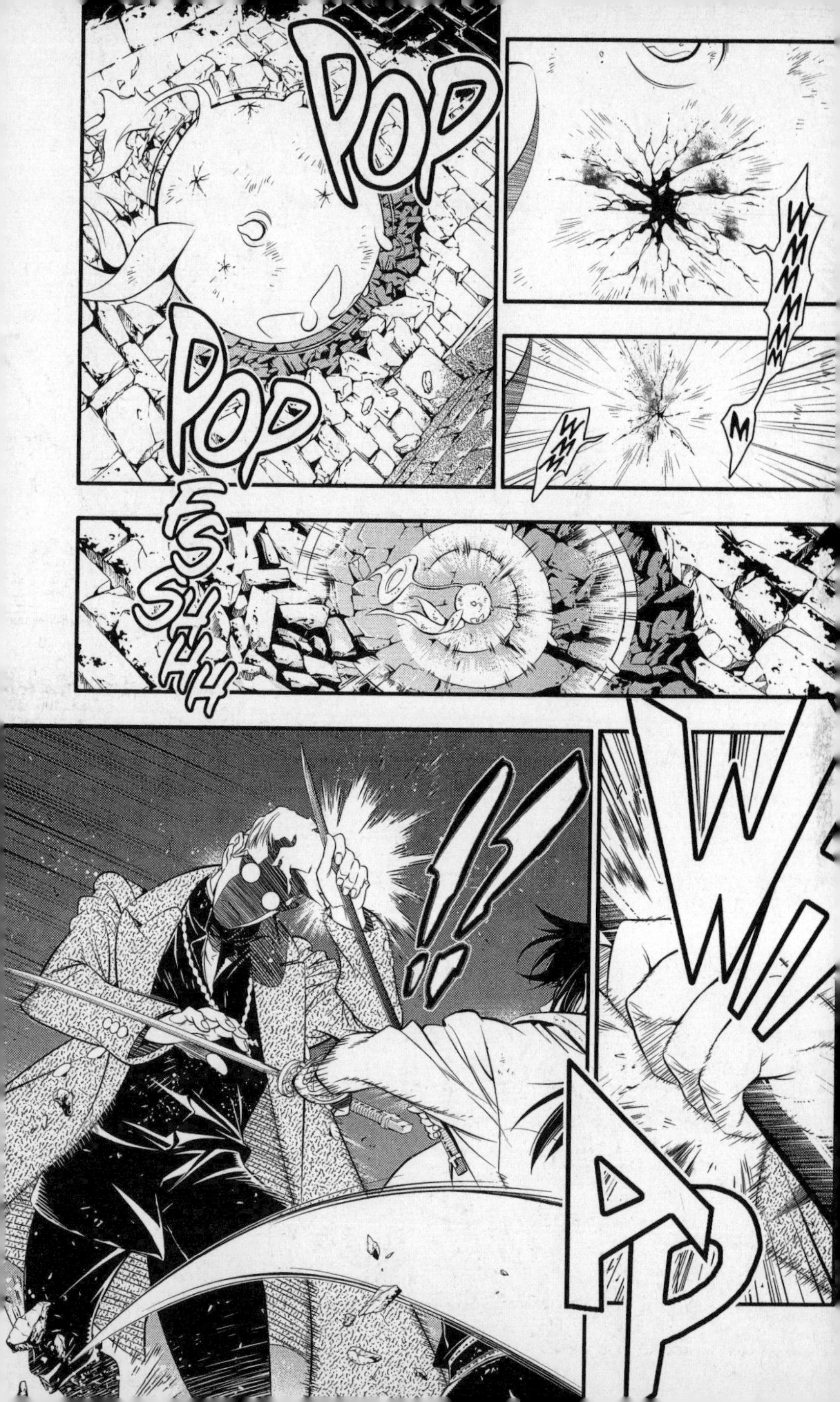
WMMMMMM
WMM
POP
POP
FSSHHH
WHAP
!!

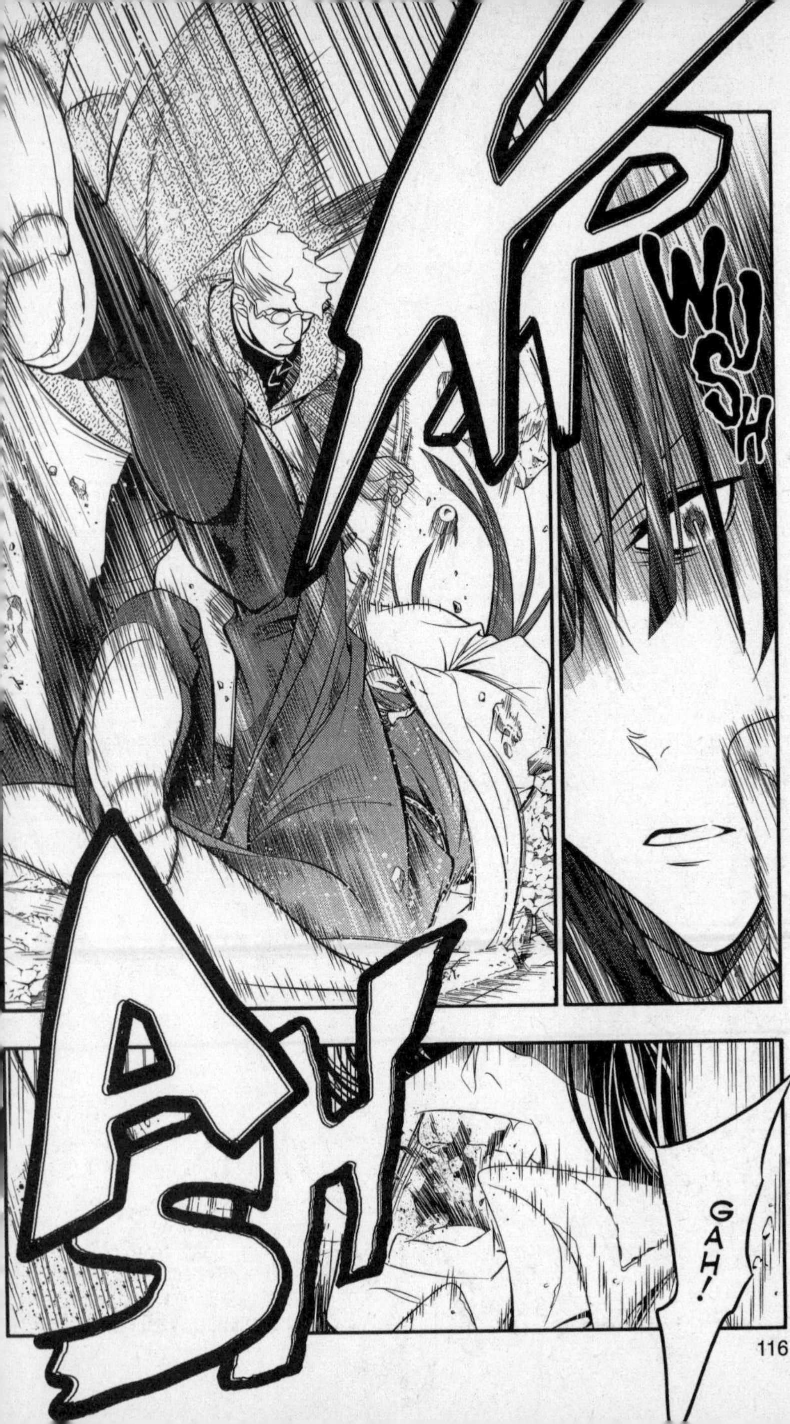
WUSH
GAH!

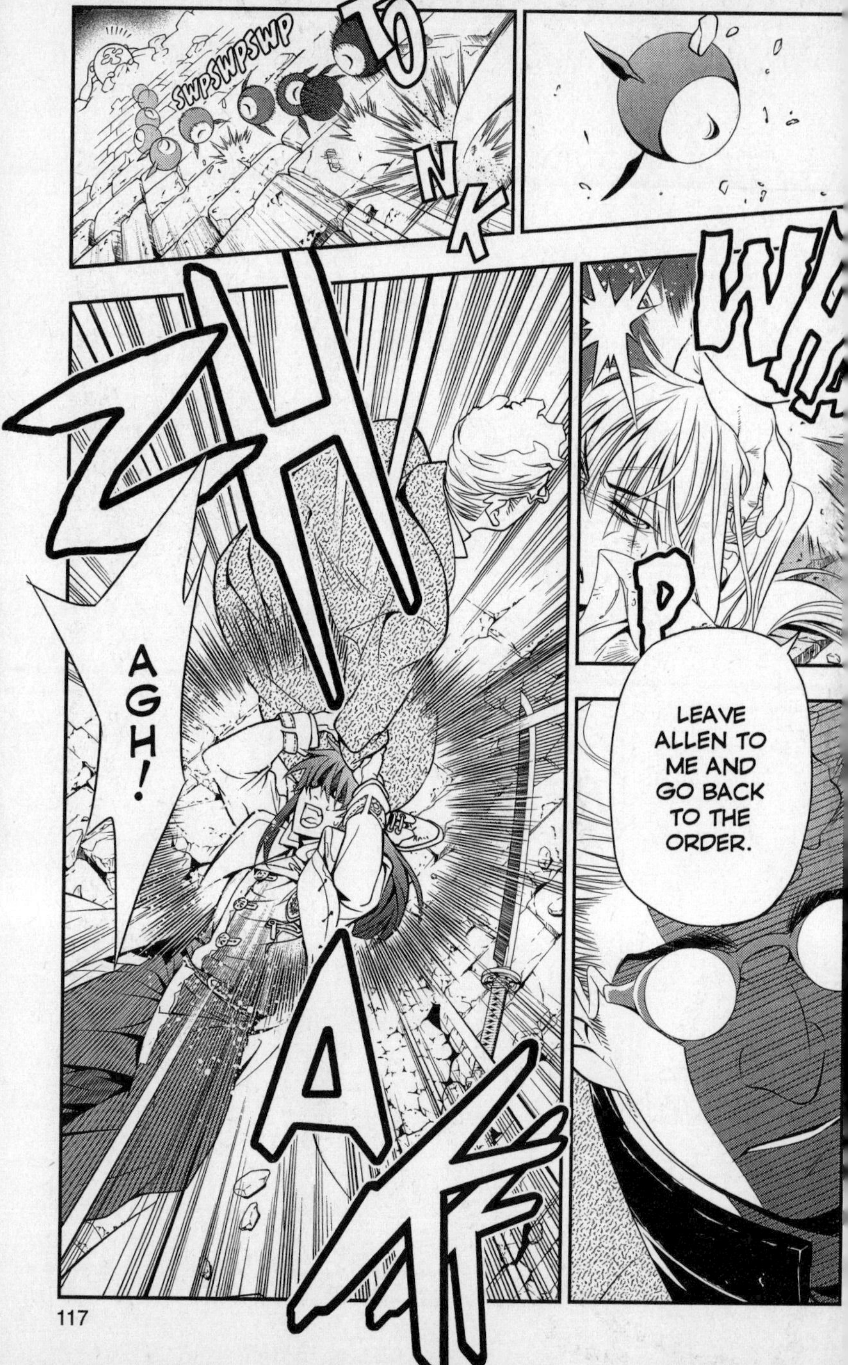
SWPSWPSWP
TONK
LEAVE ALLEN TO ME AND GO BACK TO THE ORDER.
AGH!

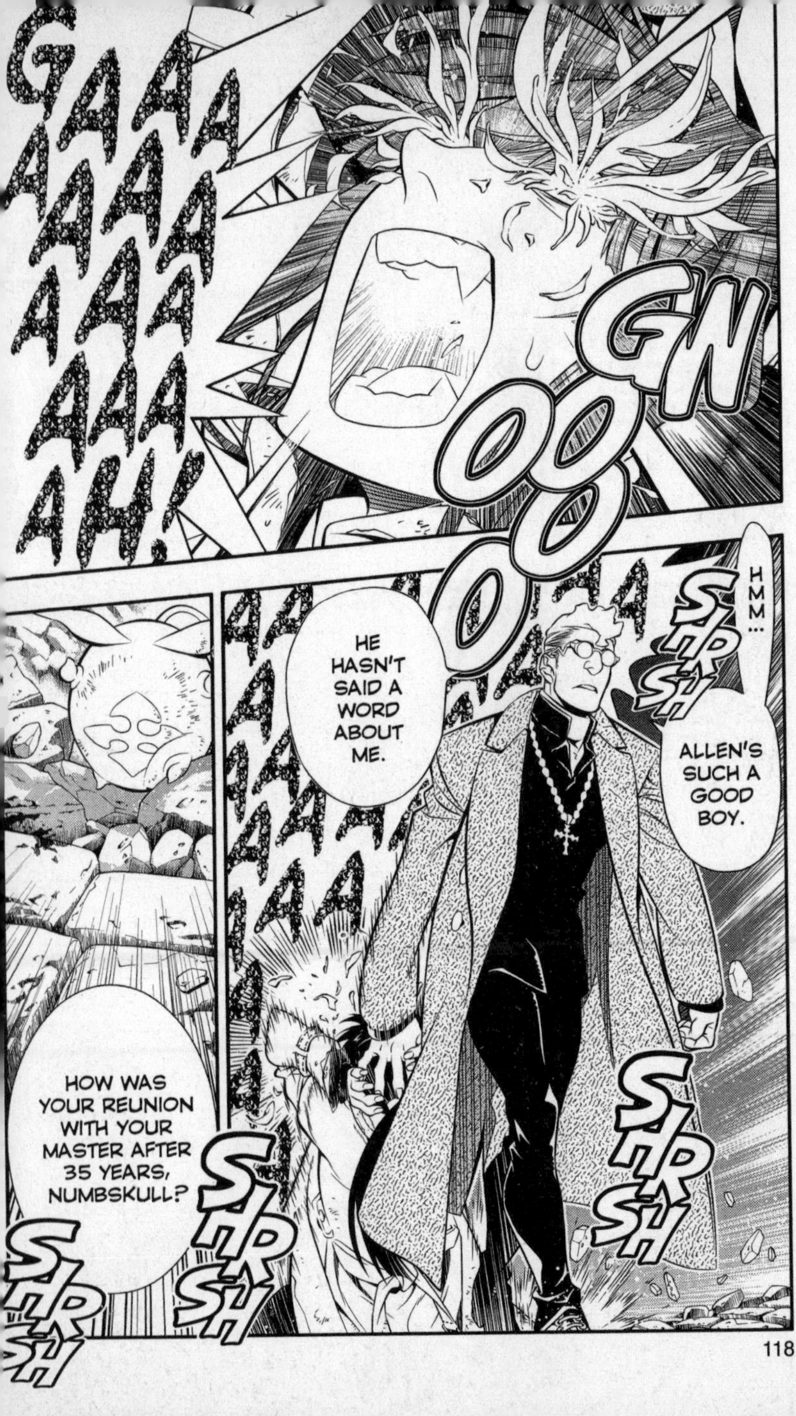
GNOOOO
GAAAAAAAAAAAAAAAAAAH!
HMM...
ALLEN'S SUCH A GOOD BOY.
HE HASN'T SAID A WORD ABOUT ME.
SHRSH
SHRSH
HOW WAS YOUR REUNION WITH YOUR MASTER AFTER 35 YEARS, NUMBSKULL?
SHRSH
SHRSH

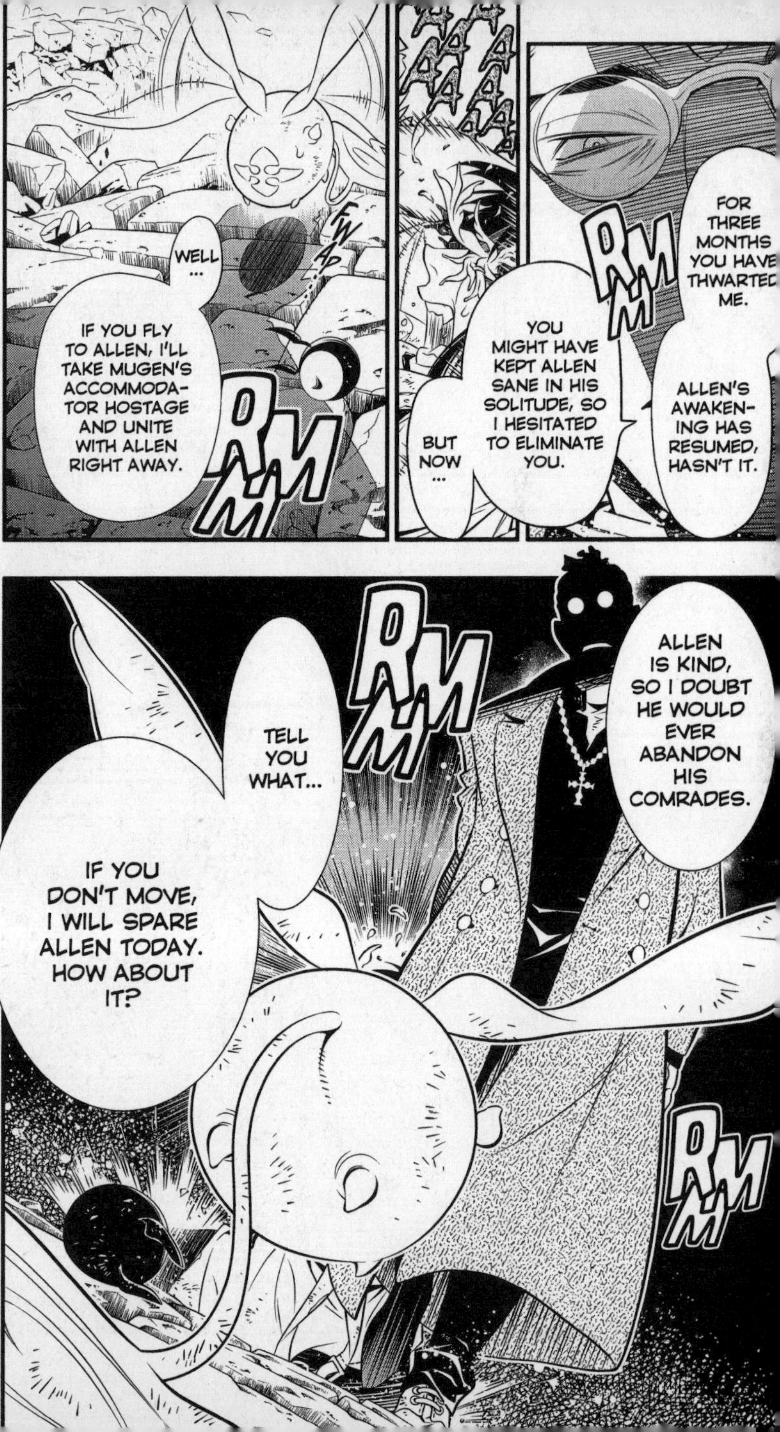
FOR THREE MONTHS YOU HAVE THWARTED ME.
ALLEN'S AWAKENING HAS RESUMED, HASN'T IT.
RMM
YOU MIGHT HAVE KEPT ALLEN SANE IN HIS SOLITUDE, SO I HESITATED TO ELIMINATE YOU.
BUT NOW ...
FWAP
WELL ...
IF YOU FLY TO ALLEN, I'LL TAKE MUGEN'S ACCOMMODATOR HOSTAGE AND UNITE WITH ALLEN RIGHT AWAY.
RMM
ALLEN IS KIND, SO I DOUBT HE WOULD EVER ABANDON HIS COMRADES.
RMM
TELL YOU WHAT...
IF YOU DON'T MOVE, I WILL SPARE ALLEN TODAY. HOW ABOUT IT?
RMM

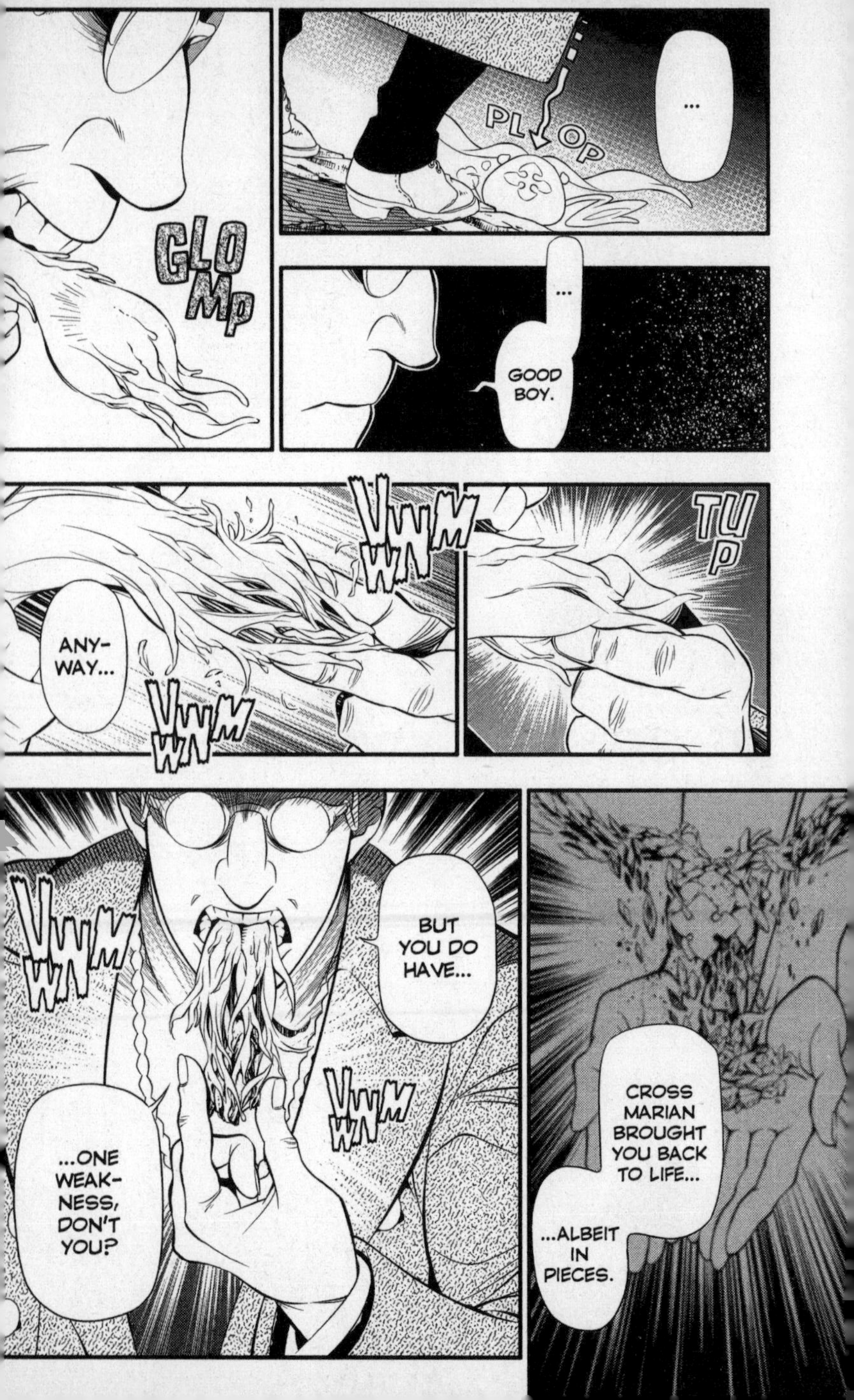
PLOP
...
...
GOOD BOY.
GLOMP
TUP
ANYWAY...
CROSS MARIAN BROUGHT YOU BACK TO LIFE...
...ALBEIT IN PIECES.
BUT YOU DO HAVE...
...ONE WEAKNESS, DON'T YOU?

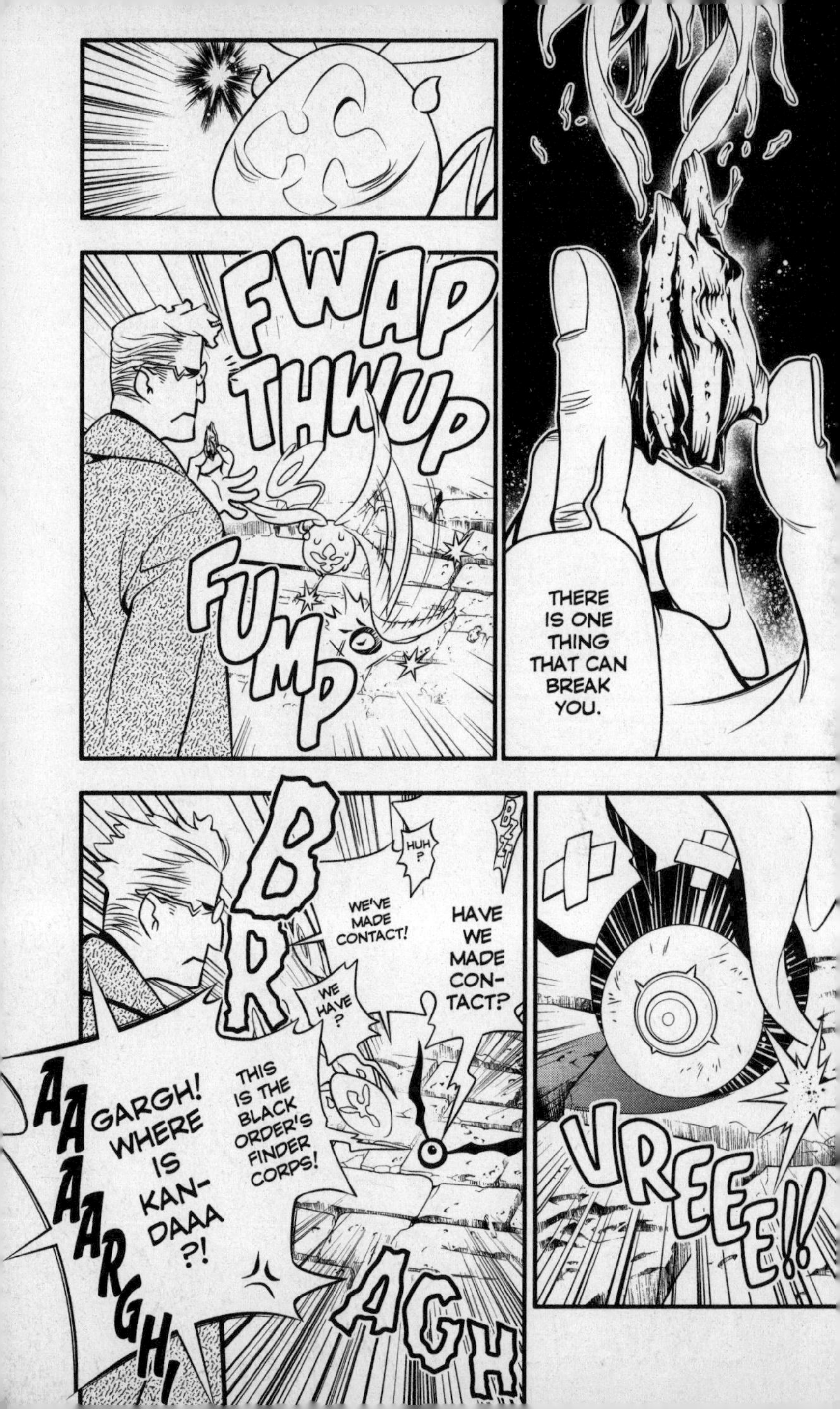
THERE IS ONE THING THAT CAN BREAK YOU.
FWAP
THWUP
FUMP
VREEEE!!
BZZT
HUH?
HAVE WE MADE CONTACT?
WE'VE MADE CONTACT!
BR
WE HAVE?
THIS IS THE BLACK ORDER'S FINDER CORPS!
GARGH! WHERE IS KANDAAA?!
AGH
AAAARGH!

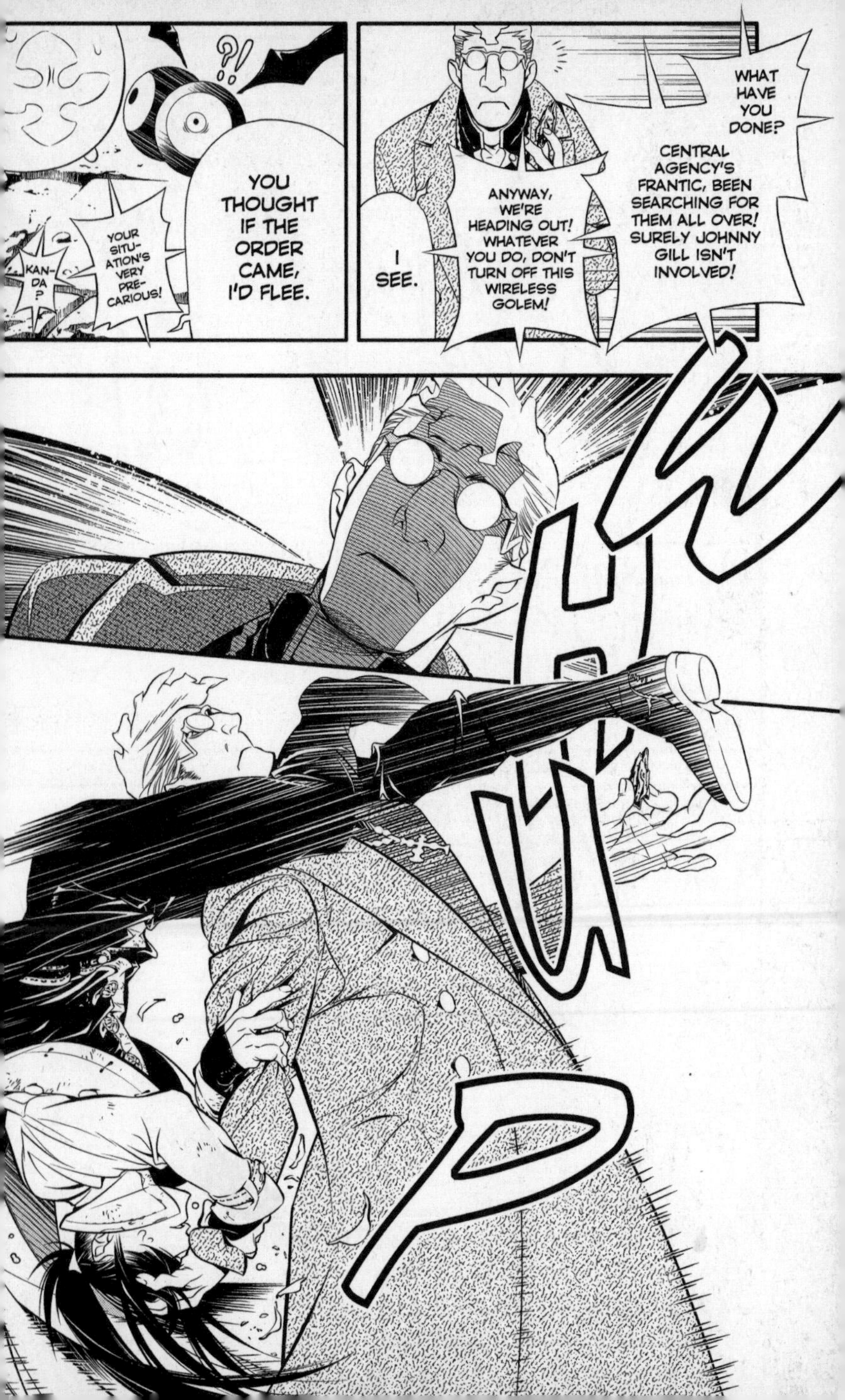
WHAT HAVE YOU DONE?
CENTRAL AGENCY'S FRANTIC, BEEN SEARCHING FOR THEM ALL OVER! SURELY JOHNNY GILL ISN'T INVOLVED!
ANYWAY, WE'RE HEADING OUT! WHATEVER YOU DO, DON'T TURN OFF THIS WIRELESS GOLEM!
I SEE.
?!
YOU THOUGHT IF THE ORDER CAME, I'D FLEE.
YOUR SITU-ATION'S VERY PRE-CARIOUS!
KAN-DA?

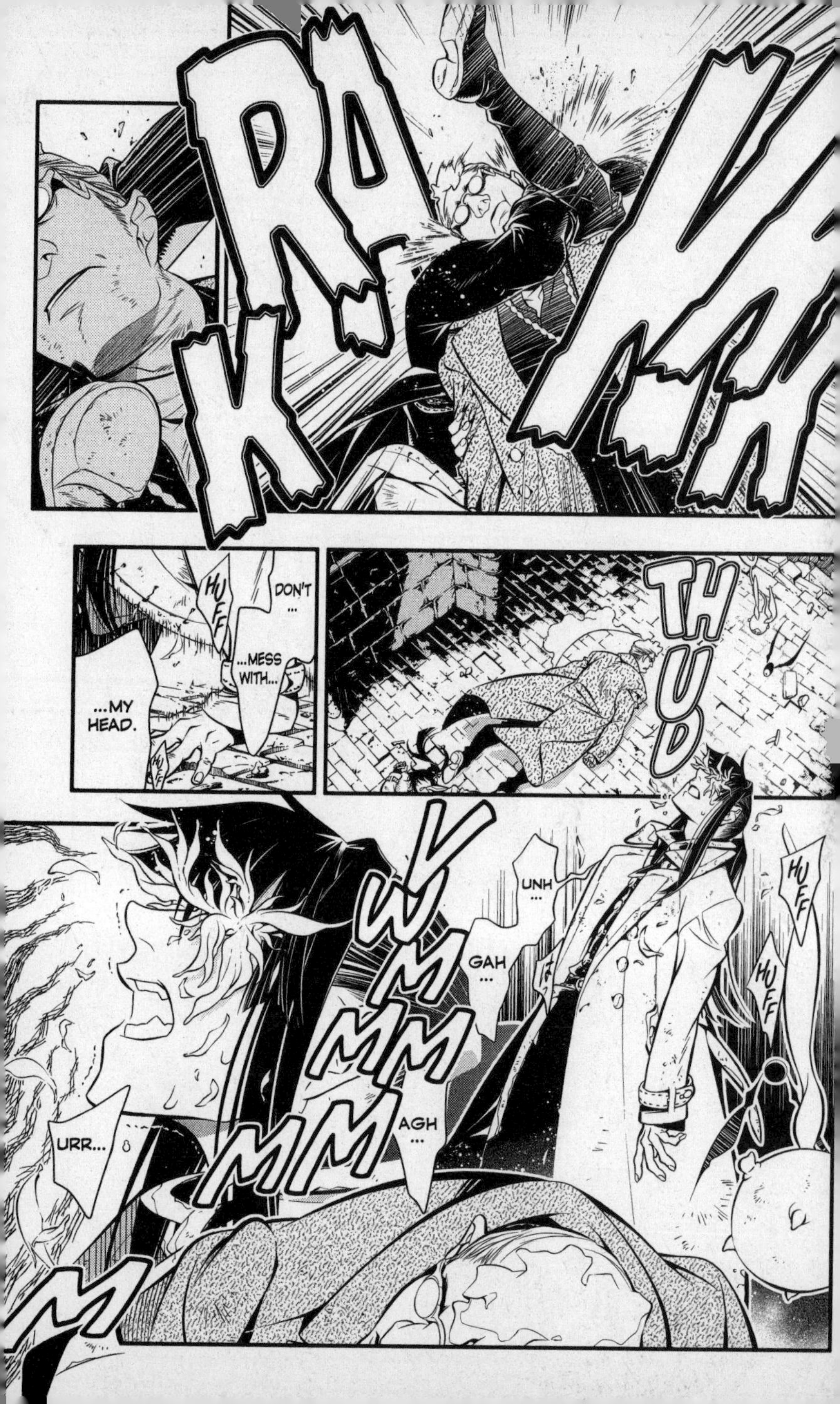
KRAKA
THUD
HUFF
DON'T ...
...MESS WITH...
...MY HEAD.
HUFF
HUFF
HUFF
UNH ...
GAH ...
VWMMMMM
AGH ...
URR...

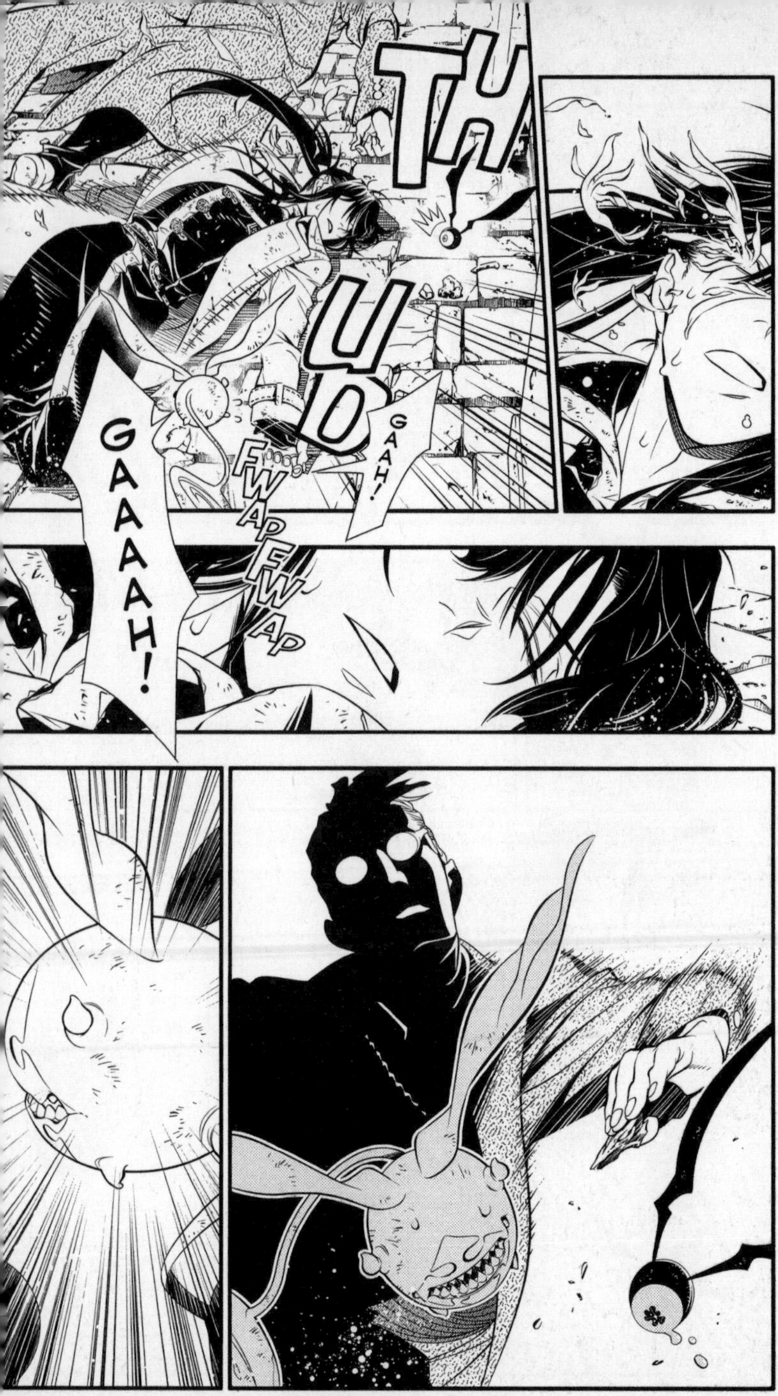THUD
GAAH!
GAAAAAH!
FWAP FWAP

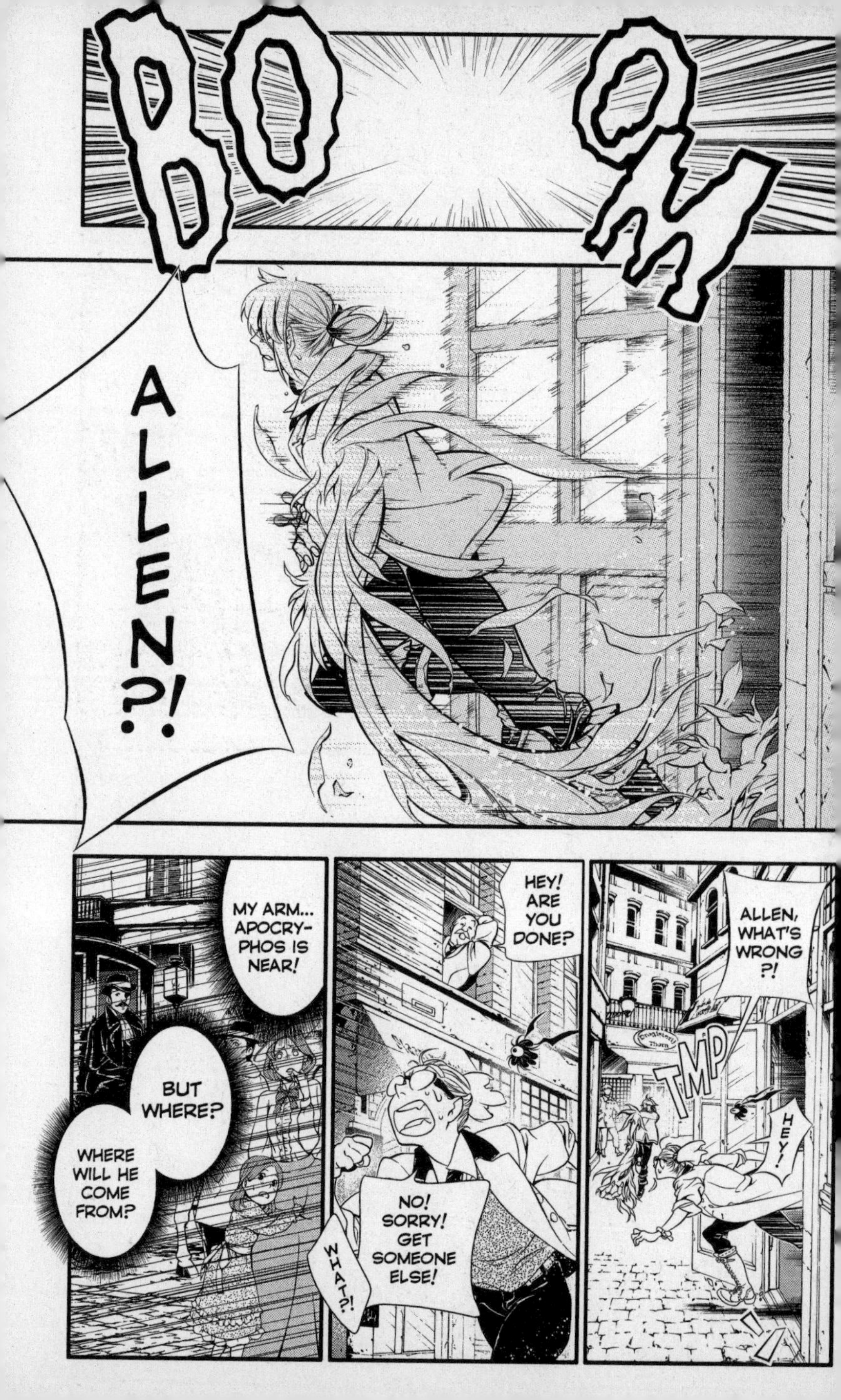
BOOM
ALLEN?!
ALLEN, WHAT'S WRONG?!
TMP
HEY!
HEY! ARE YOU DONE?
NO! SORRY! GET SOMEONE ELSE!
WHAT?!
MY ARM... APOCRYPHOS IS NEAR!
BUT WHERE?
WHERE WILL HE COME FROM?

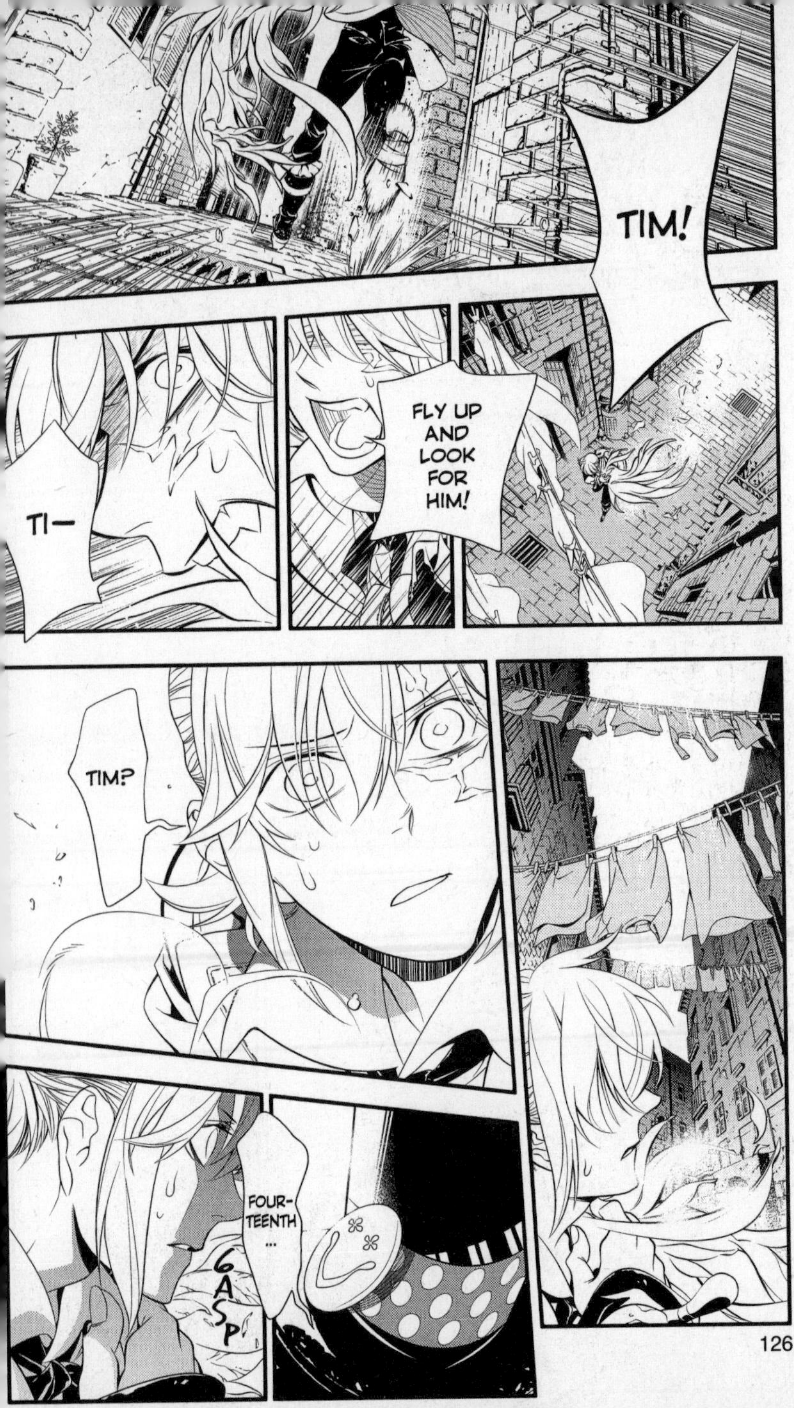
TIM!
FLY UP AND LOOK FOR HIM!
TI—
TIM?
FOUR-TEENTH...
GASP

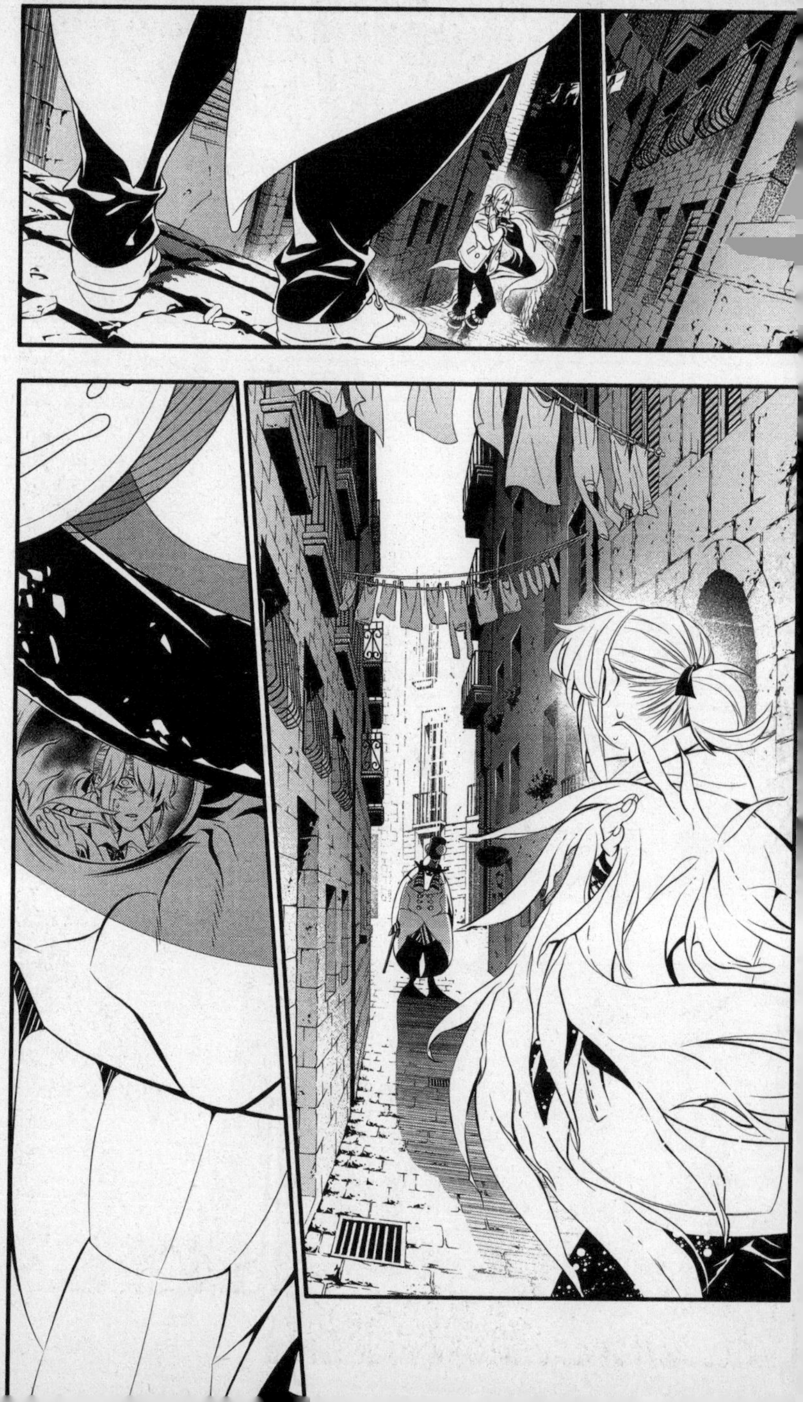

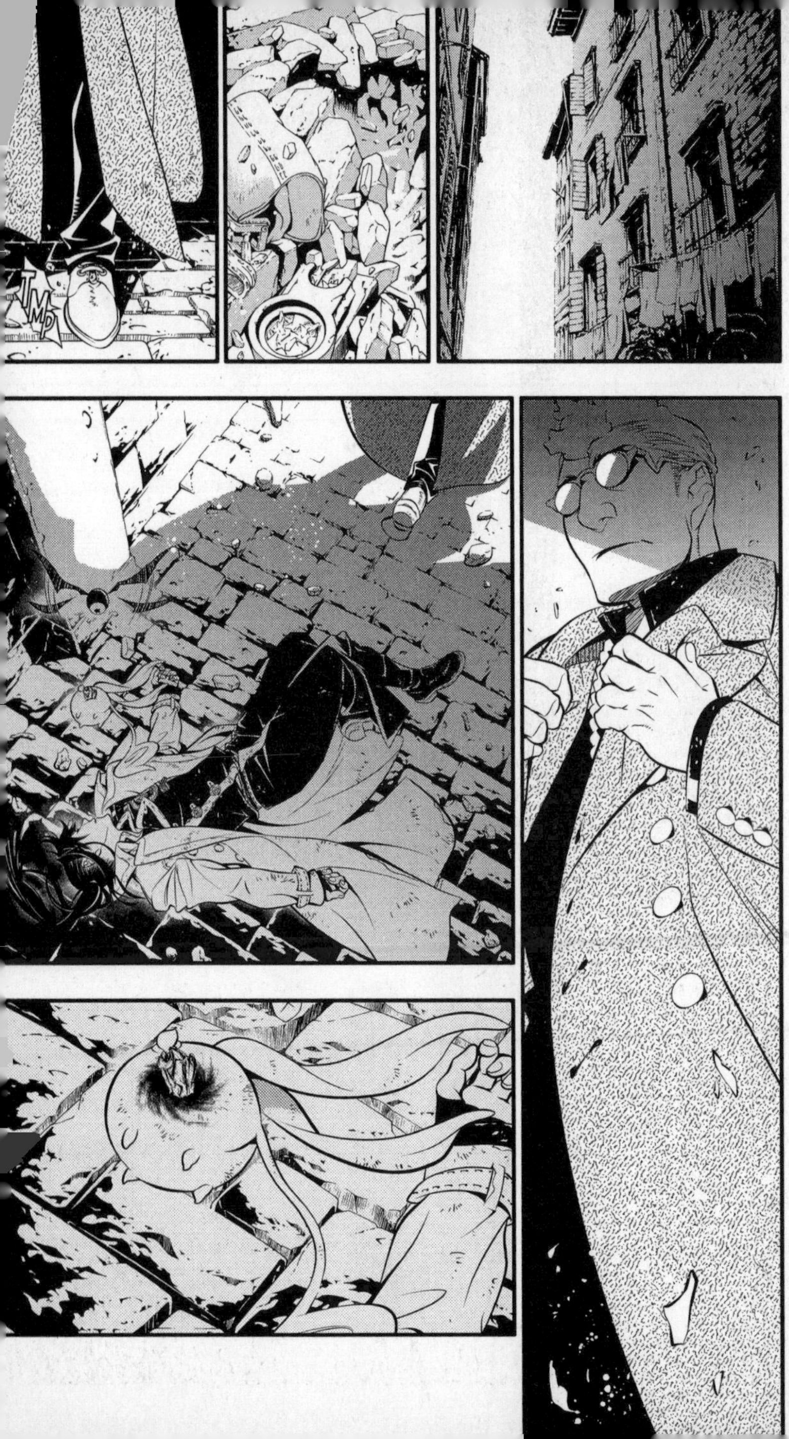
TMP

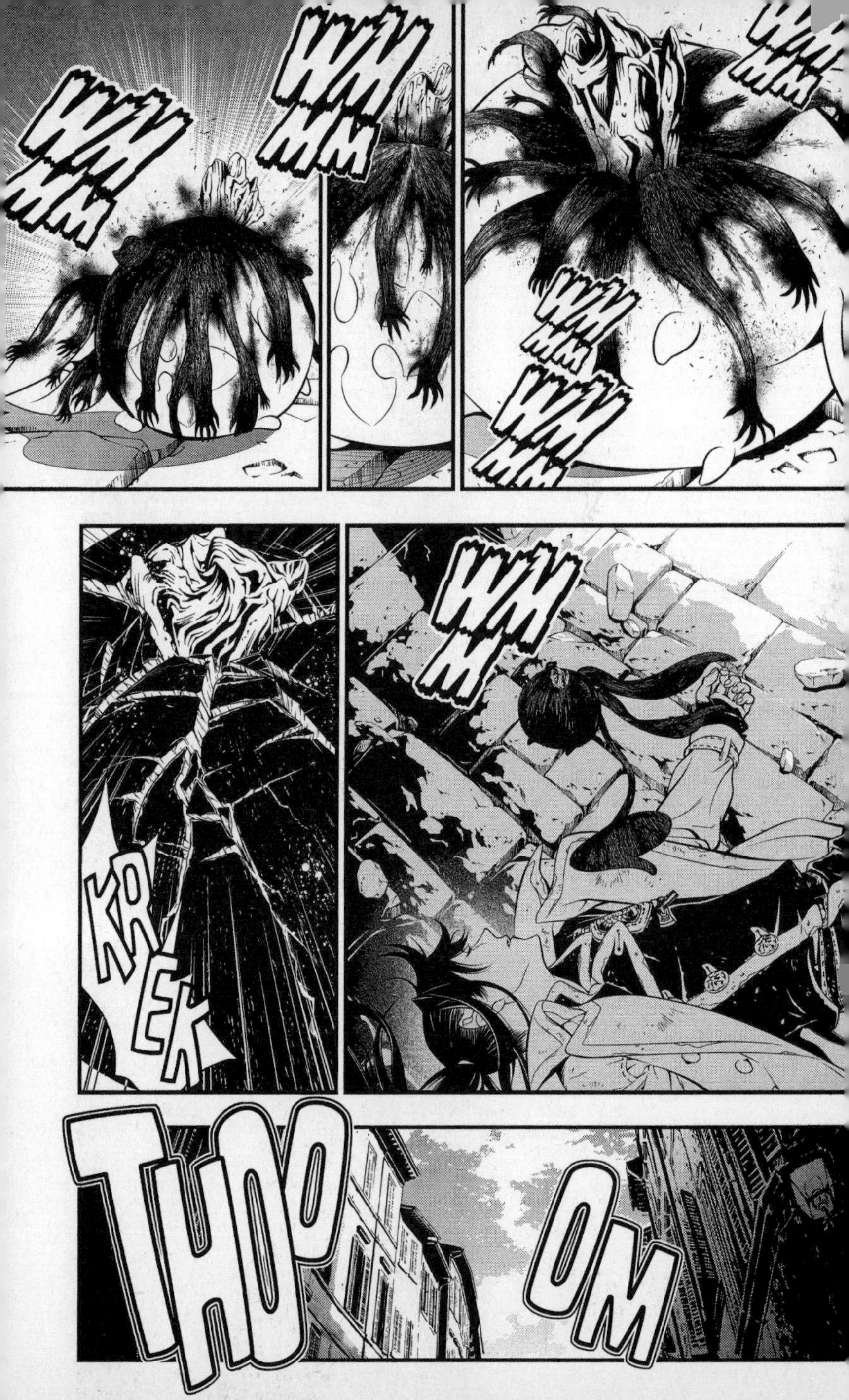
WHMM
WHMM
WHMM
WHMM
WHMM
WHM
KREK
THOOOM

KOMUI'S DISCUSSION ROOM 4

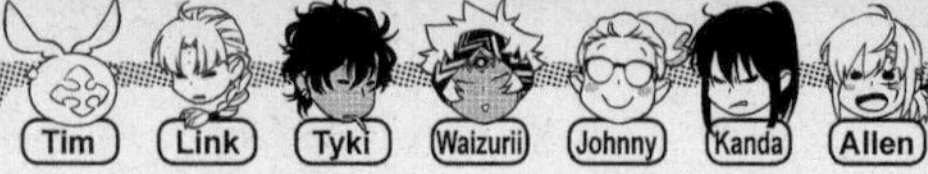
Tim
Link
Tyki
Waizurii
Johnny
Kanda
Allen

Q. When Johnny went bar-hopping, he got tipsy. Was that the first time he'd ever imbibed?

J: Of course not! ☆ I'm not a heavy drinker but I'm a grown-up! ☆

A: Johnny's about the same age as Mr. Mole-and-Wavy-Hair there.

Ty: Really? He doesn't look it! (*surprised*) That's a bit mean, boy.

J: You can't survive Science Section unless you can handle all kinds of stuff, including liquor.

W: Oh? Like what?

K: They're always concocting "health drinks." The level of toxicity varies.

Q. Kanda said he'd never had a hangover before. What kinds of booze does he like?

J: You drank tequila on the sly at HQ, right?

A: Tequila?! (*high-pitched*)

K: (How do you know that?) Well... a long time ago, I was under a spell that let nothing affect me unless it was highly alcoholic. But I don't drink it anymore.

Ty: A long time ago? How long have you been drinking?

W: Ha ha! You handled your first hangover pretty well! If not for that spell, he couldn't drink at all! Huh? (*uneasy*)

K: Peek inside my head again, Mr. Turban, and I'll kill you! (*pointing with Mugen*)

A: I've never seen Kanda drink at HQ. Why were you hiding it? Oh, right, because you're the "brooding" sort.

K: Whatever, Bean Sprout.

J: One time Lenalee saw him drinking so she tried some tequila and passed out. Ha ha! You should've seen Kanda's face! He panicked! (*laughs*)

K: How do you know that?! Even Komui doesn't know!

A: Oooh... ☆

Ty: You have a wicked laugh, boy.

Q. I think Road is sexier than she used to be.

Ty: Well...

W: Yeah.

A: Stop it, you guys! You too, Johnny! Hey, you're blushing!

J: Allen, she kissed you!

W: You know what they say about young girls in love! (*grins*)

Ty: You mean to say you haven't noticed her?

A: N-Noticed her? She crushed my left eye! That's how we met!

W: In shojo manga, love begins with hostility!

A: Well, D.Gray-man isn't a shojo!

Ty: I bet you think she's cute, eh, boy?

A: What's this have to do with the question? (*sweats*)

W: It's okay to find an enemy cute! After all, she's the heroine!

K: Lenalee.

W: What?

K: Lenalee is the heroine.

W: No, it's Road.

K: You're wrong.

W: It's Road! The heroine is Road!

K & W: ... (*glares exchanged*)

J: Can't they both be heroines? (*frets*)

W: It's Roaaad!!

A: Next! Next question! (*sweats*)

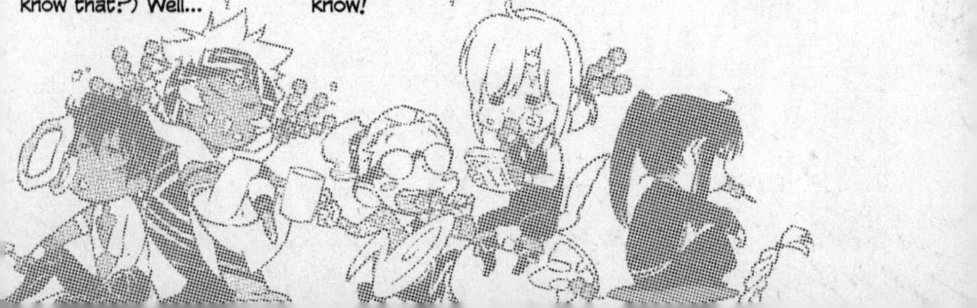

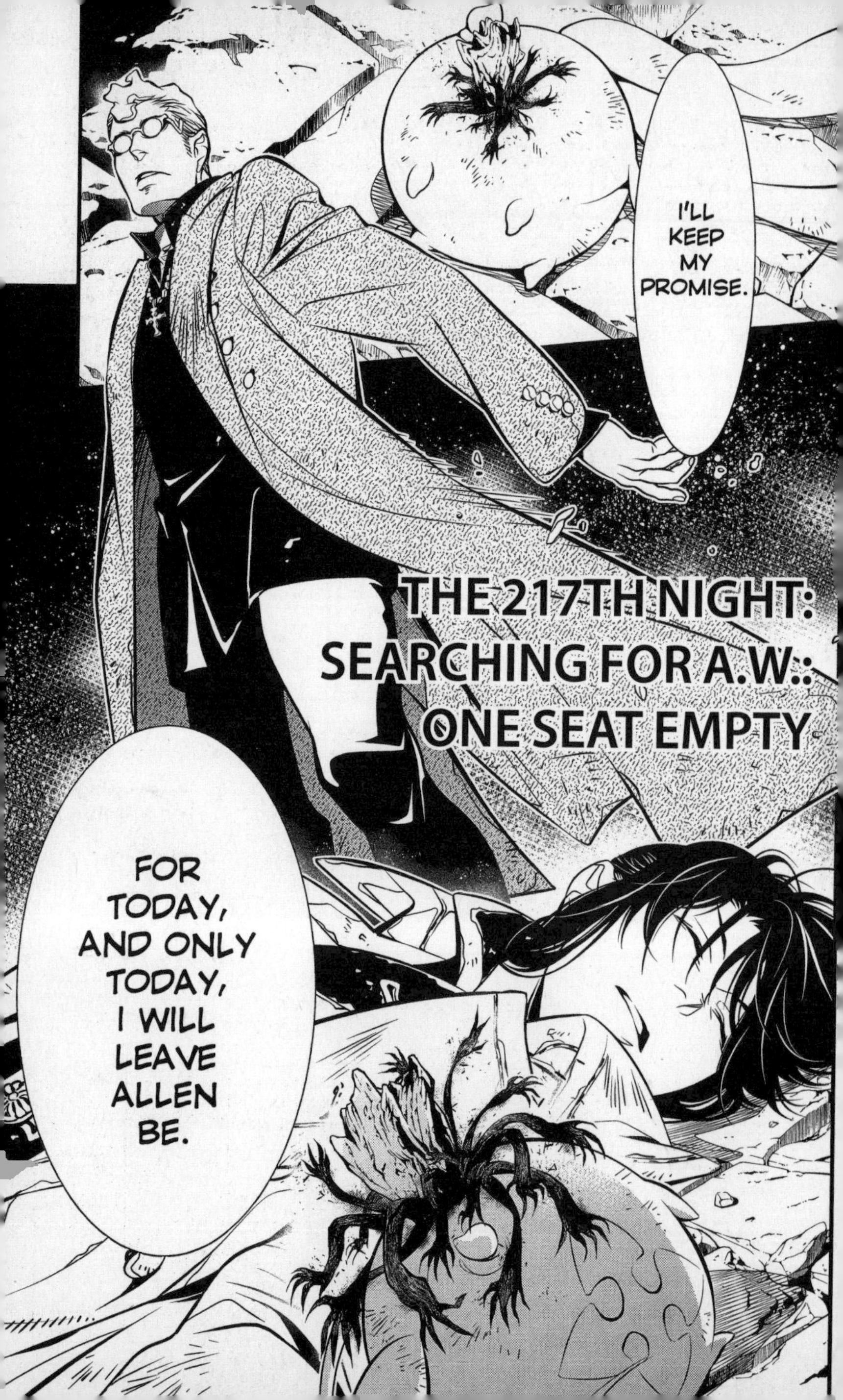
I'LL KEEP MY PROMISE.
THE 217TH NIGHT: SEARCHING FOR A.W.: ONE SEAT EMPTY
FOR TODAY, AND ONLY TODAY, I WILL LEAVE ALLEN BE.

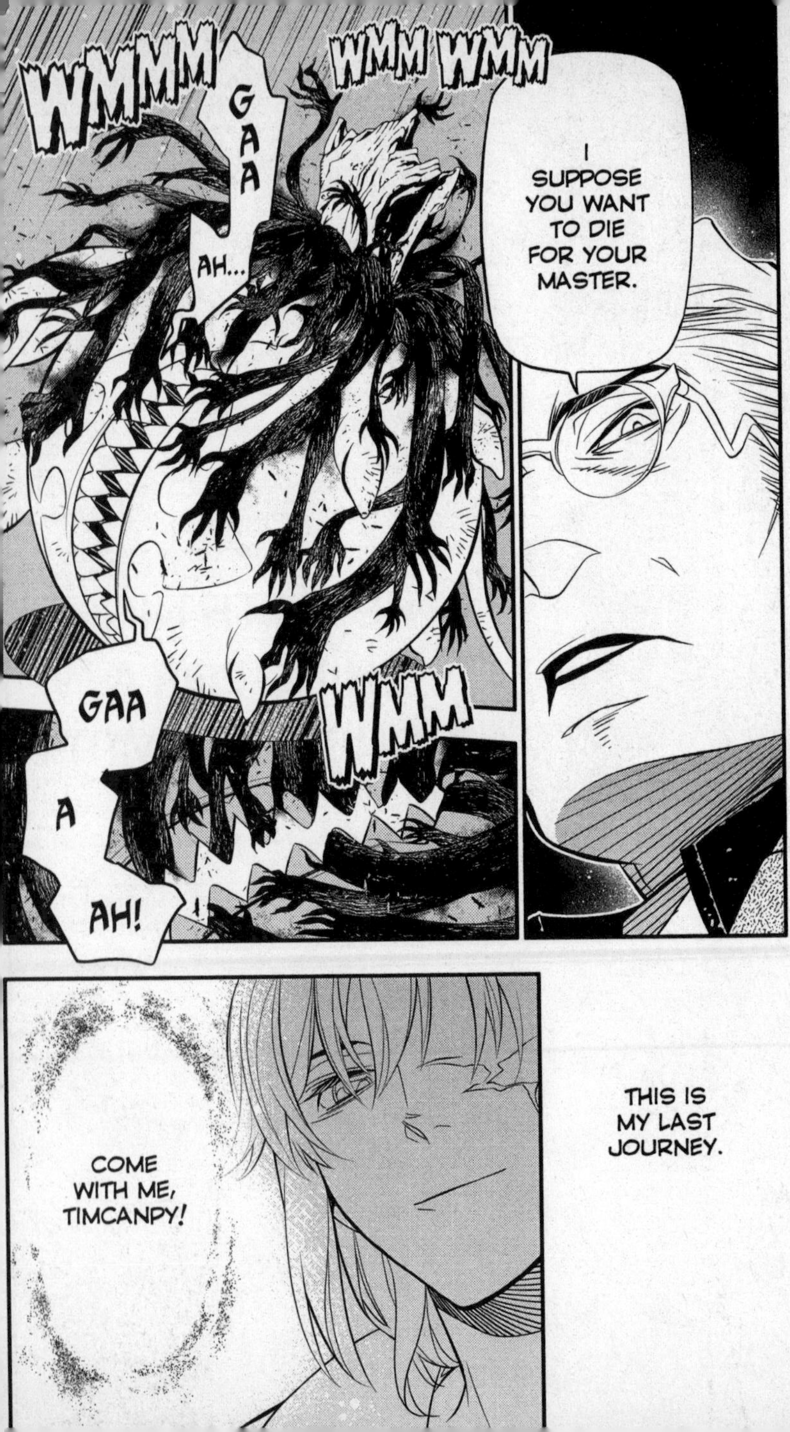
I SUPPOSE YOU WANT TO DIE FOR YOUR MASTER.
WMM WMM
WMMM
GAA AH...
WMM
GAA A AH!
THIS IS MY LAST JOURNEY.
COME WITH ME, TIMCANPY!

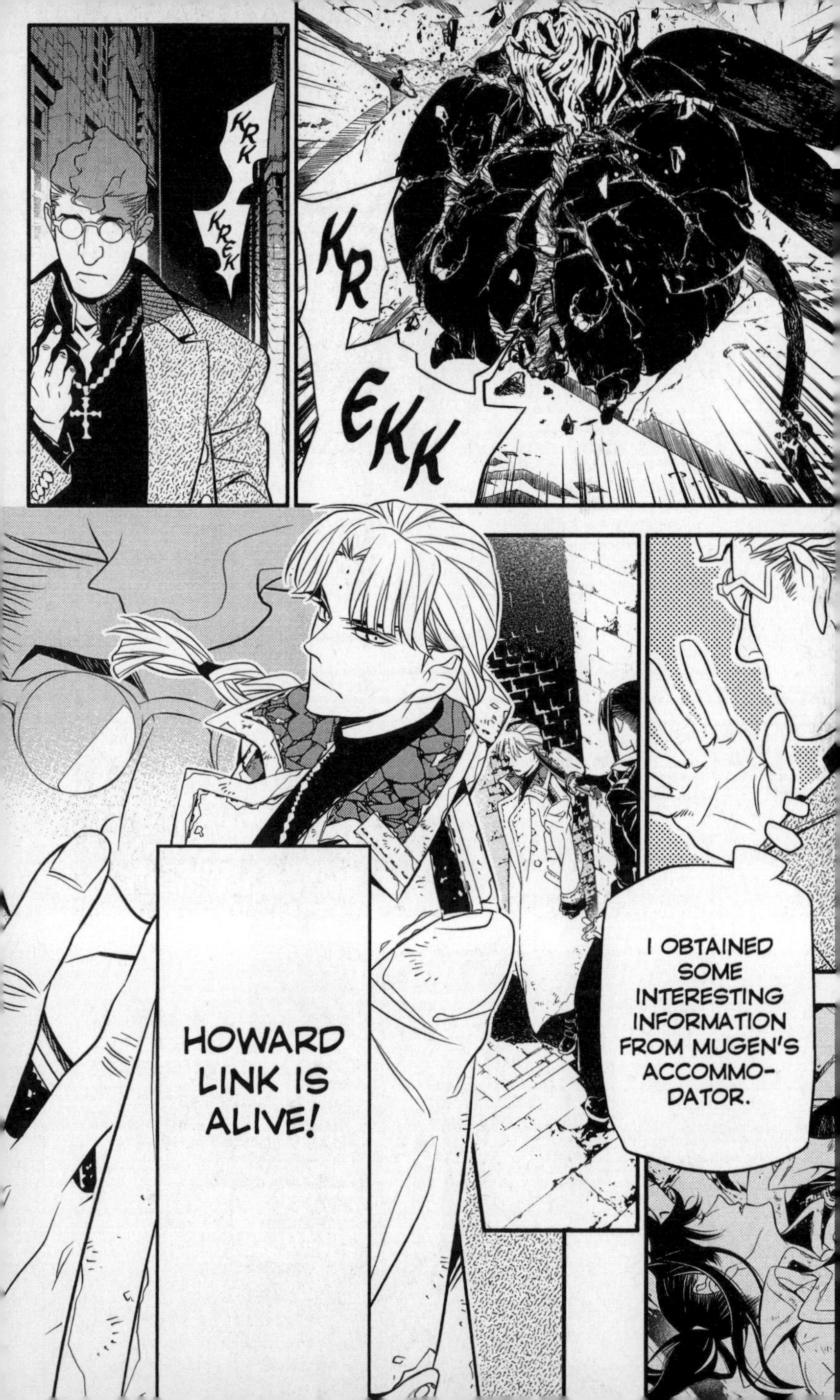
KR
EKK
KRK
KREK
I OBTAINED SOME INTERESTING INFORMATION FROM MUGEN'S ACCOMMO-DATOR.
HOWARD LINK IS ALIVE!

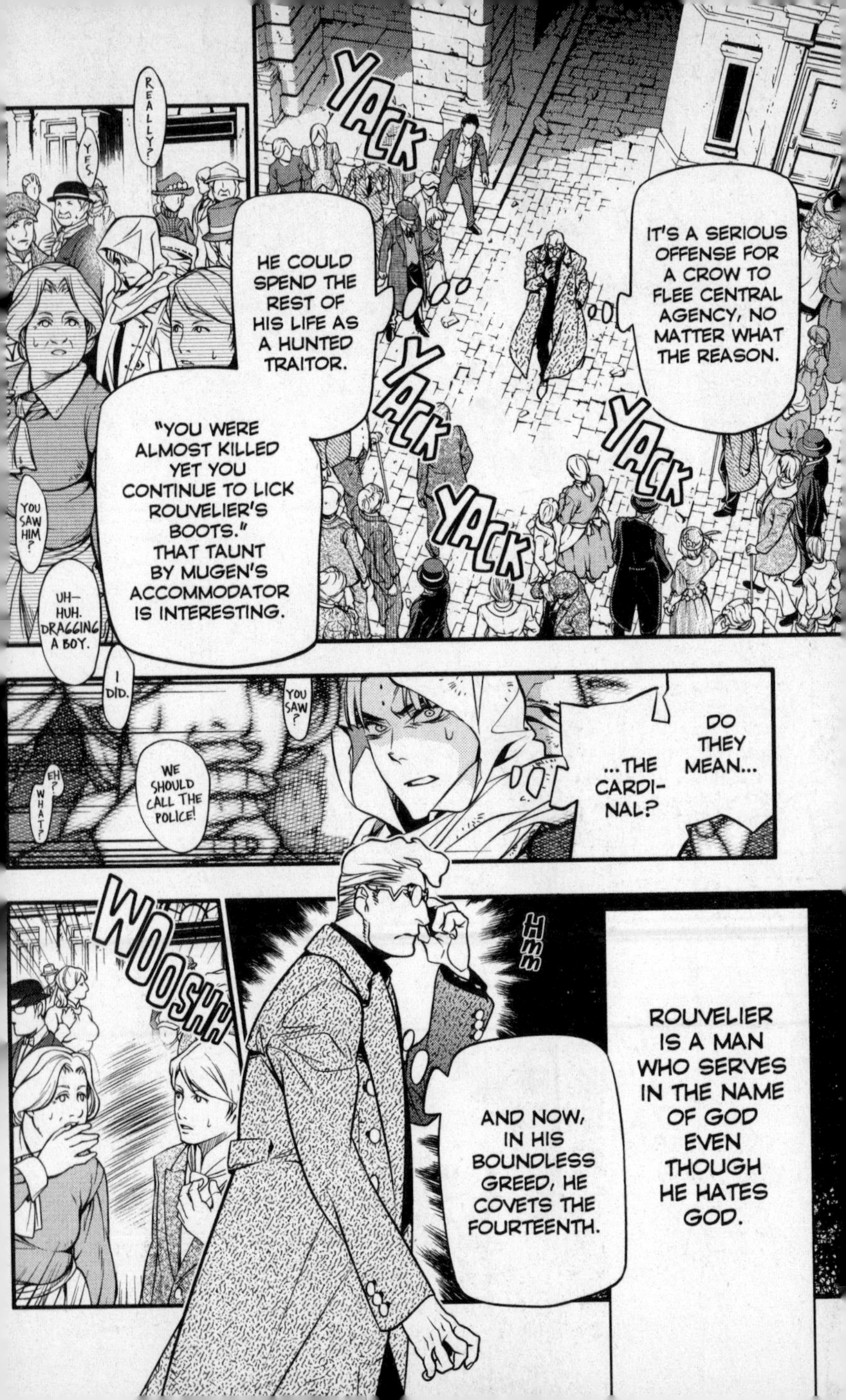
YACK
IT'S A SERIOUS OFFENSE FOR A CROW TO FLEE CENTRAL AGENCY, NO MATTER WHAT THE REASON.
HE COULD SPEND THE REST OF HIS LIFE AS A HUNTED TRAITOR.
YACK
YACK
YACK
REALLY?
YES.
"YOU WERE ALMOST KILLED YET YOU CONTINUE TO LICK ROUVELIER'S BOOTS." THAT TAUNT BY MUGEN'S ACCOMMODATOR IS INTERESTING.
YOU SAW HIM?
UH-HUH. DRAGGING A BOY.
DO THEY MEAN...
...THE CARDINAL?
YOU SAW?
I DID.
WE SHOULD CALL THE POLICE!
EH? WHAT?
ROUVELIER IS A MAN WHO SERVES IN THE NAME OF GOD EVEN THOUGH HE HATES GOD.
AND NOW, IN HIS BOUNDLESS GREED, HE COVETS THE FOURTEENTH.
Hmm
WOOSHH

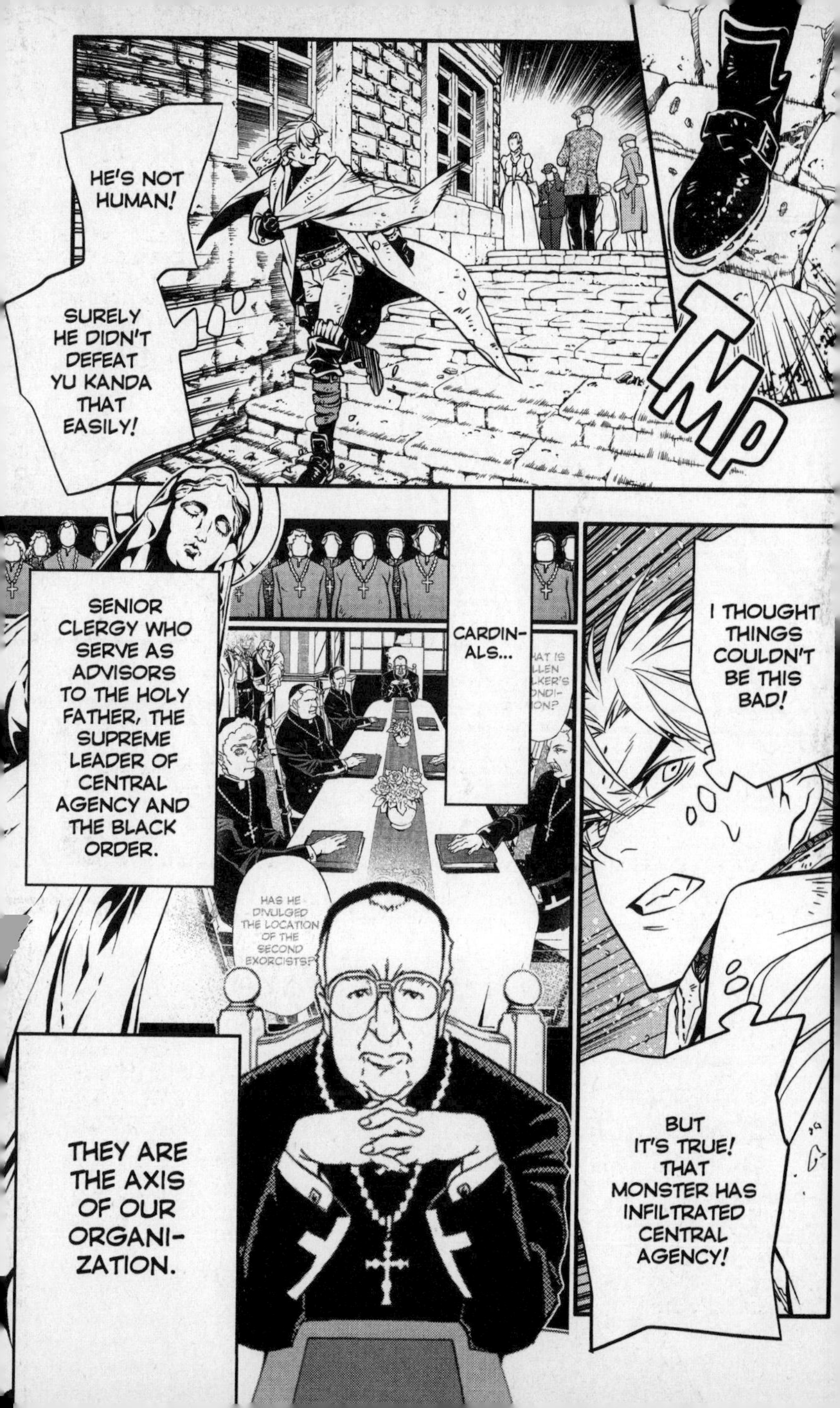
TMP
HE'S NOT HUMAN!
SURELY HE DIDN'T DEFEAT YU KANDA THAT EASILY!
I THOUGHT THINGS COULDN'T BE THIS BAD!
BUT IT'S TRUE! THAT MONSTER HAS INFILTRATED CENTRAL AGENCY!
CARDIN-ALS...
SENIOR CLERGY WHO SERVE AS ADVISORS TO THE HOLY FATHER, THE SUPREME LEADER OF CENTRAL AGENCY AND THE BLACK ORDER.
HAT IS LLEN LKER'S ONDI- ON?
HAS HE DIVULGED THE LOCATION OF THE SECOND EXORCISTS?
THEY ARE THE AXIS OF OUR ORGANI-ZATION.

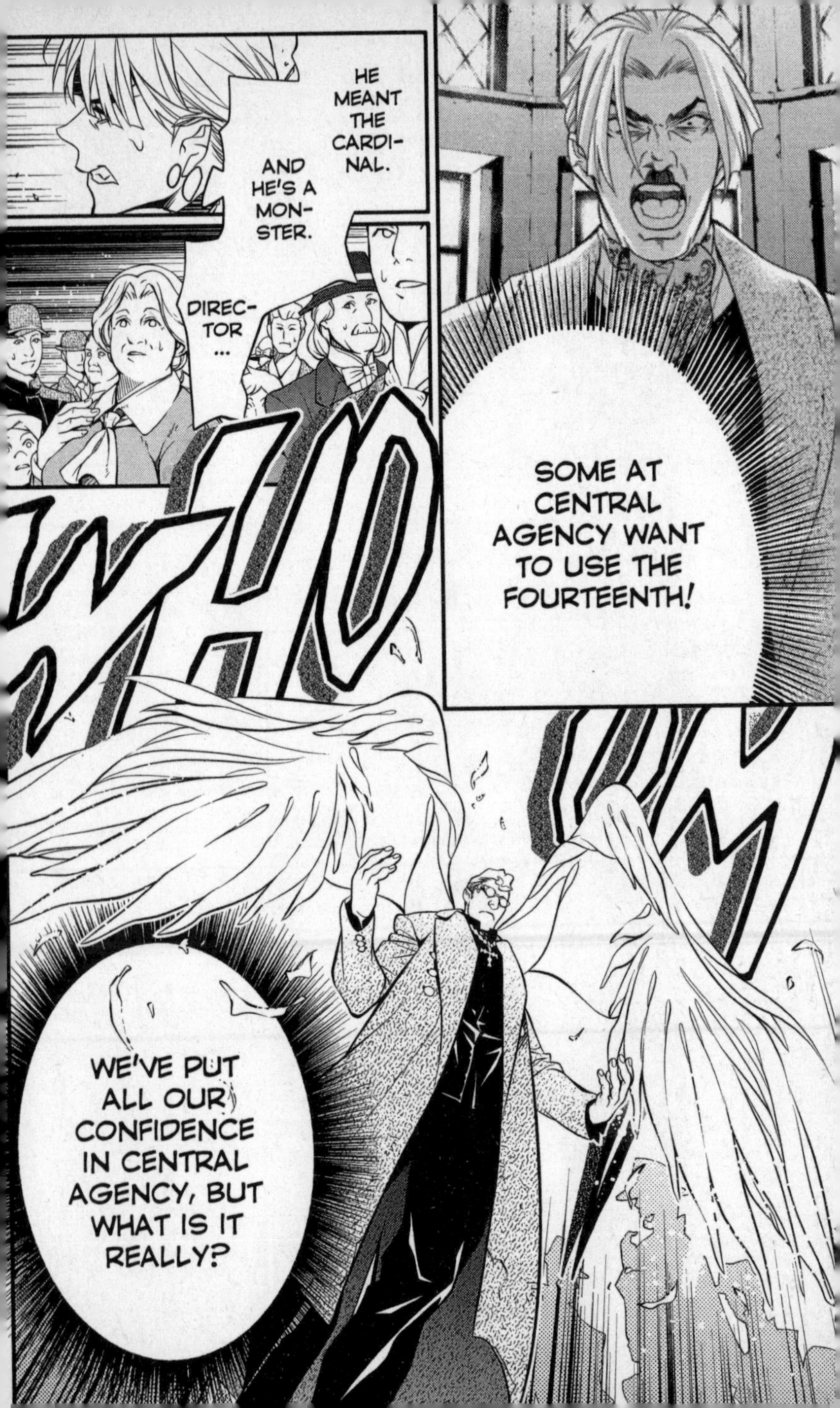
SOME AT CENTRAL AGENCY WANT TO USE THE FOURTEENTH!
HE MEANT THE CARDINAL.
AND HE'S A MONSTER.
DIRECTOR...
WHOOM
WE'VE PUT ALL OUR CONFIDENCE IN CENTRAL AGENCY, BUT WHAT IS IT REALLY?

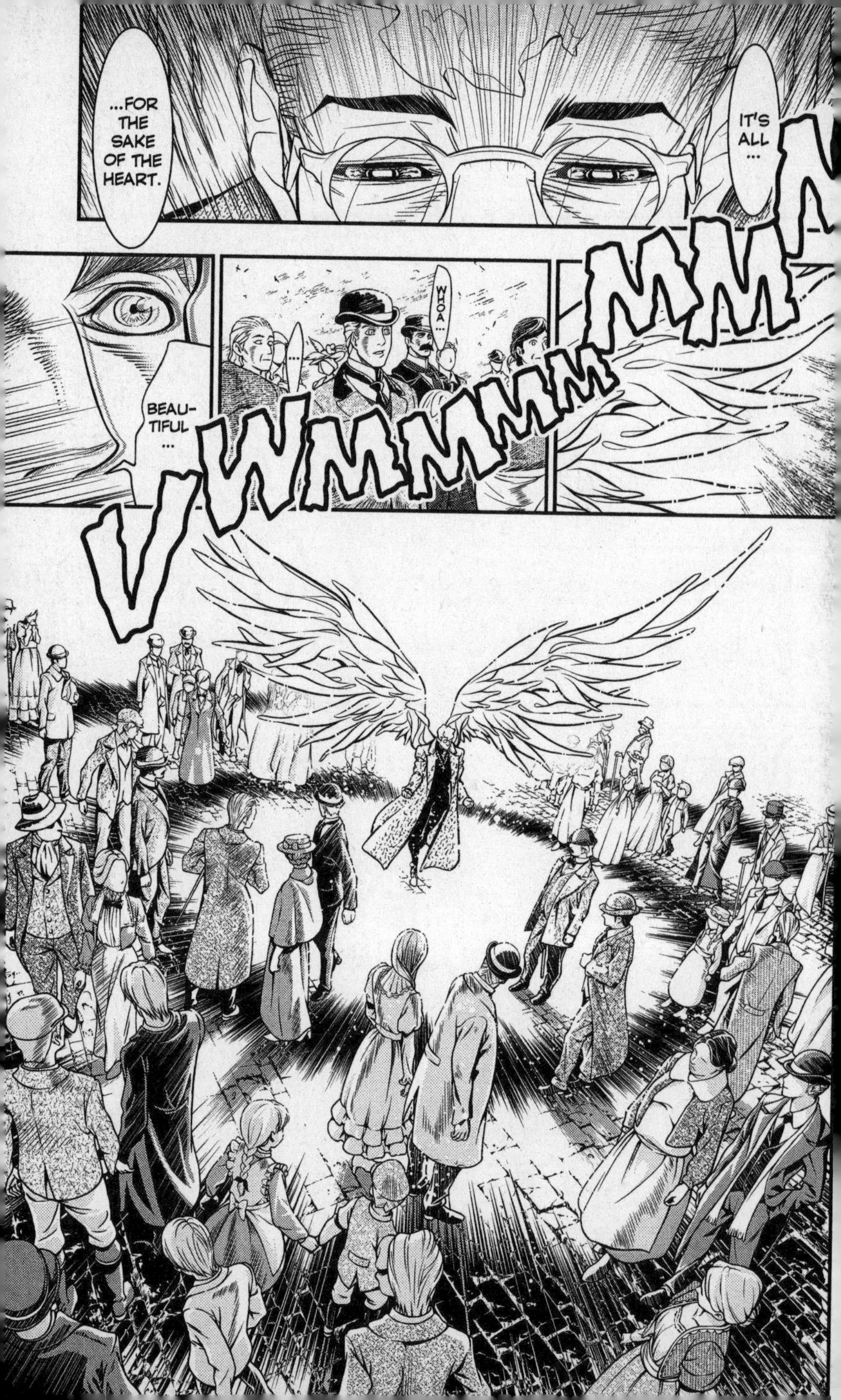

IT'S ALL ...
...FOR THE SAKE OF THE HEART.
VWMMMMMMMMMM
WHOA ...
...
BEAUTIFUL ...

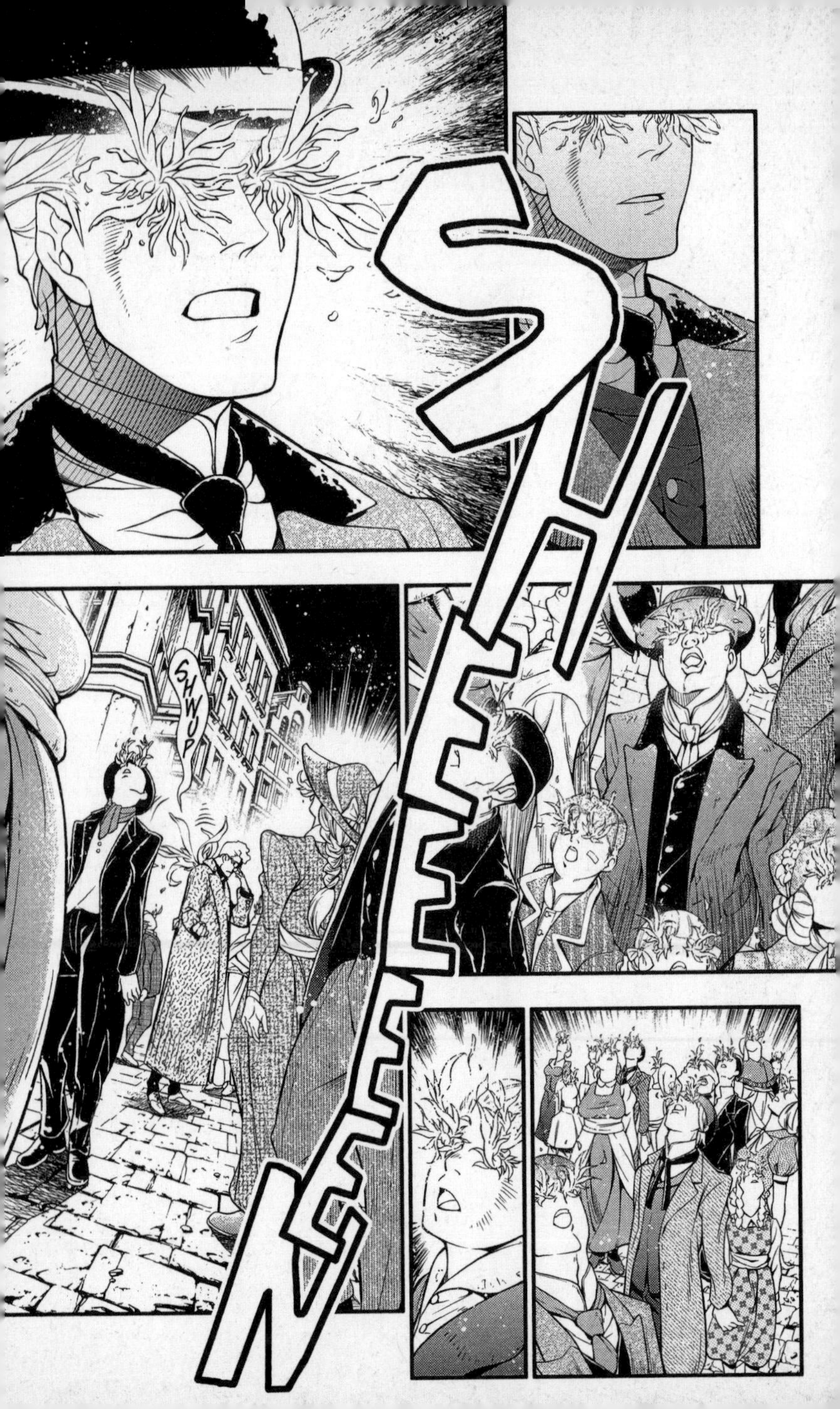
SHWUP

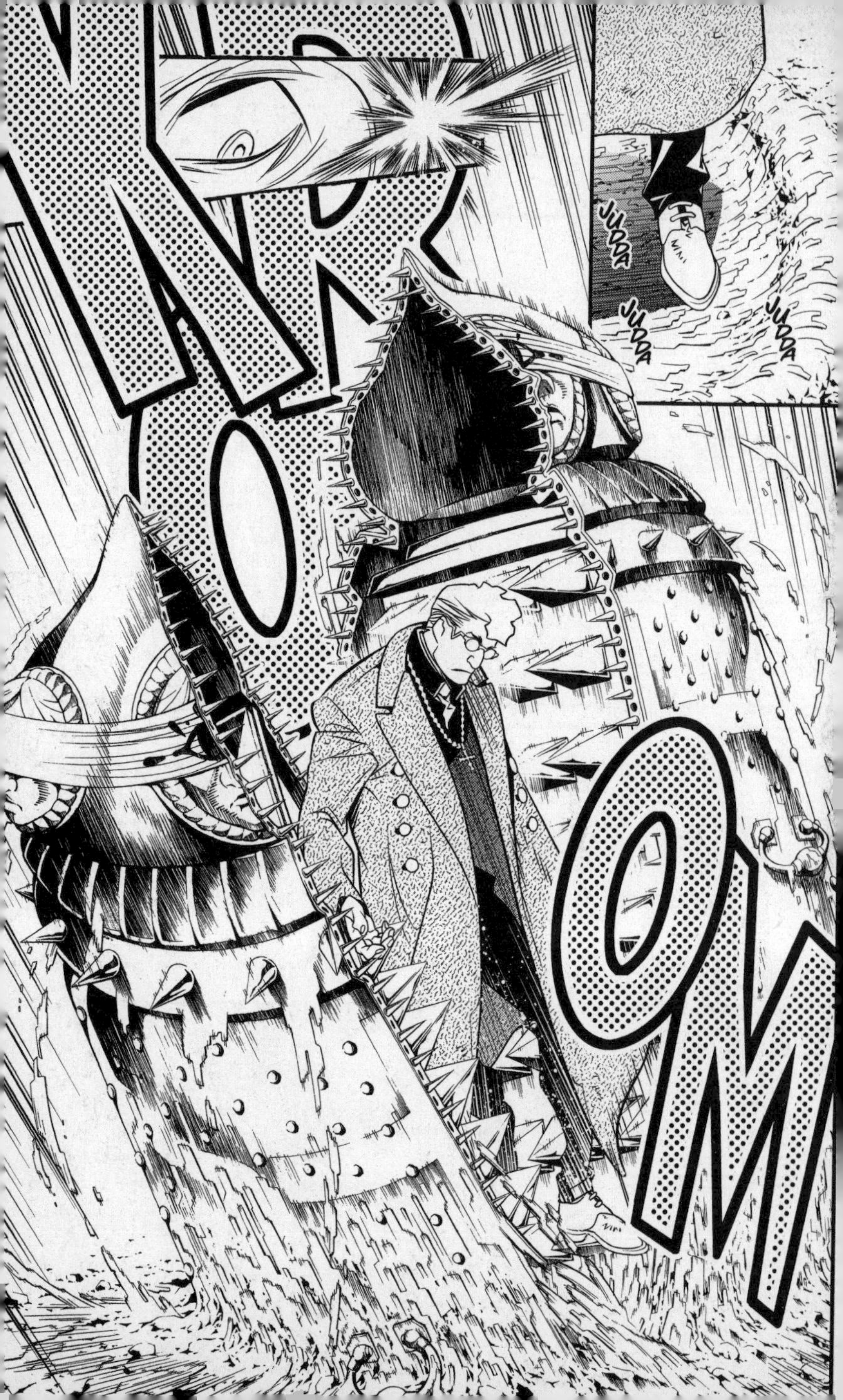
JUDDA
JUDDA
JUDDA

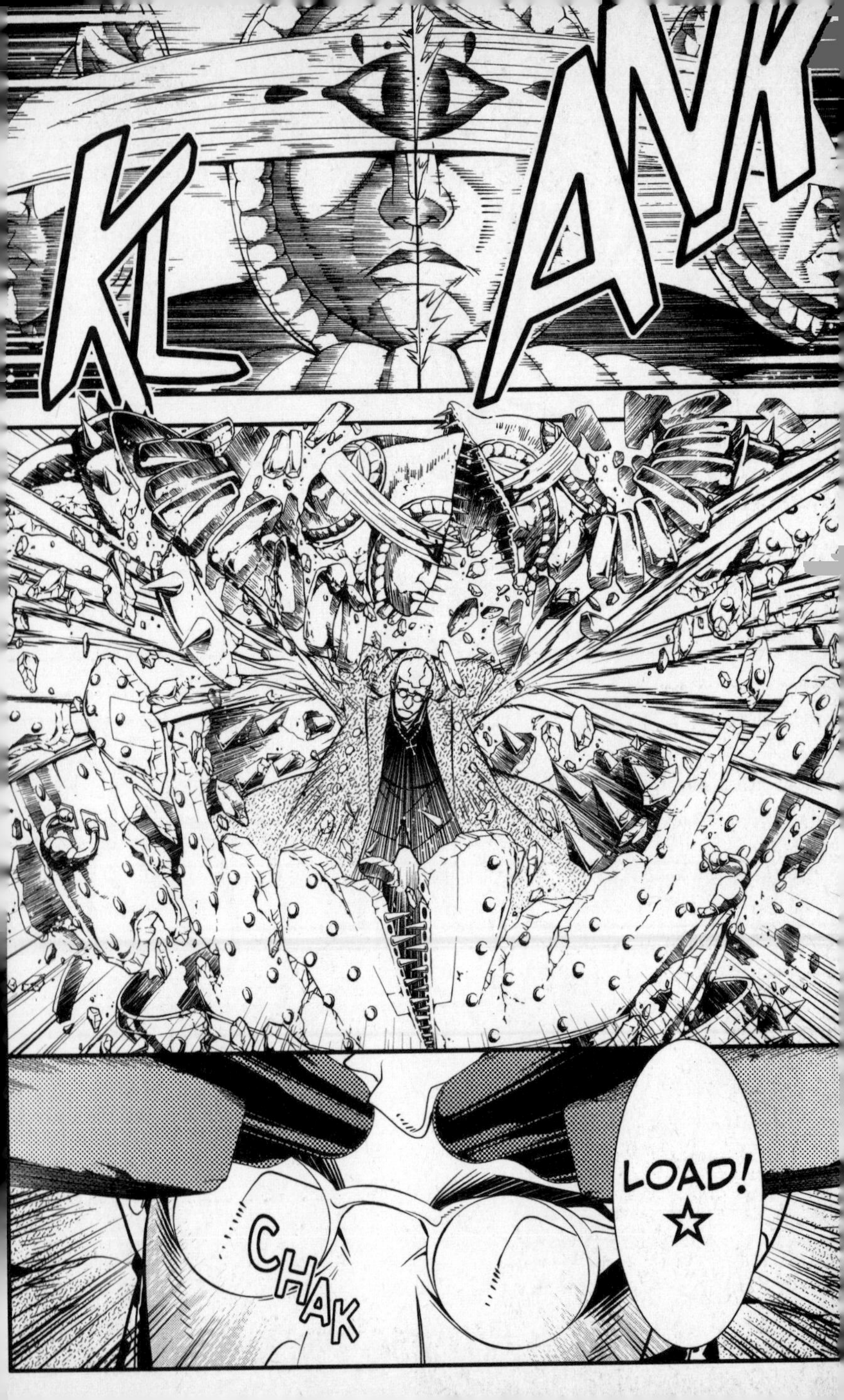
KLANK
LOAD! ☆
CHAK

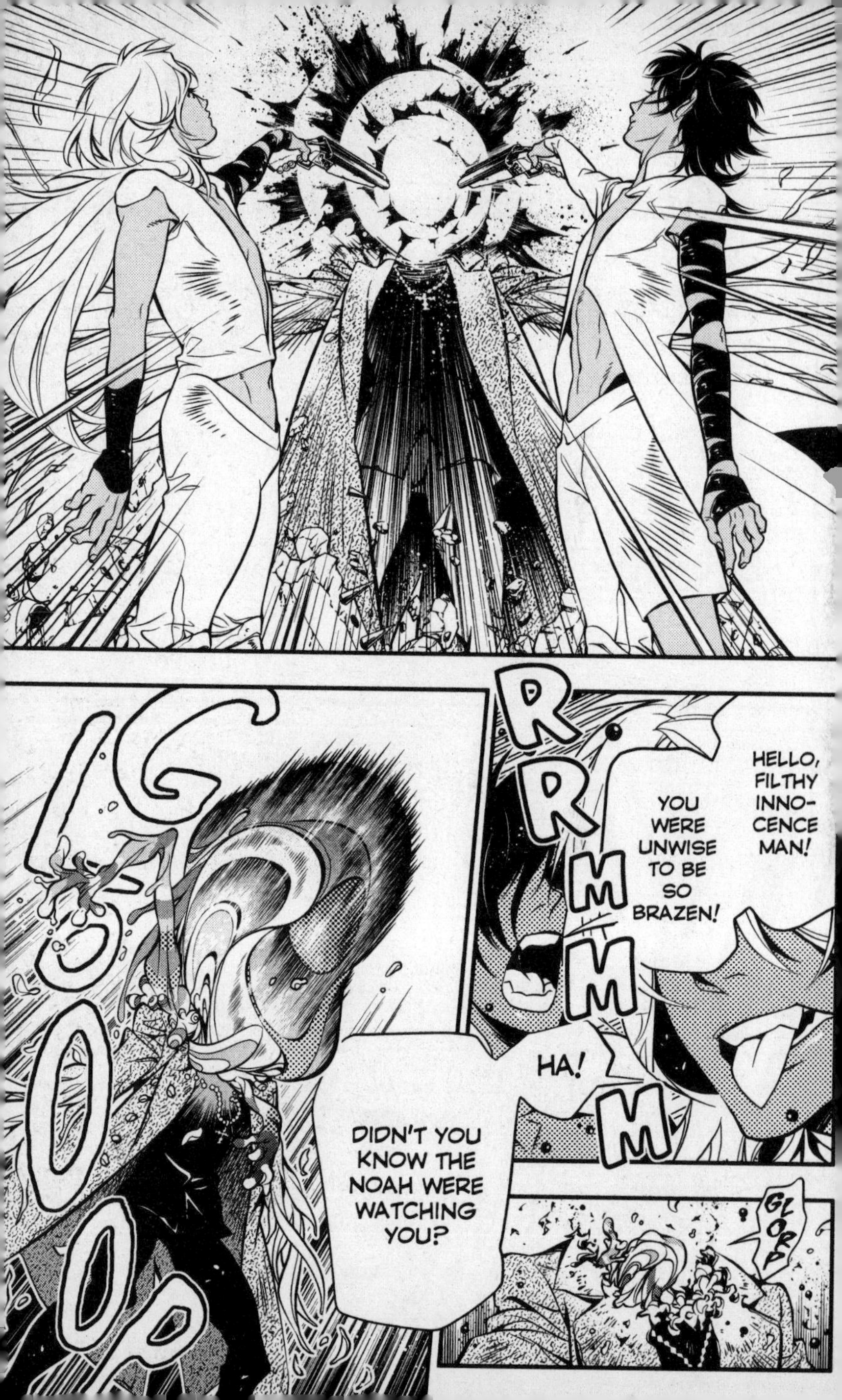

RRMMMM
HELLO, FILTHY INNOCENCE MAN!
YOU WERE UNWISE TO BE SO BRAZEN!
HA!
GLORP
GLOOOP
DIDN'T YOU KNOW THE NOAH WERE WATCHING YOU?

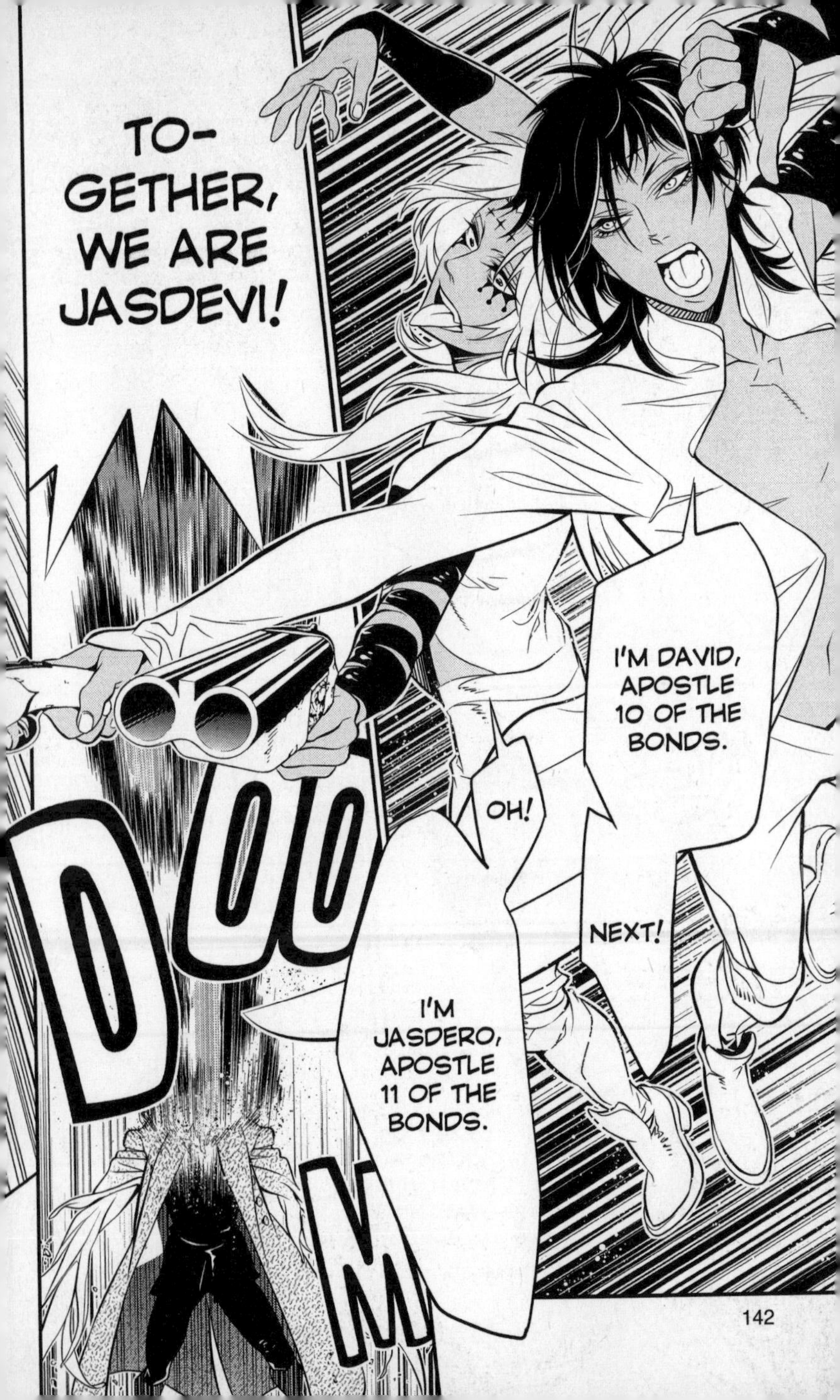
I'M DAVID, APOSTLE 10 OF THE BONDS.
NEXT!
OH!
I'M JASDERO, APOSTLE 11 OF THE BONDS.
TO-GETHER, WE ARE JASDEVI!
DOOOM

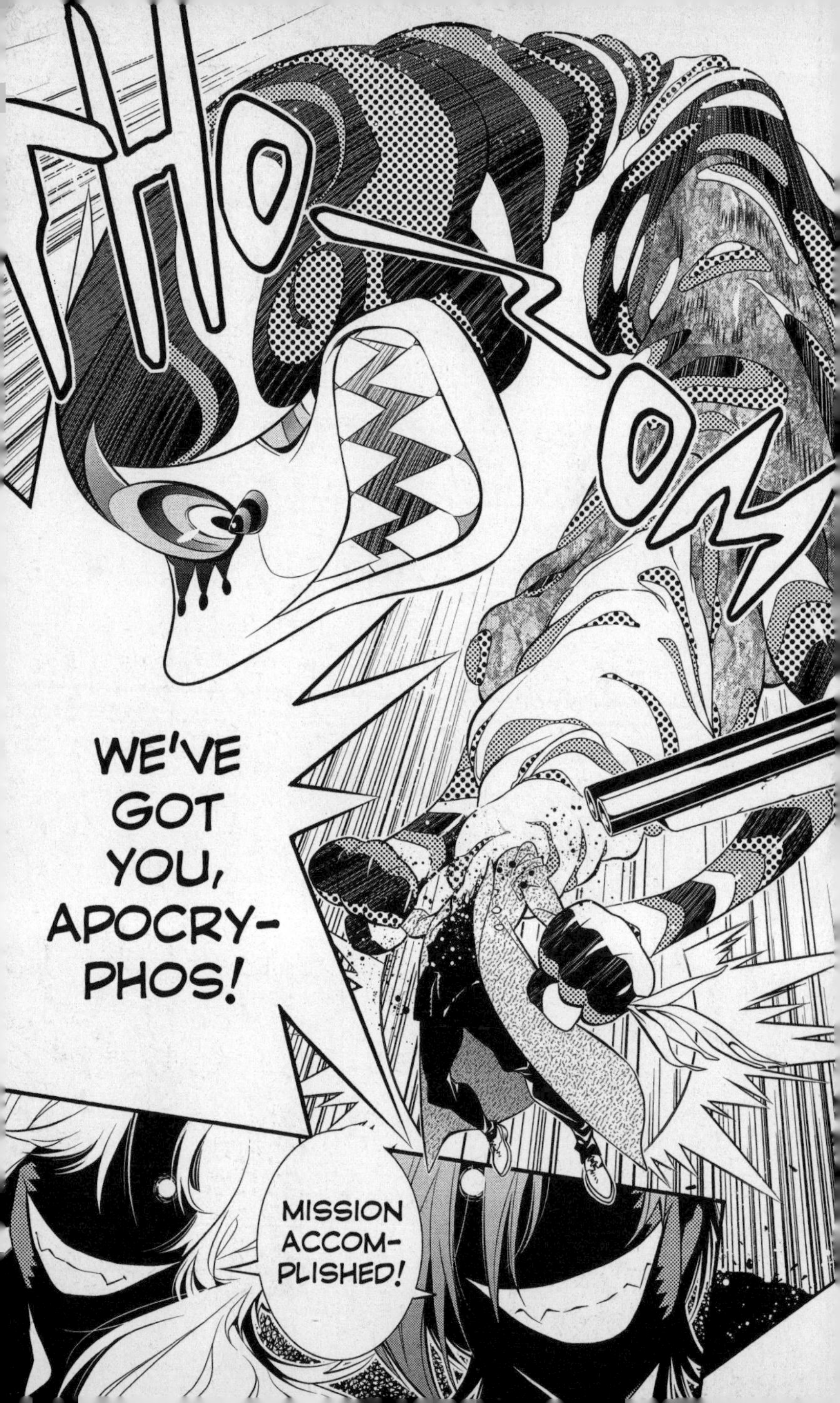
THOOM
WE'VE GOT YOU, APOCRY-PHOS!
MISSION ACCOM-PLISHED!

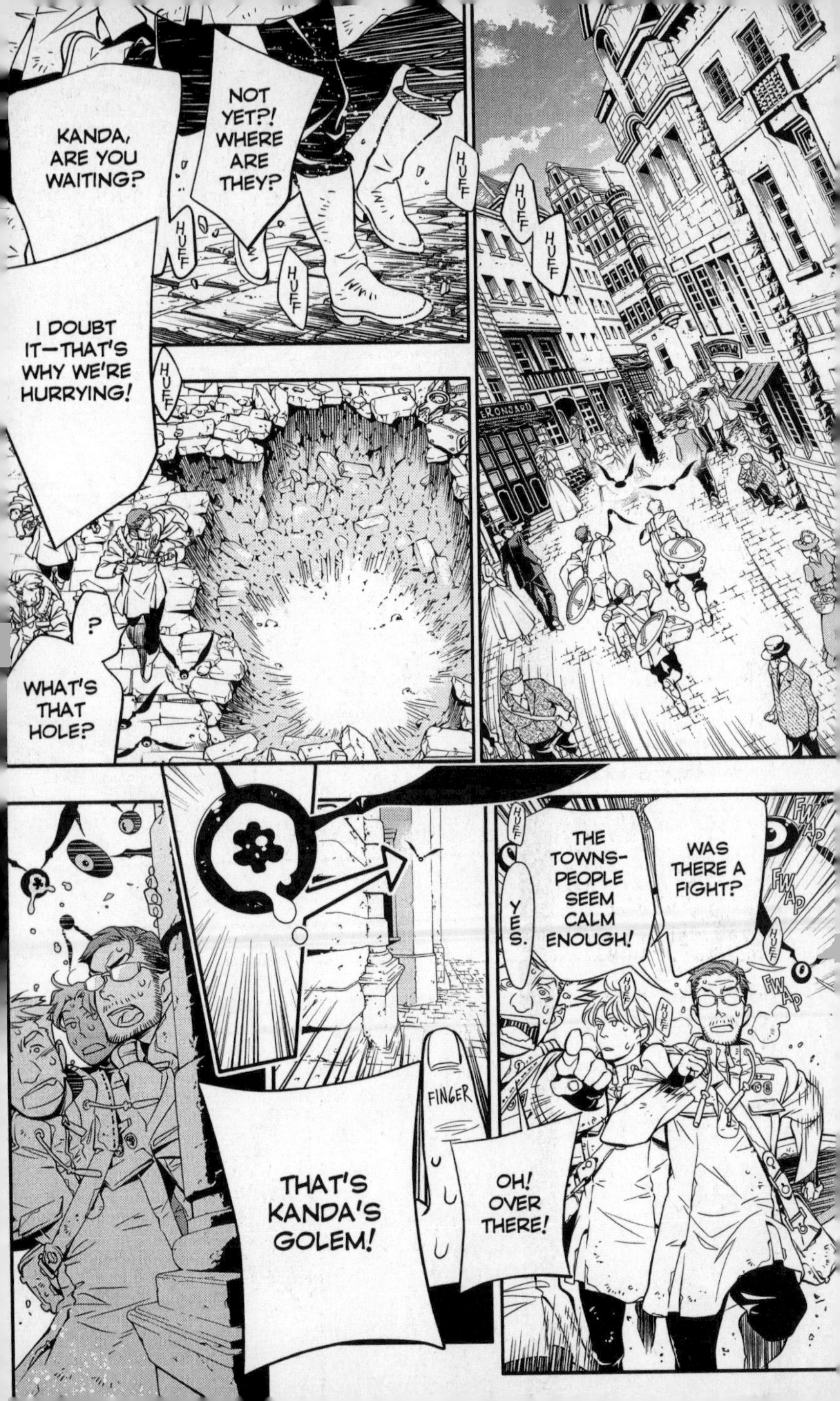

HUFF
HUFF
HUFF
NOT YET?! WHERE ARE THEY?
KANDA, ARE YOU WAITING?
HUFF
HUFF
I DOUBT IT—THAT'S WHY WE'RE HURRYING!
HUFF
?
WHAT'S THAT HOLE?
FWAP
WAS THERE A FIGHT?
THE TOWNS-PEOPLE SEEM CALM ENOUGH!
HUFF
YES.
FWAP
HUFF
FWAP
HUFF
HUFF
OH! OVER THERE!
FINGER
THAT'S KANDA'S GOLEM!

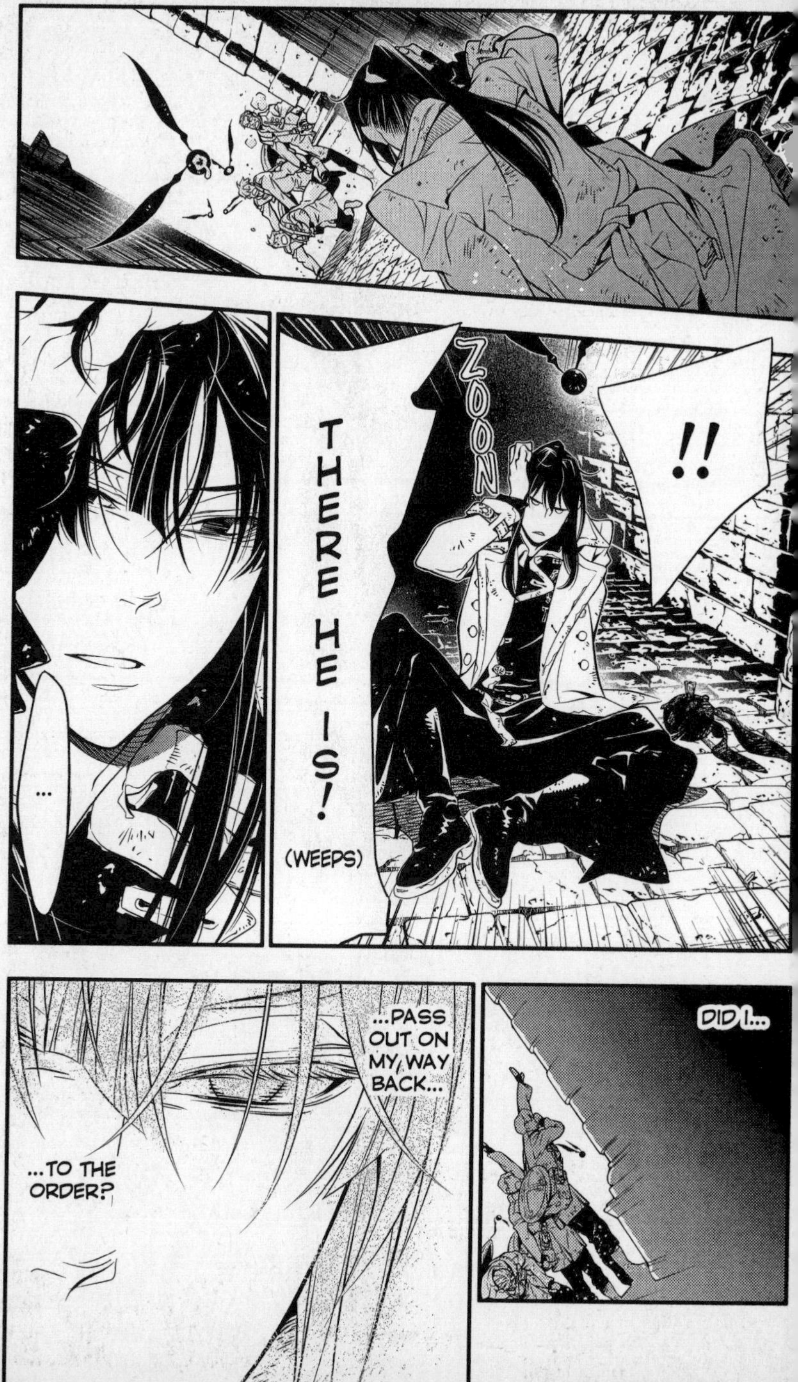
!!
ZOOON
THERE HE IS!
(WEEPS)
...
DID I...
...PASS OUT ON MY WAY BACK...
...TO THE ORDER?

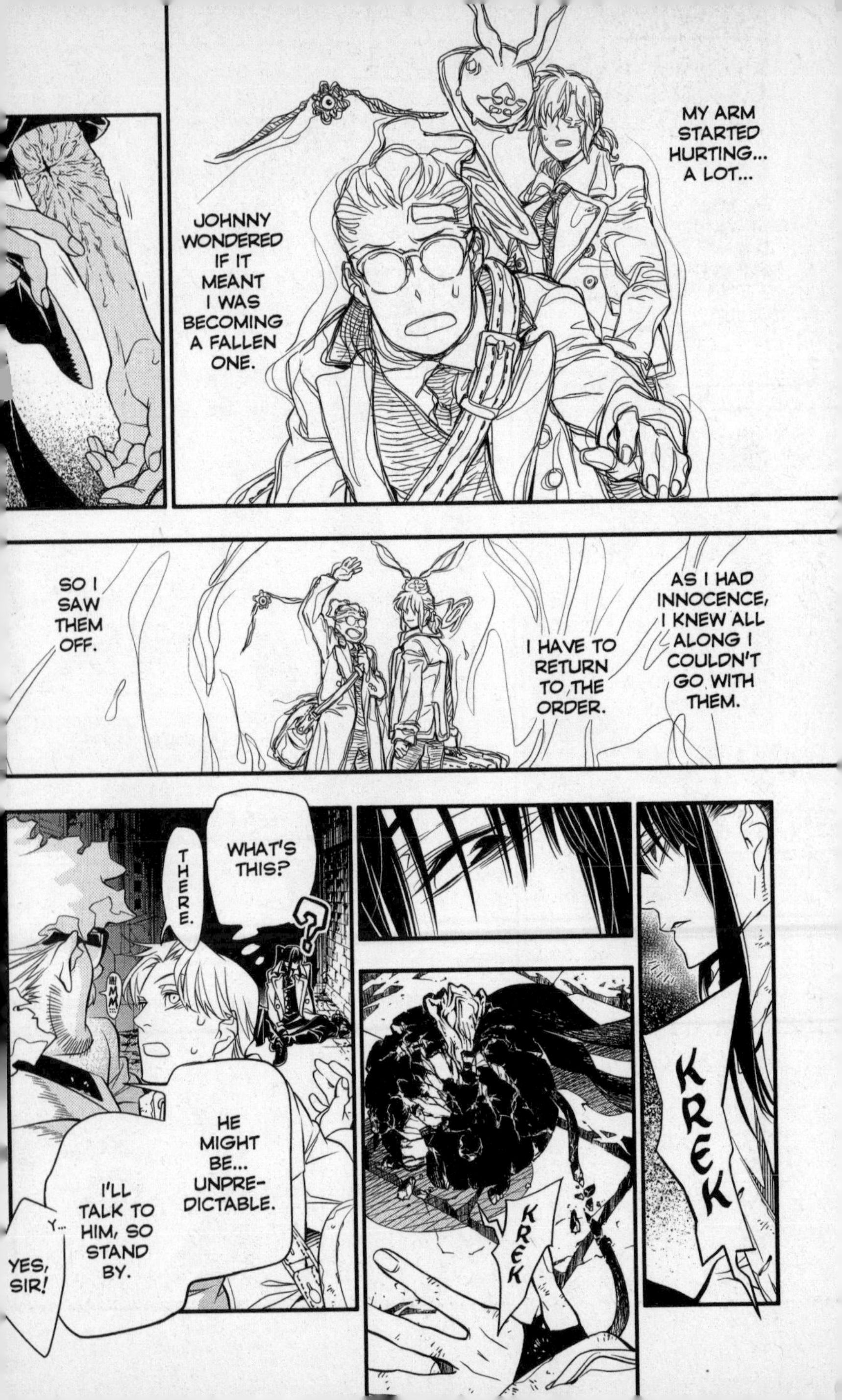
MY ARM STARTED HURTING... A LOT...
JOHNNY WONDERED IF IT MEANT I WAS BECOMING A FALLEN ONE.
AS I HAD INNOCENCE, I KNEW ALL ALONG I COULDN'T GO WITH THEM.
I HAVE TO RETURN TO THE ORDER.
SO I SAW THEM OFF.
KREK
KREK
WHAT'S THIS?
THERE.
?
HE MIGHT BE... UNPREDICTABLE.
I'LL TALK TO HIM, SO STAND BY.
Y...
YES, SIR!

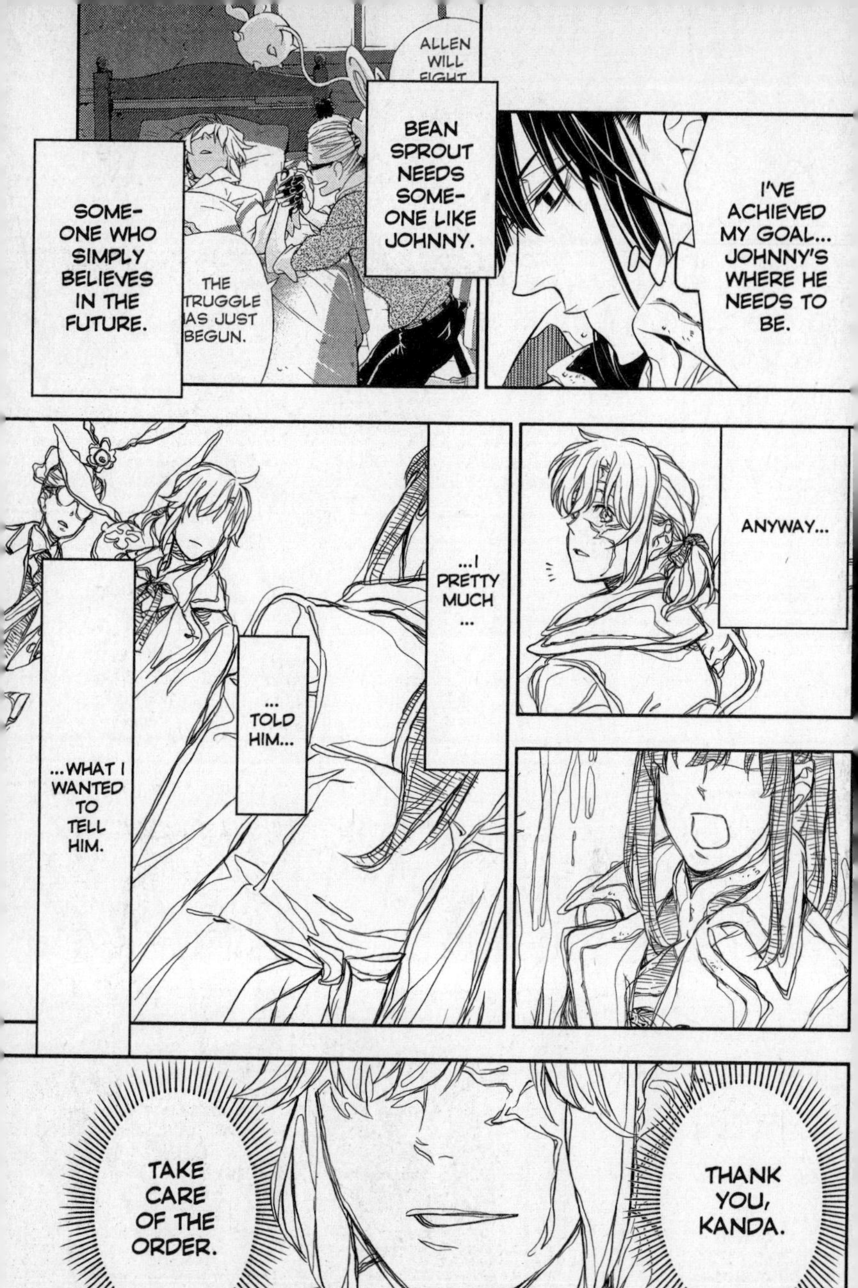

I'VE ACHIEVED MY GOAL... JOHNNY'S WHERE HE NEEDS TO BE.
BEAN SPROUT NEEDS SOME-ONE LIKE JOHNNY.
ALLEN WILL FIGHT
THE STRUGGLE HAS JUST BEGUN.
SOME-ONE WHO SIMPLY BELIEVES IN THE FUTURE.
ANYWAY...
...I PRETTY MUCH ...
... TOLD HIM...
...WHAT I WANTED TO TELL HIM.
THANK YOU, KANDA.
TAKE CARE OF THE ORDER.

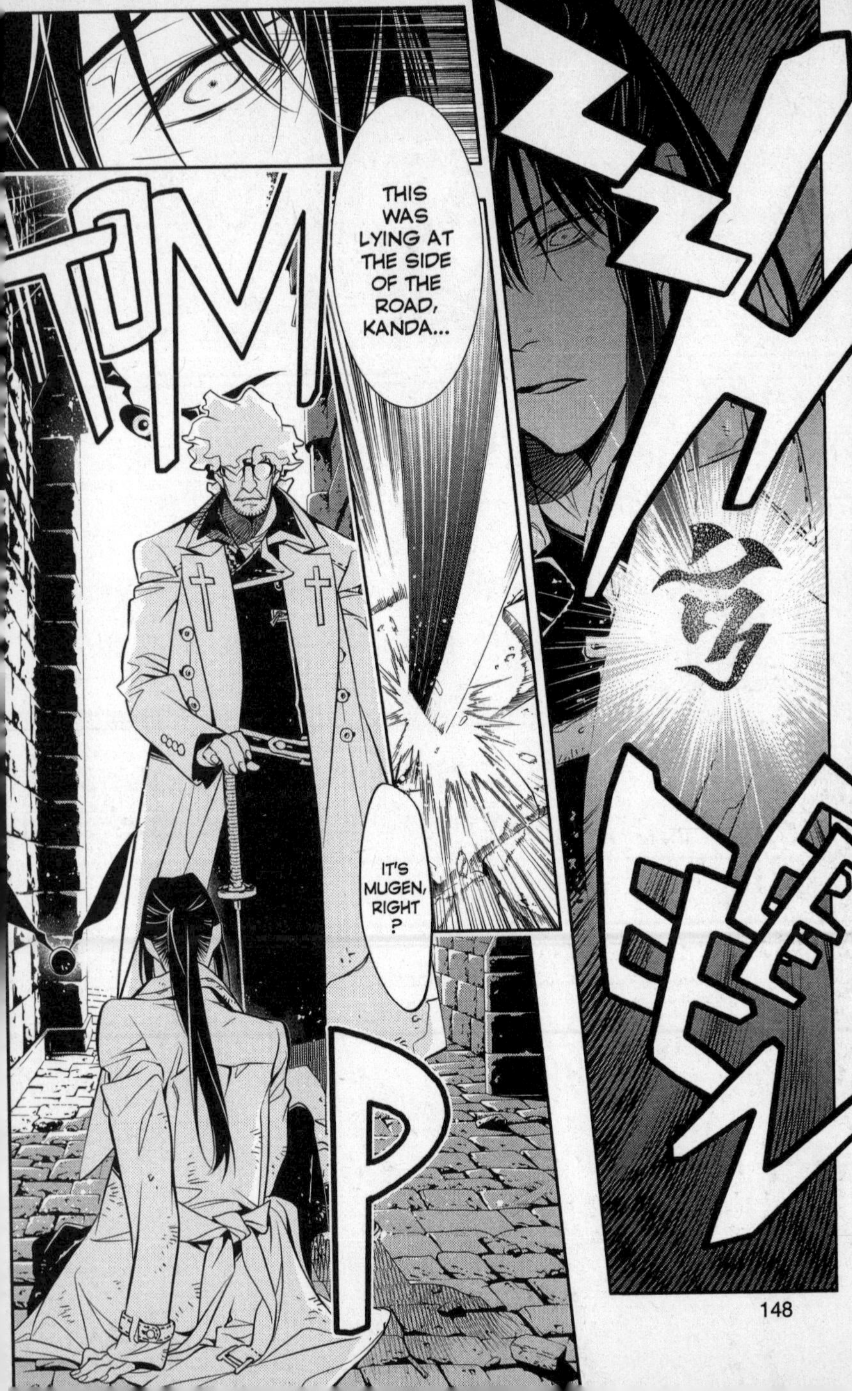
THIS WAS LYING AT THE SIDE OF THE ROAD, KANDA...
IT'S MUGEN, RIGHT?
TOMP

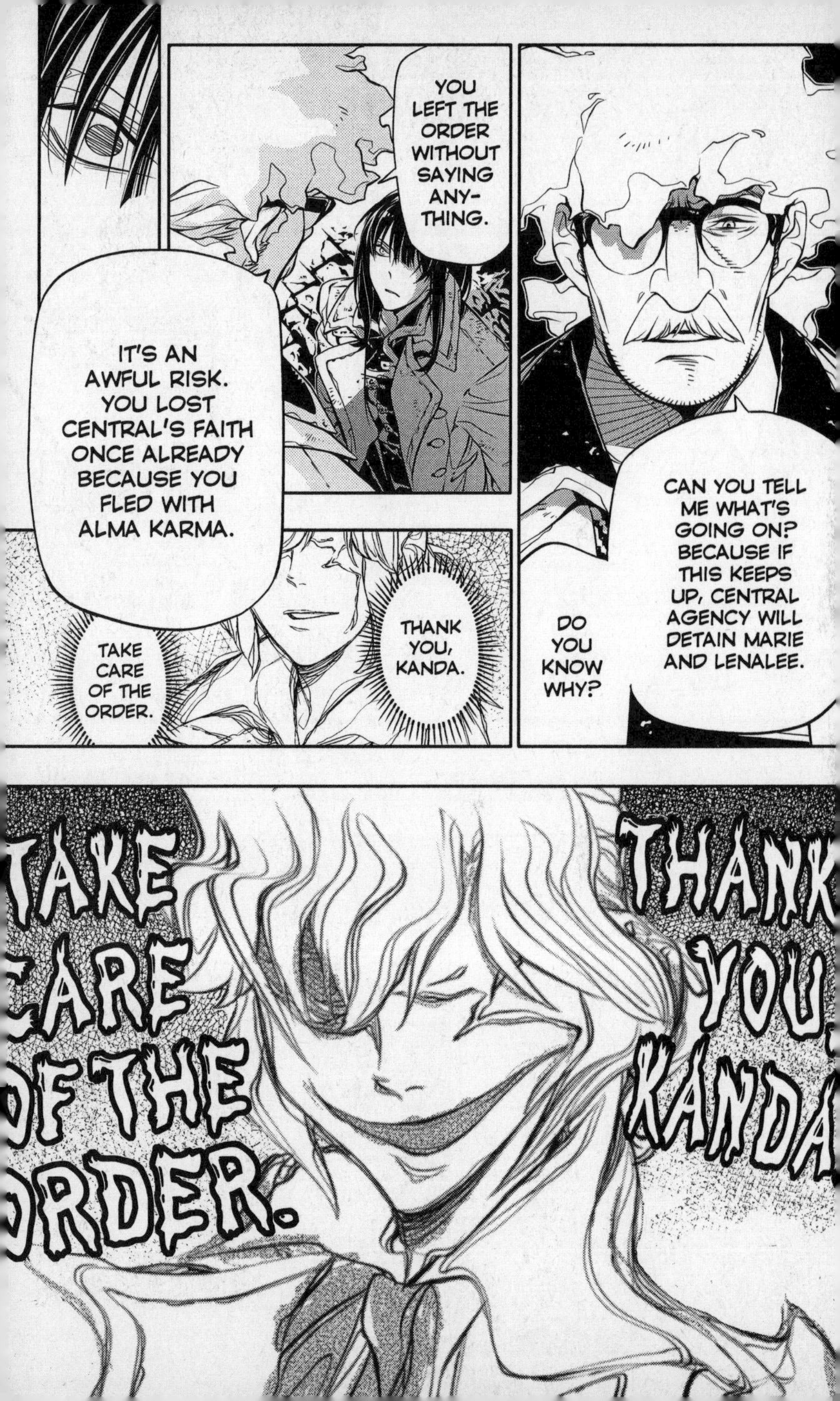
CAN YOU TELL ME WHAT'S GOING ON? BECAUSE IF THIS KEEPS UP, CENTRAL AGENCY WILL DETAIN MARIE AND LENALEE.
DO YOU KNOW WHY?
YOU LEFT THE ORDER WITHOUT SAYING ANY-THING.
IT'S AN AWFUL RISK. YOU LOST CENTRAL'S FAITH ONCE ALREADY BECAUSE YOU FLED WITH ALMA KARMA.
THANK YOU, KANDA.
TAKE CARE OF THE ORDER.
THANK YOU, KANDA.
TAKE CARE OF THE ORDER.

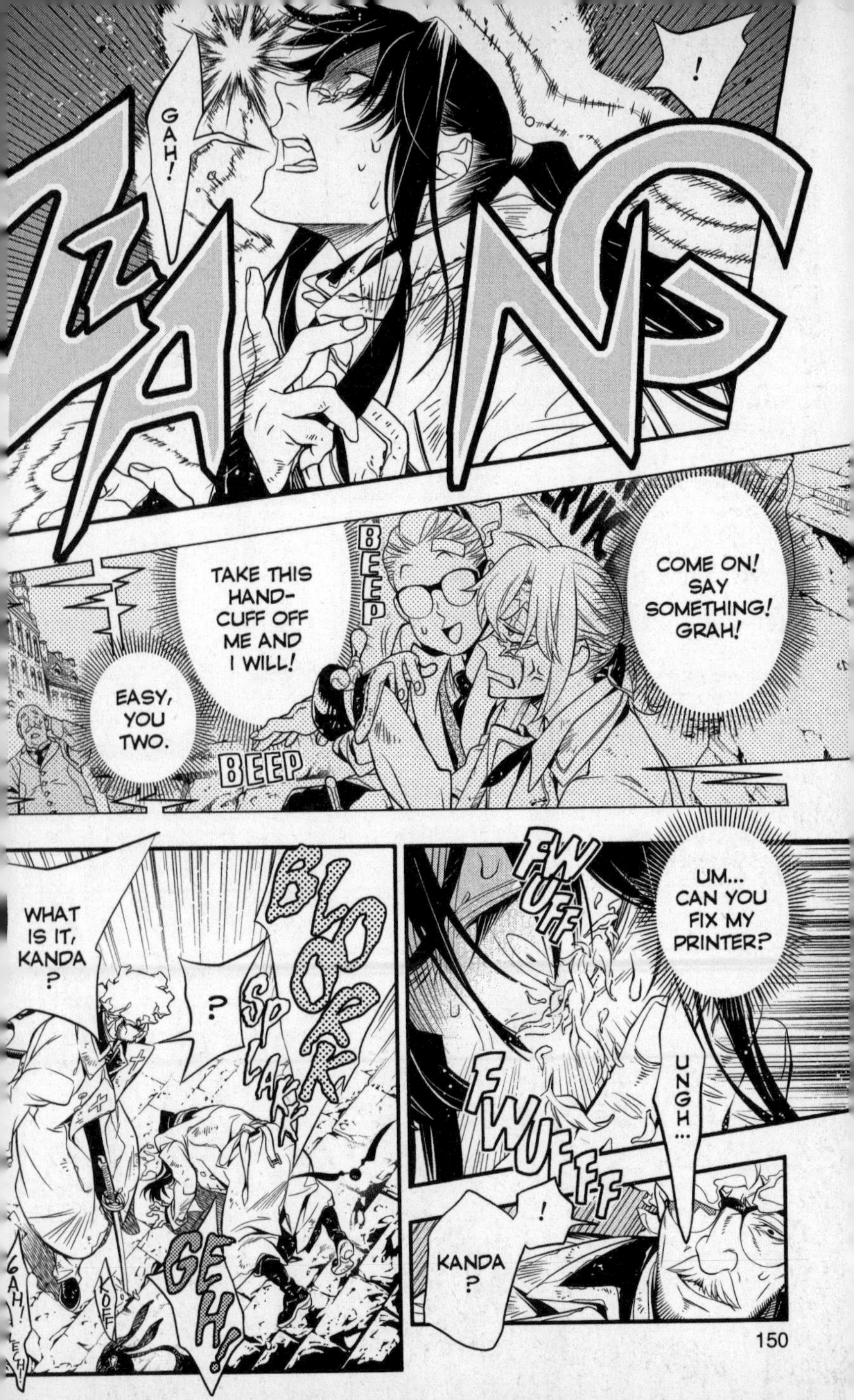
!
GAH!
ZZANG
COME ON! SAY SOMETHING! GRAH!
BEEP
TAKE THIS HAND-CUFF OFF ME AND I WILL!
EASY, YOU TWO.
BEEP
FWUFF
UM... CAN YOU FIX MY PRINTER?
UNGH...
FWUFFFF
!
KANDA?
BLOORK
SPLAKK
?
WHAT IS IT, KANDA?
GEH!
KOFF
GAH! LECH!

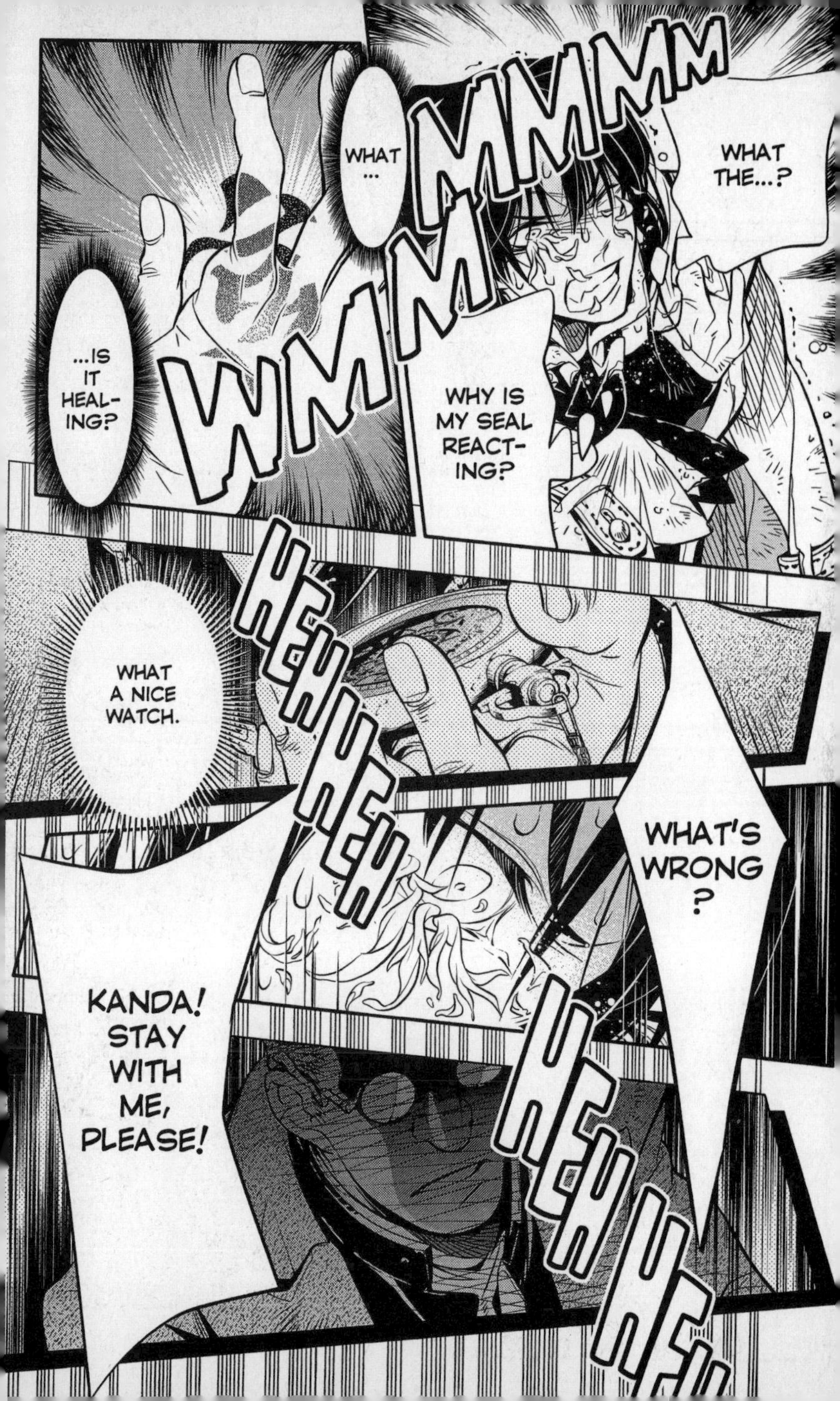
WHAT THE...?
WHY IS MY SEAL REACTING?
WMMMMMMMMM
WHAT...
...IS IT HEALING?
WHAT A NICE WATCH.
HEH HEH HEH
WHAT'S WRONG?
KANDA! STAY WITH ME, PLEASE!
HEH HEH HEH HEH

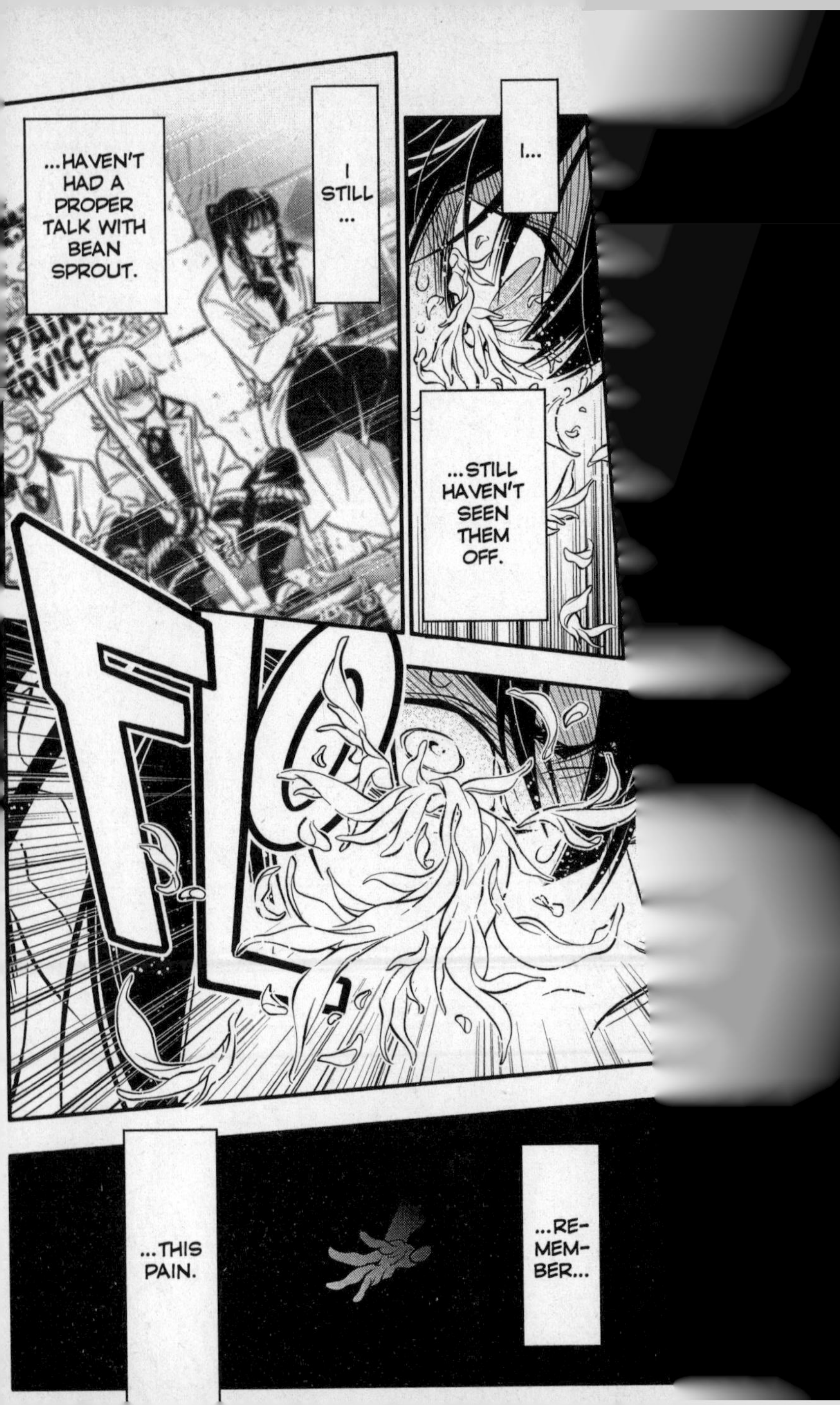
I...
...STILL HAVEN'T SEEN THEM OFF.
I STILL...
...HAVEN'T HAD A PROPER TALK WITH BEAN SPROUT.
...RE-MEM-BER...
...THIS PAIN.

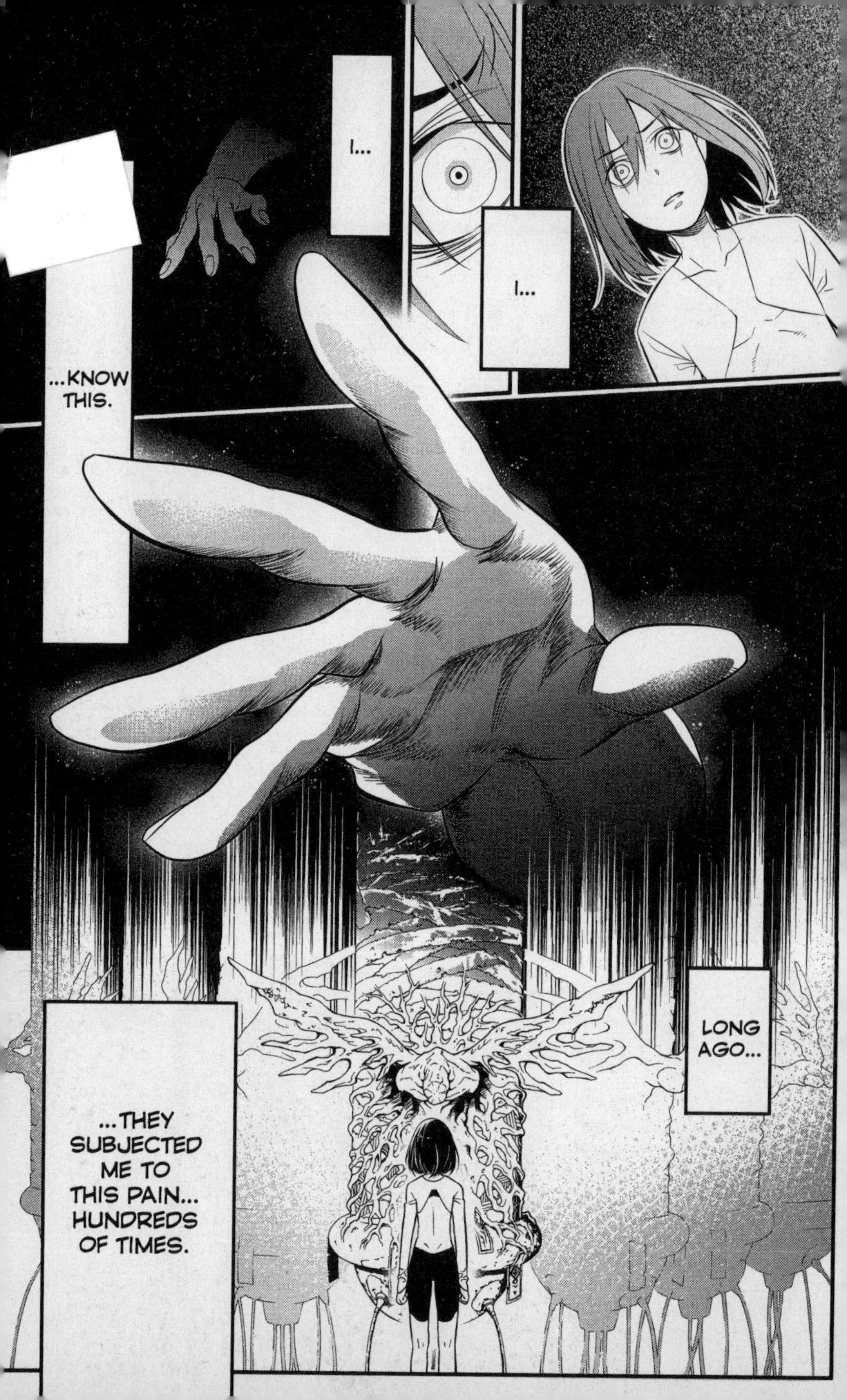
I...
I...
...KNOW THIS.
LONG AGO...
...THEY SUBJECTED ME TO THIS PAIN... HUNDREDS OF TIMES.

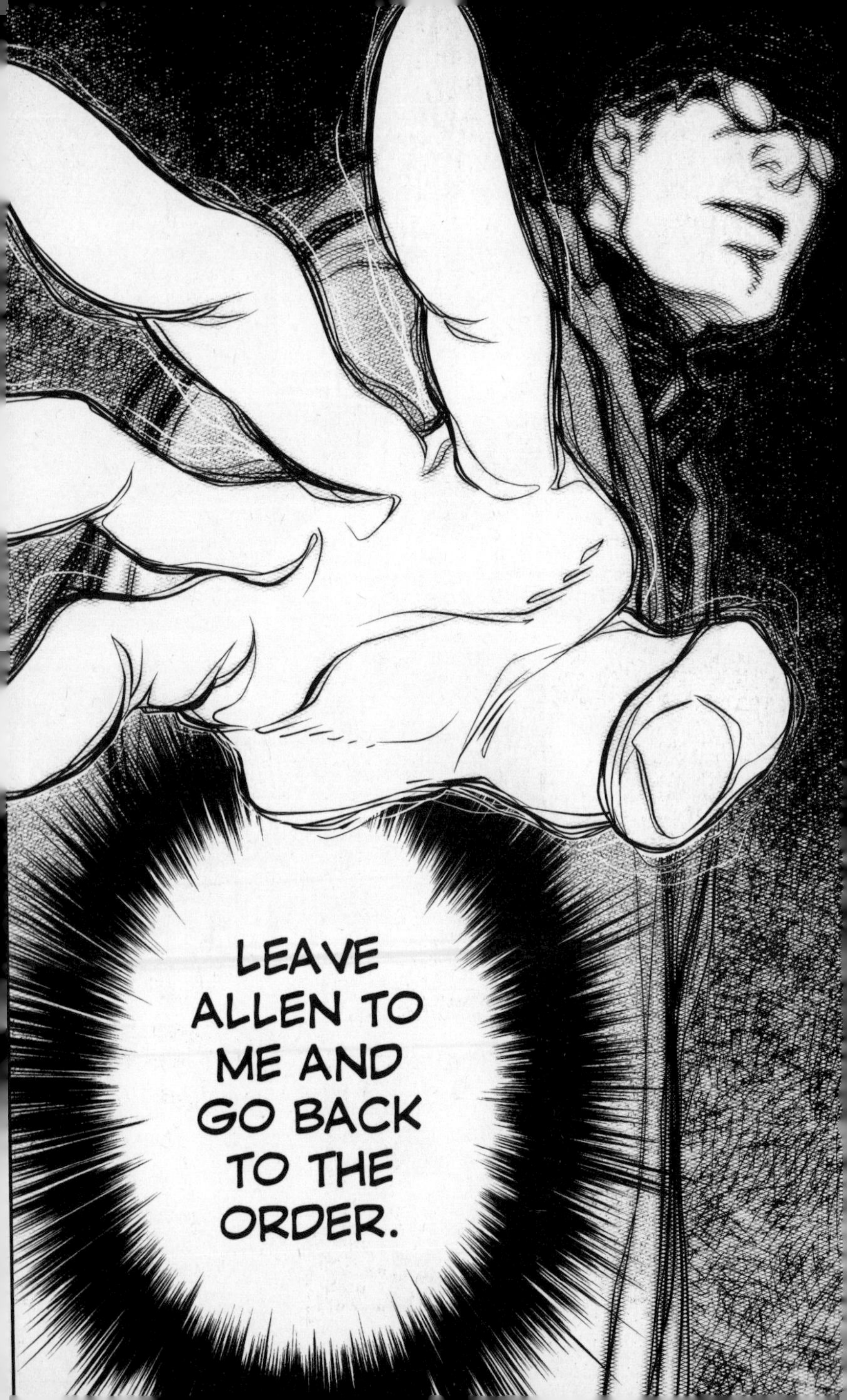
LEAVE ALLEN TO ME AND GO BACK TO THE ORDER.

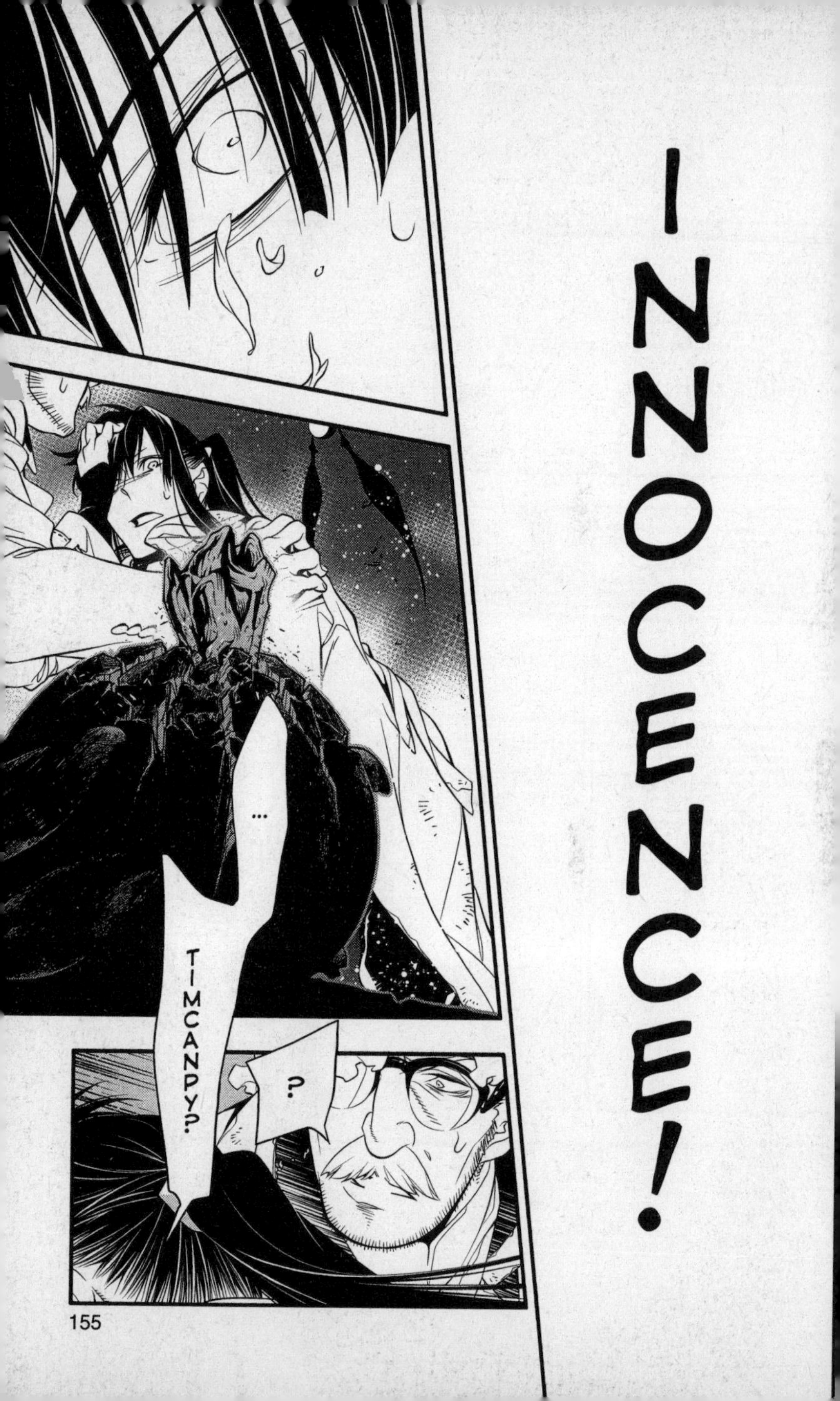
INNOCENCE!
...
TIMCANPY?
?

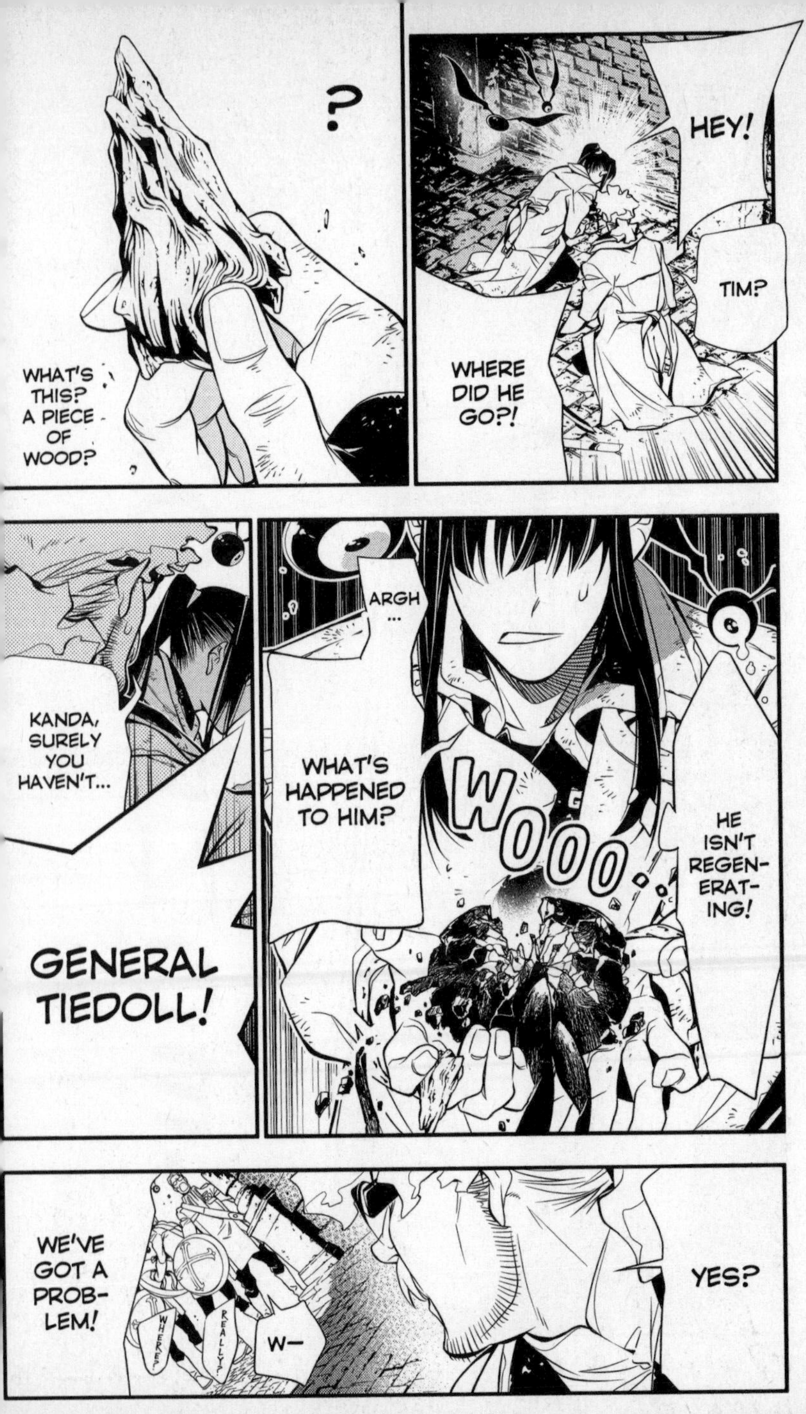
HEY!
TIM?
WHERE DID HE GO?!
?
WHAT'S THIS? A PIECE OF WOOD?
ARGH...
HE ISN'T REGEN-ERAT-ING!
WHAT'S HAPPENED TO HIM?
WOOO
KANDA, SURELY YOU HAVEN'T...
GENERAL TIEDOLL!
YES?
W—
REALLY?
WHERE?
WE'VE GOT A PROB-LEM!

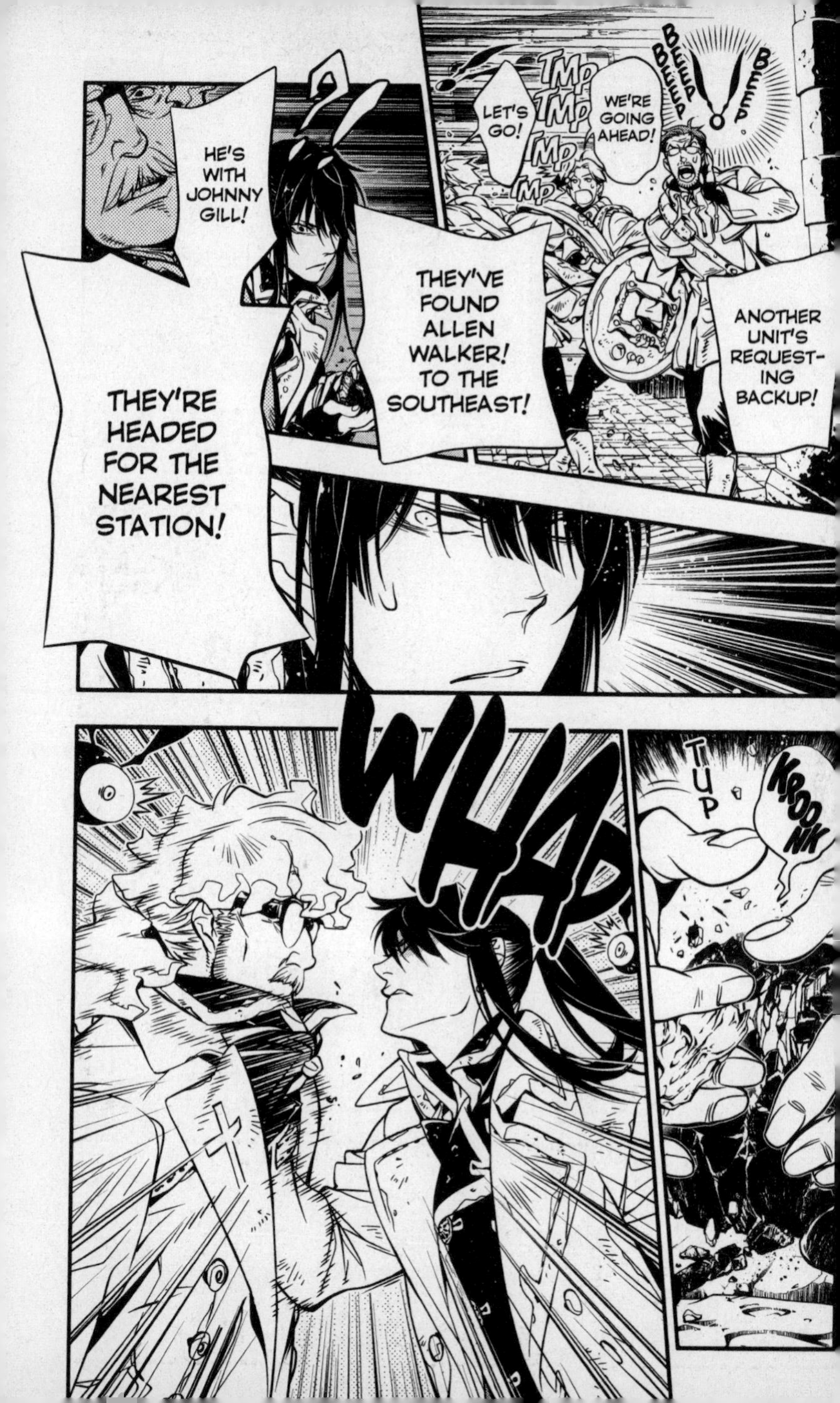
BEEP BEEP
BEEP
WE'RE GOING AHEAD!
TMP TMP TMP TMP
LET'S GO!
ANOTHER UNIT'S REQUESTING BACKUP!
THEY'VE FOUND ALLEN WALKER! TO THE SOUTHEAST!
?
HE'S WITH JOHNNY GILL!
THEY'RE HEADED FOR THE NEAREST STATION!
KROOONK
TUP
WHAP

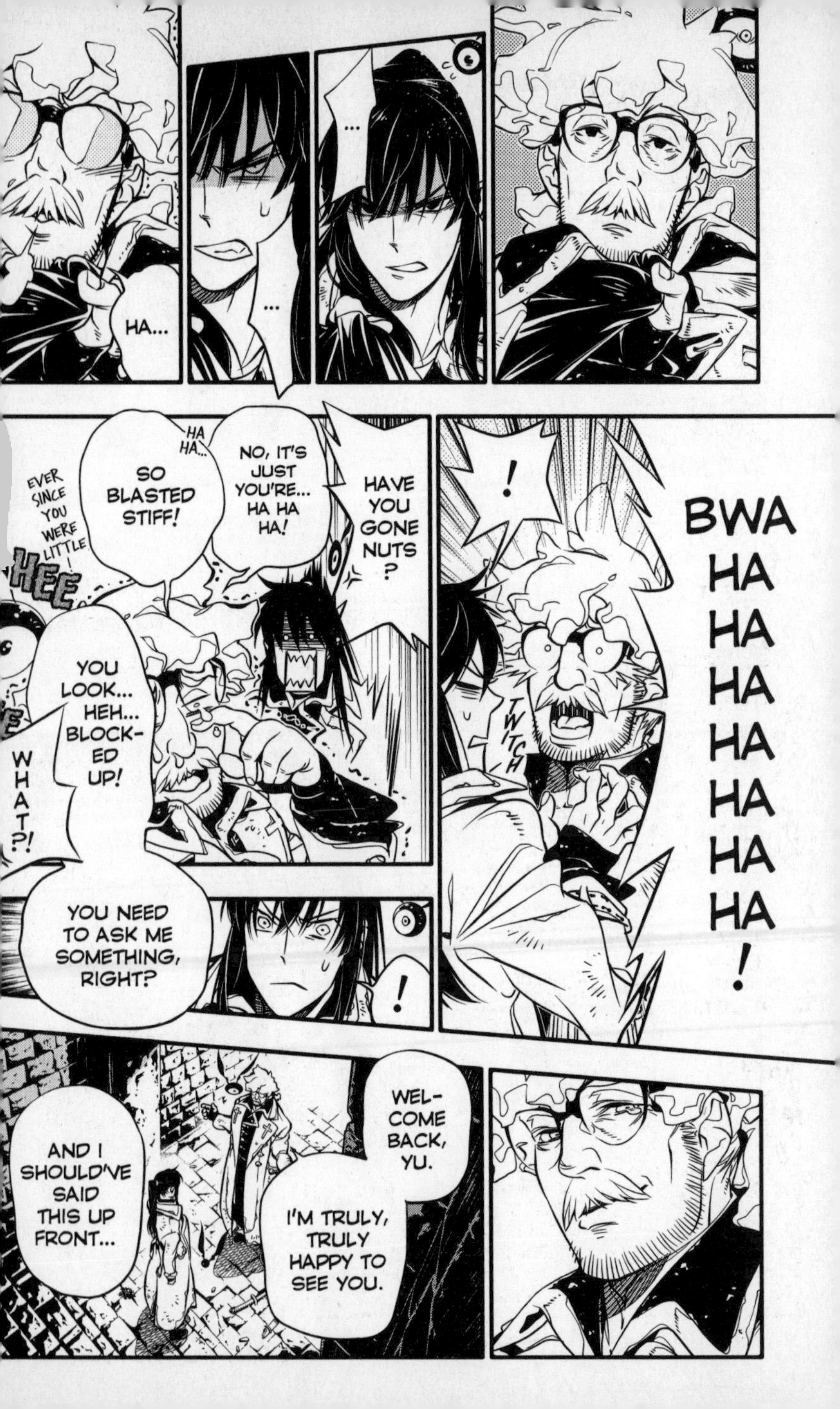
...
...
HA...
BWA HA HA HA HA HA HA HA!
!
TWITCH
HAVE YOU GONE NUTS?
NO, IT'S JUST YOU'RE... HA HA HA!
HA HA...
SO BLASTED STIFF!
EVER SINCE YOU WERE LITTLE!
HEE
YOU LOOK... HEH... BLOCKED UP!
WHAT?!
!
YOU NEED TO ASK ME SOMETHING, RIGHT?
WELCOME BACK, YU.
I'M TRULY, TRULY HAPPY TO SEE YOU.
AND I SHOULD'VE SAID THIS UP FRONT...

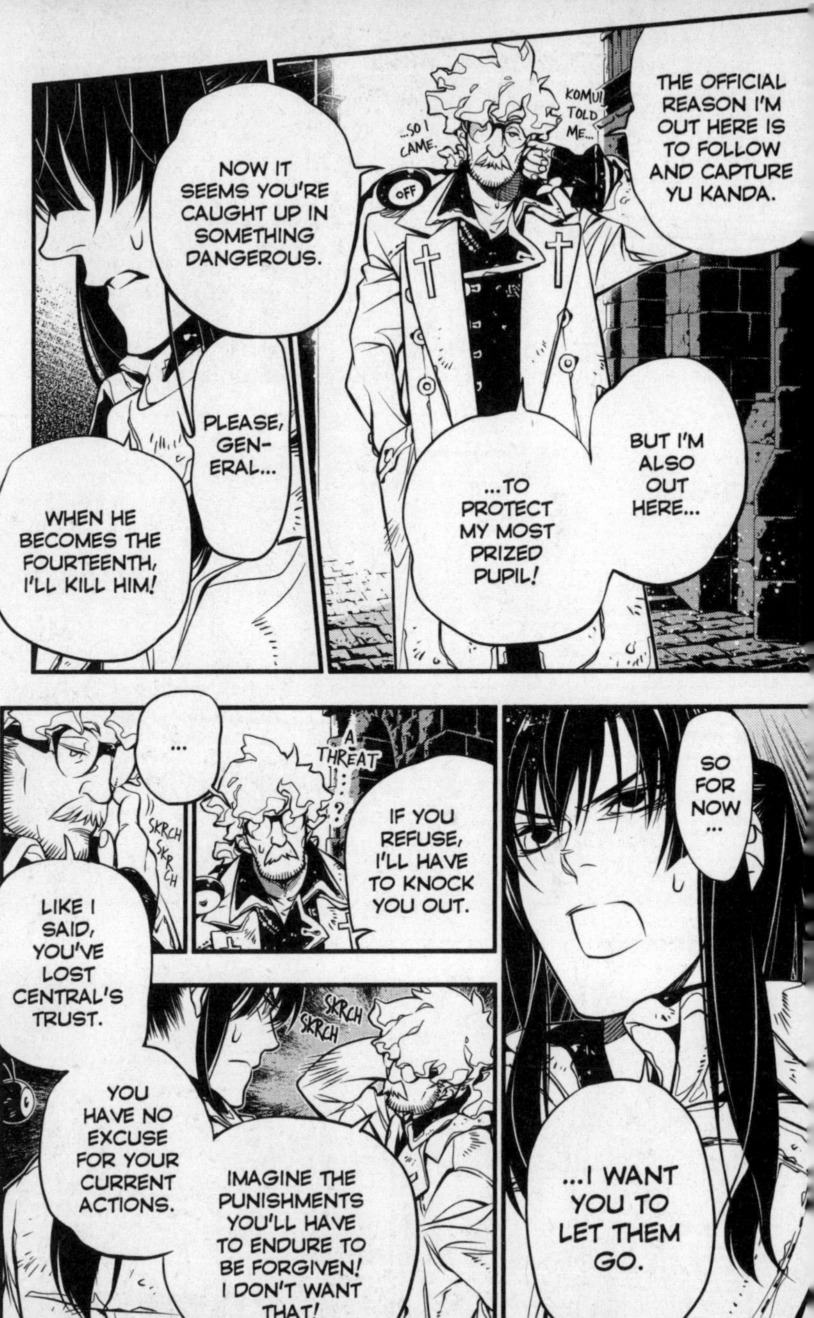
THE OFFICIAL REASON I'M OUT HERE IS TO FOLLOW AND CAPTURE YU KANDA.
KOMUI TOLD ME...
...SO I CAME.
NOW IT SEEMS YOU'RE CAUGHT UP IN SOMETHING DANGEROUS.
BUT I'M ALSO OUT HERE...
...TO PROTECT MY MOST PRIZED PUPIL!
PLEASE, GEN-ERAL...
WHEN HE BECOMES THE FOURTEENTH, I'LL KILL HIM!
SO FOR NOW...
...I WANT YOU TO LET THEM GO.
A THREAT...?
IF YOU REFUSE, I'LL HAVE TO KNOCK YOU OUT.
...
SKRCH SKRCH
LIKE I SAID, YOU'VE LOST CENTRAL'S TRUST.
SKRCH SKRCH
YOU HAVE NO EXCUSE FOR YOUR CURRENT ACTIONS.
IMAGINE THE PUNISHMENTS YOU'LL HAVE TO ENDURE TO BE FORGIVEN! I DON'T WANT THAT!

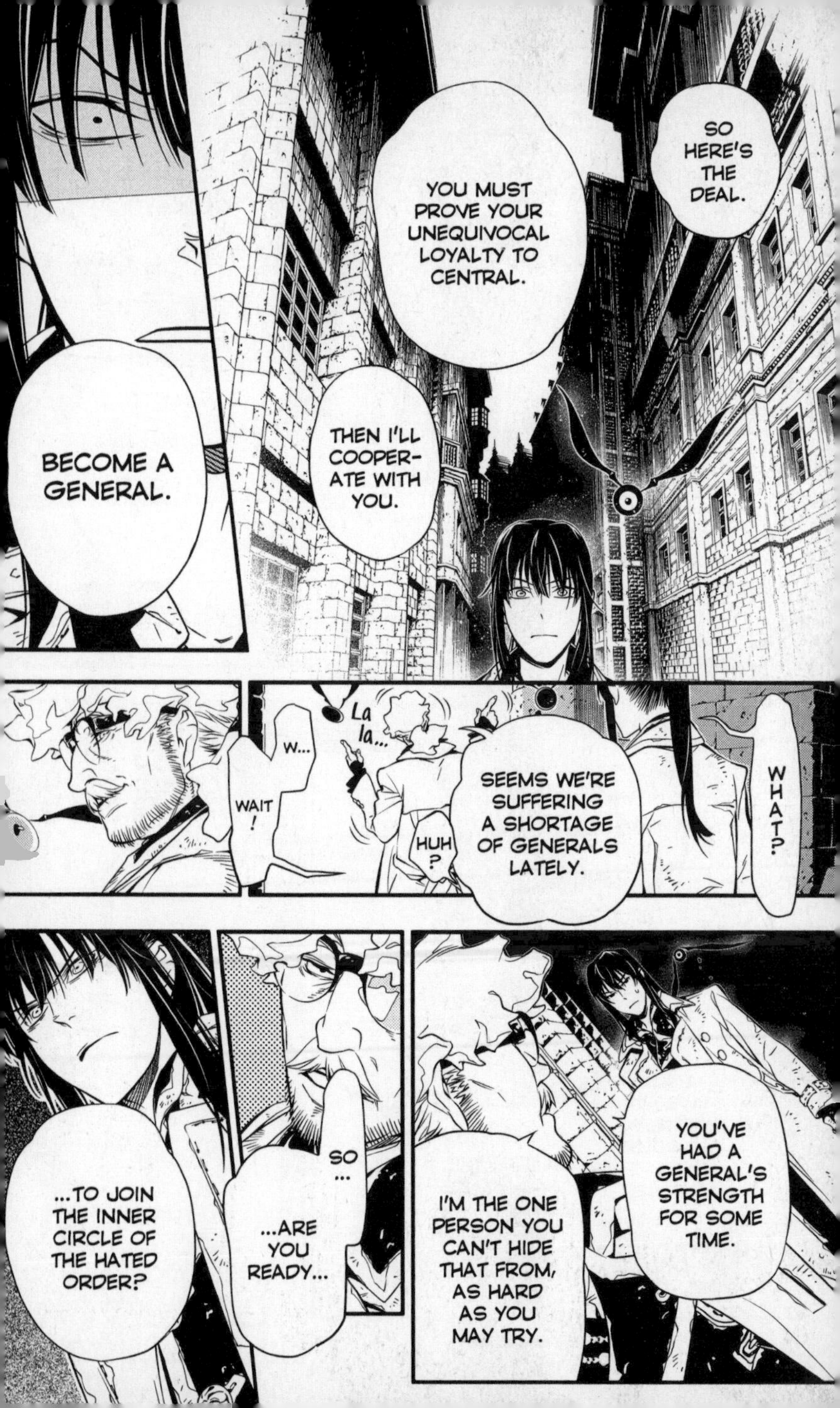
SO HERE'S THE DEAL.
YOU MUST PROVE YOUR UNEQUIVOCAL LOYALTY TO CENTRAL.
THEN I'LL COOPER-ATE WITH YOU.
BECOME A GENERAL.
WHAT?
SEEMS WE'RE SUFFERING A SHORTAGE OF GENERALS LATELY.
La la...
HUH?
W...
WAIT!
YOU'VE HAD A GENERAL'S STRENGTH FOR SOME TIME.
I'M THE ONE PERSON YOU CAN'T HIDE THAT FROM, AS HARD AS YOU MAY TRY.
SO...
...ARE YOU READY...
...TO JOIN THE INNER CIRCLE OF THE HATED ORDER?

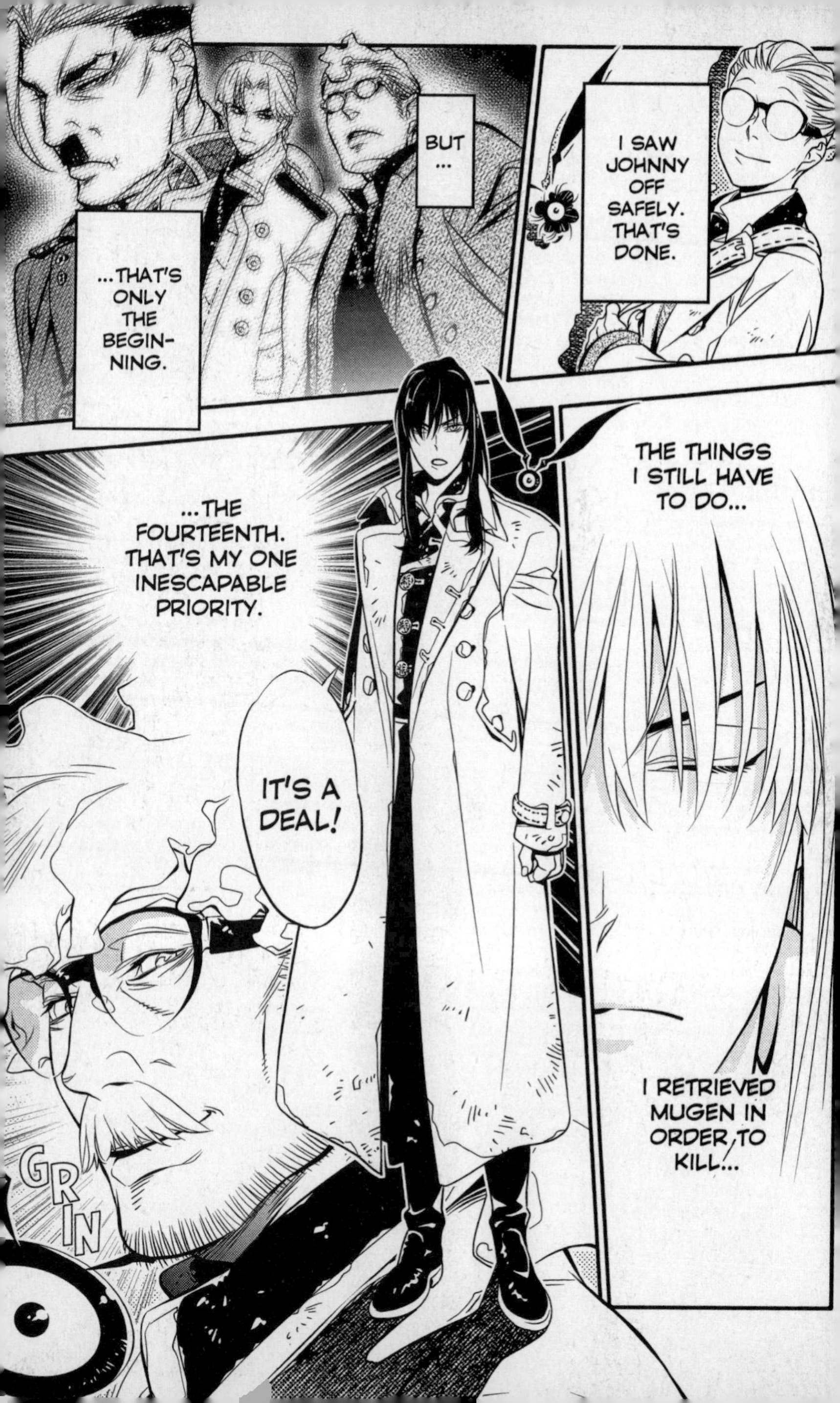
I SAW JOHNNY OFF SAFELY. THAT'S DONE.
BUT ...
...THAT'S ONLY THE BEGIN-NING.
THE THINGS I STILL HAVE TO DO...
I RETRIEVED MUGEN IN ORDER TO KILL...
...THE FOURTEENTH. THAT'S MY ONE INESCAPABLE PRIORITY.
IT'S A DEAL!
GRIN

Tim | Link | Tyki | Waizurii | Johnny | Kanda | Allen

KOMUI'S DISCUSSION ROOM 5

Q. How much is an Order uniform worth?

A: We used the decorations from Kanda's to pay for our lodging and sandwiches.

Ty: And to bet in poker, boy.

J: Huh? The uniforms we made?! (*cries*)

A: It's not what you think, Johnny! (*flustered*) I had to do it to help Krory! B-Besides, I won big!

J: You did? Then that's okay! (*smiles*)

A: Phew... (*sweats*)

W: It looks like you spend more on the make and materials than on the decorations anyway.

J: True. They're totally custom-made, extremely durable and adapted to the wearer's physique and fighting style. For example, Lenalee fights airborne a lot, so hers is wind-resistant and retains heat. Lavi uses fire attacks,

so his is heat-resistant. Krory's is extra special—his body can convert Akuma blood into energy, so we used a special fabric that readily absorbs blood. I think that one was the most expensive. Allen's and Kanda's styles are physically intense, so we focused on their uniforms' ability to absorb sweat and dry quickly. And when Akuma are destroyed, they generate a virulent gas, so we wove a fabric containing secret talismans from the Chan family. And... What's wrong, Allen?

A: Y-You really do put in a lot of effort! I just thought they were extra sturdy and nicely ornamented. (*apologetic*)

W: Yet you used it for a poker bet! Heartless!

Link: Hmph! The uniforms are a symbol of Central Agency's prestige!

A: I hear Link's voice again.

A ghost?!

K: ...

J: Ha ha! (*blushes*) Well, as to their total value, each design is different, so I can't give you a definite price. But they each run to hundreds of thousands.

Ty: Oh! Then next time we fight, I'll rough up your uniforms!

A: You do anyway! Hundreds of thousands... hundreds of thousands! And I've ruined several of them! If I'd only known! (*stomps*)

K: If you'd known, then what?!

Q. In Volume 23, Tim was eating his master's tobacco. What's his favorite food?

Tim: Gaah!

A: Yep... He likes chewy stuff.

Ty: Is that what he said? It sounded like "Gaah!" to me. Ow! Don't bite!

Tim: Gaaaah!

A: He says he can't help biting you whenever he sees you.

Ty: You're definitely lying now! Ow! Stop that!

W: Did you bite your master, the Fourteenth, golem? He has naturally wavy hair!

A: I forgot about that. Gaaaaah! ♡ (*high-pitched*)

J: Ha ha! ☆ Are you mimicking Tim?

K: Creepy...

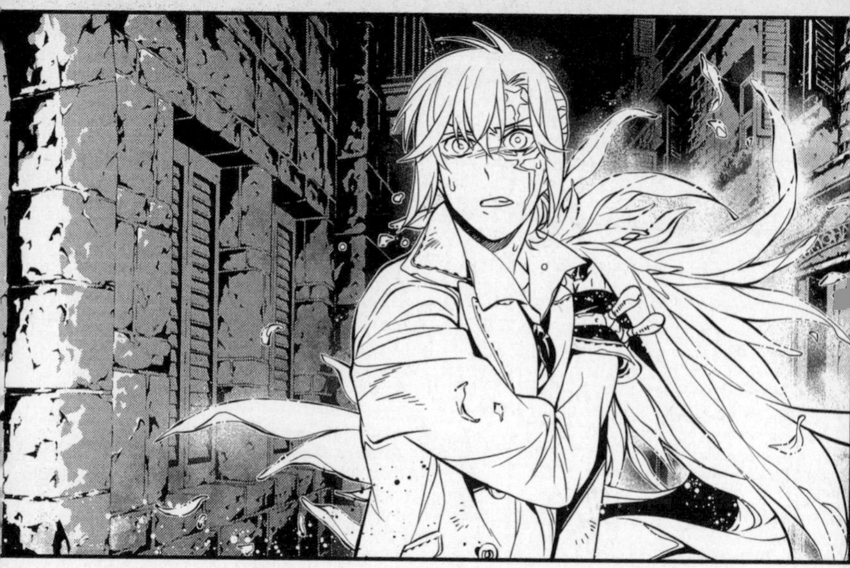

THE 218TH NIGHT
SEARCHING FOR A.W.: D

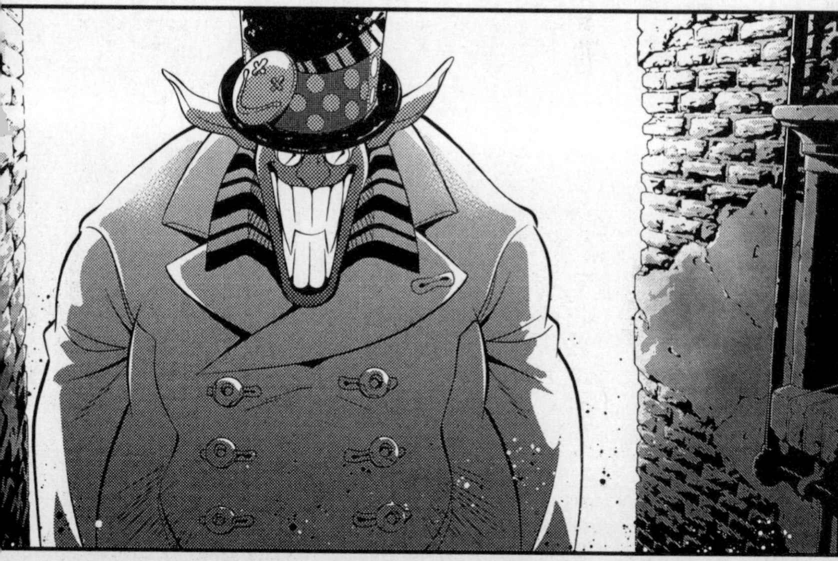

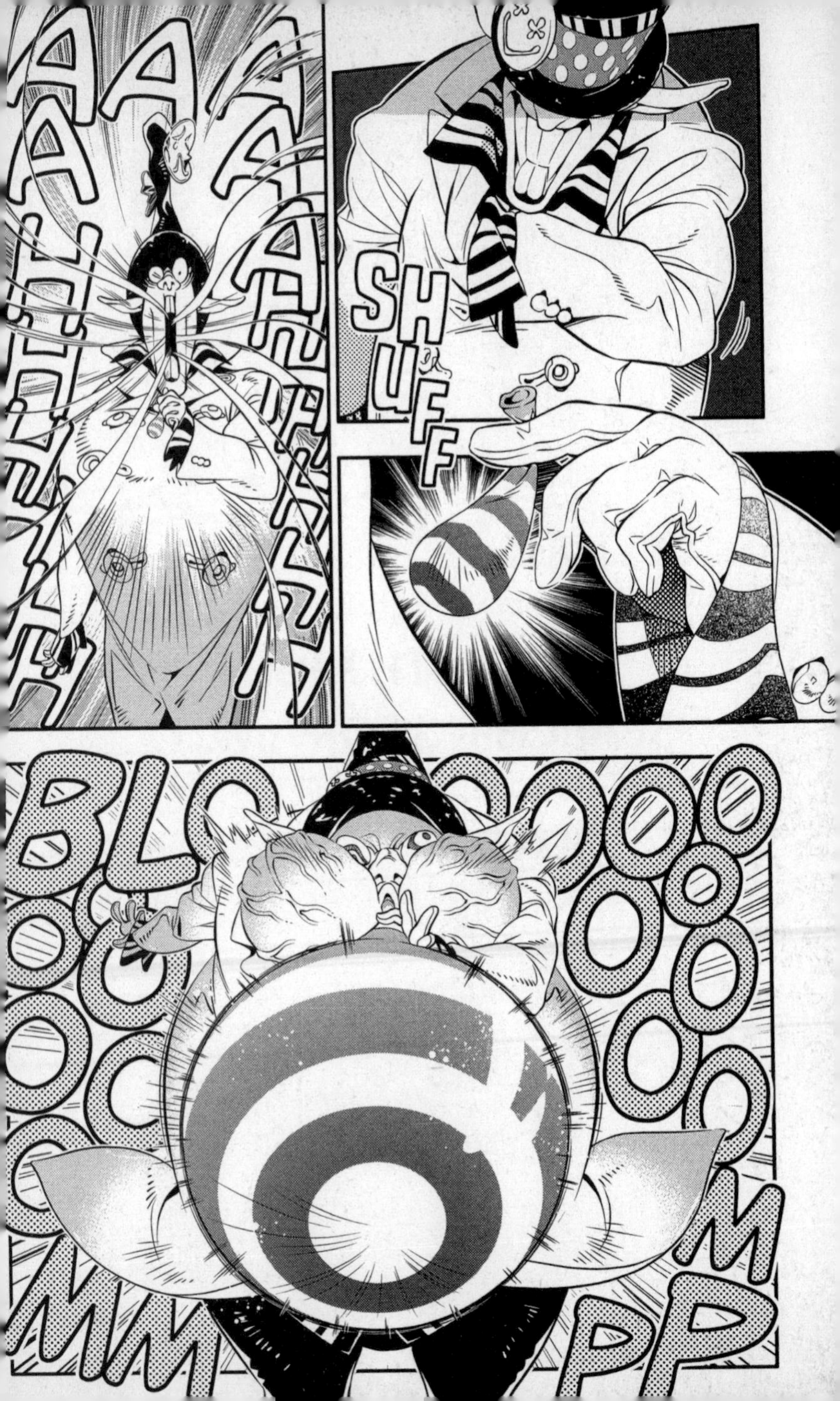
SHUFF
AAAAAHHHHHH
BLOOOOOOOOOOOOOOMMMPP

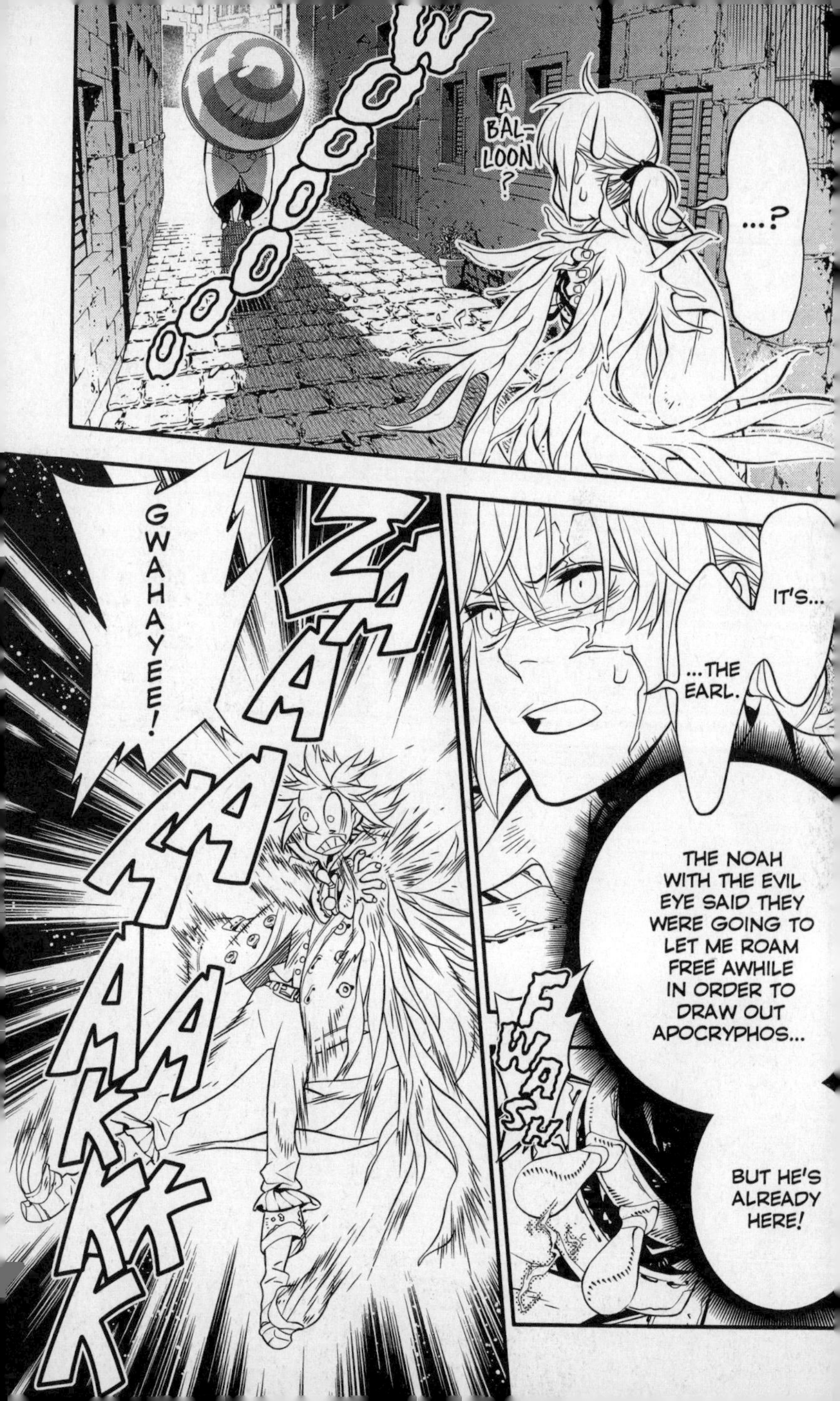
...?
A BAL-LOON?
WOOOOOOOOO
IT'S...
...THE EARL.
THE NOAH WITH THE EVIL EYE SAID THEY WERE GOING TO LET ME ROAM FREE AWHILE IN ORDER TO DRAW OUT APOCRYPHOS...
BUT HE'S ALREADY HERE!
FWASH
ZAAAAAAAKKK
GWAHAYEEE!

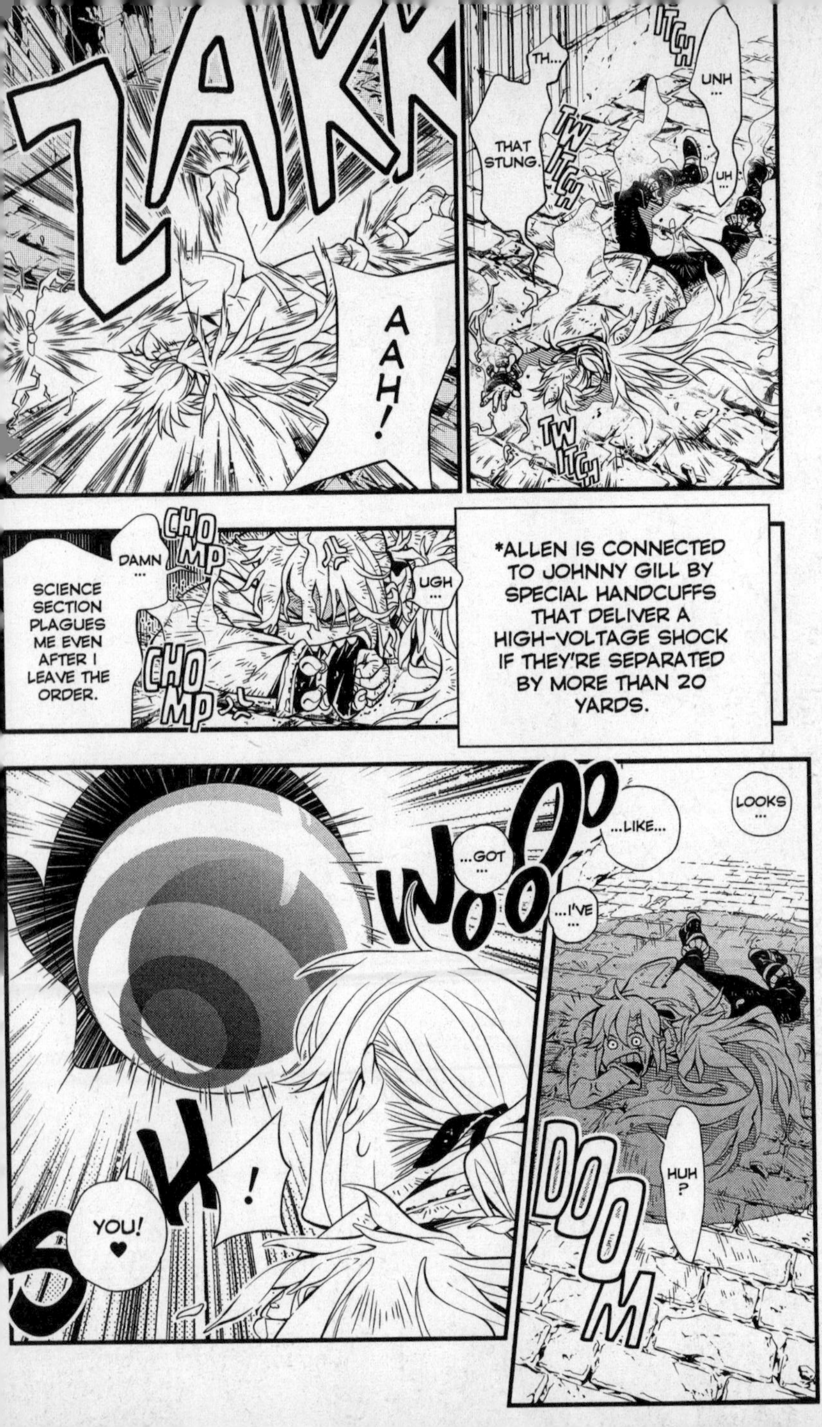
ITCH
UNH ...
TH...
TWITCH
THAT STUNG.
UH ...
TWITCH
ZAKK
AAH!
*ALLEN IS CONNECTED TO JOHNNY GILL BY SPECIAL HANDCUFFS THAT DELIVER A HIGH-VOLTAGE SHOCK IF THEY'RE SEPARATED BY MORE THAN 20 YARDS.
UGH ...
CHOMP
DAMN ...
SCIENCE SECTION PLAGUES ME EVEN AFTER I LEAVE THE ORDER.
CHOMP
LOOKS ...
...LIKE...
...I'VE ...
...GOT ...
WOOO
HUH ?
DOOOM
SK !
YOU! ♥

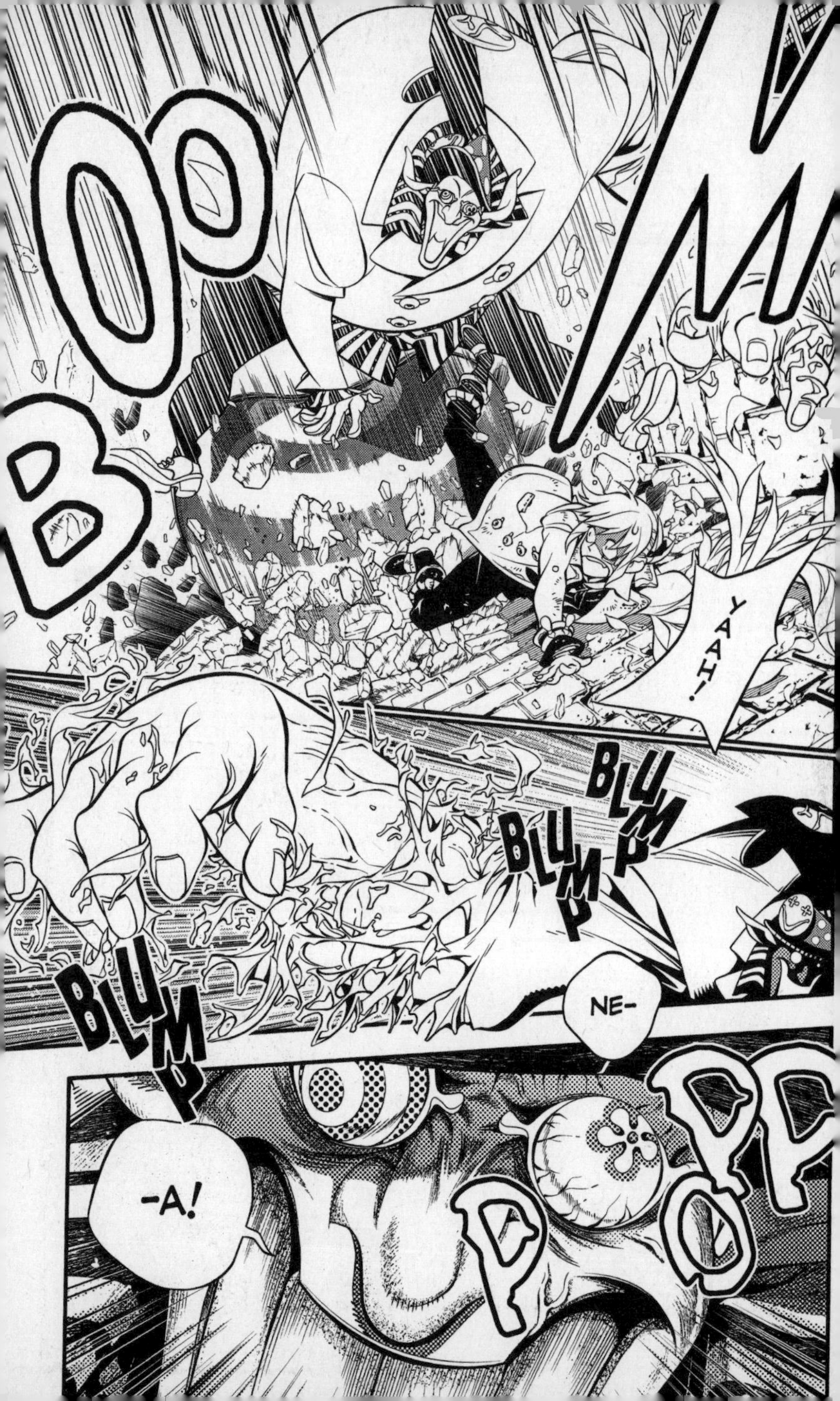
BOOOM
YAAH!
BLUMP
BLUMP
NE-
BLUMP
-A!
POP POP

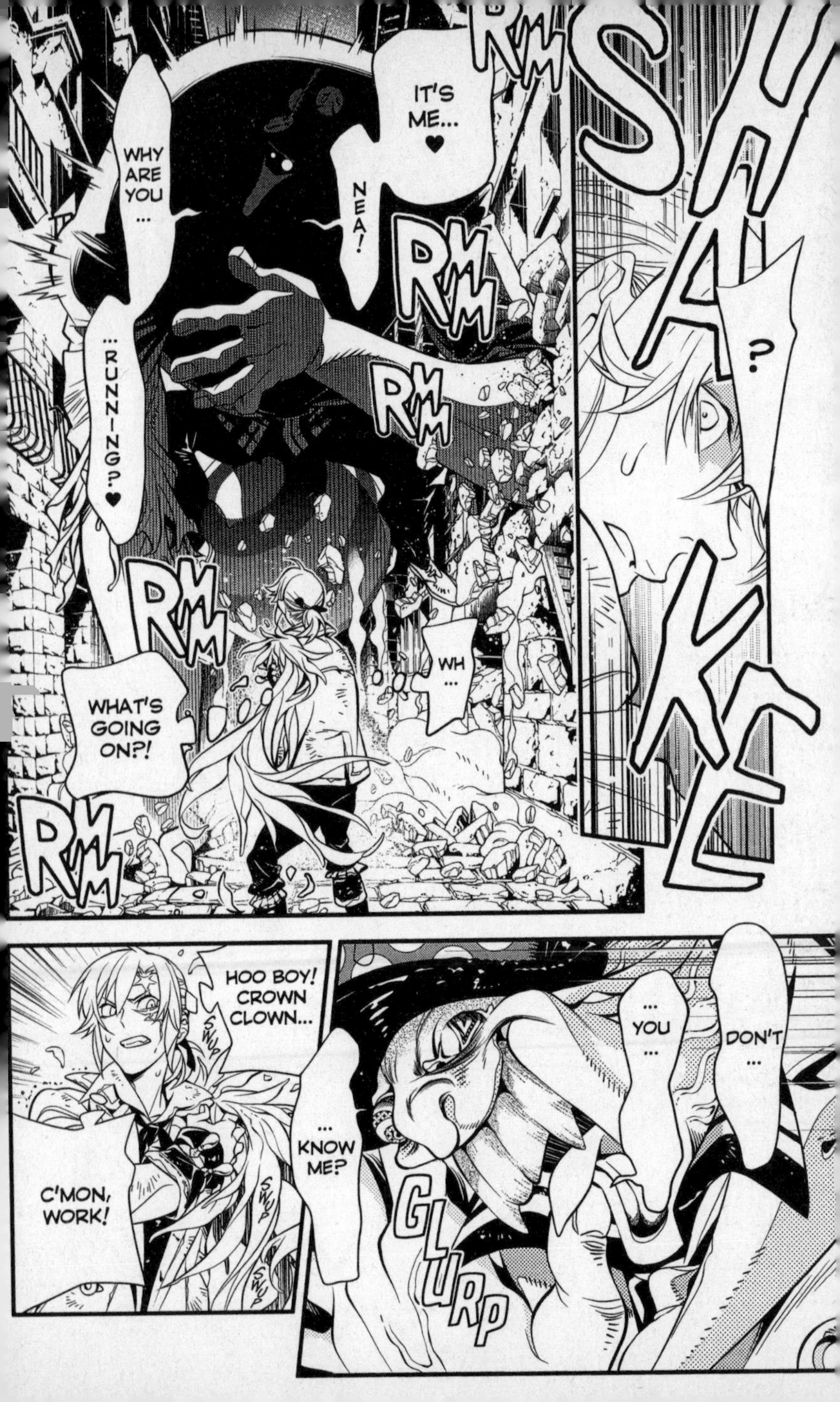

?
RMM
IT'S ME... ♥
NEA!
WHY ARE YOU ...
... RUNNING? ♥
RMM
RMM
RMM
WH ...
WHAT'S GOING ON?!
RMM
DON'T ...
... YOU ...
... KNOW ME?
GLURP
HOO BOY! CROWN CLOWN...
SWUP
C'MON, WORK!
SWUP
SWUP

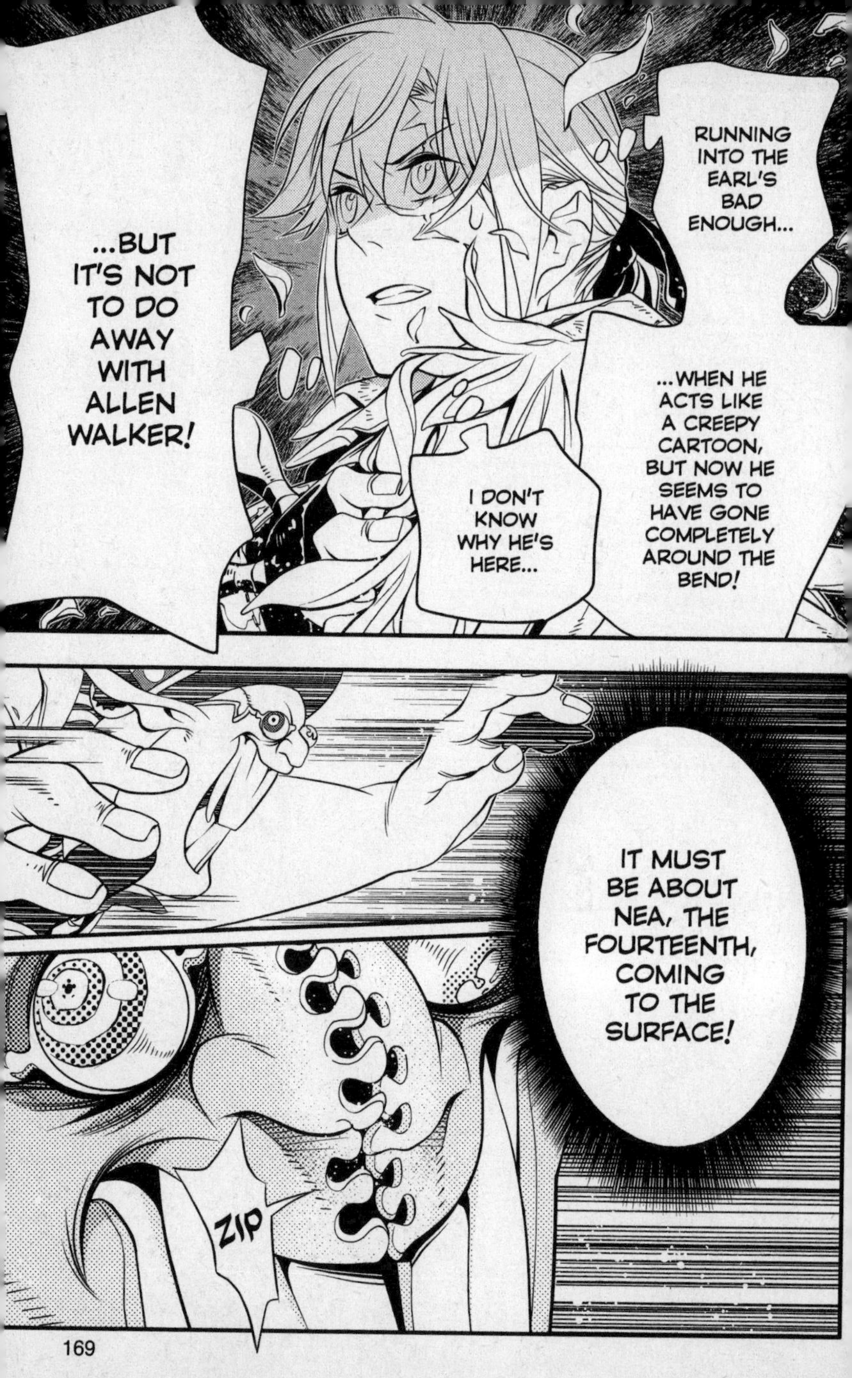
RUNNING INTO THE EARL'S BAD ENOUGH...
...WHEN HE ACTS LIKE A CREEPY CARTOON, BUT NOW HE SEEMS TO HAVE GONE COMPLETELY AROUND THE BEND!
I DON'T KNOW WHY HE'S HERE...
...BUT IT'S NOT TO DO AWAY WITH ALLEN WALKER!
IT MUST BE ABOUT NEA, THE FOURTEENTH, COMING TO THE SURFACE!
ZIP

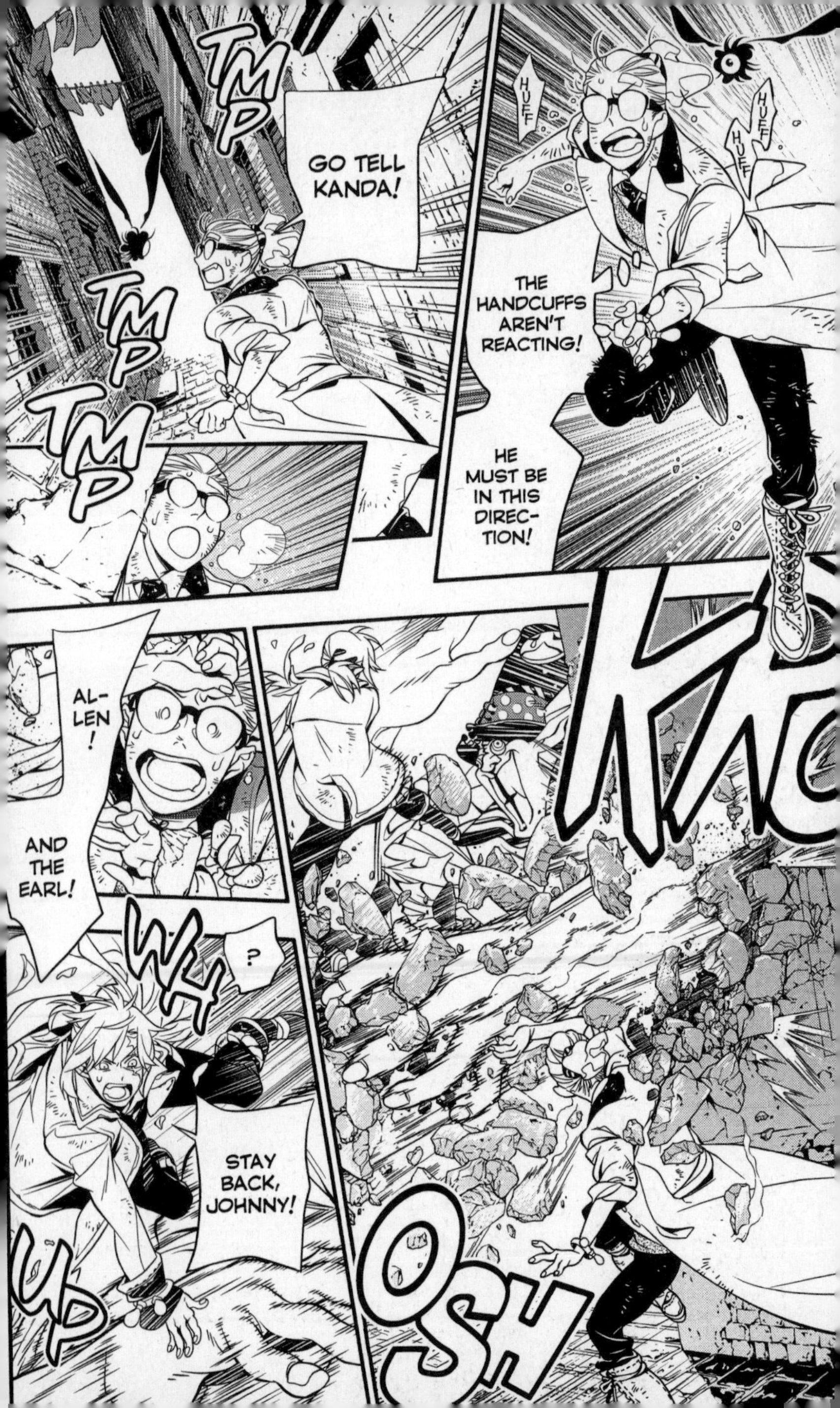
HUFF
HUFF
HUFF
THE HANDCUFFS AREN'T REACTING!
HE MUST BE IN THIS DIREC-TION!
TMP
GO TELL KANDA!
TMP
TMP
AL-LEN!
AND THE EARL!
WH
?
STAY BACK, JOHNNY!
UP
OSH

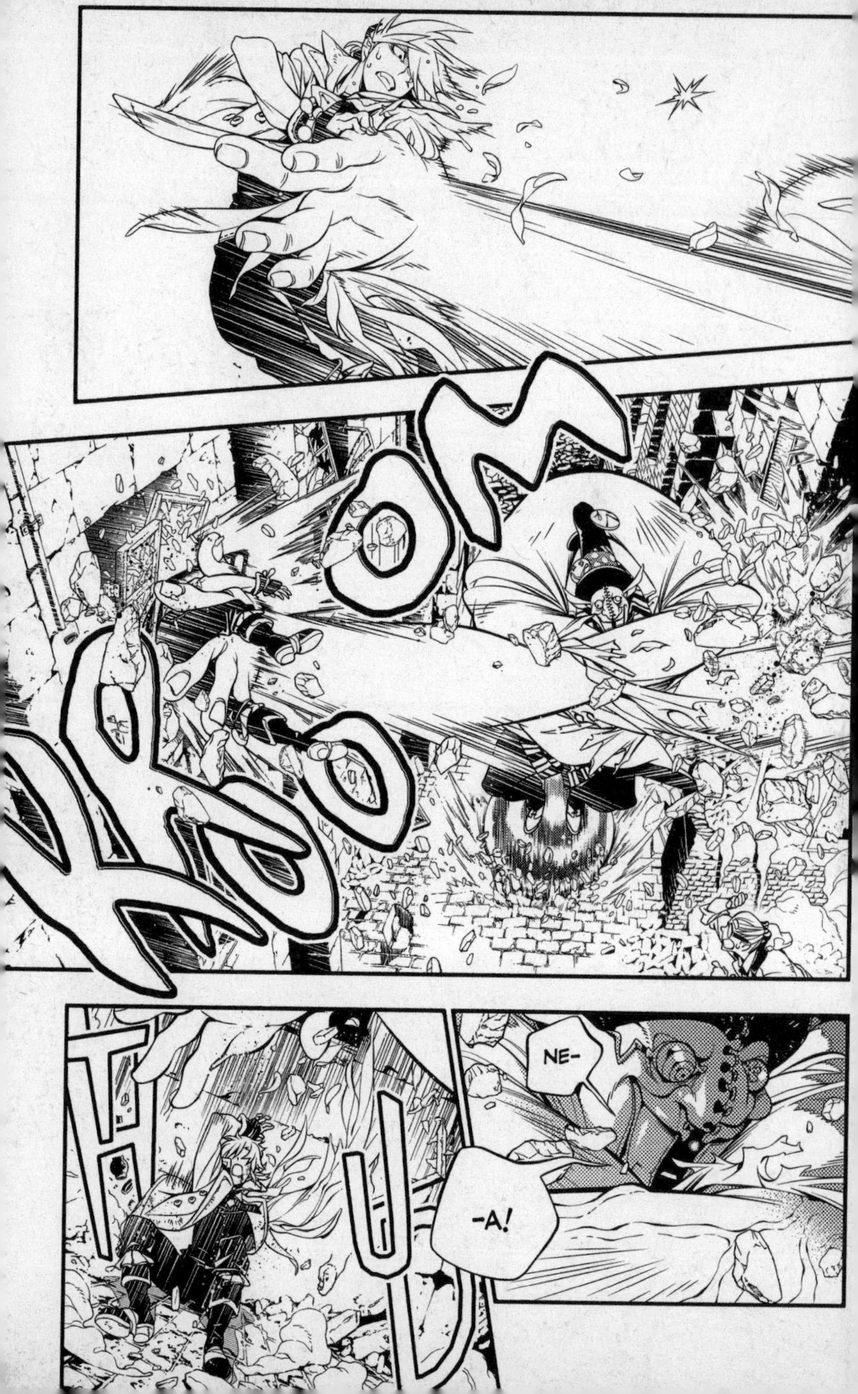
NE-
-A!

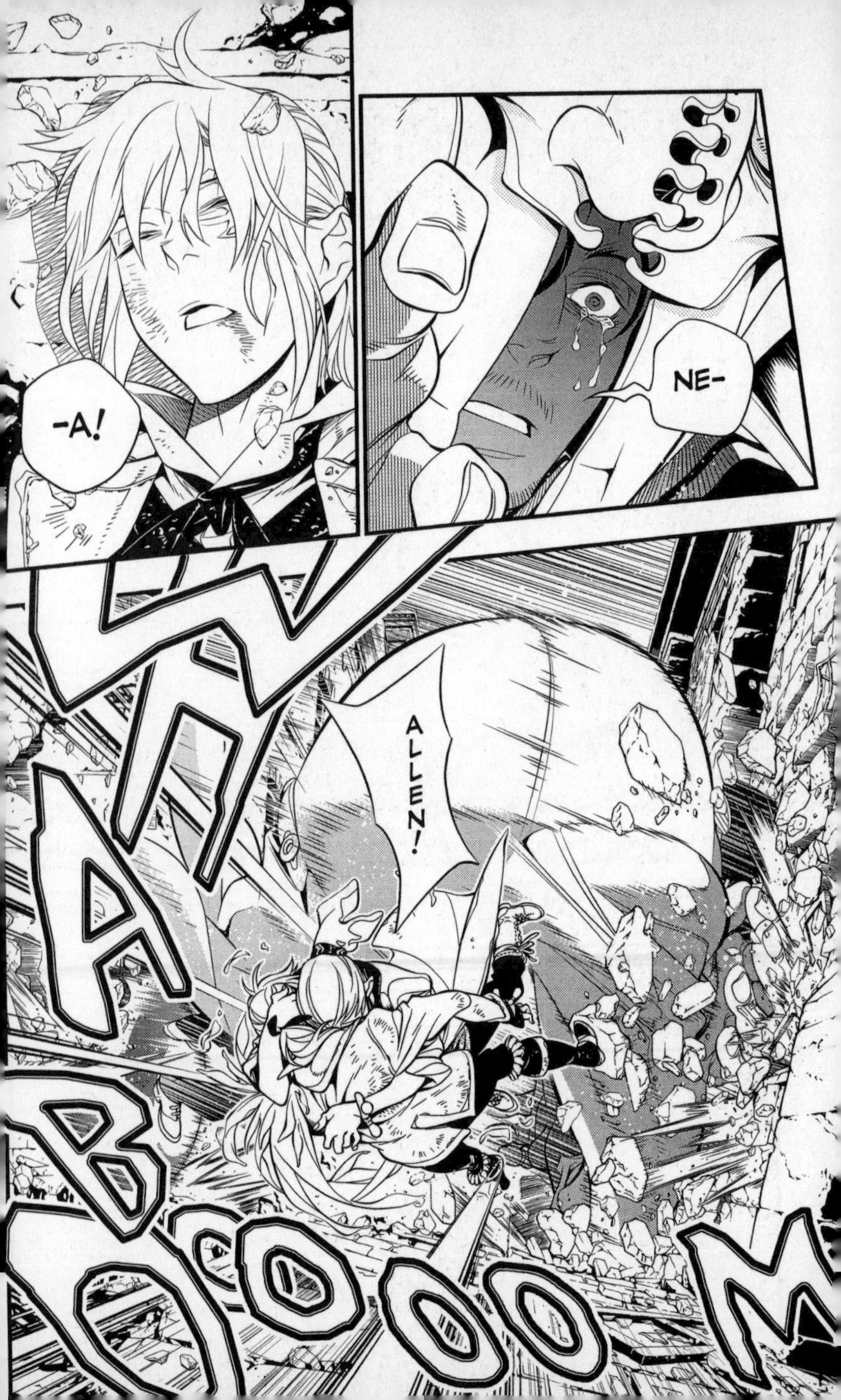
NE-
-A!
ALLEN!
KA
BOOOOOM

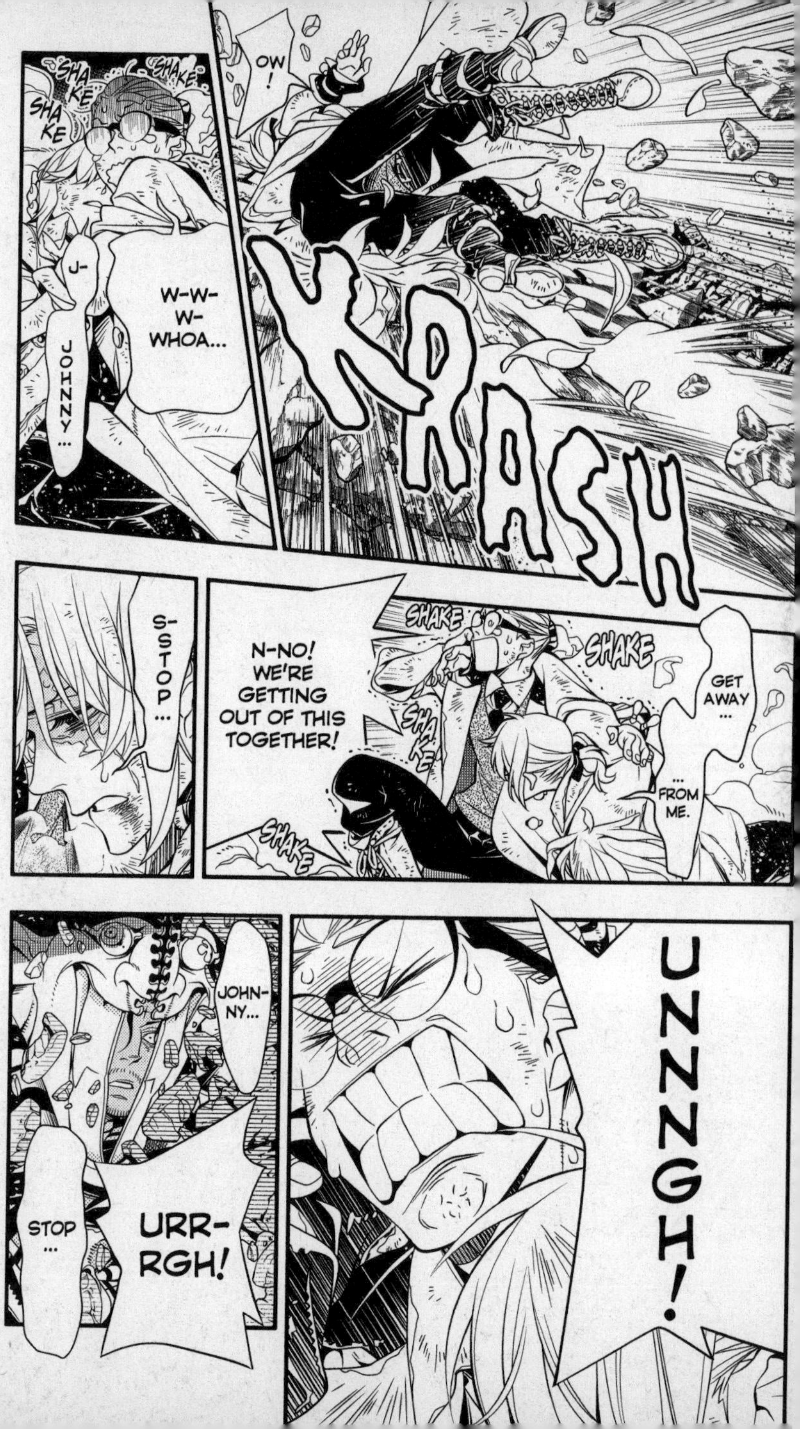
OW!
KRASH
SHAKE
SHAKE
SHAKE
SHAKE
W-W-W-WHOA...
J-
JOHNNY...
GET AWAY...
...FROM ME.
SHAKE
SHAKE
SHAKE
SHAKE
N-NO! WE'RE GETTING OUT OF THIS TOGETHER!
S-STOP...
UNNNGH!
JOHN-NY...
URR-RGH!
STOP...

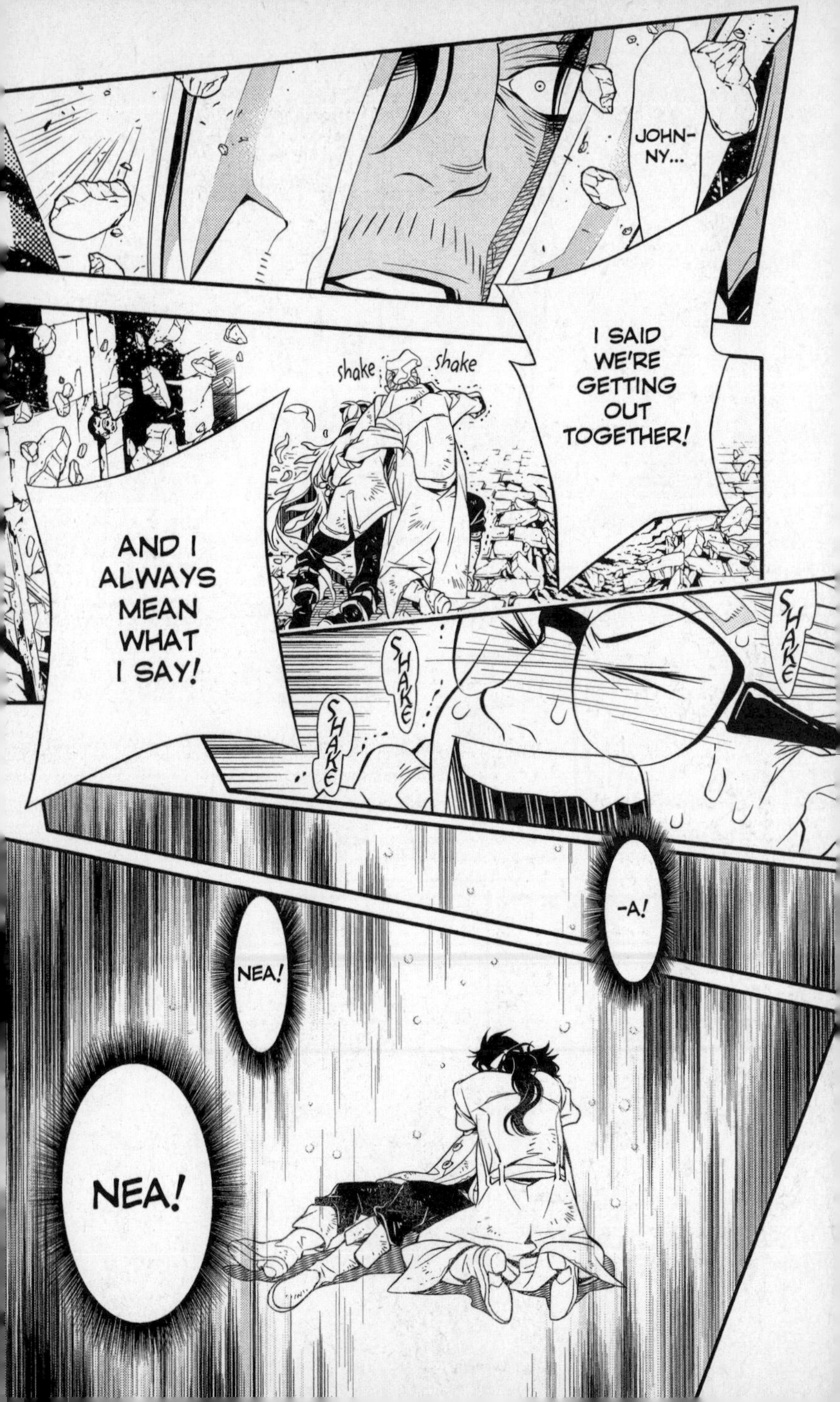

JOHN-NY...
I SAID WE'RE GETTING OUT TOGETHER!
shake shake
AND I ALWAYS MEAN WHAT I SAY!
SHAKE
SHAKE
SHAKE
-A!
NEA!
NEA!

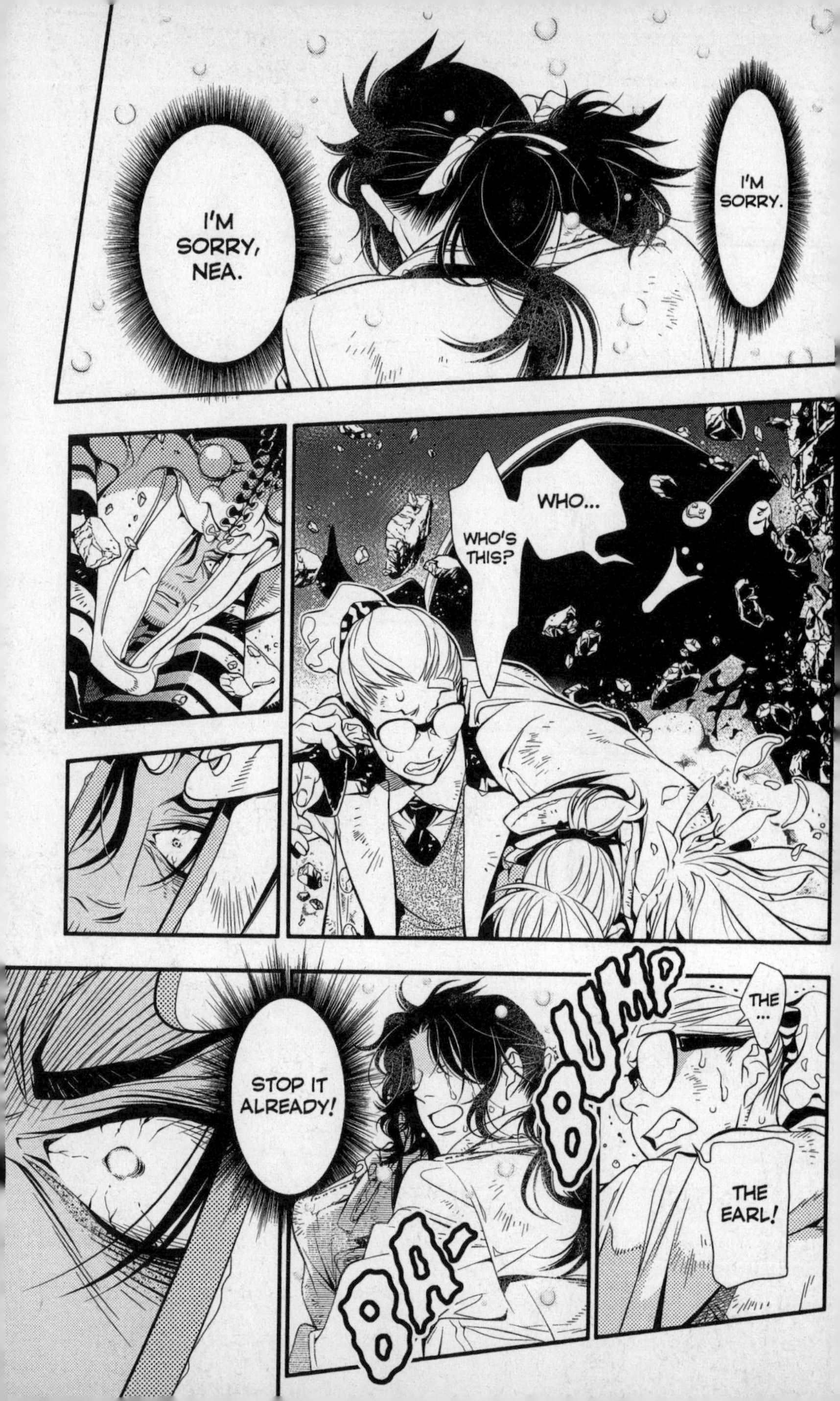
I'M SORRY.
I'M SORRY, NEA.
WHO... WHO'S THIS?
THE...
THE EARL!
BA-BUMP
STOP IT ALREADY!

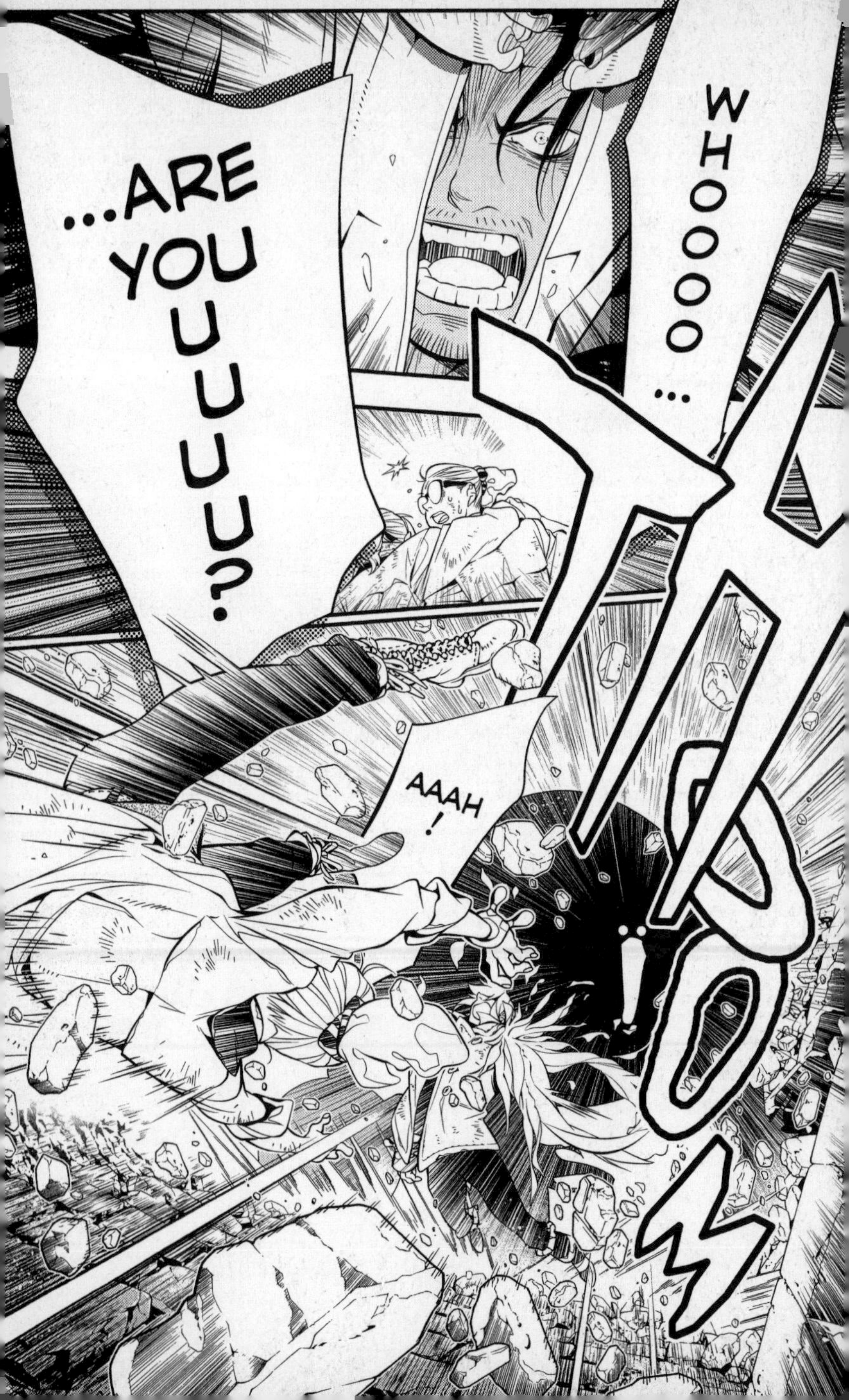
WHOOOO...
...ARE YOU UUUU?
AAAH!

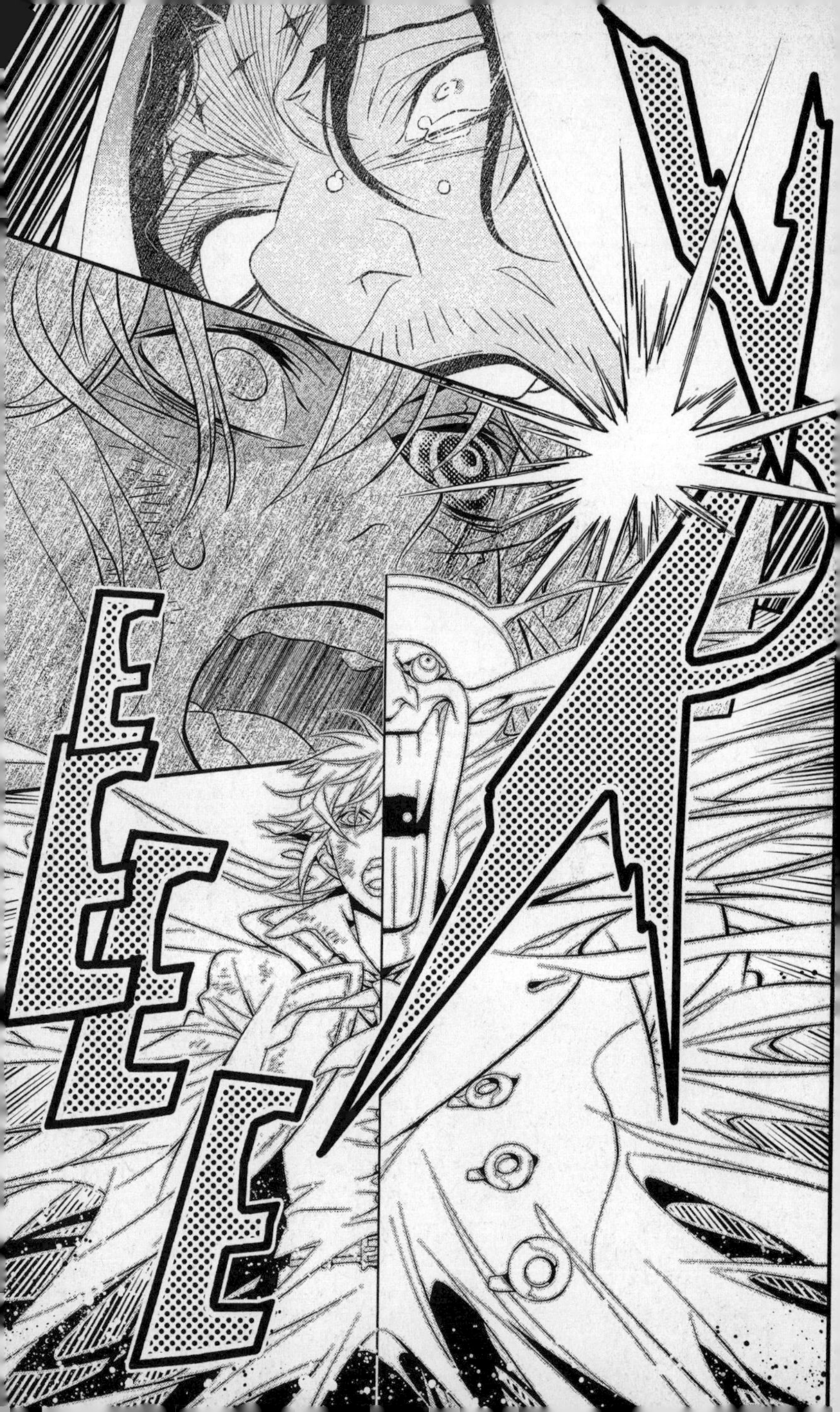
EEEE

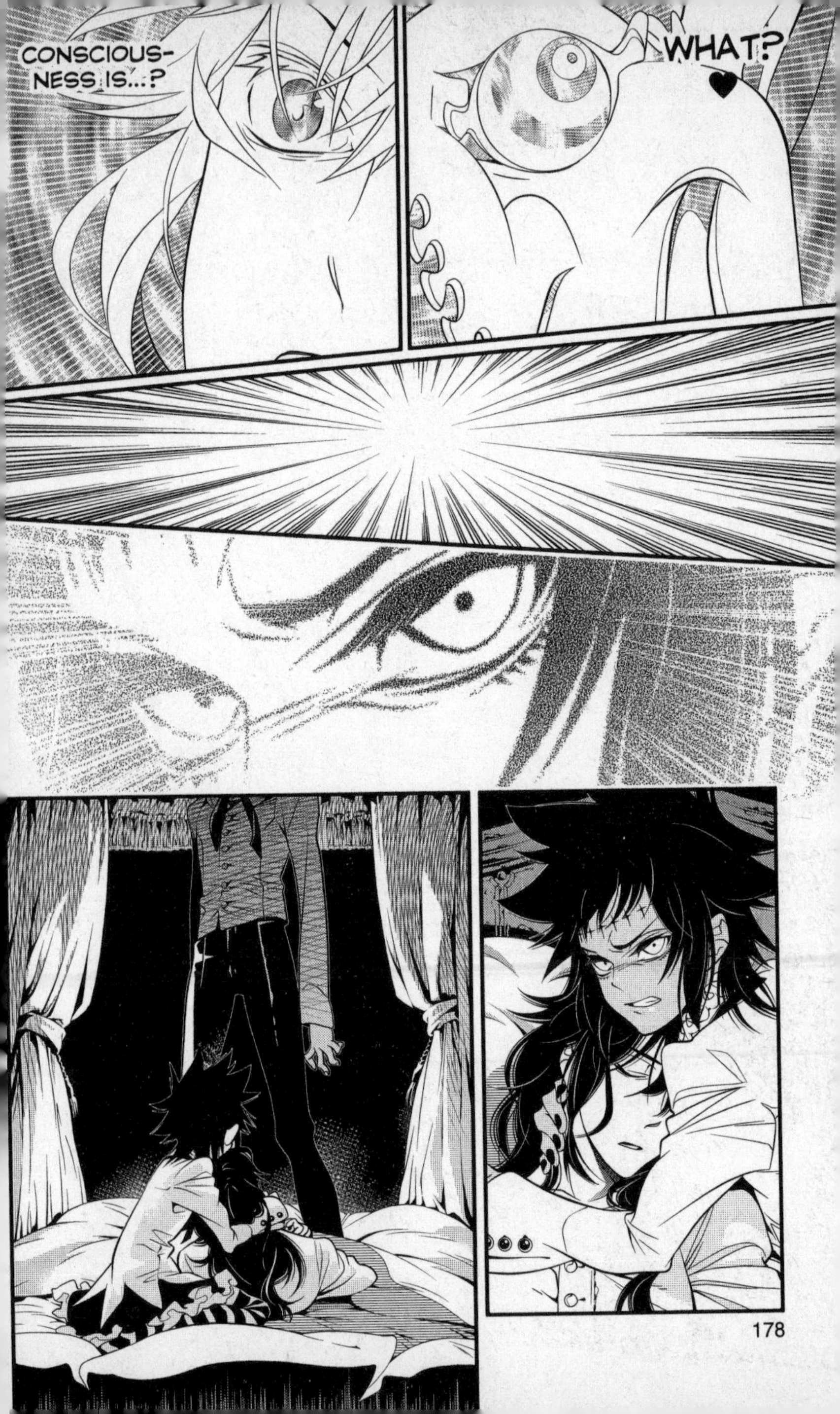
WHAT? ♥
CONSCIOUS-NESS IS...?

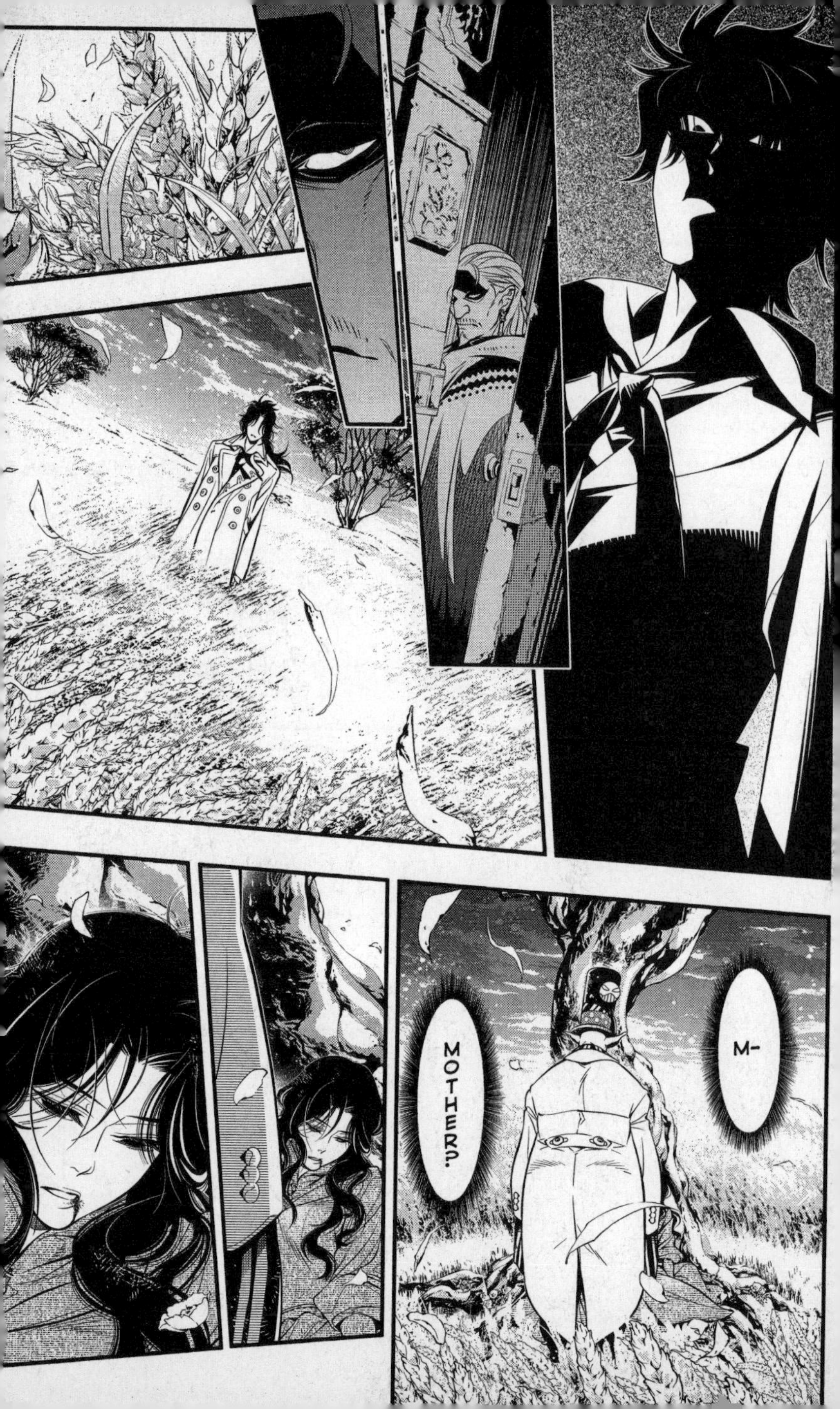
M-
MOTHER?

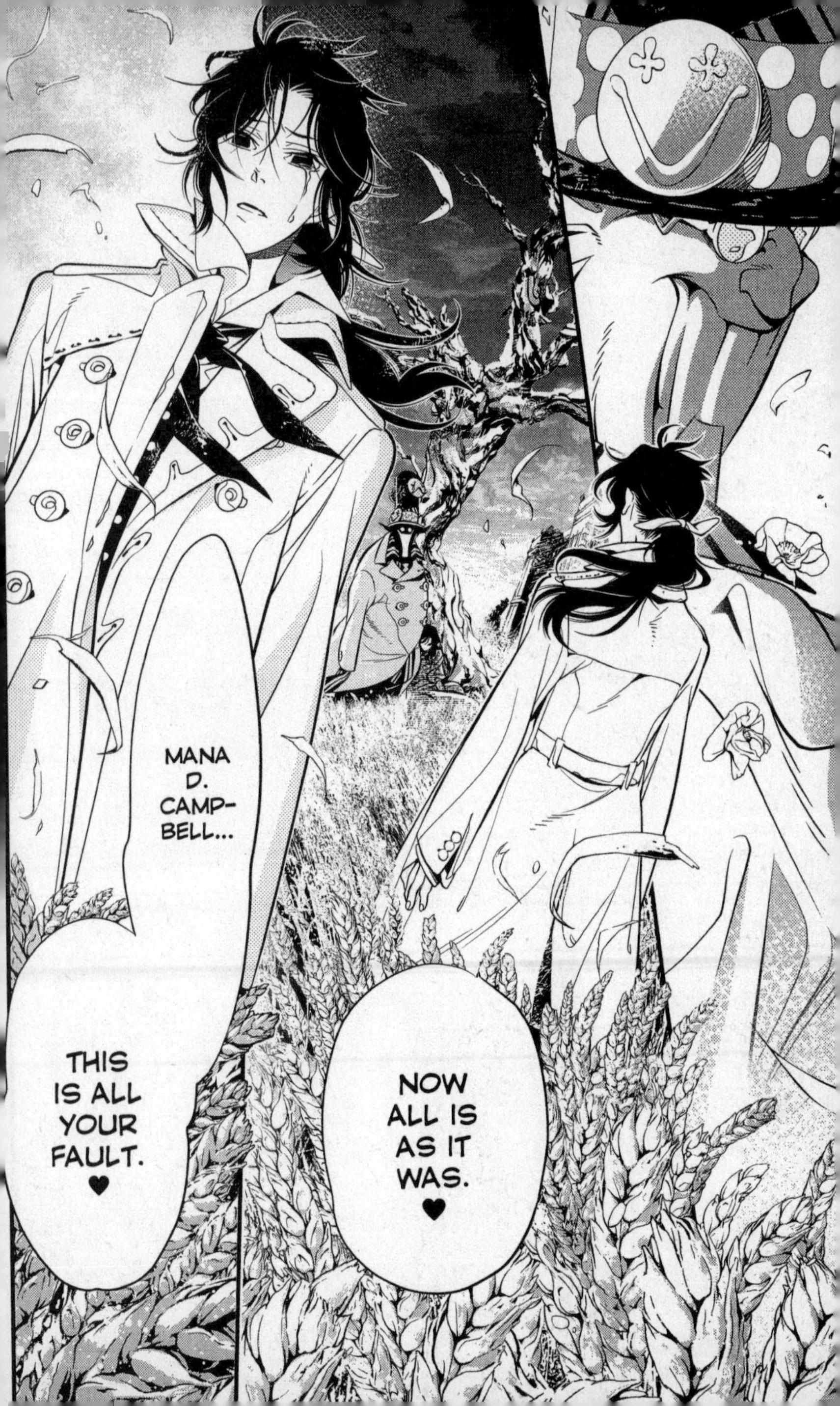
MANA D. CAMPBELL...
NOW ALL IS AS IT WAS. ♥
THIS IS ALL YOUR FAULT. ♥

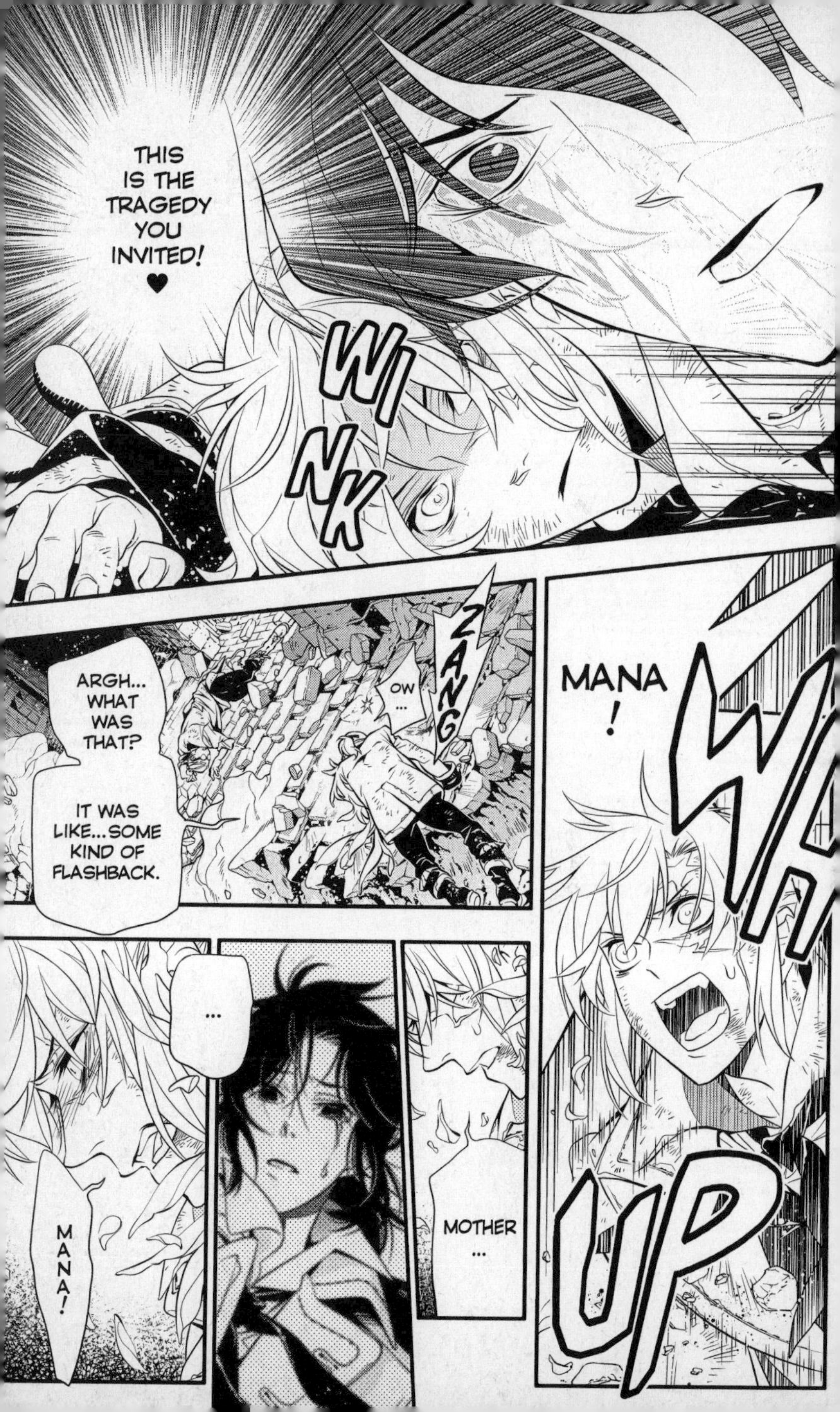
THIS IS THE TRAGEDY YOU INVITED! ♥
WINK
MANA!
UP
ZANG
OW...
ARGH... WHAT WAS THAT?
IT WAS LIKE...SOME KIND OF FLASHBACK.
MOTHER ...
...
MANA!

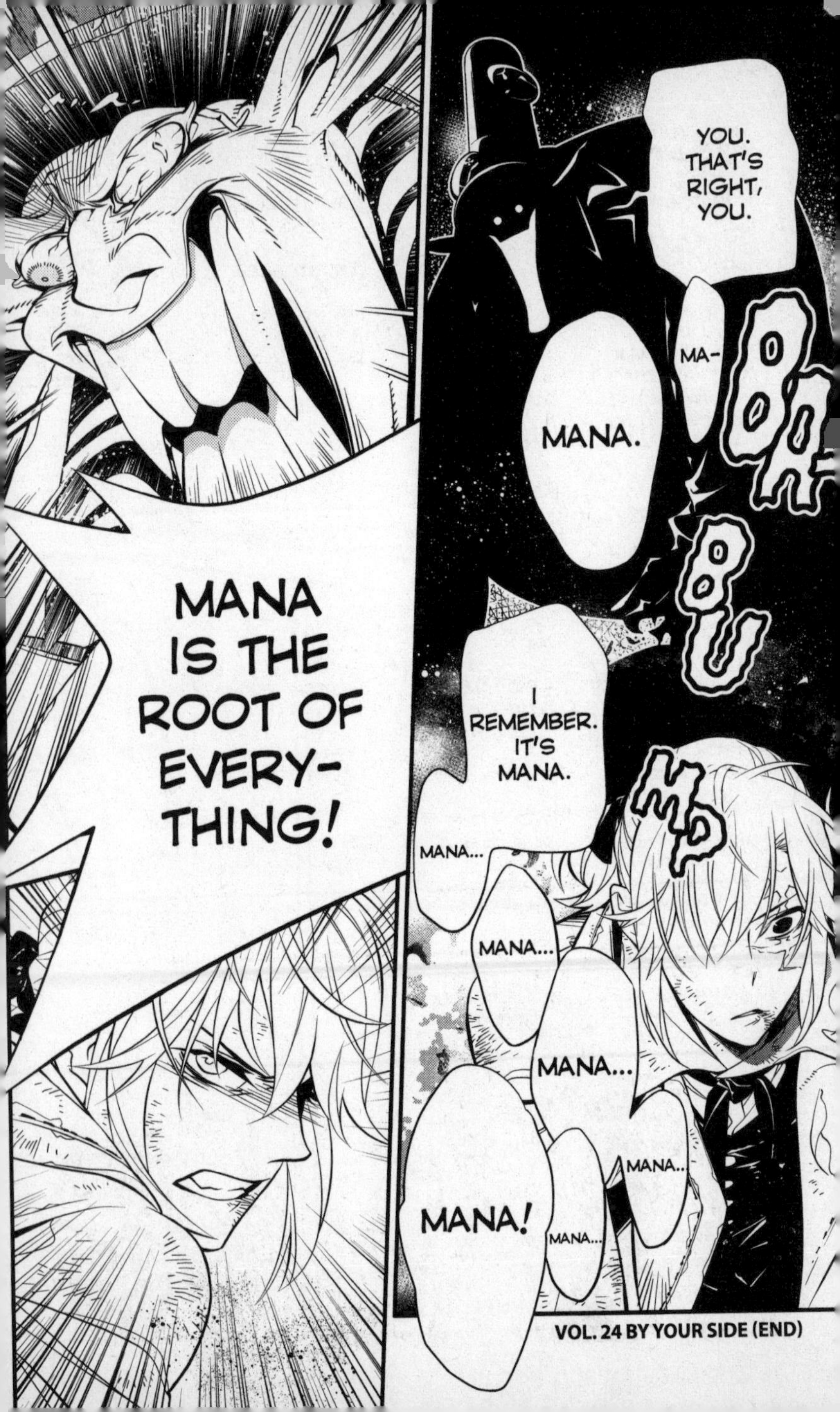
YOU. THAT'S RIGHT, YOU.
MA-
MANA.
I REMEMBER. IT'S MANA.
MANA...
MANA...
MANA...
MANA...
MANA!
MANA...
MANA IS THE ROOT OF EVERYTHING!

VOL. 24 BY YOUR SIDE (END)

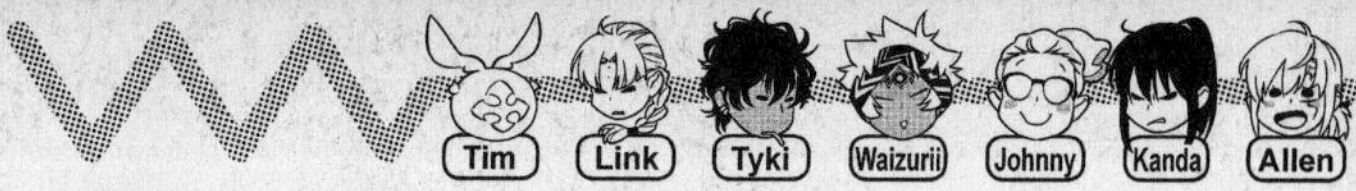
Tim
Link
Tyki
Waizurii
Johnny
Kanda
Allen

KOMUI'S DISCUSSION ROOM 6

Q. So where's Lavi?

A, J & K: ...

W: Hey, if you look at me like that, you won't get any dango.

Ty: How nice that everyone's worried about Eye-patch Lad. Don't you think so, boy?

A: Yeah, I guess.

J: You think that?!

K: I doubt that rabbit is in his grave.

W: Are you sure? Hoshino's pretty rough on D.Gray-man characters!

Ty: Well, if you run into Eye-patch Lad, go easy on him.

A: Go easy on him? When I see him, I have to tease him. I wonder why? Just because he's Lavi maybe?

J: Maybe because he's like a big brother to you.

A: Marie would make a better one. He's calm and steady and big. It would be great to ride on his shoulders. And Jerry's the mother. And Link too. Lavi's more like...the local *NEET. Kanda is... oh, I don't wanna go there.

NEET: *Not Educated, Employed or Trained*

K: Then don't.

W: And there are two mothers.

J: What about me? Huh?

A: Johnny and Lenalee and Krory are classmates!

Ty: And me? What about me?

A: The local lecher.

Tim: Gaaaaah!

A: And Tim's my brother, of course! (*hugs*)

W: And Road and I are the youngest kids! That's five siblings! Here's to family, Big Bro!

A: No way!

Link: There's hardly any space left! So wrap it up!

A: (Gah!) There's no mistake! It's the ghost of Link!! (*flees*)

J: I heard him too! Waaah! (*flees*)

K: (These guys are so stupid.)

W: You know, I like the dango that guy Jerry made. I'll ask Dezaiasu to take him on as our cook!

Ty: I'm so tired.

The End

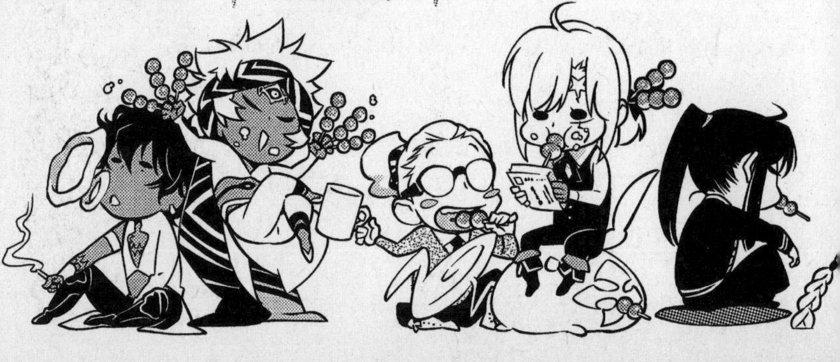

You're Reading in the Wrong Direction!!

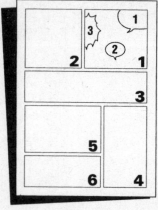

Whoops! Guess what? You're starting at the wrong end of the comic!

It's true! In keeping with the original Japanese format, **D.Gray-man** is meant to be read from right to left, starting in the upper-right corner.

Unlike English, which is read from left to right, Japanese is read from right to left, meaning action, sound effects and word-balloon order are completely reversed... something which can make readers unfamiliar with Japanese feel pretty backwards themselves. For this reason, manga or Japanese comics published in the U.S. in English have sometimes been published "flopped"—that is, printed in exact reverse order, as though seen from the other side of a mirror.

By flopping pages, U.S. publishers can avoid confusing readers, but the compromise is not without its downside. For one thing, a character in a flopped manga series who once wore in the original Japanese version a T-shirt emblazoned with "M A Y" (as in "the merry month of") now wears one which reads "Y A M"! Additionally, many manga creators in Japan are themselves unhappy with the process, as some feel the mirror-imaging of their art skews their original intentions.

We are proud to bring you Katsura Hoshino's **D.Gray-man** in the original unflopped format. For now, though, turn to the other side of the book and let the adventure begin...!

—Editor